Frank, Evie & Liz

Inside Their Quiet Lives

Betty Powell

BP Publishers
Tulsa, OK 74145

BPpublishers@gmail.com

Printed in the United States of America

ISBN-10: 1-5152-2191-1
ISBN-13: 978-1-5152-2191-3

Cover design: This universal hand sign used by the Deaf Community includes I, L, and Y to indicate "I love you."

Subject heading: CODA (Child of Deaf Adults)
Autobiography of my life experiences with my deaf parents.

Note: In my research, I found the Minnesota School for the Deaf has also been referred to as the Minnesota State Academy for the Deaf.

I dedicate this book to my dear daughters,
Julie, Vicki, Marci and Connie.

In honor of their deaf grandparents,
Frank and Evelyn Niklaus.

Growing up in Minnesota, working and raising their two children in Wisconsin, they retired to Minnesota living out their lives close to their brothers and sisters. Frank and Evelyn lived eighty-nine and eighty-seven years of the twentieth century in which they celebrated sixty-two years of marriage. I loved them dearly!

In Memory of:

Jerry Powell	1933-2009	My beloved husband of 55 years.
Donna Mae Walters	1933-2003	My lovely cousin and close friend.
Tomas Kulka	1959-2003	My sweet son-in-law whose life was too short.
Bob Niklaus	1930-2002	My cousin, another CODA, who prompted me to write my story.

Acknowledgments:

I wish to thank my daughter, Marci, for her patience with me while editing this book, bringing it to life for me and hopefully, for you, the reader.

I also extend my appreciation to Barbara Weems, my friend and neighbor, for her encouragement and assistance in self-publishing this, my first book!

Frank and Liz (1934)

ABOUT THE AUTHOR

*A*s the daughter of deaf parents, Betty has read books and articles by Children of Deaf Adults (CODA) as well as educators of deaf children. Others are written by professionals such as counselors, social workers and speech therapists. There has been a tremendous growth of technology benefiting people with a wide variety of hearing loss, from the small decibel loss to the profoundly deafened.

Unfortunately, from her perspective as a CODA and a professional interpreter for the deaf; she still sees a lack of social education that leaves many in the deaf community with a social stigma that affects not only the individual deaf person. This stigma effects his family members, co-workers and peers. Deaf people have declared their disdain to using either the word *disabled* or the word *handicapped*. Betty whole-heartedly agrees. However, she states that deafness does put a person at a *disadvantage* when relating to the *hearing world*.

In this book, Betty is the character known as Liz, while Frank and Evie are her beloved parents, now deceased. Bobby is Liz's only sibling. Some characters have been given fictitious names. Evie was born profoundly deaf into a family of hearing parents and siblings. Her mother had contracted the measles while pregnant with Evie. Frank was the ninth of ten children. The three youngest children became deaf after suffering with scarlet fever. High fever is still one cause of deafness in children today.

Frank and Evelyn attended the Minnesota State Academy for the Deaf in the early 1900s. Both Betty and her brother have normal hearing. She has been blessed with four daughters and seven grandchildren, all with normal hearing. Her brother has three children, all also born with normal hearing. Betty will always be grateful to her parents for giving her an incredibly unique life with the bonus of talents and skills necessary to become a professional interpreter for the deaf.

Betty Jean (Niklaus) Powell has now retired from full time work with the Deaf as an interpreter and consultant. Prior to retirement, Betty was a free-lance interpreter. Certified with the national Registry of Interpreters for the Deaf (RID) and the Oklahoma Registry of Interpreters for the Deaf (OKRID), she worked through the Oklahoma Department of Rehabilitation Services (DRS), the Communication Services for the Deaf, the Tulsa Public School systems; Tulsa Jr. College, Tulsa Vo-Tech School; Sign Language Referral Services and the Tulsa Speech & Hearing Association. Her final employment was with Sorenson Video Relay Services as a Video Interpreter, a wonderful way to end her career. As a grass-roots member of OKRID, Betty received a "Lifetime Achievement Award" in 2012. She was extremely proud of the inscription which read "In recognition of your exemplary service to OKRID and the field of interpreting." Betty was the first interpreter in Oklahoma to serve in court to a deaf juror and the third interpreter to do so nationally. She gained a contract with DRS becoming the first to deliver a telephone relay service to the deaf in Eastern Oklahoma.

Mrs. Powell has a degree in Psychology with sixty graduate hours in counseling and religion. Her husband, Jerry, now deceased, was a retired high school teacher of Union High School in Tulsa. Retired after twenty years with Air Force Bands, he played the saxophone and clarinet in the Tulsa Community Band and the Sounds of Music big band style; as well as working with the Union High School Key Club, sponsored by his Southeast Tulsa Kiwanis Club.

Having raised four daughters, Betty also enjoys seven grand-children now. She enjoys bowling as a hobby and stays active with the United Methodist Church. Danny now roams her home, the sixth collie Betty has owned over the last fifty years.

Looking out the window on a rare winter day in Oklahoma where snow left high drifts making driving difficult and even churches to cancel services, she thought this might be a good time to "start my book."

CONTENTS

1

There's a Special School for Us?

*C*lass pictures! Fine! How tedious to get back into that white dress with all the pink pearl buttons down the front, hand stitched by Mama's weather worn hands. After all, poor Mama is almost sixty now, a dairy farmer's wife who works so hard every day including milking those cows. Eew! I'll never marry a farmer! I just hope that Frank finds a decent job soon so we can have a family and live a decent life. Of course there were no promises for jobs these days, especially for those who were deaf. But Frank was not lazy. Evie just knew he would be successful out in the world!

However, today, Evie's thoughts were focused on the dress. Mama never really was a good seamstress, not as good as Molly's mama. Evie couldn't believe her eyes when she saw the lovely garment her roommate unwrapped earlier that day. But, Molly was originally from California so her mother knew the newest styles. My mama never paid much attention to fashion. Evie's thoughts were racing today. Oh, silly me, the truth is I had told her that I just want to be comfortable. Still, I do want to be pretty. All girls want to look pretty.

Brother Ray always said my beauty came from within, whatever that was supposed to mean. I like the way I look on the outside; but I don't know what I look like on the inside! What a silly thing to say. I think he just says sweet things to me because that's his duty, watching over four sisters after his older half-brother had married and moved away. Evie had always looked up to her big brother, Ray, and believed that she was his favorite sister. Why else would he always give her compliments, even when she was wearing overalls and gathering eggs in the barn. But, Evie mused, it is true when I look in the mirror I like what I see.

Oh, my face is not especially pretty but my blue-violet eyes draw a lot of attention. My sisters always say they are jealous of my eyes because of their contrast to my dark hair that Erma says is ink black. Since she is the oldest sister I take her words seriously. I don't know about her compliments so much but I am lucky because it doesn't take much time to fix my hair with just a brush through the shoulder length locks and a comb through the bangs. Hmmm, I wonder if I should let Molly trim my bangs a little today.

All of these thoughts were running through Evie's head as she prepared for the traditional graduation pictures to be taken in a couple of hours. Of course, Evie reasoned, Molly came from a rich California family who owned three large farms here in Minnesota. But it seemed Molly's father spent much of the year here while his wife worked for some Hollywood people in California during the winter months, joining her husband for the summer on one of the largest farms in Minnesota. Even her mother's name was fancy, Adriana. She always dressed in sophisticated clothes herself. Molly said she bought some of the dresses ready made in a stylish store so that she would know what fabric to use as well as what pattern to choose for her daughter's clothes.

Molly's dress for graduation was plain white, but dreamy. The tight fitting bodice gave way to folds of soft taffeta gathered around her waist. The finishing touch was the pale blue lace overlaying the skirt. With her long curly auburn hair becoming a flaming-red against that white dress, Molly's eyes were flashing green. Oh well, Evie thought, Mama and Papa will not be here for the picture-taking time anyway. Maybe I don't need to wear this dress today after all. Signing to the mirror as she often did, "Anyway, me dress wear? Say no one! I can wait and wear graduation covered with robe! Perfect," she laughed devilishly. But no one could hear her.

The image in the mirror showed a slim body in a white cotton slip. Her hair had been cut in the new "bobbed" style that everyone said was very flattering on Evie; but she had her doubts. Mama had also made a big white hair ribbon at least four inches wide that she had already decided against wearing, no matter if it did hurt her mama's feelings. The white dress was made from some new kind of material called seersucker. Mama's note that came with the dress in the mail promised Evie that it would never look wrinkled like the cotton dresses she had made for her all during these years here at school. She really didn't care. It was ugly. Oh, sure, there was a pretty rayon collar trimmed in white ribbon and a couple of ribbon bows on the sleeves and pockets but Evie still didn't like it. "Don't like," she signed to herself as she threw it on the bed.

Looking at the other things strewn on the bed and across the room on her chair and desk; she suddenly felt sad about graduation because it would mean leaving this room, her roommate and the beautiful school. It would mean going out into that big world of hearing people she could not communicate with in her language of signs.

Careful not to sit on the dress, she sat down and put her head in her hands and tried not to cry. After just a minute she felt a hand on her shoulder. "Hey, wrong what, Evie?" her roommate signed. "Don't smear powder face. Soon go pictures," Molly signed as she looked at her new gold watch that her parents had given her as an early graduation present. She stepped over to the window and signed excitedly to her friend, "I think see Frankeee walking across campus." She exaggerated the "eee" on her lips so that Evie could lip read that name on her mouth. She knew Evie loved to see it but Evie didn't know how much Molly loved to say the name.

Molly didn't always use her voice even though her mother had insisted on her doing so. But she did love to say Frank's name as she looked at the handsome picture on the dresser of Frank in his uniform. Some people thought it strange that the boys at our school were required to wear uniforms but this place has been known as the Minnesota Deaf Academy during its 59 year history. She was sure glad they didn't require the girls to wear uniforms though because she loved to dress up in clothes that made her look so much more sophisticated than her classmates. Molly and Evie agreed that uniforms sure flattered some of the boys, especially Frank.

His dark piercing eyes seemed to be smiling all of the time. His thick brown hair was always falling in his face causing him to run his hand up over his forehead to brush the hair back, making him look much younger. Frank was not especially tall, probably just shy of six foot; but he walked with a proud gait that all the girls admired. He'd been a pretty good basketball player.

Pictures were hanging in the library of the School's sports teams over the years. Frank's brother, Karl, had been a real football star so his pictures were more numerous than Frank 's. However, both girls would rather look at Frank 's pictures. They loved to look at the different ones of him in a baseball uniform, a basketball uniform and of course, the uniform of the school. Now, they agreed, it was hard to believe that it was time for the graduation of the class of 1922.

Molly and Evie had been such good friends. However, Molly knew that Evie never suspected that she, herself, was crazy about Franklin Niklaus too. Molly had caught him looking at her in the classroom more than once. When he saw her looking at him he would just grin that sweet boyish way, then look away quickly. She prayed that Evie would never know, at least not until after they had left the campus for the last time. Molly had plans.

After graduation when everyone had gone home she would catch Frank and reveal those plans confessing her feelings to Frank. To Frank that is, not to Evie. Molly refused to feel guilty because Evie had confessed to her that Frank had never really declared that he loved her. He treated her as a good friend and always sat with her at all school events, walking her back to the dorm with a friendly kiss on the cheek. Well, yes they had held hands during the silent movies, stolen a kiss now and then and hugged each other laughing at Charlie Chaplin. But, no, he had never told Evie he wanted to be any more serious in their future. He made no commitment or plans with her for after graduation.

To be honest, Evie had to admit that Frank had not mentioned anything about the future. Molly realized then that Evie didn't even seem to know that Frank had accepted a job working on one of Molly's papa's farms just north of here this summer. Then Molly would have the opportunity to bring him lunch and water while working out in the fields. They would sit in the shade under the old maple tree. How exciting that would be. Anything could happen and she intended to see that something memorable would happen.

For now, Evie was her best friend and Molly would not cause any trouble this close to graduation. Jumping up, Evie grabbed Molly's arm, pointed to the dress, and shaking her head negatively, signed, "What wear? Not wear that! I look like baby." As a good friend, Molly sweetly answered, "I have dress. Worn one time party my house. No one else see yet. Wait. Show you."

An hour later, the girls were both ready for pictures looking lovely in their nearly matching dresses of soft silk and lace. Walking toward the field, Evie waved at Frank as she saw him approaching slowly. Returning the wave, he started signing from afar, complimenting both girls on their looks from their hairdos to their pretty white pumps.

As he came closer, he touched Evie's elbow and drew her around to face him. He quietly gestured close to his chest so that Molly would not see, asking Evie to step around the corner with him. They were standing at the corner of the Administration Building where the pictures would be taken with a background of beautiful thick green vines growing up the brick walls. As she stood there trying to politely get away from Molly she decided to just be honest so she signed, "Someone want talk me alone," pointing around the corner. "Find you later. Okay?" Molly slowly smiled, nodded in affirmative and continued walking. Someone, indeed, she mused. It had to be Frank.

As she walked, she wondered what Frank wanted to talk to Evie about on this graduation eve. Would he make plans to see her after graduation after all? Could he possibly want to spend some time with her this summer? Did he really care for Evie seriously? That would ruin everything!

Molly's mind turned swiftly to the letter she received in the post just yesterday. It was a very tempting invitation from Aunt Mary out in California. She had also written to Molly's mama asking her to let

Molly spend the summer with her to meet some really nice young deaf people in the Fremont area.

Mama had said it would be a wonderful opportunity for Molly since Aunt Mary worked at the School for the Deaf and was a real leader in the deaf community. By the time Molly arrived back in the dorm room, she had decided it would be foolish not to take advantage of that invitation. She would "broaden her horizons" her mother insisted. Sometimes Molly could really understand her mother's desire for her to use her speech more and use proper grammar. Understanding English grammar had made it a little easier to read her school studies but it didn't really get through to her writing skills.

Perhaps she would meet some more educated young people in California because that school had a good reputation for deaf education. Of course, this Minnesota school was also known for academic success. It was just that Fremont was in the wonderful state of California which was a natural attraction in itself. Molly's mother had her heart set on her daughter attending Gallaudet University in Washington, D. C., the only four year college for the deaf. She heard that all of the teachers there used sign language and some of them were deaf teachers. How wonderful that would be for a smart young lady such as Molly.

She often imagined herself as a good teacher in that school after she received her teacher's certificate. Molly also realized that Adriana knew some important people who would help make sure that this would happen for her daughter.

Molly was interested enough in the idea that she did take the tests for admission but had not heard the results yet. Right now, she thought only about this summer, her chance to spend time with Frank and to visit her aunt in California. After sorting it out, Molly made up her mind. She would go to California for part of the summer! I could just wait until the end of June so that I could help Mama on the farm for a few weeks and have a chance to talk to Frank as planned. Yes, that's what I will do! So, it doesn't matter what Frank had to tell Evie today, I doubt very much that his plans to work for Papa will change. After all, he said that he needs the money.

At supper that evening, all the students were too excited to eat much. The teachers in the dining room observed dozens of hands moving so fast they soon gave up on trying to read any single conversation. They were able to catch some making plans for the summer but no one seemed to be talking of the future. They did not see any signs used about Gallaudet College or stories related about searching for employment. A few couples were obviously signing only of their recent engagements and impending marriages. Some of them already had jobs lined up through their family members.

A very interesting conversation, involving several of the girls, seemed to be centered on the fact that they were leaving here, a place that they had been so comfortable living in. A place they preferred to call home. This led to individuals sharing their story about how they had been brought to this school so many years ago. Some of the students were already in their mid-twenties, having come here late just as Evie had started school here when she was ten. Two of the teachers were fascinated with Evie's story and could not help but eavesdrop even though they knew it was poor manners.

Thinking again about her mama, Evie said she was so surprised when her sister told her that their mother had married at the age of sixteen. Evie's father had been married before but his wife had died with some disease, leaving him with a little boy to raise. Evie could not imagine a sixteen year old girl taking care of a little boy as well as her husband's desires. She had her household duties and the farming chores, all expected of a housewife on a farm. Adding five more children to the family, naturally, Anna and Julius were both busy people. They owned a small dairy farm in Minnesota. For a few years they had also raised turkeys that were sold to the local turkey plant which employed a hand full of the local housewives who plucked and cleaned them by hand before packing them for shipping across the state.

It was years before they realized their little Evie could not hear anything. The doctor believed Evie had been born deaf because her mama had the "bad" measles while carrying her. Mama was a good mother and a good cook; however, she just didn't know what to do with a deaf daughter. She tried to communicate to Evie that she had to be very careful around the house and scolded her sisters when they did anything to upset her.

Evie was never blamed for anything that went awry. She was more or less placed on a pedestal and told to keep out of the way. It was too dangerous for her to go too far outside because the men were out on tractors plowing; or too busy with all sorts of tools and machinery keeping the farm profitable. Alice and Erma soon learned that they must be responsible for Evie but they didn't seem to mind. They taught her how to dust and polish the big old player piano that mama loved to play. Unlike other families, it never occurred to these sisters that perhaps their mother, Anna, was actually spoiling Evie. They each felt a need to protect Evie from the outside world.

When the girls gathered around Mama and began to sing, Evie held back, only able to sing with guttural sounds, drawing nasty looks from her sisters. She did not know how to enjoy the music. One day sweet little Alice put Evie's hands on the side of the piano to feel the deep vibrations that made her body tingle with something they called rhythm. From that time on, Evie learned to enjoy music and count the beat with which to move her hips.

Erma, the eldest, would sing the words she read on the music sheet. Evie decided not to pay attention to Erma's singing; however she couldn't help but think of Erma as a second mother. After all, she was ten years older, and always appeared as serious and stern as Mama looked.

Her younger sister, Alice, was just the opposite. She was always cheerful, unless harassed by her brothers. Alice loved everyone and it seemed everyone loved her. She always laughed and tickled Evie under her arms, running away so that Evie would chase her. She and Lydia, the baby sister, taught Evie how to have fun with games like jacks and hopscotch. They developed their own gestures so that Evie understood their moods and could express hers somewhat. It was fun for Evie to entertain Baby Lydi too. Evie really found very few times to be a real part of the family and feel happy.

Finally at age nine the public school accepted Evie with the condition that her sister would be the teacher's aide if and when needed.

Alice did her best to keep Evie informed on the school subjects and always helped her with her homework. But, she never knew what the teacher was talking about and really could not read. She didn't know what was wrong; just that she was not comfortable with communication. All she knew were gestures and mime along with a few home signs such as drink, milk, walk, work, clean and hungry.

It was suggested by the teacher that each family member have a sign for their names so Evie would know who they were talking about but there really was no language used that Evie could understand. Her older sister's name was simply signed with the right hand indicating "big" or "tall." She also gave the same gesture for her older brother so she added a gesture that looked like a curl below the right ear to give a feminine annotation to sister.

There were really no distinguishing looks about her siblings. First, the eldest boy was a half-brother and did not look like anyone in their family even though he shared the same father. The only true brother was of average build with the same brown eyes as their father and two sisters. Evie was the only one who matched her mother's blue eyes and black hair that always attracted compliments from visitors. Erma had a quiet kind of beauty probably due to her personality. Evie could only remember one time when she saw Erma laugh. That was when Ray fell from the hayloft onto a sleeping skunk in the barn. Of course everyone had laughed during that incident. Poor Ray! He had to take three baths that day!

All of the girls were of average build. There were six years between Erma and Evie and then just two years between the three younger sisters. The two younger girls were given rather unique signs; Alice had a slight limp so this became a gesture for her name and since Lydia was the youngest, the mime of rocking a baby in the arms was her name. Simple mime such as drink, eat, and sleep, along with facial expressions for anger, sadness and happiness were all used in the family, much as they are in any family of growing siblings. This had worked when she was a little child but when she entered school she had nothing on which to base the words found in a book or noted on the blackboard. Evie tried to read the teacher's mouth as it moved just as she had her father's mouth, but to no avail. What were mouth movements if you knew no words?

Bringing her thoughts back to the present, Evie looked up at her table mates just in time to catch the questions coming to her. The other girls around that dining room table were finally able to get Evie to get to the point; the story was supposed to be how they got to this school! Evie laughed and signed, "OK. Now I tell!" She shifted her weight in her chair and soon had the girls spellbound again as she continued her personal story:

Finally a life-changing event happened! One day soon after Evie's ninth birthday, Evie's teacher brought someone to their home to meet her parents. Mama (Anna) and Papa (Julius) were of German descent following the tradition of serving sweet cakes and coffee before beginning any conversation. Their house was quite spacious with an open dining and living room allowing comfortable living room furniture and a large dining table with eight chairs. Papa greeted their guest at the front door and brought them through the little sun porch into the front room.

Here he took their coats and hats and hung them on the coat rack just inside the front door. He knew that the house gave the appearance of comfort as well as a certain richness expressed through the polished walnut woodwork trim and the lovely dining room built-in cabinets. Papa was proud of the home he had provided his family and was always happy to have proper company such as Evie's teacher and this woman she brought to visit. Yet, Evie detected deep concern etched into the deep lines of Papa's face.

He needn't have worried his graying head about this smiling lady. She was very respectful of his place in this home. Evie tried not to be impolite as she stared at the tall lady at Papa's side. Then she realized that Papa was telling the lady who she was as he put his hand on Evie's shoulder and gave it a gentle squeeze. She smiled timidly and made a slight curtsy as Mama had taught her to do. The woman smiled kindly to her and moved her hands in a strange manner moving one palm smoothly over the other open palm. Then her two forefingers poked up in the air, facing each other, touched softly,

22

and ended with one forefinger pointing to Evie. All Evie could do was continue smiling. To her father's surprise, she then took the lady's hand and led her to a seat at the dining room table. Evie missed the quick explanation given by the lady to her parents; telling her the meaning of the gestures. "Those are signs meaning nice to meet you," she said. Anna walked around the table to the teacher and led her to a chair directly across from their guest, then sat down next to her. Everyone quickly took a seat and gave Evie nods of pleasure as they awaited their treats.

Evie was not aware of the polite comments being made about the delicious apple tarts and wonderful coffee while her two sisters began clearing away the dishes, taking them into the kitchen. Evie was allowed to sit with the four adults but as usual no one tried to include her in their conversation. However, the fact that she could remain at the table with them was enough for Evie to realize that this woman was here to talk about her. She didn't know if she should be afraid or excited about the whole situation. How Evie wished that she could understand what was being said. All she could do was continue to stare at the charming lady.

She was not beautiful but there was something attractive about her. Evie wondered if she had any children and then noted that she wore no wedding band. Her dark hair may have been long but it was wrapped into a bun behind her head neatly covered with a bright colored hairnet. The orange of the hairnet matched the big bow on her white blouse. Evie continued to watch her and turned her eyes ever so slightly to her mother and father to see what their expressions would tell her about the conversation. Using her lip-reading skills, she thought she caught the teacher saying the word school more than once.

Little did Evie know that this woman was here to tell her parents about something that would be a life-changing experience for Evie. Mrs. Emerson proceeded to tell them about the state school for the deaf in a town just a hundred miles away from them.

She told them about sign language used by the children and the teachers in this school. The children would live at the school and come home for holidays or special events that the family desired.

Evie did not know what they were talking about as no one could really explain it to her. They soon tried to include her by showing her a picture of a building that looked a little like the school where she and her sisters attended. But there were other buildings and a lot of beautiful grass around the buildings. One picture showed several children standing in front of the largest building. Mrs. Emerson pointed her finger from here to there to show that it was far away. Evie tried to understand what they were trying to tell her.

Even after they left that afternoon, she sat and thought about the gestures she had seen and the pictures that were shared. Everyone seemed very quiet at the dinner table that evening and her sisters did not even communicate to her in a teasing way as they normally would. Why did everyone seem so serious, she wondered. If they were planning to go on an extended vacation they would be smiling and happy. However, if they were actually going to move somewhere else, that would be serious. Had her teacher complained about her? Were her parents disappointed with her? All these thoughts whirled about in Evie's mind until she fell asleep that night in her own comfy bed.

The next morning Mama washed Evie's hair with rainwater collected during the early hours of the day. This was a special treat as the water was so soft that it left her hair feeling like silk. The girls all took turns using whatever water they collected until it was gone. Usually it would mean two of them would wait until the next rainfall. It was something to look forward to. Today was very special for Evie as Mama pointed to the high stool, indicating that it was Evie's turn for a haircut. She always enjoyed this time sitting quietly and taking in the scents that were on her mama's clothes, apron and hair; scents that only Mama had. It was fun to figure out what the scents were; with today's odor strongly of pancakes and the maple syrup she had served for breakfast. When Mama was finished she gave Evie a hug across the shoulders, giving Evie a whiff of her hair which smelled like rose petals. Despite the fact that Anna rolled her long gray locks into a tight bun on the back of her neck, there were always a few loose curls around her face. She was not a beautiful woman, but to Evie she was an angel, and so strong to carry out all the chores around the house and barn. Evie wondered if she would grow up to do the same things for her husband and children. Those thoughts were quickly dispelled as she realized she did not want to think of what her life would be when she became a woman. Best not to ponder long in that direction.

A few days later her mama and papa took her for a long ride. Evie thought the family was simply enjoying a pleasure ride in her papa's new car, the first one their family had ever owned. Even though her sisters were in school, Mama had gestured that Evie would not go with them that morning. She didn't know that in the trunk of the car was a blue suitcase packed with her clothes. With no one to talk to but her dolly, she settled into the back seat for what seemed like a long ride.

Eventually, they stopped to buy gasoline and she saw the man working there point up the hill and papa leaned over to mama and she looked up there too. When Evie looked up the hill she thought it was a beautiful sight. Julius soon began driving up that winding road while Anna and Evie were looking at some lovely homes surround-ed with gardens growing profusely. Slowing down near the top of the hill, they turned into a gated drive but since the gate was wide open they drove in toward a large red brick building that looked very much like a school. Stopping again, Anna stepped out of the car and gestured for Evie to get out.

Papa walked quickly to the rear of the car and pulled the suit-case from the trunk. Abruptly taking Evie by the hand they walked up to this huge dark brick building with mama trailing behind them. Finally at the bottom of several steps leading up to the front entrance, Julius stopped and waited for his wife to catch up with them. Evie began to feel a little sick to her stomach and looked at her mother with a questioning expression. Gesturing, she pointed to the suitcase and made the number one with her forefinger then pointed it to each of them. Anna knew Evie was questioning why there was just one suitcase, but she just forced a smile and waved her forward.

Upon entering through a huge doorway they were directed to an office where they talked with a rather stern looking gentleman. Evie was led to a third chair where she waited patiently while the adults moved their mouths back and forth across the large wooden desk. She had absolutely no idea what they were talking about so seriously but she somehow sensed that it was not good. Little did she know that this was to be one day of her life she would never forget. After what seemed like hours to Evie, everyone got up and shook hands. The man behind the desk went out the door with them, turning into another office, leaving the three of them alone in the hallway. Papa walked toward the door they had come in. Trying to stay strong, Mama could not hide her feelings any longer.

When Mama gave Evie an unusually tight hug, Evie knew something was very wrong. She had never seen her mama with this look of fear on her face. Was she angry? Or, was it sadness? It was never easy to discern her mother's emotions. What had Evie done to cause her parents to do this? Evie was only sure of one thing, Mama had never acted this way before.

Why was she walking away from her toward the entryway? Evie ran after her, gesturing to go with her as she grabbed her sleeve. Shaking her head negatively, Evie made it as clear as she could – she did not want to stay in this strange place! Mama paused long enough to look her daughter square in the face, mouthing "No. You stay." Then Mama turned her back to retreat down the hallway at a faster pace. Evie stared after her in disbelief. She watched her mother walk right past Papa who was sitting on a bench waiting, and on out those big doors without another look back at Evie. Papa simply nodded his head in Evie's direction and joined his wife before the door closed behind them.

Evie was so frightened. At that moment a tall lady from another office stepped up beside her. Looking up at her, Evie remembered that she was the pleasant lady who wrote something in a book in that first office before her parents had left. She had shaken hands with Mama and Papa and waved a friendly goodbye as they left her area. When she turned to take Evie's hand now, she first pointed to herself and made a sign that looked like she was writing with a pencil. It was a few days before Evie learned what that indicated. This was her *name sign*. Since she was the office secretary the gesture showing the right hand writing into the left palm was given to Mrs. Taylor. Everyone here was given a name sign so that they did not have to spell out a whole proper name to identify someone. When using a friend's name in a conversation it would save a lot of time to just make the name sign. Evie thought this was a wonderful idea.

In fact, it had really been given to Evie already while still in the hearing school. Someone there had given Evie a piece of paper on which were printed pictures of hand shapes for each letter of the alphabet. Evie was given the letter "E" on her ring finger. "E" was for her name of course, then placed on the finger because she wore a beautiful birthstone given to her by her parents. It was very rare that a young student wore any ring so this "identified" Evie to the students and teachers here at this school. It was fun learning name signs for everyone she met along the way. Some placements of name signs would indicate long curly hair, a scar on the face or hand, a smile, a dimple, or in the case of one male teacher, a mustache.

Mrs. Writing kindly took Evie by the hand and led her down the long gray hallway to the side door, across the grass to a little sidewalk that led to a smaller building. As they walked, she noticed some children-playing ball outside who waved and gestured to the lady and smiled as though they were happy. That was a little comforting, but she still didn't know where she was or why she was here. She tried to dry her tears as they continued their walk. She noticed other buildings but didn't pay much attention as the lady pointed them out to her. They soon entered the dormitory and climbed to the second floor where Evie would see for the first time the long room with six beds where she would spend many nights to come.

She was glad she was left alone then to lay on the bed and cry out her fears. A few minutes later five girls came into the room all gesturing to each other in a happy fashion. They each gave Evie a quick hug and pointed to their individual beds. Two of them brought her some sheets and a pillow while the dark-redhead helped her make the bed. That was how she met Molly. Her name sign was an "M" at the side of her mouth moving slightly as though smiling.

Eleven years later, sitting here at supper with all her friends, Evie still remembered that day vividly. She sighed as she finished her story and smiled sadly at all her friends around the table. Little did she know then, when the day came for her to graduate and return to the "outside world," she would cry because she was leaving. It was Molly who had introduced Evie to sign language. After just a few weeks she was expressing herself pretty well to others as life at the Minnesota State Academy for the Deaf had begun. Now she had told this story with her beautiful rendition of American Sign Language "soaked" up for communication such as this. "I wonder what boys talk about?" she signed with a frown on her face as she looked across the room.

The boys were really remembering things today too. Each one recalled good times with their friends here at school and didn't know how they would cope without them out in the world on their own. Molly and Evie had had many late night chats about this very thing. It was so wonderful here at school where everyone communicated with sign language, including teachers using signs in classes. Tests were written in simpler English as there seemed to be no way to write American Sign Language. Conversations went on for hours with almost all of the graduates talking about their visits home during holidays where communication was so difficult, so sparse.

Evie's thoughts drifted toward home. When comparing Evie's family to those of others in their stories, she realized she was fortunate to have sisters and brothers who always loved her. Some of the other students' stories were of abuse, physical and mental. Evie vowed she would show more affection to her family when she was home this summer.

Each time she went home she learned some new fact about her family. Best of all, the family members were striving to use the manual alphabet that helped her learn more about the "outside world." Evie remembered one day when to her amazement, Alice and Erma told her that she was not the only one unable to communicate at all times. They wrote notes to explain that mama and papa spoke in German when talking to each other and only their older brother, Ray, understood them. Evie had no idea that people of other countries spoke a different language. That was so interesting!

It seemed that in Germany people were very *formal* even to their neighbors. This helped Evie to understand why her parents at home were somewhat *stiff*. That was a sign she learned at school when she learned from her sisters that formal really means *stiff* or *strict*. The girls all laughed when Evie showed them a sign for *strict* as opposed to a sign for *stiff* or *formal*. *Strict* was two fingers curled over the top of the nose with a mean look on the face; while *formal* used an open palm with the thumb making tiny vertical circles against the chest, while having the expression of a high-browed person.

However, they all agreed that it seemed the German manners really were quite *stiff*. This would affect their showing any affection toward one another. Hugs were very rare in the family. Evie was almost glad she could be at the school for the deaf where everyone hugged for no reason at all and without embarrassment. Here at school, it was so different where all the girls greeted each other with a warm hug when leaving for home and returning for a new semester. Any exciting moment they shared would begin or end with a hug. This is how we communicate, thought Evie.

Communication. Evie and Molly knew this was going to be a real problem "out in the world." This was more and more evident as the classmates shared their individual "outside" experiences during this senior year. Now, she realized as she looked around the room that this would be the last time they had supper together. Evie knew that almost no one had been able to make plans beyond summer because jobs were very rare for deaf men to say nothing of deaf women. That's why the older girls preferred to think only of marriage and starting a family.

Many of the fellows had taken vocational courses during this last year that their teachers said were certain to lead them to the job fields of printing, painting, baking and farming. Frank had even learned something called linotyping and had been told he would have no problem finding work with a newspaper. He told Evie just that afternoon that if he got a job he wanted her to marry him! She couldn't believe it! She said she would wait for him for as long as he wanted. They exchanged addresses so that they could keep in touch. Evie couldn't wait to tell Molly!

However, now was not the time. She snapped out of this reverie and brought her attention back to this lovely dinner that all the seniors were enjoying this evening. Now was the time to watch her friends as they shared their stories with great enthusiasm!

Frank told about the time he and his brother, Karl, had gone out to check on their rabbit traps. "We boys were allowed to set traps outside of two miles from the school buildings. We were only allowed to do this for the school kitchen staff. The school cook actually made a delicious rabbit stew and often paid us a few cents for the rabbits that encouraged our keenness for hunting. We hung the skins on the back steps railings and after they dried out some of the boys would take them into town and sell them. Sometimes they would get as much as two dollars for a good animal fur.

"But this one particular time we found a skunk still alive in one of the traps! Oh, my! We ran dorm, soaked bath, smell bad! We really didn't know what to do with the clothes except to stuff them in a laundry bag. The housefather tracked down the stench and sent us to the Principal's office where we were scolded royally." Yet, today they laughed about the incident.

Billy had a story about hiding all of his underwear, saying he had none, because he didn't like to wear underwear! He had to work a week in the laundry as punishment. When the house father forced him to smell his own pants he learned quickly that he had better wear the underwear from then on! This brought on a lot of laughter throughout the dining room with the girls trying hard not to picture the scene, as they giggled politely.

Of course the boys had to review their sports events, teasing Frank about the time he had missed a free-throw. Reminding him it would have won the school championship over the Illinois School for the Deaf. But they all praised him for the points he had made over the past two years and hoped that he would be able to continue to play somewhere out in the world.

Frank believed there was no place for a deaf basketball player in local colleges or vocational teams. The only college a deaf person should really attend was way out in Washington, D.C. Gallaudet would be a wonderful place to go. Because Frank was good with writing in good English order, his English teacher encouraged him to apply. However, he put that out of his mind quickly.

He knew his parents could not afford to send him there. Besides, he really wanted to find work with his skill as a linotype operator that he had learned here at school. He had plans that he had not shared with Evie yet; plans to find work and then ask her to marry him. He knew that a beautiful girl like Evie would not be single very long.

On the eve of graduation, the girls reminisced together about the time they had helped each other get dressed for the school dance last fall. They were so excited as it was the very first time the school had held one. Evie was thrilled as she was chosen to be one of the demonstration team on stage. Ten girls had practiced a dance routine for three weeks wherein they followed the music vibrations they could feel in the wooden floor. After showing the students the steps they came down off the stage, picked partners, and proceeded to dance.

It wasn't easy for them but most of them had the steps mastered by the third song. Mrs. Writer, as she had affectionately been named, stood on stage next to the Victrola and directed the beat that accompanied the vibrations they could feel on the gym floor. They would watch her wind up the handle and upon dropping the needle onto the record she would nod her head fervently.

Evie was to begin her first step upon that nod and the others would follow. She had also learned to count the steps, one-two-three; one-two. Mrs. Writer was one hearing person that all the kids loved. She understood a lot of their signs. Her husband, Jim, had been deaf but he died of a heart attack at an early age and the school became Loretta Writer's life.

Jim had always loved to feel the beat of music and would steal a dance with her in the hallways where the wood floor carried vibrations from the band room. He was such a crazy young man and it had been very difficult to wait out his senior year before she could date him. Her college years had never prepared her for the real world of the deaf. In fact, she only had one year of sign language in the deaf education program in the school she attended.

Loretta soon learned it had not been enough for someone teaching at the state school for the deaf. She could use signs with her students so that they seemed to grasp most of what she said. But when they wanted to tell her something that had happened she always told them to slow down, which resulted in a loss of the grammar and expressions needed for her to comprehend.

Theirs was a sign language that brought in visual scenes so clearly to each other. Somehow the picture got lost when they settled into correct signs or English grammar. When they became excited it was impossible for her to understand them. It was frustrating because she wanted to be able to interact with them everywhere, not just in the classroom.

American Sign Language was the major mode of communication here; so she began to watch the students closely to catch on to this marvelous way of signs. Someday Loretta hoped to have time to research the language and work on the linguistics and credibility of signs. She was still slim and attractive with short brown hair and brown eyes that were always full of love for her students. She only wished Jim was here with her and had been able to see something like this school dance. What fun!

The school dance. This was just another event included in their school story-telling tonight. It continued when Katherine told about the girls looking into the boys' bathroom across the campus one night because someone had forgotten to close the window. They saw four naked boys before the window was closed and they laughed and giggled all night until the housemother made them confess what was going on.

Supper was long over and it was getting late. One of the teachers stood up and walked over to the light switch, turning it off and back on. This was the way to get an entire room of deaf people to stop their conversations and look to the head table for information. Now they were given directions for the rest of the evening.

They were all told to go to their rooms to be sure their clothes were ready for graduation ceremonies the next day and to finish packing for their trips home. Many parents would be there for graduation so they were to be on their best behavior; however, there would be no time to see their parents until after the ceremonies.

Evie and Molly knew their parents would be there. Evie's sisters would come too. They had never been to the school in all the years that she had been there. Of course she had gone home on all important holidays and for the summers. She had been nine years old when she came here and now she would be twenty in just two months. Wearing long braids when she first started school she now had her hair bobbed like the other girls here. This framed her beautiful high cheeks and blue eyes. Evie considered herself average in looks but Frank and others always complimented her on her beauty.

A very nice letter with a crisp ten dollar bill inside from her mother was received by Evie. This was to be her graduation gift. Mama had apologized that they could not give more but Evie had known not to expect more. She tucked the bill away in a secret compartment of her suitcase and vowed to keep it for any emergency that might arise. Frank's mother had died two years ago of tuberculosis and his father could not come to graduation. It was really nothing new to his seven older brothers and sisters because Karl had graduated this school just last year.

When Frank came to school he was told that his sign name would be a *k* on the forehead moving to his chin. That was because Karl had the sign of *k* on his forehead as his name started with a K. Since Frank was his little brother, his sign would be starting like Karl's but then dropping like it was little on the chin. Then when their younger sister started school they gave her one with the *k* starting on the chin and then dropping to the chest. Everyone caught on quickly to name signs. Sometimes the signs would indicate something like a scar, a hairstyle, or something easily identifiable.

Evie, though, had been given the sign of *e* placed on her left hand palm down because of her lovely birthstone ring. Her parents had given it to her on her sixth birthday. Since coming to this Minnesota School for the Deaf, Evie had not seen any other girl wearing such a ring, except Molly. Molly had two rings, one her birthstone and one antique looking with a beautiful opal. Molly had never shared who gave her the rings and Evie never asked. Even though they had been roommates for all these years there were still some things they just considered private.

Today, Frank's sister, Mandy, still had two more years of school ahead of her; so the two of them would catch an early evening train home. It was just one hour on the train to their little hometown where Father would pick them up with Jennie, their old horse, pulling their worn carriage. Karl, Frank and Mandy had all become deaf as a result of scarlet fever when they were just toddlers.

Frank's family had learned of the School for the Deaf early on so they all had a real advantage because they could communicate together at home too. They shared information and felt they had a good education with hopes of a bright future.

At school, Karl and Frank were trained in the printing business while Mandy learned to sew and cook very well. Mandy was a plain girl but had a terrific memory. She knew everybody's birthday and where they lived. She always appeared to be happy. She already had a serious boyfriend. They were already making plans to be married in three years. George was also trained as a printer and had an uncle who promised to help him get into the newspaper in Illinois where he worked. This was fortunate, indeed.

Evie invited Frank to meet her parents after the ceremonies and he was happy to comply! Evie hoped this would result in a good experience for her parents and sisters as they watched Evie and Frank signing to each other. Mama and papa stood quietly as Molly and a couple of other friends came along to say goodbye. Evie could not help but beam with pride as she introduced her deaf friends and teachers to her mama through writing notes after finger spelling the names.

She was careful to spell out their proper names, Julius as her Papa who did not even try to acknowledge the introductions. But, when she spelled out Anna for her Mama, she had shaken hands with Frank and the teachers with a smile. Evie knew this was somewhat of an effort for her mama and that she had done so to please her. Now the time had come to say goodbye to Frank and Molly. She excused herself from her parents for a few minutes, gesturing for them to wait for her in the car.

When she returned to them for the trip home she was in tears. Trying to console her, Alice carefully spelled out *b e a u t i f u l*. She continued to gesture happily, telling her she was impressed with the school campus and they all thought it was a beautiful graduation ceremony. Getting no response, Alice spelled out the name *F r a n k* and with a teasing expression, she hugged herself tightly! However, no one could stop Evie's tears so they finally just left her alone huddled in the corner of the back seat.

Evie and Frank's wedding (1928)

2

⤳

Will We Work? Will We Marry?

Alice and Erma chatted quietly about the wonders of deafness and what might lie ahead for their little sister. What
did their parents expect of them? Erma was married now and Alice
was engaged. Alice's fiancé was a farmer and they would live with
his parents not too far from Mama and Papa. Erma and her husband
lived in the city where he had a good job as a carpenter. They had
a lovely little brick home that Alice loved to visit. They were both
well on their way to their own separate lives, no longer really members of the household of their father. Of course, their sister, Lydia,
was still in the home with no real plans of moving out.

Alice wanted to share all this news with Evie but was not sure
just when or how. Would this make her happy for her sisters or
would she feel more alone than ever? What did Evie's future hold?
What could it hold for any deaf person? Even if she were to marry that boy Frank someday, could he really provide for her? What
kind of job could he hold? Oh, dear Lord, please take care of Evie.
Having finished that prayer she decided she must take Evie one day
at a time. For now, Evie would be living with her parents. Would she
be able to work at a real job?

Would she be able to marry? Surely father would not expect
them to take on any responsibility for Evie in her adult years, would
he? As though reading her mind, Julius spoke, never taking his eyes
off of the road in front of them. He loved this car and never took any
chances of having an accident or allowing the rocks on this gravel
country road to scratch the hood or doors. "Your mother and I have
been considering allowing Evie to go to Chicago with her cousin,

Irene. She seems to think she can go to the same school and learn sewing with the new sewing machines. The teachers at Faribault said Evie has already learned on the machines they have there so she should adapt quite well. Her cousin is willing to have Evie as a roommate for that one year and promises to look after her safety.

However, we do not want Evie to get a job in Chicago as her cousin plans to do. We hope something will open up in Winona at their clothing factory." "Oh! Papa! That sounds like a good plan," Lydia said with excitement. "What does Evie think about it?" "Oh," Papa quickly responded, "she doesn't know about this yet. We wanted to wait until school was out and we are home again before we discuss this. Irene said she would come for a visit and help us explain the whole thing to her." "I see. Yes, that will help because Irene is learning signs in a church class. Isn't that a good idea for a church to do?" Lydia replied. Papa had no more to say on the subject as he concentrated on the road again. The rest of the family was quiet, each lost in their own thoughts about Evie.

As it turned out, Irene did very well in describing the whole situation to her cousin that summer and before too long they were making their plans to put Evie on the train along with Irene. It all happened so fast but Papa had been clear on his plans and Evie did not want to fight him. After all, she really had no other plans for her future except for a faint hope that Frank would ask her to marry him some day! Anyway, if she could tell her friends that she was going to Chicago that would really impress them.

At first, Evie thought a year away from Frank would be too long but she realized he would be working on that farm as long as he could before searching for a job. That search could be as little as a week but it might stretch into months. She had received two letters from him stating just those facts. He said nothing about marriage in his third letter after receiving Evie's news. He wished her good luck and said he hoped she found a job in Winona the following year. She decided to keep on writing letters as often as she could.

Chicago was exciting, indeed! Their apartment was on the third floor over a small grocery store. It was small with just one bedroom that Irene claimed and a fold-a-way bed in the little front room for Evie. Evie didn't mind though because she loved looking out the window at the El-train in the distance and watch the bright lights flashing below. She could buy groceries downstairs and soon learned to cook a little for herself and Irene. They took turns fixing a light meal in the evenings but each fixed their own breakfast and packed their own lunch to take to school. They walked together to the bus that took them to the sewing school so they wouldn't be late for class; then walked home each afternoon so they could look at the store windows and dream.

Evie caught on quickly to the workings of the new sewing machine, bringing smiles and a pat on the back by the teacher almost every day. There were ten girls at the machines and sometimes she would see three or four of them chatting with each other and laughing. She never knew if they were laughing at her or some story they told. Once she saw the teacher scold them with her finger pointing in their faces so that they all stopped talking and concentrated on their work. Irene never wasted time talking and seemed to love the work they were learning. Three months went by quickly.

At Christmas time, Irene said her boyfriend was coming to visit for three days and asked Evie to be nice to him. But, Evie never got to meet the boyfriend because her father sent her a train ticket to come home during the Christmas break from classes. Better than that, she received a letter from Frank the same day, telling her he would be home for Christmas too. Evie could hardly contain her joy as she shared the good news with Irene. They both laughed and promised to share their Christmas stories when they were together again in January.

Unfortunately, Frank was only able to visit Evie at her parents' home for one day. His brother brought him to Altura in his old pickup truck. They arrived in time for lunch, when introductions were made all around. Frank 's brother talked with her brother, Ray, all through lunch. Frank signed to Evie that he was glad they could talk in sign language and keep the conversation to themselves. He told her that he really thought he would soon have a job in Wisconsin.

"Job linotype operator small town newspaper!" he signed, excitedly. Evie was so enraptured by the happy expression on his face that she scarcely knew what he had said. "Evie! Did you understand what I just said?" Frank signed impatiently.

"What? Job? Where? When?" Evie signed sharply, as though she had just awakened to what he had signed. Frank repeated his information and added the fact that he thought maybe they could get married that next summer. "But, Secret! We should not tell any-one yet. Wait until happen for sure. Okay?" Frank signed in a small framework so that he would not attract attention. This was fun, having their own private conversation and keeping a secret.

But with the whole family at the table, this solitude did not last. Alice was tugging on Evie's dress sleeve, gesturing and mouthing, "Why you happy, Evie?" Erma had given Evie and Frank both a pad of paper and a pencil. Evie wrote down that they were just catching up on news of friends from school. Evie politely enquired of her mother that she and Frank be excused from the table. Soon they re-layed that they were going for a walk to acquaint Frank with Altura.

Alice, being Alice, put a stern look on her face as she followed the couple around all the rest of the day. That was really difficult for her to do because she was warm and kind, by nature. Besides she loved Evie. After a short while, she found a grassy spot on the side of a hill and sat down to watch them.

Earlier, all the family members had talked about how their school had been a good decision for Evie. Also, from what they could glean, for all young deaf people who found a mutual language they could enjoy within their own community. Yes, the family was thankful for the teacher who had referred them to that special school.

The young couple took a long walk around the edge of town and managed a few minutes to sit down on a park bench holding hands. Frank's brother soon came in his truck waving Frank to come on board using enough gestures to tell him that they had to get home before dark. Frank quickly gave Evie a sweet kiss on the mouth and waved goodbye. She could feel that kiss for an hour and would not dare touch her mouth until bedtime.

Evie so wanted to share her news with someone but decided Frank had been right. He didn't know that he had the job yet and even if he did it might take more than just a few months to find a place to live. For now, she would be living in Illinois, while he might be living in Wisconsin, and her parents still assumed she would get a job in Winona. Evie would need patience and *life* would just have to wait.

Evie, Frank, Liz and Trixie (1935)   *Frank, Bobby, Evie, and Liz (1938)*

Bobby, Liz and Trixie (1937)

3

Can We Raise Our Own Children?

Dear Evie and Frank,   *August 8, 1931*

Congratulations on your new baby daughter! Thank you so much for the picture. She looks like a little doll. Do you know yet if she can hear? I sure hope so. But it is okay if she is deaf because she will have you as deaf parents and you can all communicate. Everything will be fine. I am so sorry that I have not been in touch for so long. I just did not feel like writing letters. Now I must write and tell you how wonderful it is to know that you two are happy as parents now!

I am so jealous. Of course we were fortunate in having our lovely baby boy, Johnny, for five years. It took us two years to get over the loss of that precious child. We blamed each other for that terrible accident. Then we decided we should really try to have another child. But, Sam and I have not been lucky to have any children yet. In fact the doctor has told me I will not be able to conceive.

After that accident last year it seems my insides were torn up so much that it would not be good for me to try to have a child. So now we are talking about adoption. I am so busy with my students at school that they are like my own children. Yet I know Sam feels cheated. I will let you know if we adopt. I wish we could come to see the baby. My goodness, we haven't seen you for years!

Yet, I feel you are still my dearest friend! You and Frank looked so good when we saw you at the reunion in Faribault.

Neither one of you had changed much in five years. We had so many good times together during our school years. So many memories to cherish forever.

One of my fondest memories is the day of your wedding. You were so beautiful, Evie, in that gorgeous brown velvet dress. Your mama did well by you. The church was so beautiful. I wish we could have heard all the words that the minister said. Alice did her best to tell me what your promises were but I long to hear every word of the marriage vows, don't you? And then, I remember when it was time to see you off at the railroad station!

What a comical scene that was. Watching Frank and your papa lifting that mattress onto the baggage car was funny! Then Karl carried all your boxes filled with wedding presents into the car in which you would be riding. You truly were fortunate to receive such nice gifts and I was so afraid for you to put that lovely china on board. I made sure your sisters had packed it well. My dear Evie, it was so hard to say goodbye to both of you then and again at the reunion!

Life here in California is still as exciting as it was the day I came. It's hard to believe I've lived here many years already. I thank my Aunt Mary every time I see her. Again, Evie, and you too Frank, congratulations on your first baby!

Love, Molly and Sam
P.S. Look for a small package in the mail soon!

Evie read the letter three times before folding it up and slipping it into a tiny drawer in their antique desk that mama and papa had bought for them when they came to visit two years ago. They said they found it in a used furniture store and told Evie they wanted her to have it. She was somewhat disappointed though, when Mama told her their reason for this gift. Papa was the one who put an unusual smile on his face as he carefully handed Evie a note that he had already written. "My Dear Evie, This desk is to be used by you to practice your writing skills so you will not fall far behind Frank." Evie had never realized how her parents must have assumed that Frank would write good English grammar because of his job.

But Frank had told Evie that this just was not true. All he did was copy what was already written out for him. He had to really concentrate to get all of the wording in the right order. Because of that his fellow workers bragged on what a good linotype operator Frank was because he was always focused on his work and did not waste time with idle chit chat or ogling the front desk secretary. Frank never let on that grammar was a problem for him so Evie did not tell her parents Frank's secret. He had a good job, was good to her and seemed to adore their daughter. For now that was more than enough to keep their marriage strong.

That evening they read Molly's letter together and decided that she was genuinely jealous of them and that sure was a pleasing thought. But they both envied Molly, her good grammar and life as a teacher in a school for the deaf. Life had been good to all of them in the outside world after all. Except for Molly's loss of her son. That was so tragic.

Frank had his own memories of Molly that he never shared with his wife. It was only when they received this letter from California that these memories came forward in his mind again. He tried not to think about Molly; yet he couldn't help but reflect on those events of his youth. For the rest of that evening he pretended to be reading the newspaper but was really recalling his time with Molly. He couldn't help but let his mind drift back to those youthful, care-free days.

That first summer Frank had gone to work on Molly's family farm. At least he worked there for one month. That month was full of a mixture of young blood aroused by a beautiful redhead and a guilty conscience when reading letters he received from Evie. It was absolutely impossible to resist Molly! She was there, in the barn, all of the time. In the fields he would naturally sit with her to eat the lunch she brought to the men; after all, they could communicate with each other. Frank did not intend for that communication to develop into a body language. Yet how could he deny his feelings when she pushed him down playfully and jumped fully on him with a deep kiss. Of course nothing happened during the daytime as he had to get back to work. All the while he was stacking the sheathes of wheat in an orderly fashion, he could still feel Molly's delicate bosom against his chest. What an exquisite body she had!

In the evening, Molly would sneak into the barn where Frank's mattress waited for him after supper. He always told her he was too tired to chat much. However, by the third evening her visit lasted into the wee hours of the morning. She would allow him to take a nap and then awaken him in the middle of the night. Then she would hurry back to the house and sleep all morning until her mother awakened her to help prepare lunch for the men in the field. This soon became a habit that Frank did not really want. Yet, he could not resist. Besides, what could he do about her? She was the boss's daughter!

Frank could not believe how easily he fell in love with her soft, shapely body and her bubbly personality. Yet he felt a different kind of love for Evie and could not erase her from his mind. Eventually, unfortunately for Molly, she was caught! Neither Frank nor Molly had considered that their lovemaking was noisy and would be over-heard by the other workers in the barn. One of the men decided he should tell Molly's mother because they were so young and after all, they were deaf! They couldn't ever marry, could they? Frank was not really sorry that Molly was forced to go through with her Aunt's plans to spend the rest of the summer in California.

After that, Frank was too embarrassed to stay on at the farm with Molly's family. He took his friend's advice, caught a ride on an open railroad car, that took him north to Canada where his broth-er Karl was working on a huge grain farm. Even though the work was hard it had been a fun summer for them. On Saturday nights they would take a hot bath, put on some clean shirts and dungarees and walk into town.

There they had free movies outdoors right next to a little saloon where they learned to communicate an order for a bottle of beer. Both young men were good looking enough to attract attention from the girls even without the uniforms of the academy. However, they never got past the first awkward attempts at communication before the girls would turn their attention to some other guys. Hearing guys of course! That did not really upset the brothers as they still wrote letters to their girls from school. The whole experience certainly helped Frank to forget about Molly. He had received one letter from her not long after she departed for California and he chose not to reply. He never shared the story of his passion for Molly with his brother but he did say that she had flirted with him; so he came to Canada to get away from her. Karl had no reason to believe otherwise.

Karl's girlfriend, Emily, surprised him with a visit to the farm in Canada! It just so happened that her parents were taking a train through Montreal. It wasn't much of a visit really; just a half hour at the train station before she rejoined her parents and continued their trip. When October rolled around, Frank and Karl were told they were not needed again until April. Since both had managed to save some money they stopped by their home for a few days visit. This was long enough for them to renew their promises to each other that they would not live like this on poor dirt farms again! They assured their father that they did not need money and were careful not to let him know of their meager savings. When they said their good-byes, they decided to save their money by hitchhiking to Wisconsin. There they stopped at cities along the way to fill out applications at the local newspaper offices. Surely someone, somewhere would need a linotype operator!

That was then and this is now, Frank realized as he awoke from his day dream with Evie's hand shaking his sleeve and signing, "You fell asleep! Hard day at work? Come help!" Frank helped with the dishes as they swapped stories of how the day had been. The subject of Molly's letter was not brought up again.

Evie told Frank she was so thankful for her new neighbor, Sally, who tried to use a new sign every day and was doing well enough that she could let Evie know if she heard the baby crying too long. "Makes me feel safer. Know Sally helps." "Yes, good. Will only let you know if baby cries too much. Not change diapers or feed baby. That your duty," Frank signed softly, with a smirk on his face. "Oh! Naturally! I know!" Evie retorted sharply. She wondered why he felt he had to make that clear to her. Of course she wouldn't ask Sally to do anything else. But if Sally *offered* to, then she would not turn her down!

Evie spent the rest of the evening cleaning the kitchen while Frank entertained the baby with silly faces and a rattle. It was kind of exciting to watch Liz's face light up with surprise when Frank would shake that silly looking rattle. She must be able to distinguish this as a noise unlike any other sound in their house. Evie already knew that it would be important to watch her baby's reaction to unusual movements around the house to learn what things were okay or not okay to do. One time she knew Liz was frightened into crying when Evie dragged her chair across the kitchen floor so she knew not to do that again. These little things that make sound would be interesting to note. Of course, the chair had vibrated when dragged on the floor and Evie knew immediately that must make noise. However, there were other things she didn't know, like the day she hung up a picture, using a hammer and nail. She was determined to pay attention to sounds so that her baby would be comfortable and able to sleep as needed. Learning to be a good mother was not easy.

The next day after dinner and dishes were done, Frank asked Evie to sit down and pay attention to him. "I have news. Bad news today." Looking at Evie's anxious facial expression, he continued, "Mr. Furly came work today gave note for us. Finish this house sold. Must move out month end!" Evie almost dropped her dish and set it carefully back into the water. "Oh, no. Where go?" Evie signed. Frank put his arm around her shoulder and led her to the table so they could sit down. "Me see sign "For Rent" two blocks," Frank signed as he pointed his finger three times at the window indicating the direction to take to the house with the sign. "You, me, Liz walk now," he continued as he walked over to the closet and brought out the baby carriage.

Their new home was an upstairs apartment. The three of them shared one bedroom for a year. Never comfortable with this arrangement, Frank finally found a two bedroom house for rent in a neighborhood not too far from the school that Liz would soon attend. Evie was quite comfortable in this house and relaxed enough to enjoy taking care of her daughter. Liz was soon signing everything they could throw at her. They were surprised at how easily she caught on to their sign language. However, they had letters from Emily and Karl stating how their daughter signed so well by age five and now their son was learning quickly too. So they knew to expect this and yet they were surprised and proud of Liz. Emily had also written a cautionary statement in her letter. "We have been told by members of the Deaf Club that it is not a good idea to teach your children to voice everything you sign to any 'hearies' around! Also, even more importantly, we should not expect that our children understand enough of what they hear from different people to translate into signs for us.

"I think this might be true. Our five year old certainly does not have the vocabulary to put into words what we sign to them. It is really too much to expect a child to sign to us the words that they hear. Maybe we need to wait until they are ten or twelve to trust their translation. Yet, it will be important for us to build a trust with our children so that we can always see that they are doing their best to be honest and not making up stories. It certainly will not be easy. So, always be aware of this."

When Liz was five, Evie discovered she was pregnant again and was not too sure she was happy about it. "Me, mother, me hard do," she shared with Frank that evening when she had learned the news from her doctor. "But you good daddy. Thank God!" She would never forget the day that Frank had seen an ad in the paper for puppies for sale near their home.

That evening he took Liz by the hand and walked to the sale. The lady showing the puppies soon realized that Frank was deaf and didn't feel she could trust the little girl to communicate the deal for her. However, she soon found out she was quite wrong. Frank simply gestured with the fingers shaping the scissor blades and pointed to the puppy and then to his own ear. The owner interpreted his gestures correctly and nodding in the affirmative, said, "Yes, his ears were clipped and have already healed." Liz waited patiently while her daddy wrote a note probably asking how much the puppy cost. Before long she had the puppy in her arms and they were returning home. After walking a couple of blocks Liz put the puppy down long enough to sign to her daddy, "Thank you! Puppy precious birthday present." Frank quickly picked up the wandering puppy and grinned down at his daughter. He loved the way she signed precious with her little fist keeping the touch to the chin for just a little longer than necessary and pulling it straight down slowly. Frank was amazed at his own daughter's quick response to a new sign and her clear understanding of the subject in question. He continued to hold the puppy in his arms as they walked into the house and found Evie in the kitchen. When she turned to see what he had she jumped back and signed, "What animal?" Frank drew closer to Evie and took her hand to pet the puppy's head before he placed her into Evie's arms.

Evie touched the puppy and stroked her smooth head as the puppy looked up at her with big black eyes that seemed to pop out from a white streak running down her forehead and circling her mouth. "Remember? Sale, Larsen's puppies! Liz birthday." Nodding in agreement, Evie slowly turned to Liz and signed in a deliberate manner. "You responsible puppy. Food, water give. Teach potty out." Liz nodded strongly and looked to her daddy for some kind of instructions on how this was to be done. Frank took her by the hand and led her to the basement where he had put out a doggie dish for food and one for water. He laid out some newspaper and pointed to a box he had fixed up with an old worn out jacket and gestured, *sleep*. Then he put a little pink collar around the pup's neck and attached a leash leading them outside for a romp around the yard. This was one of the happiest days Liz could ever remember. At supper that evening they had all decided on Trixie as the puppy's name.

Evie reflected again, she would never forget that day. It was a day that Evie knew for a fact that Frank was a natural at being a daddy, and she was sure glad of that. She wished she could say the same thing about herself in the role of a mother but it just seemed difficult. Once a friend had given Evie a good suggestion. "Make an eight inch by ten inch sign to hang on the buggy when you take baby Liz out for stroll. On this sign you first print these words with a black crayon. PLEASE TALK TO THE BABY." Evie had done exactly that. What fun! What a good experience for the baby! Some people actually took the time to write a note to Evie too. They were simple notes about how pretty or sweet the baby was. All she would do in response was nod her head in the affirmative and give a big smile. She never wanted to get into a conversation. She was happy that the baby got all the attention. Frank was usually comfortable with writing notes, just the opposite of her. Even after five years she would direct people's attention to her daughter rather than try a conversation on her own.

Maybe it was this way because she actually felt jealous of her own daughter. The fact that she could hear and talk to everyone who came into her life seemed so overwhelming to Evie. At the same time, she was thankful that Liz would be able to translate for her with strangers in the future.

Why had they chosen such difficult names for their children? Their names were vocally hard to say. When trying to call to them, Frank and Evie used the strongest voice they could muster. Liz seemed to understand when she heard Evie's way of saying it, but it was not that easy when she heard her father's voice. Frank and Evie often discussed what it would be like to hear what voices sounded like. They knew they made sounds with their voices or throats because Liz let them know when they made too much noise.

One night they had two friends in for a game of cards. Neither of them were totally deaf, just what Liz called "hard-of-hearing." They could speak fairly well, audible enough for most folks to understand. But, to Liz, their voices still sounded like they were in a well. One of them wore a hearing aid behind his ear but his wife preferred not to wear one. She had told Evie that it was really difficult to get those aids balanced well and she had a headache after wearing hers for an hour or so. Why wear them when visiting with deaf friends who used sign language; her favorite way of communicating.

This particular evening Liz had been in bed a couple of hours and everyone assumed she was long asleep. With surprise, the adults saw her come walking into the room with tears in her eyes. "Wrong?" signed Evie. Liz signed for all to see, "You funny noises. Baby Bobby scared. Me sleep not!" Frank told her he was sorry they had awakened her, as he picked Liz up and carried her back to her bed. The card game soon ended as a discussion arose about how they had made *noise*. No one had done anything to cause any vibration on the floor so how could they have produced "*noise?*" Evie poured everyone a cup of coffee as they retired into the living room into comfortable chairs. Fred swore that he and his wife had not used their voices all evening. However, he had been laughing pretty loudly and pointed out that vibrations of the throat made noise. His wife joined her hubby by noting how she knew she often made guttural vibrations when she became excited. Frank admitted that he was yelling "Out!" He said he often did this when playing cards, when slamming down his last card. Fred and his wife had no children and were reminded by Evie that it was important to keep quiet when the kids were asleep. This subject of *noise* was to remain a wonder to them all as they bade each other good-night.

The next morning Frank and Evie told Liz how proud they were of her helping Bobby. They were fully aware that Liz insisted on calling her baby brother, Bobby; but they had been advised this was just a normal phase for a sibling who had been an only child for six years. So they had ignored it, using his real name when they spoke of him. As Bobby grew, it seemed he just would not sign to his mommy and daddy like Liz did. He really seemed to depend on his big sister too much to communicate for him. When he was ready to go to school he still did not want to use sign language when other kids were around. His parents decided that was just the difference between boys and girls; but Liz did not appreciate this at all.

She grew up thinking her little brother was nothing but a pest. He was definitely spoiled by mom something awful! But when she asked her mother why she loved her baby brother more than she loved her, she was surprised at Evie's response. "You my first baby.

I worried and nervous all time. Funny story tell you." And, with that, Evie signed a long story that did help Liz to understand her mother a little more.

During the first three years of Liz's life, their home had been in a house where an older lady lived upstairs in her own flat. Evie worried about having a crying baby downstairs and did everything she could to keep Liz from crying. This made a busy day for Evie. She couldn't concentrate on her own work more than ten minutes because she had to stop and go peek in on the baby. Mrs. Johnston had figured out a way to let the Niklaus' know if their little girl was too noisy. She would pound on the pipes that went through their first floor ceiling bringing heat up to her level. This vibrated their floor so that Evie got up to look into the bedroom to see if baby Liz was awake or crying. Of course things were a little better as Liz grew and started walking.

This happened one afternoon when Liz was almost three years old. She was nowhere to be seen! What a fright! Then she noticed that the bathroom door was shut and when she opened it there was Liz crying. Apparently she had got up from her nap, gone into the bathroom and closed the door and locked it. She had just learned how to do that. Then she could not get it open. There was no way of knowing how long she had been in there and Mrs. Johnston never offered to tell them. Evie pondered on how to prevent such an event again as she held her child in her arms until she fell asleep.

At long last, Frank and Evie bought a home of their own. They actually had the house built from the basement up. Everything smelled new and Evie couldn't get enough of the fresh oak scent in her kitchen cabinets. Liz was eight and baby brother was just two. Having three bedrooms made the new house all the more of a wonderful move. They were so proud to have been able to build a home and afford the mortgage payments. Evie was especially proud of Frank as he continued with his employment at the *Merrill Daily Herald*.

Evie and Liz grew a little impatient as they waited for the building to finish. They would walk the few blocks from their present home to the site where the new house was going up. It was interesting watching the walls go up and then looking inside as they finished the walls with boards and plaster. Finally, when they actually moved in, they thought it was a palace! With the three bedrooms, Bobby didn't have to share a room with anyone. Liz was so glad that he had his own neighborhood friends and she didn't have to keep a close eye on him so much anymore. He could sign some but never seemed to want to use it as much as Liz did. However, she really didn't mind clarifying messages that he was trying to relay to their parents. She felt all grown up and it was true that she knew just as much as they did even though none of them realized this or the impact this would have with the family.

Liz had so much fun decorating her room with her own things in the way she wanted them. Evie let her pick out a lovely new pink bedspread at the nice furniture store down town. She chose pink because her Shirley Temple doll had on a deep pink color polka dot dress so she could set in the middle of the bed and continue to be her *show* doll. Lying on the bed with her doll, she reflected on the day when Aunt Lydia had given it to her for her fifth birthday. Aunt Lydia was somewhat sophisticated in her actions. As young as Liz was, she had noticed how this younger sister of her mother's had always appeared more stylish than the older sisters who lived in Minnesota. She had her hair cut and clothes that looked like the ladies in the Sears catalog that Evie kept in her bedroom. But, to Liz, her mother was the prettiest sister of the four girls in that family. Lydia had only one son, so apparently she enjoyed buying a doll for her niece; but she had asked Liz to promise to keep it for *show* only, not to play with it at all!

After her aunt's visit, Liz had asked her mother just what did she mean, for *show*? Evie said it was simple enough to understand, "Play doll? No! Pretty look shelf," she signed. Liz was somewhat disappointed because this was the only really pretty doll she ever owned. She thought it would be so nice to put pretty doll clothes on her and show her off to her girlfriends in the neighborhood. But she had dutifully put the doll on top of her chest of drawers and said nothing. However, now in this new house, she put it on her bed. She was sure her mother would have forgotten about her promise to Aunt Lydia. Not only that, she could argue with her mom that she was old enough now to know how to take care of such a pretty doll. As it turned out, Liz did not need to have that discussion with her mother after all.

The following year Santa brought her a doll for play. It was even bigger than the Shirley Temple doll and had real hair and eyes that open and shut when she would lie her down on the bed. "Oh," Liz signed excitedly to her parents, "this play doll. Eyes wink! Name Winki," and with that she cuddled the doll in her arms and pretended to rock her back and forth. Then she said out loud, "Winki, I'm so glad Santa brought you to me. Now I have a friend to talk to at night. I love you so much!"

Liz would talk to Winki every night after saying her prayers. She would tell her of the day's events and ask her to keep secrets when she didn't want to write them into her diary. But, she still would ask Trixie to come jump on the bed with her when she wanted some interaction after certain incidents. Trixie would lick her cheek and nuzzle her chin if she heard tears or words of fear from Liz. Liz just knew that Trixie understood everything she said to her. Sometimes Liz didn't know what she would do without Winki and Trixie to console her. She didn't know why she couldn't seem to tell her mama or daddy the things she told her doll and dog. But she didn't let it bother her much because she was happy most of the time.

She sure was happy the day that her daddy finished making her a dollhouse. It was beautiful. Liz could not believe her eyes. It was huge with three rooms down stairs and two upstairs. He even made some tiny furniture to set around the living room, kitchen, bedroom and bathroom. Frank had been secretly building this in his neighbor's garage and finished it in time for Liz's eighth birthday. It was January and there was snow on the ground but he insisted that they carry the kitchen table outside and set the dollhouse on top of it so it wouldn't get wet. Then Evie got out their family camera and took a picture of Liz in her snowsuit and hood, holding Winki, standing proudly beside the dollhouse. Her daddy had built this for her! She just couldn't believe it!

What a delightful day that was. Liz knew she was one lucky little girl to have such a wonderful daddy. She knew that both her mama and daddy were so good to her to give her such wonderful presents! First it was Trixie, then Winki, and now this wonderful dollhouse. She would be the envy of all her friends in the neighborhood. And that she was. Of course by this time Liz had all but forgotten the day when her baby brother was born. That event changed so much in her life. People had put her into a role now that she was much too young to fulfill.

When Liz approached the Hospital desk the day that Bobby was born she was only six years old. Yet the Hospital staff used her as a translator. They queried Evie and Frank through Liz, asking all the normal questions and then satisfied that Liz was able to relay all of the information to her parents; they asked if she knew what they would name the baby. She looked at her parents and could see that her mother was under a lot of stress at the moment as Evie signed frantically, "Baby please. Now. Now!" So she turned to the lady to say, "My mama says that she needs to go get her baby now!" Sensing the child's urgent voice, the nurse standing by, looked at Evie and said firmly, "That's true. You and your Daddy can wait out here. We will take Mama to get your new baby." With that she pushed Evie in the wheelchair through the big double doors at the end of the hallway. Frank took Liz by the hand and led her to one of the hard leather chairs in the waiting room. He gestured for her to sit down in a matching chair just across the corner space from him.

Noticing some magazines and children's books on the lamp table, she hoped to have a chance to look at one because there were none at her home. She pointed to them with an inquisitive look on her face looking at her Daddy until he nodded and handed her a children's book. Slowly shaking his head he signed, "Read me no. Tired." As Liz opened the book she thought to herself that Daddy was worried but she didn't understand why. She didn't really know anything about how Mommy was going to get that new baby. She thought about how she had answered the lady at the desk about the baby's name. She really didn't know what her parents wanted to name a new baby. What a silly question to ask a little girl like me she thought. Bobby and Jane were just names she had heard from her friends in the neighborhood; names she thought were cute. She also knew there was a Bobby, Jack and Betty on the radio show that she listened to after school.

She never saw her mommy and daddy talking about the baby. So she assumed it was a private thing that they could not tell her about. It had never bothered her and was not any problem right now so she decided to try to read the book in her lap. Soon she was nodding her head, fighting off the sleep, but her daddy brought her a pillow and told her to curl up and take a nap.

The next morning Liz woke up in her own bed with the sunlight streaming through her window. She wondered how this happened. There had been just one other time when she had gone to sleep at one place and awakened in her own bed the next day. Sometimes she imagined that God had carried her there. She had read somewhere that God would take you to Heaven when you were asleep. This seemed like a comforting idea.

Suddenly, Liz realized what had happened that caused her to wake up like this in her own bed. Where is Daddy, she thought as she jumped up and walked the short hallway to her parents' room. There he was, still fully dressed, sleeping on top of the covers, snoring loudly. She had told him once how his snoring had awakened her one night. Immediately she was sorry she had done so because that brought up another long discussion about the sounds our body can produce. Her descriptions of snoring included heavy breathing, soft breathing, steady breathing and the sounds of choking or catching one's breath when laughing too hard. Liz never wanted to alarm her dad, so she learned to keep many sounds to herself. Over the course of time there were incidents when she and her brother would accuse one another of squealing, screaming, muffling a laugh or a cry of anguish. Dad would catch them in their actions demanding a clear explanation.

Liz planned to ask her dad in the morning whether Evie had got a new baby. If she did, what gender was the baby and when would they be able to bring it home. She dressed in a hurry as she heard him getting up, using the bathroom and going into the kitchen. By the time she walked into the room there was a definite aroma of coffee, and bacon in the air. At her light touch on his shoulder, Frank turned to face his daughter with a bright smile. "Scrambled eggs okay?" he signed. With an affirmative nod from Liz, he added, "Sit down, eat, and then I will tell you all." Liz noted his complete English sentence and recognized this as a request not to be argued with as she sat down to enjoy her breakfast.

Her father's story covered all three of Liz's questions and more. A baby boy was born at such and such a time, weighing such and such pounds. Evie and baby were doing well, but both would need to stay in the hospital a few days before Frank could bring her home. Liz wanted to ask why but decided not to complicate things until she was sure about the meaning behind the stay in the hospital. "Will you go to work today, Daddy?" Liz signed fearfully. She didn't want a baby sitter, especially if it was that lady who came last time. She was so relieved when her daddy told her he was taking a week off… a week's vacation from work. She jumped up, hugged him and thanked him for breakfast. Frank was moved by the gesture, signing "You welcome. Go nice your bed and mine, read book, later we go to hospital see our new baby!"

Even though Liz was a little frightened to be in the hospital again, the actual viewing of her new baby brother was so exciting she forgot to be careful of what she said to the nurse. "That's my brother, Bobby?! He's sooo tiny! How can he play with me? He can't make snowballs or slide down the hill on my sled! Why didn't my mother get a bigger boy? Oh, my gosh! Don't tell my Daddy I said that! He is happy with a baby boy!"

Three days later Liz awoke to a strange odor in the house. Again, she had been brought home and put into bed without knowing what happened. She did remember that they had been in the hospital wait-ing room where a deaf couple had come to see the new baby. They lived in a town a few miles outside of Merrill so they had surprised Evie and Frank with their visit. After visiting with Evie for a short while they could see she was tired so they decided to gather in the waiting room to chat with Frank before heading back home. Or so they said.

What Liz did not know was the plan to bring Evie and the baby home late that afternoon so that their friends could help get Evie settled back into her home and introduce the baby to his new sleeping quarters. So, now, the next morning, Liz had a big surprise awaiting her. After the strange odor was identified as sweet powder, the quiet of the morning seeped into Liz's mind. It was so quiet in the house she was almost afraid to get up. Why didn't she hear her mother in the kitchen? Why didn't she hear her daddy when it had been time for him to go to work?

Then she heard a baby crying! Oh, my! Where was a baby? She jumped up out of bed and ran into her mama's bedroom only to find it empty. She listened closely and heard the baby's cry coming from the kitchen now. There she found mama holding the baby over her shoulder and pacing the floor. Does mama even know how hard the baby is crying?! Then Liz realized Mama was crying too. Liz slipped away back into her bedroom to ponder on why her mama was crying when she had said she wanted to get a baby for the family. Mama seemed so happy to tell us it would be nice to have a baby brother for Liz when I did not feel excited at all, in fact I really didn't care. She wasn't sure that she cared about having any baby in the house. Would she have to share her bedroom? Would she have to take care of the baby?

That was the beginning of a new life for Liz and for everyone in the family. Liz soon learned that her mama needed privacy when she fed the baby and that she would cry easily herself for no obvious reason. Her daddy was usually not at home when the baby cried. In the evening, Frank often asked Liz to help them by letting them know when the baby was crying. Liz couldn't help but wonder what would happen after Christmas break was over and she had to go back to school. But, when she was home she would let her mother know when the baby cried hard, and she did that always.

But it wasn't long until little Bobby had a routine of eating and sleeping that you could "set your clock by," said one of the neighbor ladies that came to visit. At this time they were living in a nice little two-bedroom house but the landlord had to evict them as he had sold this house. They had no choice but to move to an upstairs apartment that was not comfortable but her daddy told her that it was just temporary and she should laugh about it as though it was an adventure. Liz could sense that things were not too happy between her mama and daddy. It seemed to her that the new baby had caused some kind of problem but she didn't have any idea what it could be about. Liz tried not to think about it and sure enough, in a few months things seemed better and her mama was not crying anymore, so Liz felt better.

Then one day Liz was so surprised when her daddy announced that he had plans to build a house in another part of town. It was such fun driving over there on weekends to watch the men working, putting up the two by four studs for the walls and division of the room. Then later they could walk through and see where the rooms would be. It was so funny to see the sinks and bathtub in before the walls were done.

She would run down the boards where the steps would be built later, on into the garage which was already finished so that they could store things that should not get wet in the rain. At times like this, Liz was so glad her little brother was growing up fast so he could play with her. And he was a cute little boy so all of Liz's friends did not mind if he tagged along with them as they played tag or hide-and-go-seek in the yard.

Soon the roof was on and it was time to move in! What a happy day that was for Evie and Frank. Their joy spilled over to Liz so that she began singing songs to Bobby while they were getting settled into their bedrooms. Her daddy even put up a pretty white picket fence across the back yard so Evie could have a garden without worrying about Trixie digging it up. Later he built a beautiful archway with latticework and two benches to sit on. He was proud of his handiwork and Evie smiled brightly as he finished the painting. She was proud of him too. When her parents were happy Liz was happy too. So she didn't complain when one chore became several chores as Liz was asked to go next door and call to the utility companies to connect their electricity and change their address with the water company as well. Of course, the neighbor helped her by confirming the information given on the phone.

Evie even asked Liz to call to the local dairy and ask if they would deliver milk to their new home. The lady on the phone insisted that she talk to either Mr. or Mrs. Niklaus because she was not allowed to take orders from a child. Liz felt a little brazen as she answered, "Then you will need to send someone over to our new address to write notes with one of my parents because they are deaf and cannot use the phone." Since this was a small town the lady consented. The very next morning a milk truck pulled up at the curb and a nice young man came to the door with notepaper in hand. Liz had already related the phone conversation to her mother so she was prepared to fill in the form. However, the first note that Evie wrote to the young man was, "Please. Daughter me help." He smiled and nodded in the affirmative. With Liz's translation of the questions on the form, Evie finished in a few minutes and placed an order for the next day. Liz looked at the list to choose items to be delivered while her mother circled "two quarts milk." With an imploring expression, Liz signed, "Please. Ice cream?" Evie laughed as she handed the card back to the milkman. With disappointment written on her face, Liz repeated, "No ice cream! Daddy likes cottage cheese on list." Again Evie politely shook her head and waved goodbye to the milkman as she turned to return into the kitchen. "Nice try kid," the boy called back over his shoulder as he headed back to his truck.

Liz knew that her mother would not order cottage cheese. Evie hated cheese! Whenever Frank brought home cheese of any kind she would wrap it in wax paper and put it into a jar with the lid shut tight. Then she would place that jar in the rear of the refrigerator so that she did not have to look at it. Poor Frank had to remove everything in front of that jar every time he wanted some cheese. Neither Liz nor Bobby liked cottage cheese but they both loved regular yellow cheese. Their daddy would sneak a slice onto each of their hamburgers when he grilled outdoors. They would grin their thanks and keep the bun tightly over them so that their mother never knew.

One day when visiting their Aunt in Minnesota, Liz asked, "Aunt Erma, do you have any idea why my mother hates cheese so much?" "Hmmm." Aunt Erma shook her head slowly. She was deep in thought for a minute and then she started laughing. "Oh my, yes! One time Evie and I were privy to a private tour of the dairy barn at your Uncle Ray's farm. In other words, we were looking in places that were off limits to we kids. He had a special space in the room where he would leave a certain amount of milk to coagulate. That means it would turn from a liquid form to a solid. Then I don't know what they added. I think it was some kind of bacteria to make it into cottage cheese. Uncle Ray's family would eat it. I can remember another time when our mother had forgotten to put the bottle of milk away and Evie happened upon it first. She opened it and the sour smell immediately hit her nostrils. She screamed. When your grandmother came into the kitchen Evie was pouring the stuff into the sink. She saw the thick, smelly stuff and said something we couldn't understand. I bet she was saying cheese!" "I'm sure that had something to do with it. Thank you for sharing that story. It's funny to us but I bet it was very serious to mom at that time," Liz commented giving her Auntie a big hug. Liz wanted to approach her mother about this but she just never could figure out how to do so. She decided to just let it go because of the difficulty in communicating something humorous to her mom without upsetting her in some way.

But, now, we are in a new home, Liz mused. Life will be so much better for her mother! At first her friends were a bit timid when they met Evie and Frank. They were afraid because they didn't know how to talk to them. So Liz taught them some signs like "Hello, good-bye, thank you, nice, and please." Along with that, some learned the manual alphabet that soon became a fun game. They were more comfortable then around her folks; maybe too comfortable. Finger spelling could be used across the room or across the playground. Anywhere, even in school.

Much to Liz's chagrin, two of her friends were caught cheating on a test using finger spelling. Of course the teacher sent Liz into the principal's office with the two offenders. Liz explained that she only intended for this to be used in communicating with her parents. The principal listened to all three of the students' explanations, pondering on what punishment he should inflict upon them. First Mr. Zee turned to Liz and said, "I do understand why you taught your friends sign language. This was mighty kind of you. I have heard stories about how well you communicate with your parents that way. However, you just didn't realize how others might use that in a wrong way." Then looking the other two square in the eyes, the principal regained his role and wrinkling up his big forehead, he said loud and clear, "I will excuse you this time but I don't want to see this sign language or gesturing in the classroom again! Understood?" All three declared simultaneously, "Yes, Mr. Zee!" Pointing to Liz's friends, Mr. Zee added, "and you two will remain after class to help your teacher clean the blackboard and anything else she may ask you to do.

"Then you will write fifty times, 'I will not cheat on tests!' Understood? Now get out of here!" The principal then escorted Liz and her friends to the door so that they could return to their classroom. Liz was so embarrassed when walking back into the room, fearing that the rest of the students would laugh at her. Instead they all looked relieved as the teacher continued her lesson for that hour. Furthermore, after school was out some of her friends were waiting for her to relate to them the whole story of what happened in the principal's office. She tried to remain humble about the whole experience but she felt on cloud nine as she walked home. Of course she did not tell her parents about this incident. She just didn't see any reason to confuse them on this issue. Instead she sure did tell Trixie about it that night as she crawled into bed. When saying her prayers she asked God to forgive her two friends for cheating in class.

Evie was especially proud of Frank as he continued his employ-ment with the Merrill Daily Herald. Not only did that make Evie proud, but it was nice to have such good reports from school about Liz. Miss Brown often sent home notes telling them how Liz was such a smart little girl. She had no problems with her speech and was the best speller in the class. The teacher seemed surprised at this; so Evie wrote her a note stating that Liz's daddy read stories to her almost every night before bedtime. Evie knew the teacher couldn't believe it but it was true.

Frank would sign and fingerspell children's books that he brought home from the library. He also received a newsletter monthly from their alma mater, called "The Companion." It was filled with news about deaf people. Some stories carried the problems of the deaf community forward for all to learn about and eventually there would be a story of how that problem had been solved. This newsletter also included a story for children, urging deaf parents to read the story to their hearing children. Always faithful to the promptings of his beloved alma mater, Frank would read the story carefully to himself and then do his best to sign it carefully to his daughter, trying to include each word on the page.

Frank didn't know if Liz was catching all the words he had to fingerspell. He had to admit that there were times he did not know the meaning of some words so he could not put a sign to it because it might not even be the right concept. Thus the fingerspelling. Liz didn't tell her daddy that she would ask her playmates when she was outside playing hopscotch or hide and seek about the words that she wanted to understand. They usually recognized them because they were reading the same books at their homes. Eventually parents of these children learned of Liz's parents deafness and invited her into their homes for meals or just to watch and listen to her interact. She was always accepted as a good playmate for their child. They were surprised at her out-going personality and her pleasant smile. She didn't seem to have any problems with language, English or listening skills. In fact, Liz was probably the smartest among the neighborhood kids and she certainly had a natural beauty about her when signing to her parents. "Sign language is so intimidating," one mother told Liz. Liz didn't even know what the word meant and always signed it as *difficult*. She always laughed and said, "It's sure easy for my mom and dad!"

The kids of the neighborhood loved Frank. He would spend two hours every evening outside pitching a ball with the boys during the summer months. After all he had been a good player in High School and this was an opportunity for him to coach. The youngsters loved him because he was not intimidating like other coaches who yelled at them. Mr. Niklaus would stand behind the plate when they had enough kids to play a game and they understood when he waved his hand in the right direction and called out as loudly as he could, "Strike" or "Ball." The words may not have been that clear but they learned quickly just how they sounded from his lips. Frank was a fun coach and they learned a lot of baseball signs from him. They found it interesting that some of his signs were already used by referees.

After they bought their beautiful new house, Frank spent a lot of time in his garage making wooden lattices. Then he set it all up in the backyard making an archway with a trellis on both sides so that Evie could have those vines with purple flowers growing on them. He completed the backyard with a latticework fence and painted it all a shiny white. Evie and Liz loved it. They planted a garden behind the fence and Trixie never offered to bother the area. In the winter Frank would build snowmen for Liz and Bobby. He didn't stop with one snowman but would make a horse, putting wood and cardboard on for a saddle and let the kids ride with him holding the reins. They could tell by his gestures they were riding up a hill or down a hill. They knew if it was windy or raining so they'd lean forward and hold tight to the horse's neck.

The older kids would be building a fort in their backyard and after a fun snowball war, he would tell them to sit on the porch and warm up a little. If Evie were in a good mood she would bring them cups of hot chocolate and some of her oatmeal cookies. Laughing, they would tell Liz that everything was *hunky dory*. Of course the only way to put that into signs was to tell Evie that "everything good." They said Mrs. Niklaus was the best cookie maker in the whole neighborhood. Evie never "talked" to the children so they would sit and watch Liz communicate with her folks as they enjoyed their treat. A couple of the neighbors were watching all these activities going on in the Niklaus' yard. One said to the other, "I would never have thought that deaf folks like that would be able to handle a job, have a marriage and keep their children happy! What a wonderful family they are to have as neighbors."

4

Does Daughter Know More Than We Do?

*L*iz was probably eight years old before she realized there seemed to be no other people in their area like her parents who could not hear or talk. But she knew they were not the only deaf people in the world because she went with them to Wausau to deaf club meetings and also to church meetings. There was a deaf minister who would come to a school building there once every three or four months. Liz would sit in a desk and color in her coloring book. She would watch the little man with his black mustache, in the black suit, as he stood up front and signed to the group of twenty deaf folks. It was a bit hard to understand his finger spelling as his words seemed to fly off his hands. He often looked angry and would flail his arms up to Heaven so many times.

Thinking he would fall off the step stool, Liz was really watching close at times because she didn't want to miss it happen. There was a pretty lady who came with him and she always closed the service signing a lovely hymn while Liz's mom and dad tried to copy. No one ever told Liz who she was but she assumed she was the pastor's wife. She was able to talk and would always ask Liz how she was and encouraged her to sign the song with everyone. Sometimes she was asked to come up front and sign with the lady and the deaf folks would give her a hug afterwards. Liz wondered if she could sign that gracefully someday. But she didn't give it much thought and absolutely no practice. She still didn't know what that would be called, a translator?

Liz was going to Sunday School and church with her neighbors when an opportunity came along that required her parents approval.

When Frank read the information that their neighbor gave him he was really in favor of it. With a big smile, he nodded to the mother and signed to Liz that it looked like a good thing to do. Liz couldn't believe he approved so quickly and gave him a hug around his neck. It was quite another thing to get Evie to agree but in the end she said yes too. But for some reason, Liz didn't feel like hugging her mother for her acceptance.

This was when Liz had her first and only experience with a church summer camp. The camp was made up of log cabins that sat close to the waters of Green Lake in the southeast part of the state. It was beautiful there but there was something intimidating about the whole event. Oh, it had been fun because her friend, Mae, from church and neighborhood, went with her. They had enjoyed the crafts classes and hikes in the woods as well as swimming. The food was good and most of the adult leaders were friendly. When it came time for the evening campfire discussions about God's word, she became rather anxious. Actually, it was frightening because Liz didn't know much about the subject of being *saved* and someone was continually urging her to stand up and confess her sins so that she could become *saved*.

When she tried to take up this discussion with her parents after returning home, they had no idea what she was talking about. It was not until she was a few years older that she felt comfortable about this subject. At that time she was visiting a United Methodist Church with her new friend. One Sunday morning after church, she asked her friend if she would mind waiting for her for a few minutes as she wanted to stop by the minister's office to ask him a question.

Naomi said that was fine, her parents were always visiting with people for a while. Walking quickly, Liz knocked on the Pastor's door and asked if she could speak to him. After he waved her to enter, she quickly asked him how she could know she was saved. The gray-haired minister could see that Liz was very concerned about the subject, so he stroked his chin to show that he was taking her seriously. After a minute of this demonstration, he asked Liz to sit down in a small chair across the desk from where he sat in a large leather chair. Finally, he grinned and said with a positive demeanor,

"Yes, my dear girl, you are saved! Furthermore, if someone asks you if you have been saved the answer is always yes. So, you ask me, How do you know you are saved?" Looking her straight in the eye, Reverend King asked Liz, "You do know the story of Jesus and how he loved all the little children?" Liz replied happily, "Yes, I love that story!" "Ok, then, do you know how Jesus wanted us all to love each other and Him?" Again, Liz nodded in the affirmative, simply saying, "Yes!" The kindly pastor continued, "If they ask you to recite the day and time you were *saved* you have this answer: 'It was on a Friday afternoon around three o'clock over two thousand years ago!' How could that be? Because at that time Jesus Christ died on the cross for all of our sins forevermore. All you have to do is continue to love Jesus as He loves you. Just believe that He is with you always!" Liz was ecstatic! Of course she was saved! She thanked the Reverend and skipped down the hall to catch her friends for her ride home.

Liz was so relieved and happy to understand this message that she hurried home to tell her parents. Frank's face immediately broke out in a big smile as he pulled out his Bible to find the verse in the scriptures that he said he had read many times. Evie was not at all sure she understood what either Frank or her daughter were trying to say. Evie still questioned the fact that there was a God. If there was a God why did he make people deaf? Liz really had no answer for her mother's desperate question. She promised her that she would ask her minister that question when the opportunity arose. That night Liz tossed and turned in her bed as these mixed emotions worked through her mind. Jesus had died for our sins but somewhere he said that because we accepted him as our Lord and Savior did not mean there were any promises that we would have good lives. In fact Christians had suffered for thousands of years in one way or another. So why did God let them suffer? Why didn't God do away with handicaps and diseases? As she finally fell asleep she promised herself that she would study the Bible more to find the answers.

One day after a service with their deaf group, Frank and Liz were waiting by the car for Evie and Bobby when a young man came by and stopped to give Evie a card. She turned around and handed it to

Frank as they both frowned at each other. Liz was actually frightened when her dad started signing angrily to the stranger. He was
so vehement that she did not take time to read his signs but jumped
into the back seat of their car. Liz did not like the looks of the fellow,
with his hair long and a scraggly looking beard. He was dressed
decently though. Soon she saw that the frightened man had quickly
walked away and then started running until he was out of sight. Liz
slowly got out of the car and asked, "Daddy! What? Why mad you?"
Frank quietly signed, "Man deaf maybe?" His face expressed doubt
and frustration. "Sell needles thread card. Print 'I am deaf. I cannot
find work. Please help with $1.00.' Me, other deaf, don't like! Can
work, deaf! Can!" Liz was a little young to understand this but she
knew she would never buy from a deaf person on the street if she
ever met one again. She certainly recognized that her father was
proud of his job and somehow that made him proud to be deaf.

There was to be only one other time that Liz saw her father that
angry. One day Liz was told to meet her daddy after school so he
could take her to the dentist. She was not to go into the Tribune
building and bother anyone. Instead she was to wait in the family car
parked on the road or parking lot just behind the Tribune. Frank was
sure he would be out to meet her in just ten minutes after she would
arrive. Liz dutifully walked downtown where she found her dad's car
on the side street and climbed into the passenger's seat. Ten minutes
would not be enough time to start her homework so she just stared
out the window. She was looking at the backside of a brick building
down an alleyway and noticed two men yelling at each other. One
man had an apron on and pushed the other one down, yelling something as he turned and went into the building. The scruffy looking
one got up slowly and came walking down the alley toward the car.
Instinctively Liz locked the car doors and sat quietly.

The man was still coming toward the car and stopped short of
Liz's door and said, "Hey, little girl, bet you don't know what this
is." Before Liz could close her eyes or say a word, he had opened
up his pants to show his bushy hair. Quickly Liz slid to the floor and
felt her heart beating a thousand miles an hour! What was she to do!

Then she heard a familiar loud raspy voice yelling, "Go! Go!" and as she opened her eyes slowly she saw her Daddy's broad shoulders against her door. Everything was still for a moment but then she heard footsteps running away, back down the alley. Frank looked in at Liz and asked in signs if she was okay. His handsome face was contorted with such anger that his brown eyes seemed dark and black. "Ok, Daddy. Me okay!" Liz signed swiftly.

Walking slowly around the car, Frank looked around the area and finally opened the door with his key and slid into the driver's seat. After putting the key in the ignition he turned to Liz and she saw tears in his eyes. But he smiled and said, "You right, lock doors. Man drunk." This was one of the rare moments that Liz felt her daddy's love strongly even though he never said the words. I wonder why I don't say those words to Daddy, she thought, she realized she never heard or said, "I love you" to either one of her parents. She decided then to keep a listening ear out to see if her hearing friends said that to their hearing parents. It was surely something too personal to actually ask her friends about. That was all that was ever said about the incident. Liz often wondered if he had related the whole story to her mother. As far as she knew, there had been no conversation about it.

That evening Liz held Trixie in her lap for a long while, telling her about what had happened. Again, Liz wished she had someone to share this trauma with but somehow she didn't think she should tell any one of her friends. Somehow it just seemed too dirty to talk about. "But, it's okay, Trix, 'cuz I learned today how much my daddy loves me!"

Rosie was Liz's good friend who lived just across the street. Rosie was an only child and had everything she wanted, even naturally curly blonde hair. There were a dozen dolls lined up on a shelf in her pretty bedroom. But, Liz was not jealous. She was happy. Liz had only one doll. This was a doll that Auntie Lydia had brought her all the way from California. It was a Shirley Temple doll and the envy of all the girls in the neighborhood, even Rosie. So this doll became Liz's swap toy. Whenever she wanted to play with someone's special toy she would trade Shirley Temple for a limited period of time. One night Liz wanted to give her doll a bath but since water was so limited her mother had denied her that pleasure. She was to wait until Saturday when she took her own bath. In a dream that night, Liz started to walk in her sleep like she had done a couple of times before. Apparently, she thought of the doll as her baby and took her into the kitchen and put her in a pan for a bath. She couldn't reach the sink or the water bottle so she got out a footstool for help. Still unable to reach, she pulled a chair over, put the footstool on the chair and climbed onto the table to step over to this ladder she had fashioned for herself. As she stepped over to the ladder the stool slipped off the chair and Liz took a hard fall onto the floor. This caused a loud vibration that was felt in Evie and Frank's bedroom. They came rushing to the kitchen to see what was going on.

"Liz sleep-walk again," signed Evie to Frank. They struggled to get Evie out of the tangled mess and onto the couch. "Liz, up, see walk can," Frank signed to Liz. Liz was completely confused. Is this what Auntie Mable meant when she said Liz was walking in her sleep when last she visited them in Minnesota? It seemed that Liz had walked in her sleep down into the basement where Granma kept her home made root beer that Liz loved so much.

Oh, that had been a grand summer when Liz stayed at her Auntie's farm and spent nights at her different cousins' farms as well as at Granma's house. On the farm she was treated like a special visitor but she tried to remain polite and do her share of the work along with her cousins. She wasn't sure why she had been allowed to stay here in Minnesota for the whole summer but she thought it was maybe due to the new baby in her house. Mommy was having a difficult time with him as he cried so much. Daddy thought Evie should visit her mother and get some help on how to cope with this new little one. So Frank took a vacation and brought the family for a visit.

Then Liz's cousins had begged her parents as well the aunts and uncles to let Liz stay for the summer. She was so glad that they had. She always wanted to know more about collecting eggs from the chickens, milking the cows, and above all to ride a pony. Liz decided not to tell her mommy and daddy that she never once was homesick.

Oh, but when hot August came with the sounds and smells of the farm she was ready to go back home. She also learned that she was highly allergic to the hay filling up the silo in the barn. Aunt Mabel told Liz she was restricted from the barn when the men were harvesting the wheat. Yes, Liz was ready to go home.

Liz had her first train ride ever and made the trip home all by herself. That was fun too. When her aunt put her on the train, she spoke to the Porter who was the first black man that Liz had ever seen. He was to keep an eye on her niece and Liz was to let him know if she needed anything. Liz was so happy to receive a big storybook from her Auntie Erma as a farewell gift. She held it close to her until she was settled in a big leather seat on the train.

The Porter told her his name was Joe and if she needed anything to call for him. As the train began its chugging, Liz waved out the window to her Aunt Erma and settled back with a little sigh. Wow! She was to be on this train all by herself for two hours. It was a little scary so she opened her new book and looked at all the pictures. To her surprise Joe came and asked if she would like him to read her a story from the book. Shyly she accepted his offer and soon it was time for him to do his duty as they pulled into a station. He told her to sit still as this was not her destination. That was a big word to add to her vocabulary, destination. A nice lady across the aisle then chatted with Liz a little while and gave her an apple to eat. By the time she found a place to trash her apple core Joe was there to tell her that the next stop would be Merrill. As they pulled into the station she could see her daddy waiting for her. Joe took her suitcase and helped her down the steps.

"Do you see your mama?" he asked. "No, but my daddy is here!" she exclaimed as she tossed her curly permed head and grinned up at him. Joe turned to see a handsome man come toward them and then stopped in awe as Liz gestured something to the man and he signed back. This must be some of that sign language I've heard that deaf mutes use. Liz turned to this kindly porter and said, "Joe, I want you to meet my daddy." Then she signed to her father, "Man name Joe nice. Help me time off train." Frank offered his hand to shake Joe's hand and felt a warm hand in his. "I knew your daughter was a smart

little girl. But I didn't know she could sign. God bless you both." Liz
simply signed to her daddy that Joe had said it was nice to meet them.
Liz found herself changing people's words often. For some reason a lot
of people said "God bless you" and somehow Liz felt that it was said
with sympathy and she didn't want her parents to think that people felt
sorry for them. She hoped God would forgive her for this "little" fib.

Liz realized that God had other things to forgive her for too. She
had a real love for candy and rarely had any pennies with which to
buy some. Temptation got the better of her though as she saw her
mother putting her change on her dresser after a trip to the grocery
store. This was before they bought their new house. They had no
plumbing in the house and had to use an outhouse for their potty.
She took the change and hid it in the outhouse up high on a board.

Then when Rosie asked her to go to the candy store with her she
took it with her and bought a big bag of candies, trying to eat most of
them before it was time to go in for supper. She hid the rest out in the
outhouse. Needless to say supper was not inviting and she excused
herself telling her folks that she had a tummy ache. Concerned about
that, Evie entered her room later to ask if she wanted some soup.
When Liz shook her head in the negative her mother looked sternly
at her and asked if she had eaten all the candy. Liz was frightened
and signed, "You know about candy?" Evie gave her one of those
ugly looks that Liz hated but was never really frightened by.

Evie then explained that Rosie's mother had seen the girls with
so much candy and thought it was strange so she came over and
wrote a note telling her about the girls going to the candy store.
Evie knew that Liz had taken the missing coins. Her daddy came in
then and told Liz that he would have to put this in the newspaper the
next day because all crime had to be reported. For a moment, Liz
believed he would but then she saw the twinkle in his eyes. She tried
not to smile as she signed, "Please don't do that, Daddy! I'm sorry!
Never do again!" Liz learned a lesson that day!

Liz loved her Daddy but he had one habit she hated; he smoked
cigars! Yuk! She would sign to him, "Stink," but all he would do
is laugh. Thank goodness he would only smoke one after dinner

and Liz always threw the used cigar into the trash as soon as it had cooled off. Every evening she took Trixie out for some exercise. Sometimes they would walk around the block but most of the time they just played in the back yard, throwing a stick for her to fetch. Trixie was the best birthday present Liz ever got.

She followed Liz everywhere and curled up at the foot of her bed every night. Ever since that day, Trixie became the only one that Liz could talk openly to and it sure helped to express some of her frustrations with family communication. How good it was to have someone to communicate with in a very special way.

Liz stewed and stewed about the fact that Rosie had told her mother about the coins. She decided to get even. There had been some boys in the neighborhood that played Kick the Can with them out under the corner street light at night which was usually a lot of fun.

But lately she had not liked what the boys were saying to them. They talked about "Father, uncle, cousin and Kate" and even though Liz didn't know what that meant, Rosie giggled every time. Liz didn't know how to tell her own mom or dad about that but maybe it was time to tell Rosie's mom. She would tell her about her showing off her stockings and panties to the boys in the street! And about the time the girls went down to the store to buy socks and the clerk asked Rosie to show him her pretty panties and she did! That will teach her a lesson Liz thought and it did!

Evie wished she could talk to her daughter about intimate things but she could not communicate with her well enough to do so. She thought about asking Rosie's mother if she would include Liz in her discussions with Rosie about growing into a young lady. But Liz was only ten so there was plenty of time for that. On Saturdays Evie always baked a pie and cinnamon rolls for the weekend. Then she would make fresh buns and cook hamburgers for lunch as Frank was through with work at noon on Saturdays. They "put the paper to bed" early on Saturdays. That was one idiom that hearing people used that she thought was very clever. But most of the idioms she read did not make any sense at all. She didn't even know that word, "idiom," until they had gone to a Deaf Club meeting over in

Wausau. The Club here in Wisconsin was not as big or as nice as the one in Minnesota.

Over there, a rich benefactor had donated his home to the Deaf community when he died. It was a lovely three-story brick home with a wide porch stretching over three sides. The younger people could play pool or billiards on the second floor while the senior citizens enjoyed card games on the first floor. Everyone could enjoy the bar and its cozy tables and chairs on the third floor. They even had a dance twice a year with music provided by a group who played drum, piano and clarinet. They danced to the vibrations on the wood floor.

Frank and his two special buddies seemed to never tire of chatting about their school days and their trip to Pikes Peak. They thought it was so neat they experienced one time they were glad they were deaf. Other folks were complaining about their ears hurting but they didn't feel anything at all. They had planned to drive all the way to California where they were to see Molly. Unfortunately, after they drove the climb up to Pikes Peak and back down, they had car troubles. They pooled their monies to repair the car, canceled the rest of the trip and headed back home. They repeated the story over and over and how lucky they all had been.

Now Frank added, "Not only to make a safe journey but to arrive home in time to answer letters they had waiting for them. That was when Frank had received an offer to work in Wisconsin on the Daily Herald and asked his brother to make a call and appointment for an interview." Now his buddies wanted to "catch up" on Frank's news. So he told them his brother, Karl, had gone to work in Illinois on a small town newspaper not far from Chicago. He had married his lovely Emily and written that he was very happy. Baby sister, Mandy, had also found a nice deaf fella in Illinois and after they were married they lived close to Karl and Emily. They were fortunate in having many deaf friends in the Chicago area where they could fellowship every month.

The fellows went on to relate their own stories. All five of the men were now living in separate townships at least an hour's drive from each other. It was so good to be here now together at the Club discussing these past events. They agreed that life in the "outside world" was getting better all of the time but they could never really chat like this with the *hearies* they worked with or folks in the neighborhood. So few people knew sign language. When they were apart, letters were the only way to communicate but they were few as they all found it a chore to sit down and write their news with clarity.

Here they could discuss the world events in a manner that allowed everyone their time to say what they wanted to say. They were all concerned about the Depression. They read about people who were hungry in the United States. What would their President be able to do? It seemed there had been a terrible drought in the Midwest and farmers lost their fields of fruits and vegetables. Thank goodness for the Club here in Wausau where they could meet every three months to discuss these important events.

Saturdays were special for Bobby and Liz. Their daddy only had to work until lunch time, and Evie loved cooking on the grill making lunches fun for the family. Little Bobby loved eating the hamburgers with big sweet onion rings, covered in mustard, just like his daddy; while Liz imitated her mom and ate the hamburger separate from the bun with just a little catsup. The apple pie had been baked that morning but it was saved for Sunday; while the cinnamon rolls were a treat on Saturday night after the dishes were done. To close out the evening, they often played some card games. Of course they had to quit by nine o clock to take their baths and lay out their clothes for Sunday school the next morning. As Frank tucked each of his children into bed he would remind them to say their prayers and always thanked God for Liz and Bobby in his own prayers. Life was good.

This Sunday was going to be a special one. There was to be a different kind of birthday celebration for Frank and Bobby. Their birthdays were the same day so they always had birthday cake with candles for Bobby and an apple pie for Daddy. For the first time Evie and Frank would take both their children to the movies. It would be fun explaining the story of *The Wizard of Oz* to their parents afterwards, Liz thought. She would make notes during the movie of at least the main characters' names.

But that opportunity never came because when they arrived home a strange car was parked in front of their house. Frank recognized his boss behind the wheel apparently waiting for him to arrive home. The man jumped out and came up to Liz pulling her arm over to her dad, saying she needed to help him tell her Daddy something important. "Tell your dad that he must come to work. We are putting out an 'Extra' today," Frank could see that his boss was very serious and somewhat upset. He simply nodded his head and signed "Why?" Mr. C replied, "Tell Frank that the Japanese bombed our ships in Pearl Harbor this morning and when he comes down to the paper he will read the whole story as he is typing it!" With that, he jumped back into his car and drove off.

Liz had no idea what he was talking about but she did her best to relay it to her dad. She had to think carefully on how to spell Pearl Harbor and Japanese. She didn't even know Frank's boss's name. She had only seen her dad spell it once a long time ago and today all she could remember was that it started with a C. Evie and Frank stood there like statues except for their hands moving too fast for Liz to understand. Clearly it was a conversation between just the two of them, so Liz and Bobby went into the house. She watched out the window as her dad got into his old Plymouth and drove off with Evie waving goodbye. Her mother looked so perplexed that Liz knew better than to ask her questions. In just a few minutes, Evie sat down with her sewing basket and proceeded to mend some clothes. This was a clear indication that she didn't want to be bothered. So, Liz retired to her bedroom with Trixie and told her what had happened. Anyway, she had her own questions. Who are Japanese people? Where is Pearl Harbor anyway? And what is an "Extra?" Liz had signed a little more than normal, hoping that would suffice. Frank had asked her no questions so she assumed he understood. At least he knew he would understand more when he got to work.

Liz was disappointed that her dad didn't come home until after her bedtime. Evie had fixed them a light supper and retired to her room telling Liz that she had things to do in their bedroom. Liz really didn't understand what was going on until she went to school the next day. After saying goodbye to Bobby at his classroom she went on into her own. There the teacher was already talking to the boys and girls about war. War? What was that? All day that day the teachers taught their students about the First World War and America's place in the history of the world today. It was a bit overwhelming to Liz. The other kids told of what their parents had told them and what they had heard on the radio, but Liz had nothing to share because none of that information was given to her at home. But, she was proud to relate how her dad had been called to work on the Extra newspaper edition.

Some of her friends were quite impressed with that story. Liz didn't know why she didn't tell her parents about that, but she did not think they would appreciate her talking about their personal business. That evening was quiet at home as usual. Frank was buried in his newspaper, stopping only long enough to sign something to his wife that did not include Liz. So, Liz decided to move herself and her homework into her bedroom. Before crawling into bed, she wrote the day's events into her diary.

A week went by before her daddy started pointing out the war stories in the newspaper to Liz asking her to read and then come to him with any questions. He also took this opportunity to teach Liz a sign for *war*. The sign used both hands with all fingers straight out except for the thumb. This looked like each hand forming the number four. Then pointing the hands at each other, move both hands in the same direction, back and forth as though forming an arch. This made the two hands look like they were in conflict to grasp a certain space to own.

Months later, with the whole idea of war still new to Liz , a letter came from her Aunt Mable addressed to the whole family. They read and re-read the news slowly. It was very sad news. When their son, Earl, Liz's cousin, had enlisted in the Seabees everyone became more aware of what was going on over there. Aunt Mable explained that she wrote this letter because her husband, Ray, was having a tough time living with the news. Sadly a telegram came to Earl's parents that he had been killed while in a submarine close to

Okinawa. Ironically they were not in action at the time as some of
the crew had gone into shore for a short leave. But he had remained
on board saying he wanted to write his girl a letter.

The ironic fact was that the sub was really a sitting duck for a
Japanese torpedo boat. Later his parents were told that the torpedo
hit the side of the ship exploding the room exactly where Earl had
chosen to sit to do his writing. Evie and Frank talked it over and
wrote a quick reply to Mable's letter stating that they were coming
to Minnesota for a visit soon.

That following month they arrived at Ray and Mable's home to
find that Earl's girlfriend from Florida had come to visit too. This was
the first time anyone had met her! But Earl had mentioned her several
times in his letters. She lived in Florida where he had been stationed
and she had accepted his engagement ring before he shipped out.

Darlene was a beautiful brunette! Earl had dark brown hair with
brown eyes and was so handsome. Mable couldn't help but think
of what beautiful children she and Earl would have had. It was still
so hard to accept that her son was really gone! Gone forever. She
could see that her husband, Ray, was hurting even more than she.
His weathered face seemed to have added more lines around the
eyes since that telegram came. Ray had always thought that Earl
would take over the farm and allow him to take some time off for
himself and his wife. They had worked so hard to keep the dairy
going. Of course they had a second son but he had always been one
to run around with his buddies and have fun. He never showed any
interest in the workings of a farm. Ray just couldn't picture him
staying on the farm very long.

His thoughts were interrupted by this lovely girl as she politely
asked questions about the cows. She was so naïve about farms that
Ray finished the thoughts in his mind with, "Oh, God, maybe she
would not have wanted to live on a farm after all!" They were pleasantly surprised and thrilled that the girl stayed a week on the farm,
enjoying her visit immensely. She brought pictures and told stories
of the times she and Earl had shared together. Liz had felt privileged
to be visiting there at the time and observing the emotions of all.

She felt so sad for her Aunt Mabel because she could see that she wanted to enjoy Darlene's visit but was still sad about losing her son, Earl. Everyone seemed happy that she had come to visit and it was difficult to say goodbye, knowing they probably would never see her again. There really was no reason for Darlene to even stay in touch with this family anymore. Liz heard Uncle Ray tell Darlene to go on and lead her life as fully as she could. "Earl would have wanted you to find another decent man and have a family and lead a good life." Tears were shed as she got on the bus one cool, rainy morning and Liz waved goodbye for as long as she could see waving hands from the vehicle. Life seemed sad this day. All because of this thing called *war*!

A few weeks later Liz's parents received another letter from Aunt Mable. This time the news was about Earl's younger brother, Les. He had been excused from the draft because he was the only son remaining on the farm. However, not waiting for his father's permission, Leslie joined the Army and was shipped out to Germany before long. He was wounded in battle and came home with an honorable discharge. Liz was sure he had satisfied his desire to get even for his brother even if it was a different enemy. He left a beautiful blonde girl right here in Altura. Liz could see that they were really in love. She almost felt glad that she wasn't old enough to have a boyfriend going into the war.

Liz never forgot the day that Leslie came home as she was lucky enough to be in Minnesota at that time. Leslie had been gone for two long years. Liz was thrilled when she was invited to go along with Donna Mae and her family to the city to meet his bus. It had been so romantic! Leslie's girlfriend had come with them, of course. She was the first one to jump out of the car and run to the bus station. Everyone was filled with excitement watching her run to him as he got off the bus. In just two long steps, folding her in his arms, he picked her up off of the ground holding her in a long hug. Just like a movie. He was so handsome in that uniform with his arm in a sling.

Liz had never seen such emotion expressed from Aunt Mable and Uncle Ray before! They were good farm folks who worked hard and had a good dairy business started now. Raymond was Evie's older brother, always so kind to Liz's parents. She guessed that was why he was her favorite uncle. Anytime Evie and Frank came to Minnesota he would ask them to play a game of cards, something called "500." This was the one way Ray felt that he could communicate with them and they loved it. They would actually laugh together as Ray attempted to bid making the signs for each suit. Spades was the only one that he could never remember. All it was, Liz told him, was to use the hand like it was actually digging like a spade. Clubs seemed a silly one. It was a simple knock on the forehead as though hitting yourself with a club. Hearts, and Diamonds were easy, just point to the heart or a ring. Frank always kept score and Evie would write notes asking Ray about the family. Mable was always busy in the kitchen cooking or baking something delicious to have with their coffee later that evening. We all looked forward to a slice of her award-winning creamy apple pie.

Donna Mae was Liz's favorite cousin. They were absolute opposites in looks. Donna with her naturally curly blonde hair and blue eyes sparkling all of the time; and Liz with her long dark braids and deep chestnut brown eyes. Liz was very upset about her hair because Granma insisted that she brush it fifty times every morning and it was almost impossible to get out all the snarls. In fact Granma got so frustrated with it she insisted that Liz get a haircut before she left for home in Wisconsin again. She set the appointment and practically dragged Liz to the beauty shop. When they were through with her she cried. All the long rich hair was gone and in its place was a head of curls permed on by the beautician. Granma took her picture and when she saw it later she cried again. She knew she was chubby but she really looked fat now! Thank goodness it grew out a little before it was time to go back to school that fall.

Donna was her favorite but there were other cousins on the farms surrounding the little town of Altura that were great too. And here she was in the car with Donna and her family bringing Leslie home from the war! All the way home in the old Plymouth truck I could hear Mable saying a prayer of thanks to God. That was the first time Liz really thought much about prayer. This was somehow different than just saying a bedtime prayer or giving a prayer of thanksgiving at meal times.

There wasn't much of that in her own home anyway which Liz assumed was because of her parents' deafness. She didn't know that Evie and Frank had a difference of opinion about prayer and about God. They had attended worship services and Bible study in school of a Lutheran nature but when they left the school they had never pursued any religious study of any kind. Frank had a Bible he read from daily but only in the quiet of the evening when Evie was busy with her housework, sewing or tending to the children. And then he would only have time to read a few scripture verses as it was so difficult to understand. Evie made it clear that she really did not believe there was a Supreme Being. If there was a God why would he let people be deaf, blind or crippled? "God real? No! Why me deaf? God not real!"

She was really bitter about the subject so Frank preferred to keep religion to himself. There were times after that that Liz would think of that moment and wish that she had been able to answer her mother's question with something positive; something comforting. But she had never been able to do so. Frank was so happy when the neighbors offered to take Liz to church and Sunday School but even then he did not know how to discuss these matters with Liz.

Her neighbor, Carol, had come over one day and said, "Liz, you should try to visit with God every day but you should certainly visit with Him every Sunday. Come to Sunday school with us and we know you will enjoy it." Liz asked Carol to come in and ask her daddy's permission. Frank was so pleased he simply replied, "Thank you. Happy me Liz church with you." And so it happened that Liz heard some of the sweet stories about Jesus and how much he loved people. She brought her good friend, Mae, to Sunday school later and the two of them joined the confirmation class that met every week for a year. She learned something of the history of the Bible and read some of the amazing stories in the Old Testament.

She knew that her Daddy read the Bible because it was on the table next to his chair. The worn cover indicated that he held it many times even though she never saw him reading. She assumed he would read either early morning or late at night after she had gone to bed. Frank had sat in the same wingback chair for all of Liz's life. One day she asked him when he bought that chair and he smiled, signing, "Chair wedding present ourselves. We buy 1928." An end table held a small lamp, that Bible and some paper and pencils on it. On the other side of his chair was a cigar stand. Evie had told Liz some time ago that it was a wedding present from her sister, Erma. Henry, her husband had carved it from wood and finished it with varnish so beautifully. There were times when Frank would entertain Liz and Bobby by blowing rings of smoke into the air. They were perfect circles and they would both clap their hands in applause. However, sometimes Liz hated the smell from her Daddy's cigar and she even told him so. He seemed at peace when smoking and reading his newspaper and she never wanted to interrupt a pleasant time for either one of her parents. Those times seemed so rare. Actually, Liz was surprised that her mother never said anything about his smoking so she sure didn't feel that she could do so. Yes, deafness did present relatively few problems for the family. Liz wished they had a radio so that she could listen to some of the programs that her friends talked about. The news might even be important such as when the war began. But her father insisted that the newspaper was enough for them.

He did feel some guilt when Liz almost got lost in a snowstorm that winter. Frank had driven to work safely in the early morning but when it was time for school, Evie decided that it would be too rough for Bobby to walk there with her. She told Liz that she could go alone and be sure to put on her snow pants and boots as well as hood up on her jacket. Liz looked out the window at the heavy snow falling, grabbed her mittens and headed out the door. It was so white everywhere she could barely find her way to the sidewalk leading to the school building. When she got there the doors were closed and she felt frightened. Did this mean the Janitor was late opening the doors or she was too early for school? She thought maybe everyone was having difficulty getting there so she just started walking around in the snow making a circle that they could play "tag" in later.

She and her classmates loved to make a big pie in the snow and the one who was "it" started in the center and had to remain on the lines that formed the pieces of the pie to catch someone to tag. Trudging through the deep snow Liz made the largest pie she had ever made. She was really cold and wet when she finished and checked the doors again only to find them still locked. She went back to her tag circle and when she saw that the snow had almost filled in all the lines she made, she realized that this was really an unusual amount of snow, even for Wisconsin. So she decided to head back home.

Everything was so white she could not tell which direction to walk but took the best choice she could make. After a long while she knew she had made a wrong choice. She could see nothing familiar, not even a house. Where was she? The snow was drifting now as the wind blew stronger and her fingers and toes felt numb. She was so tired and all she wanted to do was sleep. Suddenly she felt big strong arms pick her up and carry her as she went to sleep. It was warm here and when she opened her eyes she could see it was the back room of a grocery store she had been in before.

"Oh, George, she's awake now. How are you my dear? We know who you are. You are the little girl whose mama and papa can't talk or hear. They're deaf and dumb, aren't they? What's your name?" Liz answered quickly, "Yes, my name is Liz Niklaus. I was going to school. What happened?" Turning to her husband, the woman said, "Oh, George, she didn't know that there was no school today because of the storm." "No school?" Liz asked. "Right! They announced it on the radio early this morning. Oh, your folks wouldn't have heard that. What a shame. Let's see, your papa works at the newspaper doesn't he? George, call the Herald and tell them what's happened. Now, let's fix you a nice cup of hot chocolate, my dear."

Frank had to wait until later that evening before he could manage to get through the roads to pick her up and take her home to a worried Evie. "Me happy Bobby and I stay home," Evie signed to Frank. Liz wanted her mother to hold her and comfort her but

85

this was just like any other time when Liz might have hurt herself a little. "Mom does love me but she doesn't know how to say it," she reassured herself again. Evie did tell Liz that she should take a hot bath while she fixed a bowl of hot soup for her. It wasn't long before Liz fell into bed exhausted. She felt frightened. This day's experience gave her a feeling of insecurity that she had never reckoned with before. Was she old enough already to be responsible for herself? Could she really take care of herself? She remembered the prayer, "Now I lay me down to sleep. I pray thee Lord my soul to keep. But if I should die before I wake, I pray thee Lord my soul to take." What did these words really mean? She didn't want to die … especially in a snow storm where no one might ever find her again!

Liz thought sure her daddy would buy a radio soon. Well it wasn't really soon, but that following Christmas the family gift under the tree was a small radio which would sit in the kitchen not in Liz's room as she wished. Liz began doing her homework in the kitchen every evening, listening to Fibber McGee and Molly or Jack Benny. If there had been no one to play with after school she would come in and listen to Jack Armstrong and Captain Midnight. It was so neat to hear adult voices in the house. Sometimes she could have her friend, Connie, in to listen to the stories with her and Evie would have a treat like marshmallow and Kix cereal bar.

Connie lived just a block away but was two years older than Liz so she did not spend much time with her. She was a pretty girl and Liz often tried to copy her hairstyle. One day Liz told Connie that she loved her name. Connie was a beautiful name and Liz vowed that if she had a baby girl one day she would name her Connie Jean. Jean was Liz's middle name. Connie was flattered and told Liz she thought she was such a smart girl to live her life with deaf parents. Liz could not imagine how that made her smart but she just replied, "Thanks, but really, the credit goes to my parents. They are just normal happy people raising their kids the best way they know how."

5

How Long Until They're Grown?

Liz always looked forward to summer vacations in Minnesota where she could play in the barns of the farms, sliding down the hayloft, gathering eggs, and riding the horses. Oh, she was never good on the horses but her older cousin, Buddy, would lead the big horse and let her ride slowly on him when she was little. Later she was actually able to ride an old mare that trotted slowly out in the fields. Buddy had twin brothers her age who were always teasing Donna and Liz. The girls usually were allowed to stay out at the farm in the country for the day and then at night Uncle Ray, Donna's daddy, would come and pick them up to go back to their grand-mother's house where Liz was staying.

Grandma Anna lived in a big four bedroom house just a long block up the street from Uncle Ray's farm. There Liz could have a room to herself and she loved the big downy pillows with the feather quilt to match. It was lovely. There was wonderful wallpaper in each bedroom and hers had pink roses on one side and green vines on the adjoining wall.

Grandma Anna seemed very much a lady to be reckoned with. She was still pretty even though she was at least sixty. Her hair was mostly gray and she wore it in a bun behind her neck. However, her hair was beautiful because Liz had seen her brush it out at night. Grandma didn't smile often and was fairly strict with her, expecting Liz to do her chores each morning before she was allowed outside to play. There was always a neighborhood child to jump rope with and perhaps Donna would come up and join them. Then Grandma would come out and ask them to help her in the garden pulling weeds or picking the tomatoes and vegetables. When the town whistle blew twelve o clock noon, they would take their harvest into the kitchen. For lunch Grandma loved to make tomato soup which was not a favorite of Liz's but she pretended it was because she knew her cousin Donna really thought it was good. After homemade tomato soup and crackers it would be time for a nap.

Grandma still believed in Liz taking naps at 7 years old! She and Donna would lie on pallets on the dining room floor and pretend to go to sleep. Then when they could hear grandma snoring on the couch and grandpa making the same sounds in his rocking chair, the girls would whisper silly things to each other. Liz had a weak bladder and when she laughed too much she would wet her pants and grandma would get very upset!

Sometimes Liz would spend the night down on the farm with Donna Mae. That was awesome. To hear the rooster crow so early in the morning and hear Earl and Leslie, her two brothers in the next bedroom up as they argued about who would get into the bathroom first. Sometimes Liz would peek out the door to see one of them still pulling on their overalls. They were both big fellows sharing a bedroom smaller than her own room at home. Their room was a total disaster with clothes tossed everywhere. Just the night before, Donna had shown Liz gum stuck on the back of the headboard of their bed. Yuk!

This was the first time Liz felt fortunate to have her own room with no sisters to have to share space with. But down deep she wished she had a sister and not a pesky little brother. Donna always slept through all that early morning hustle and bustle; but anxious to start her day, Liz would wake her up soon after the sun came up. Donna would toss her blond curls up in the air and yell, "Liz, it's only six a.m.!" By that time the odor of sausage filled their nostrils and Liz yelled back, "OK, see you downstairs. I'll have the first pancakes then!" It didn't take Donna long to pull on her blue jeans and shirt to run downstairs and join her. One good thing about getting up early was that she could give her dad a peck on the check as he went out the door. Liz was pleasantly surprised when her Uncle Ray turned his face to her and said, "You can kiss me right there on my other cheek, Lizzie!" Feeling a bit embarrassed, Liz stepped on her tippy toes and put a light smack right where he had said. He was so sweet that Liz felt warm and happy with him and everyone in this family. It would be fun to live here with them and all their animals!

Liz was also amazed the first time she learned that Aunt Mable got up at five a.m. so that she could feed her men before they headed out to the fields. Aunt Mable always looked tired to Liz. She was trim but always wore a housedress with an apron over it. She never put on makeup or had her hair cut into any certain style like Evie did. Yet there was a certain loveable air about her aunt that just exuded sweetness and love for her family. Even though Mable was not Grandma's daughter, she had certain chores for the girls to do too. They tried to organize things so they could finish early enough to get out to the barn and take the pony out for a ride. While Liz helped Aunt Mable make pancakes or eggs for all of them, Donna gathered the dirty clothes and started the first tub of wash.

The tubs and wringer washer were on the back porch off the kitchen. Liz asked if she could be of any help and Aunt Mable sent her out to get Donna's Grandpa Brown. Liz complied with this errand eagerly as she loved to see his beehives. This was the only place in the world that Liz ever saw someone raising bees. Just the summer before, she had her first tour with her first taste and first chew of beeswax from the hives. Grandpa Brown was a quiet little man. He seemed a lot more agile than her Grandpa Hilke. Both had gray hair, alright; but Grandpa Brown was a tall, rather big man and quite talkative. He had a small bedroom behind the boys' room upstairs.

Liz knew the story of how Grandma and Grandpa Hilke had built this farm and then given it to their son, Raymond, after they moved to a house up the road to retire. Grandpa Hilke seemed to spend a lot of time in an easy chair after a few morning chores. Liz assumed he really had retired because he was tired!

Grandpa Brown, Mable's father, was probably retired too; yet, he spoke loud and clear when he talked about his bees. He had carefully explained his duties as a beekeeper to Liz in the past; so she knew to stop when she saw that he was wearing his hardhat with netting. This would mean he was in the act of handling the bees so she was not to distract them in any way. She watched him carry the bees to the hives, placing his arm carefully near the hive and returning to the open gate. As he closed the gate behind him he removed his hat and called out to Liz, "I bet breakfast is ready." After breakfast when all the men were back to work in the fields or barn the girls would help Mable finish the wash. What fun to run the clothes through the wringer not once but twice and then carry the basket out to the back-yard clotheslines. This was new for Liz because her mother didn't let her help at home. Evie didn't think Liz should do that kind of work until she was older. But here on the farm there was so much work for Mable to do that she needed all the help she could get. Liz assumed that was why Mable looked so much older than Evie even though Donna said they were only three years apart in age. Liz guessed it was all the sunshine causing wrinkles to show in her tanned face.

Sometimes Donna was jealous of Liz because the boys gave her a lot of attention. "You know, it's funny, Liz, they treat you nice even though you're a city girl. Yet, here they resent it that I live in town. Yes, we live on a farm like them but just because I can walk into town and have friends they consider me different," lamented Donna. Liz thought about this for a minute and then said, "Oh, it's probably the fact that they can impress me so easily because I don't know anything about farms. I have a dog but I didn't know that dogs could be trained to go out and bring in the cows when it's milking time. I didn't know that cows have to be milked at a certain time every day. I didn't know that a chicken might fight you to get the eggs out from under her! Stuff like that. And I hope I never see another bloody butchering of a hanging cow!

I'm sorry if it upsets you. You are my best cousin friend so please don't worry about the boys. Besides that, you are the prettiest! I wish my mom would let me have my hair cut into a cute style like yours. And boys like blondes, you know. But, no, Mom loves to braid these silly pigtails and wants my hair to grow to my waist.

(Actually, Liz was lying. It wasn't Evie, it was herself, who wanted her hair long.) And I'm fat! I love to eat. Huh!" With that remark they both began to giggle, then laugh out loud. "Whoa, I gotta go!" screamed Liz and headed toward the bathroom. "Yeah, and if you don't go when you gotta go then you'll find out that you've already gone when you get where you are going!" laughed Donna.

Both girls enjoyed paper dolls with a passion, which wasn't anything the boys enjoyed. The summer Liz was ten, they thought they were getting too old for paper dolls but when they went shopping one day and saw the newest thing on the market they had to have it! Two sets of "Gone With the Wind" characters were so much fun to dress and do role play with. They filled hours with them. But that was the last summer they played with paper dolls.

The girls spent a lot of time at their grandmother's house too. Liz understood that her grandparents' house was one of the first ones built "up the hill" away from the farms, beginning the township of Altura. There were less than a five hundred people living here now. Their house was still one of the finest in town. It was a two-story frame house finished on the outside with a creamy stucco cement instead of paint. There were four bedrooms upstairs with a small balcony off of the hallway.

At one time, all five of the Hilke children slept in three bedrooms while the folks used one. All shared the one full bathroom! Evie had also told Liz that her grandparents had finally decided to "carve" a half bath out of the kitchen downstairs with just the stool and a sink. This room soon became very popular with everyone during the day as they would not need to trek the long stairway to the one upstairs. That was one story that Liz loved because it had come directly from her mom. Her daddy would share stories a little but Evie did so rarely. Liz would repeat these stories to Trixie first because she thought them rather trivial for others to hear. Even with the new bathroom, the dining room and kitchen were both still big and roomy, large enough for family gatherings.

The big player piano was one story Evie really did not talk about as she didn't feel any significance to it. Grandmother would push her feet on the foot pedals hard, up and down, to play music that came out of those paper tubes with holes in them. This was all piano music and sounded as though she were playing the keys herself. When Liz was a little older she was allowed to play the piano canisters herself. She loved it. Sometimes she thought that Grandma played too many church songs but some of them were okay. Liz was allowed to play the old Victrola anytime she wanted. This large standing record player stood in the corner of the lovely dining room.

There were two big windows at the south side of the room which shed sunshine on grandma's green plants under them and carried the sunbeams on into the sunroom just west of the dining room. The old vinyl records were heavy but they were well taken care of. Liz thought the records were great and she was careful to put the needle arm down gently to play. Her favorite was the one that she and Donna could sing along with; "Buffalo gals, won't you come out tonight, come out tonight, come out tonight. Buffalo gals won't you come out tonight and dance by the light of the moon." They would dance around the big dining room table, on out into the little sunroom and porch. After that they would fall on the floor with laughter.

Liz loved her Grandmother's house; especially the big fern and all the lacy doilies that added such beauty to the house. The dining room had built in cabinets with lovely glass doors. Great-grandmother's dishes were proudly on display. Oh, yes, Liz loved Grandmother's house.

She knew that it was a lot of work to keep clean, yet, she dreamed of living here one day. Grandpa seemed to be sitting in the same spot every day. The only time he would go outdoors was to fix a meal for the dog and throw some chicken feed into the chicken coop. If grandmother needed help in her garden he might put the vegetables into the wheelbarrow and push it up to the back door where he would start snapping the green beans. But if she was pulling weeds he never offered to help. Liz assumed he could not get down on his knees anymore because of something called arthritis.

She had heard Aunt Alice say that he was twelve years older than grandmother so that was probably why grandmother never insisted on his help. So, grandpa would return to the house if grandmother was busy weeding or over in the flower garden snipping off some gladiolas for the dining room table. Rocking in his high back wooden rocker, he would listen to his favorite time spot on the radio. This was at noon when the village church bells tolled and a horn blew out in the country signifying it was lunchtime for the men out in the fields. Liz surmised that everyone in the village ate lunch at the same time! Liz heard the music of "Stella Dallas" on the radio and knew grandpa was sitting in his rocker listening to his favorite program. She also knew it was time to go into the kitchen and set the table for lunch.

When his program was over he was ready for lunch and grandmother never disappointed him. After lunch, Liz would follow him back to his chair and ask if she could have one of his lemon drops. Liz loved to spend the nights there as she could sleep in the bedroom that she was born in!

Evie had come to Minnesota to stay with her parents during her last month of pregnancy so that she had help with her newborn. In those days many women had their babies at home with the help of a midwife until a doctor would arrive. Liz never heard the story from her mother but her Aunt Alice told her about how excited everyone was that day! The family had no idea what to expect from Evie because she could be quite vocal when she was angry. They were not sure if she really understood what labor pains were and afraid that she would be very vocal when the time arrived. "But, she was relaxed and everything went so fast that before we knew it we heard your vocals, not hers!" Alice laughed as she told Liz about her real birth day. Liz loved to come to Minnesota to hear these stories.

The time always came to go back home to Wisconsin and get ready for a new year at school. Liz never gave much thought to what she wanted to do when she grew up beyond becoming a teacher. In fact, she was beginning to feel like she was now grown up. For the first time in her life she felt a part of her surroundings, enjoying real peers and receiving friendly and honest communication from them.

It didn't really matter that her parents were deaf. There were only a few people in this school that knew about them and that's the way she would keep it. She was old enough now to go places on her own and meet whomever she wanted to meet; no questions asked. Yet something tugged at her heart and she did not want to do the wrong things; the so-called "wild" things that she had heard of from some friends. Oh, she had been invited to home parties when their parents were out but she really wanted no part of the beer-drinking and cigarette-smoking crowd.

Two friendships continued with her old chums Mae and Nita. They'd been close since sixth grade! Every Saturday they went to movies and out to the "Greasy-Spoon" afterwards. When she had money, it was also fun to go shopping with the girls. Evie even helped her pay for a poodle permanent. The three girls went in at the same time but had to wait in line for the special curling device. Nita was first and the results were not what they should have been. Her dark red hair was naturally curly and now it was nothing but frizz. The beautician assured her that it would soften up after a couple of shampoos but Nita had her doubts. Mae's hair had absolutely no natural curl so she was still excited to get the curls, feeling confident that all would be well. This hairstyle made Mae look even taller and thinner which wasn't really the effect she wanted, but her dark blonde hair was beautiful. Liz had explained to her mother that "dirty blonde" meant not all yellow because brown hair was mixed in.

When it was Liz's turn she was really scared. What if she looked like a poodle dog? She wasn't tall but she wasn't short either, just average. She wasn't thin but she wasn't fat, just average. Her dark brown hair had been pretty but average. The only thing she wouldn't be able to do after this perm was to braid her hair and she didn't care about that at all. It was worth the pain of those big rollers pulling her hair up to the electric gadget hanging from the ceiling. The curls were good and tight and stayed high on her head! This turned out to be a flattering hairstyle for Liz and the girls were really jealous of her.

Liz really lacked self-confidence. Perhaps this hairdo would raise her self-esteem. However, when the girls went to the showers after gym class she was embarrassed about something else, her breasts. She didn't understand why they were so small compared to the other girls. Liz had big hips, small waist and seemingly small breasts. She cried herself to sleep nights thinking about them. When she mentioned them once to her mother Evie simply told her, "Grow will." But grow they didn't. It was just too difficult to feel good about herself with these small breasts. Finally, when she was a Senior in high school she saw something at the TG&Y store that seemed like the answer for this problem. They were soft breast inserts she could slip into her bra. Looking around to be sure no one was watching, she picked up the package and went right to the checkout counter to pay for them.

After arriving home she went directly into the bedroom and slipped the pair of soft pads into her bra and tried it on. Not bad, she thought as she looked at herself in the mirror. She slipped on her favorite blue sweater and stood looking at her side view. She would wear this to the school dance tonight and see if anyone noticed. At the supper table no one had any comments, not even Bobby. Feeling confident that no one would really notice, she went to the dance as planned. Of course her date would notice when they danced but he didn't say anything. Liz had the best time that night. It was great to feel self-assured that she looked her best.

Evie couldn't believe Liz would soon be eighteen. Watching Liz change into a young lady, Evie remembered how just a few years ago she had felt sorry for Liz when the family decided to make a big move. She was afraid it would affect her teen age life but it had turned out to be a learning experience for her. They moved to another town just up the Wisconsin River. The paper mill business was the reason this town had a larger population growth than Merrill.

The daily newspaper there had need for a linotype operator like Frank. A deaf couple living nearby had sent him the information. Frank was pleased to drive two hours for his interview a few days later. When they offered him the job with a good increase in salary, he couldn't refuse. He was confident that Evie and the kids would like this new town, Wisconsin Rapids.

It was a tough sell, an idiom that Frank had learned from one of his co-workers. Liz, for one was very upset upon hearing this news. She signed with fast moving hands, "Just when everyone is familiar with the fact that my parents are deaf we must move away? Just when our neighbors understand I need a little extra help sometimes with my vocabulary and social abilities. Just when we had this wonderful house built for us!"

How could her daddy do this? Bobby thought it was exciting. He wanted to move because he didn't like to go to school with Billy, the neighbor boy. They were friends before Billy's dog bit Bobby right in the face. Liz would never forget that day. She had just come home from skating with her friends. She saw the big crowd around someone in her yard. Oh, I wonder "What's going on?" she yelled as she ran up the street to their house. At the same time her daddy's car pulled into the driveway. A neighbor had Bobby in his arms and there was blood everywhere! Evie came out of the house carrying wet towels. After placing one on Bobby's forehead the three of them got into Frank's car. Liz caught up with them before they pulled away. "What happened?!" she signed frantically and screamed at the same time. Evie gestured to her to get into the car and Frank skidded out of the drive onto the street and on to the hospital.

An hour later the doctor came out of the Emergency stall and gestured to Frank and Evie to come in. Liz accompanied them explaining that she would relay his words to them. With a nod, the doctor informed them that Bobby was very lucky. He didn't lose his eye as they had feared. The teeth had struck just above the eyebrow and after cleaning the area it required a lot of stitches there and more high in his right cheek. It was a miracle that his eye had not been damaged. The doctor turned to Bobby and said, "You can brag to your friends with this story!"

Bobby was just six years old and since he was a boy, Liz told him he could be proud of a scar when he was older. He could tell other kids a scary story about bravely fighting off the attack of a

German Shepherd. The trauma stayed with him a long time and he lost all interest in Trixie, refusing to take his turn in feeding their own sweet dog. So, Trixie and Liz were even closer than ever. Who would ever have thought that Trixie would eventually teach Liz her first lesson in sex.

One hot summer day, Liz went outside to call Trixie in out of the heat and stopped sharply as she rounded the corner of the house and saw Trixie. She and another dog seemed to be tied together! Liz ran back into the house trying to understand what she had just seen. She peeked out the window at the same scene and confirmed that the two dogs were stuck! Liz yelled at Bobby to stay in his bedroom and not come out until she returned.

Before he could answer, Liz slipped quickly into the garage and wheeled her bicycle out to the street. Jumping on the bike she rode as fast as she could, heading for the Daily Herald which was almost two miles away. She just had to tell her dad what she had seen. "Daddy... daddy... daddy," she called when she arrived at the newspaper building. Liz hushed as she ran through the backdoor of the shop and found his linotype machine. Frank's co-workers were immediately alert to this little girl running through their newspaper office. One of them recognized Liz and told the others something must be wrong at Frank's home because this was his little girl.

They watched Liz sign frantically, "Trixie...dog.. two dogs.. stuck.. tied together.. What do?" But they had no idea what she was saying because she no longer was using her voice. Frank knew immediately what Liz was trying to tell him and holding back some laughter, he asked Liz to sit down while he fetched her a drink of water. "But... but... Trixie may be hurt! What do?" signed Liz dramatically. "Liz, Trixie ok. Natural. Ok. Mom explain you tonight." Reluctantly, Liz obeyed her dad's direction to return home.

By the time Liz arrived back home, Trixie was lying in the sun in her usual corner. She perked her head up when she heard Liz's bicycle and ran over to greet her with a panting mouth. Liz refilled the doggie dish with water, petting the little female on the head. "I'm sure glad you are alright, girl. I was worried about you but you seem

fine. I guess I have some things to learn about life, especially dogs."
Trixie licked her on the cheek and they both walked slowly into the
house. That evening Liz told Trixie a new family story. "I'm so glad
I have you to talk to even though you can't tell me what you think!"
she said as she finished. What a day! What a lesson! Before today
Liz had thought dogs were just for fun; to play with, teach tricks,
pet, feed and bathe.

Liz would never forget the day they had gone to the farm in
Altura and let Trixie run around free. When she came to the yard
where Evie and Frank were visiting with Aunt Mabel and Uncle Ray
she was full of mud! Evie screamed, "Izzz!" When Liz heard that
she knew she was in trouble and came running. Then she saw Trixie
and laughed! Her mother was horrified and signed wildly, "Bath
finish home before come!" Liz grabbed Trixie's collar and pulled
her over to the hose connected to the faucet at the barn. She knew
the water was cold but that was all she could think of to do at the
moment. Trixie didn't like it a bit and wrenched herself away from
Liz, running as fast as she could, crawled her way into the nearest
pig pen fence where three big fat pigs were wallowing in the mud.

Liz's cousin Les had come to the rescue as he grabbed Trixie and
held her down. He didn't mind the mud as his jeans were already
dirty from cleaning out the cows' stalls in the barn. Laughingly, he
told Liz to go to the house and bring some soap and a towel while
he would get a bucket. Soon they were both bathing Trixie in sudsy
water and telling her to behave when they were through. Of course
Liz had wrapped her in the towel and taken her directly to the car
where she stayed until they were ready to leave. That had been a fun
trip, both coming and leaving.

On the way here that day, Daddy had run over a skunk. Well,
that was terrible! They had to ride with their windows open till they
arrived at Granma's. Then everyone went into the house happy to be
away from the odor. Just an hour later Frank was to go to the store
for Granma and we could hear him hollering, "Ohhh!" Everyone
thought Frank had fallen; but when we went outside we could see
what upset him. The car was covered with flies! Grandpa brought

out some kind of spray to kill the flies; then gestured to Liz's daddy to drive the car to the garage down on the farm. Three farmhands began using a big hose on the car. Then they scrubbed with sudsy water that they had mixed with lemon oil. After wiping off everything they covered the inside of the car with lemon oil alone. The next day you could detect no odor of skunk! Thank goodness!

Yes, those were fun memories of Trixie. But today taught Liz that dogs were much like humans and she sure wished she could understand what Trixie was saying when she barked; or what she was feeling when she whined. Liz felt a little disappointed and sad that Trixie never did have puppies. She wondered if Trixie, herself, felt disappointed too. Well, best get supper started.

After peeling potatoes, Liz set the table because her mom came home from work at five o'clock sharp. She was lucky to have a job so close to home. During this war they hired many women like Evie to work in the Clothing Factory where they were sewing uniforms for the soldiers. She also earned a little money at home by fixing silk stockings for women. When they had a run in their lovely stockings they brought them to Evie to repair. She had a special needle that went up and down as she held the stocking over an egg-shaped dish. It was amazing how she could make the run disappear and the hose look like new again.

That evening, mom surprised Liz with some information about the female body that was sure difficult to understand at age twelve. As usual, when she talked to her friends they knew a lot more than she did and tried to help her catch up. One of the girls wanted to be too graphic, showing her pictures with all the parts of her body and what they would be used for some day! Yuk! Sometimes Liz felt like it was better to be naïve and just ignore the details of life! She was happy just going to school, listening to the radio and playing simple games outdoors or inside with her daddy.

At age twelve, Liz and her family had actually moved to another town. Liz still felt a little resentful even though she knew that her father had an opportunity for a better paying job as a linotype operator for a bigger newspaper, the Daily Tribune, in a larger town. She really could understand that. Wisconsin Rapids spread itself out on both sides of the Wisconsin River only one hour's drive south of Wausau. Evie thought it was a pretty town but she was disappointed when she saw where they had to live. An upstairs apartment in someone's home! She had really hated leaving their house in Merrill, one that was their own and never dreamed they wouldn't live in a house here!

Before even getting out of the car, Frank promised that living like this would be for just a few months while they searched for a house. They got out of the car and walked up the stairs to an upstairs flat he had rented in the west part of town. "Two bedrooms. Big, room for Daddy, Bobby, me; little you," Evie signed to Liz as she crossed the small living room and kitchen area, pointing behind her to a small loft. Liz hid her disappointment as well as she could, deciding she was lucky to have her own room. She quietly helped her mother unpack the kitchen dishes that evening before falling into bed exhausted.

The next morning after breakfast, her daddy took Liz and Bobby to their new school. It was located just four blocks from their apartment and six blocks from the river. When they stepped out of the car she wrinkled her nose and looked at Frank who was holding his nose. What a smell! "What that? Terrible!" asked Liz. "Paper mill," her daddy answered and laughed. Liz didn't think it was a laughing matter at all but they had no time to talk as it was time for school to start. They checked into the office and of course, the first thing the secretary did was start talking to Frank. Frank then pointed to his ear and shook his head negatively. The secretary looked down at Liz and said, "Is this your dad?" Liz said, "Yes, and he's deaf." She signed to her Daddy and he shook his head in the affirmative. "Can he read?" asked the Secretary. Liz signed that question to her dad and again he nodded his head in the affirmative. "Tell him he will need to sit down over there and fill out this paper."

When Frank saw the paper and the lady nodding toward the chairs, he took the paper from her and led Liz to a seat beside him. He started to skim down the page and then began filling in the spaces. Liz sat quietly watching the secretary as she walked from her station into another office space. She couldn't see who was in there but a man soon approached them, accompanied by the secretary. "Ask your daddy where he works," the man inquired. When Frank saw the gentleman speaking to Liz, he immediately stood up and politely offered his hand for a handshake. The gentleman smiled and shook Frank's hand and waited for Liz to ask him his question. "Work you, where?" she signed. Frank then took out the pad of paper and a pencil which he always carried in his pocket and wrote down the answer. The secretary then told Liz this was the Principal, Mr. Gray. Liz acknowledged that information with a little nod and spelled out the principal's role and name to her dad. Mr. Gray was writing a note to Frank and when Frank read it he smiled at Liz, gave Bobby a pat on the back and said he had to go on to work now and the secretary would take them to their classrooms. He shook Mr. Gray's hand, tipped his cap to the secretary, and left. He turned at the door and signed to Liz that she should remember to meet Bobby after school.

Liz decided that as long as her daddy was polite to hearing people, they were polite to him. They didn't even seem as wary as when they first walked in. In fact, she didn't think her daddy had had time to fill in all the spaces on that paper. But as long as they didn't ask her questions, she was satisfied. What she didn't know was that after taking them to their classrooms the secretary called to the Daily Tribune for more information about this Niklaus family.

Entering into the sixth grade was tough enough for Liz. Now she had to face three strange girls and twenty-two boys in the classroom. Fortunately, at recess it didn't take long to make friends with just three girls.

Nita, a girl of Italian descent, Mae, a quiet girl, and Peggy who bragged about her dad being a dentist. Liz wondered if that was a threat. If you were not nice to Peggy, her daddy would pull your teeth? But the four girls got along very well and played a little jump rope before the bell rang. Just two weeks after meeting Nita, Liz received an invitation to go to her home for an Italian spaghetti dinner.

After Evie and Frank asked questions about the family they gave their permission. Frank drove her to their home and told Liz to tell Nita s family that he would be back at eight to pick her up. Nodding in the affirmative, Liz gave her daddy a big smile as she ascended from the car.

Liz never had spaghetti of any kind and it didn't take long for her to fall in love with the special meatballs and sauce as well as the cook, Nita's mother. She was so loving, jovial and plump any child would feel comfortable with her hugs. She didn't pry into Liz's family life at all during dinner. They just chatted about school, their teacher and the town Liz had lived in before. Nita's father was not home as he was working the evening shift at the paper mill.

They laughed when Liz asked why the paper mill had been so stinky that first day when Liz came to school. She learned that it doesn't happen very often but when they are in the certain processing period of making paper and the wind is downstream then they will smell the sulphur it makes. Thank goodness it didn't happen too often, maybe just two or three times a year. Nita was a dark complexioned girl with wonderfully dark thick hair braided in a different way than Liz had ever seen. They called it French braids. "I thought you were pure Italians!" Liz quipped. "And, you are a sassy little girl!" Nita's mom retorted with a laugh. Nita had a younger sister, who was prettier than Nita but not as witty. These two girls were lucky to have no pesky kid brother, she told them. They all laughed but still asked no personal questions about Liz's parents. Liz felt like she had been adopted into a new family, especially when Nita's mother told her to please call her "Mama Essie."

In the months to come they had a lot of meals together, both at Liz's home and at Nita's. Nita even learned some signs so that she could communicate with Evie and Frank. Being Italian seemed to make it easy for Nita to gesture a lot. In fact, Liz told her that she probably knew as many signs as Bobby did. Bobby just relied on Liz to tell their folks what he wanted until he was a little older. Even then he didn't really communicate with them much. "Boys will be boys," Nita's mom would say when Liz complained about him. "Six years between you gives you different mind sets too," she continued. Liz tried not to let it bother her and got into a bad habit of just ignoring him. The only time she felt true sympathy for him was when he got bit by that dog. Oh, also when he had his tonsils out when he was just five. She had held his hand just before he went into the operating room and he told her he was so scared. Liz didn't have any experience with surgery so she simply told him that the angels would take care of him.

Yet Liz had to admit that Bobby could be fun sometimes. Times like blueberry picking in the bushes out on a nearby country road. On some Sunday afternoons, Evie, Frank and their children would load the car with buckets, aprons and gloves. Evie never let them pick blueberries without their aprons on to keep the stain as minimal as possible. Depending upon the season they picked raspberries, blueberries or blackberries. Liz favored the blueberries while Bobby would only eat the raspberries.

"They're kinda good," he would say because he never showed much emotion about any food. In fact, he was a picky eater but Liz decided to leave that problem to her mother to control. She knew her mother depended upon her to keep an eye on Bobby and often she had to call out his name to be sure he hadn't wandered too far from the area of berry bushes.

One day Liz almost panicked when he didn't answer her call. She ran out to a clearing and saw a combine picking peas off of their vines. There Bobby was, watching the men work but Liz could see that he wasn't paying attention to the movement of the machine. The corn field beside him was taller than he was so Liz felt that he could not be seen by the men on the machine. She ran calling his name until he responded by walking toward her. Realizing that the pea-picker was crossing the field between them she yelled, "Stop. Don't move!" After closing her eyes with a quick prayer in her heart she looked up and saw that the machine had stopped three feet away from Bobby. He was crying now and Liz ran again, yelling, "Okay. It's okay. Come on."

One man jumped off of the machine and waved to Liz. He watched Bobby run across the field toward his sister, before he climbed aboard again. This was one event that Liz preferred to scold Bobby herself without relating the incident to her parents. Liz wasn't even sure why she did things like this. Was it because it was really her fault for taking her eyes off of the little guy? Was it because she didn't think her parents knew how to control Bobby? Or was it just too much trouble to try to relate the whole story in sign language?

Like the time they went to the County Fair and Bobby ran off from her without telling her where he was going. She hoped he had just gone looking for the men's restroom and would be back shortly. After fifteen minutes of standing in the same place she wondered what to do if he didn't come back soon. Finally she saw some of her friends riding on the Ferris wheel and after they finished the ride, she asked them what to do. One of the boys offered to check the restrooms but came back quickly saying there was no sign of him there.

By this time, Liz decided she must find a policeman and enlist his help. The policeman quickly took control of the situation telling the kids to each cover a certain area of the park while Liz remained in the spot where she had last held Bobby's hand. This proved to be a good plan as after another ten minute wait Bobby came to this spot and said, "Gosh, Liz, where did you go? I was looking all over for you!" When her friends returned a few minutes later they chided Bobby for running off. "You scared your sister half-to-death and we've missed a half an hour of fun!" Liz thanked them for helping her, as well as the policeman who had just come back. It was the uniformed man who made a real impression on the boy as he took him aside using warnings of unpleasant possibilities that could have happened to Bobby.

Bobby began to cry and confessed that he had followed a carnival person who was carrying a monkey, eventually watching him perform before he realized he was lost. He promised the officer that he would never do anything like that again. And, again, Liz did not relate this incident to Evie or Frank. Why bother them when she felt partly to blame anyway. She actually pretended they had had a good time and described their rides on the Tilt-a-Whirl which had really occurred before Bobby got lost.

One day Bobby came home from school and recited the "Pledge of Allegiance" to Liz when Evie walked into the room and asked what he was saying. Liz tried to sign the Pledge but was not sure about how to sign some of the words. When she spelled the words to her mother she knew Evie didn't understand *pledge* and *allegiance* so Liz signed patiently, "Wait, daddy home." That evening Frank enjoyed the questions Liz had for him. It was a real challenge to explain the words allegiance, pledge, republic and indivisible in signs.

He chose the sign for *support* to use for allegiance; the sign for *promise* for the word pledge; *country* for republic and two signs, *can't separate* for indivisible. Liz was so pleased then to be able to sign while Bobby proudly recited the Pledge for them. They all applauded and patted the boy on the back. It was a rare moment for each one of them to have this feeling of pride in the family, to feel proud together. It was also Liz's first time to feel a pride in her country, with a feeling of gratitude that she was born an American.

Liz loved winter. Except for the bundling up in her two-piece snow suit and pulling on her boots, mittens and hood. Evie taught Liz how to make a lovely scarf by adding fringes all around the edges of the scarf. When it was not snowing, she was allowed to wear this to school instead of a hood. It was really a nuisance when you had to dress this way to trudge to school only to have to take it all off when you arrived. Sometimes she just left her snow pants on under her skirt. But they soon became too warm because Evie insisted on her wearing long brown cotton stockings. At first she hated learning to wear a garter belt to keep the stockings up. However, when Liz saw the other girls wearing them too she soon became adapted to them. The warm stockings were actually comfy in the not-so-warm schoolroom without her snow pants on.

The teacher actually had to spread towels on the floor of the "cloak room" behind the back wall of the room to collect the drops of moisture coming off of all the jackets and boots hanging on hooks along the wall. The classroom always smelled musty. After school hours the janitor could be seen pushing a tub on wheels around the rooms collecting all those wet towels! What a chore that must have been. Liz hoped she would never have to be a janitor.

Winter brought the family together at times in sledding, building snowmen, ice skating, and the chore of shoveling snow. Liz corrected that thought, it is not the whole family because her mother sure never ventured out into the snow for fun. But she did share in clearing off the sidewalk and driveway with a broom after they finished that chore. Liz knew there was a certain pride in keeping clean walks in the winter as well as neat yards in the summer. It was this feeling of pride in her family that brought Liz out of her shell and allowed her to sign in public no matter what the consequences.

When shopping, her mother often told her to keep her signs smaller and not cause a scene. Liz had a hard time controlling her signs as they were a part of her personality. She knew Evie's signs were small because she was a quiet, shy person and very much a lady. Perhaps Evie was a reflection of her times as a child who had been taught to sign "quietly" so as not to attract attention. To Liz, this was a new thought. This idea of *personality* showing up with facial expressions used in American Sign Language. She resolved to notice other deaf people closely and write down their personalities in her diary. Maybe someday this could be important information for people working with deaf children in schools. Liz often dreamed of becoming a teacher in a school for the deaf somewhere, even though she had never set foot inside of one!

6

Do the Children Prefer Hearing World?

Evie once told Liz that when she and school friends went shopping in the town, they were escorted by one of the teachers who kept a sharp eye on them. If she saw their signs getting too far away from their body or their faces becoming too contorted she would grab their hands and pull them down putting them together as if in prayer. Liz had laughed when her mother told her that story but Evie did not smile and signed, "Serious me. Your sign big. Make small." So Liz tried her best to do just that but only when they were in public. She couldn't help but wonder why her mother could not appreciate that she signed well. Bobby sure doesn't! Liz had already decided that her mom favored her little brother. This didn't really bother her because she felt way down inside that her daddy favored her and that was more than she needed to be happy.

Frank and Evie subscribed to a magazine for the deaf that came monthly in the mail. An insert inside of this magazine was a story printed for children. Before Liz could read very well, Frank would sit down and read the story to her. She loved to watch him sign new words along with the ever-challenging chore of reading his finger-spelling used for proper names. One month the story was not complete. It would be continued in next month's issue. Liz couldn't understand this but she waited patiently for the day to arrive. This long story was "Snow White and the Seven Dwarfs."

There were so many proper names in this story that Frank decided to make up signs for some of them. This was especially fun because he asked Liz to help him to do this for the names of the seven dwarfs. In so-doing, Liz laughed and laughed, causing Frank to almost choke with laughter. One name sign would be funnier than the last. Later that night Frank shared that part of the story with Evie and she had to laugh too. Liz grabbed her little brother's hand and laughingly said, "Bobby, isn't it so much fun when we can all laugh together about something?!"

The next month was the third and final edition of the story. That day they held onto the paper until Saturday afternoon when Evie joined them while Frank read the rest of the story. What an unusual break in routine this was for all of them. Bobby was just a three year old at that time, so Liz promised Frank that she would keep the story in a drawer so they could share it with him one day. Liz was so happy with this story she told her teacher about it on Monday. The teacher asked the class how many of them had heard this story and most of the kids raised their hands in affirmation.

Liz was embarrassed, but the teacher was kind and said quietly to her, "I know you are proud that your daddy could read you the story. I want to talk to him sometime about using the public library. Do you think he would like to know about it?" With that she turned to the class and continued, "Class, we will visit the public library on Thursday and learn how we can check out a book that we would like to read." Liz was immediately relieved of her feelings of embarrassment. She had loved Miss Ivers and truly missed her now.

Things were different now that her family had moved to this new town called Wisconsin Rapids. Liz thought about the city's name and decided she needed to find out where the rapids were. Maybe that would be a site for her parents to see some day. Those rapids must be somewhere along the Wisconsin River that flowed through the town. She could see on the map this city was right in the center of the state. Somehow that had to be important, Liz thought.

After more than a year of living in the upstairs flat, Frank decided they still could not buy a house but they could afford to rent a house in the same neighborhood. It was a cute little two bedroom with a big front porch. During the summer Bobby slept out on the porch but during the winter he had to share a bedroom with mom and dad. Liz was sure glad they didn't make her share but at the same time she felt sorry for Bobby having to sleep in their parents' room. It really wasn't right. This house was on a corner lot and they enjoyed a big yard which was the best thing about this home.

One night when it was raining hard outside Liz and Bobby had just come out of the movie theater and were waiting for their dad to pick them up. He never showed up so Liz took her jacket off and put it over both of their heads, grabbed her little brother by the hand and said, "Come on, we'll just have to run home." She didn't realize how rough she was on him until after they ran the mile in the rain and Bobby threw up all over the back steps leading into their kitchen. "Oh, you little brat! Now mom will really be mad at us," Liz cried out. After taking off their wet jackets and shoes she realized it was all dark in the house. No one was home. Oh dear, she thought, hope they're not sitting at the theatre looking for us. Liz decided she would have to clean up Bobby's mess first and then she would figure out what to do. Bobby had stripped himself, put on his pajamas and jumped into bed.

Finally she decided to get ready for bed. She loosened her braids and started her nightly ritual of brushing. Liz was proud of her thick, dark shiny hair. It was really pretty when Mama Essie fixed it in French braids, something either Liz or Evie could not manage to do. Yes, her hair was definitely her biggest asset. Her dark brown eyes were said to be "fetching" by her Uncle Karl. As much as Liz loved to laugh, her teeth often prevented her from doing so in front of strangers. Maybe someday she could get braces but she knew her parents could not afford them now. The gap between her upper front teeth was not as bad as some of her friends had, she thought. For heaven sakes, Liz, this is not the time to be evaluating your beauty or lack thereof. Suddenly, Liz heard someone crying outside her window. Was it her mother?

Fighting off sleep, she listened at the door for any sound. Hearing something she fell into bed and covered her head. Yes, it was her dad's car pulling into the driveway just outside her window. She heard his steps entering the back door into the kitchen where he seemed to stay. Probably fixing a cup of coffee Liz thought. Soon her mother came out of the bathroom and seemed to go into her bedroom. So Liz slipped into the bathroom and then right back to her room after a last look at the clock that read eleven p.m. It was a very late hour to Liz.

The next morning was Sunday so Liz dressed for Sunday school and waited for Bobby to get dressed as her mom was in the kitchen fixing toast for her. Her dad had apparently had his breakfast as he was sitting in the living room reading the Sunday paper. Bobby didn't want any breakfast and did not really want to know what his sister might have said to their mom about last night. Mom had nothing to say so Liz didn't question either of her folks. Frank nodded at her as she and Bobby went out the front door to catch their ride to church from their neighbor. How she wondered what had happened the night before but pondered more about how to ask them.

Actually, it was at this time that Liz began to realize that her mother led a lonely life. She didn't have any lady friends to talk to when she might want to let out some feelings about being a woman, a wife or a mother. Liz had been so wrapped up in her own feelings she never stopped to think about life from the perspective of being a deaf woman, wife and mother. Oh, she thought, she could say the same about her daddy but somehow he always had seemed more comfortable in his role as a deaf person. He probably communicated his feelings with his co-workers even if it was with notes. She never caught her daddy in a pensive or sad mood like she did her mother. Liz promised herself she would be more aware of her mother's feelings from now on.

That evening their Dad apologized to Bobby and Liz about missing them at the theatre. He promised that would never happen again. Nothing was said about the rain, about Bobby vomiting, or about Evie crying in the rain. This was the first time that Liz had any misgivings about having deaf parents. Couldn't they find a way to tell Liz why they had missed them at the theatre and why mom was upset?

Oh, how she wished Frank and Evie would share some of their feelings with her. Neither one showed emotions very often. Unfortunately, when they did show their feelings they were already in a highly emotional state and their communication was beyond reason. So it seemed to Liz and Bobby. Liz didn't spend a lot of time perusing the situation they lived in. After all, these were her parents and there was no way to change that fact or the life she would lead. She said a prayer now and then for her mother but somehow her heart was not in it.

One spring they were so surprised that the Easter bunny left them two live bunnies! Frank built a rabbit cage separated with a screen outside behind the garage. He told the kids that the rabbits were both females so they named them "Honey" and "Blondie." They took good care of them and loved showing them off to the neighborhood kids. Soon they were big and wanted to play outside of the cage so Liz and Bobby watched them closely until they were tired of it. The rabbits never grew tired but they did. They learned how to pick them up by the scruff of the neck and put them back into the cage. That Thanksgiving when dinner was over, Liz said that the chicken tasted different than usual but her mother didn't say any more about it.

After the dishes were taken care of Bobby said, "Come on, Liz, it's time to feed Honey and Blondie." He ran outside before Liz hung up her wet dishtowel. Again she signed to her mom, "Now think me. Chicken not look like chicken. Cut up before put table. You. Not normal." Before she could finish her comments, Bobby came screaming into the kitchen signing furiously, "Bunnies gone!" Liz caught the expression on her mother's face and knew what had happened! "What? What?" she signed with fervor.

Evie turned and went into the living room where Frank sat reading the paper. She grabbed the newspaper out of his hands and signed, "You. You tell Bobby where bunnies." Liz knew what was coming and grabbed Bobby's hand and held it tight. She recognized that lost look on her father's face. "We know can't keep rabbits long. Fat, good eat," their daddy told them. Bobby screamed again with tears pouring down his cheeks and ran off into the garage, slamming the door. Liz could hear him open and close the car door and explained quickly to her parents what he was doing. She thought one of them would go to get him and hold him and tell him how sorry they were, but neither one of them moved. Frank looked imploringly at Liz as he signed, "Ration meat now. Save stamps." Liz knew then how they had rationalized this idea of eating rabbits. "But, not chicken! Chicken not rationed know you," she signed vehemently!

Frank and Evie looked at each other in a perplexed manner. They said nothing more to Liz so she went into the bedroom, called to Trixie, and told her the sad story about the bunnies. "Don't worry, Trixie, no one will ever eat you!" she cried as she held her close and pondered the whole event. Did this mean that her parents had honestly not understood what the government had put on ration. She knew that her mother was aware that anything from the dairy was not rationed as she would send Liz or Bobby to Herschleb's for milk and eggs without giving her food ration stamps to take along. Liz knew that she could not explain this to Bobby. Liz never thought much about the war but this day she realized what effect it had upon the life of her little brother. This was one Thanksgiving she would never forget or perhaps it was one she would not want to remember.

Another time Liz hated the fact her folks were deaf was when her father had trouble at his work. She was fourteen years old and had no idea anything was wrong for her dad at the newspaper until one evening two men came to see her father at home. They were not deaf friends; they were strangers. But apparently they were not strangers to her dad as he invited them in and they sat around the dining room table while he took out paper and pencil to communicate with them. "Can your little girl tell you what we are here about?" queried the older man. He had a gray beard that offset his baldness and wore thick glasses. Liz told her dad what he asked and Frank wrote a note. The older man handed the note off to the second man and Liz guessed that he either couldn't read or his eyes were so bad he couldn't read daddy's writing. As the man read it he shook his head negatively. "Jim, what does it say?" asked the man in the glasses. "Hey, I don't really know. Frank wrote: Not daughter say. Write you."

Mr. Glasses turned to Liz, and ignoring the note asked, "What's your name?" Liz told him and he went on, "Liz, tell your dad we are quite upset with him and it's hard to write notes to explain what's going on. We do not want him to cross that picket line again like he did today!" Liz turned to her dad and signed what the man said, carefully finger spelling "picket line." She had to ask Mr. Glasses to explain picket line. "Oh, he'll know what we mean." The two men watched her with great interest. "Look at her sign!" one remarked to the other. "Yeah, and the expressions on her face look just like yours, Matt" replied the other. So, from this Liz now knew the older fella's name was Matt. But it really didn't make her feel any more comfortable. They were both acting mean she thought. And what did Matt mean by a picket line? Was that like a picket fence?

Again, Frank wrote a note to Matt. When the younger man asked to see the note Matt just said, "Oh, he's saying he has to work for a living. How can he feed his family? He can't get any other kind of job like we can." replied Matt. He grabbed Frank's arm roughly, looked him right in the face and said, "We all have families to feed! No work! Understand?" Again Matt turned to Liz and said, "Tell your dad that we are sorry he feels this way. We will have to report it to the Union. But we strongly advise that he doesn't go to work in the morning." And with that the two walked back to the front door and Frank did not accompany them as he usually did with visitors.

Liz realized her mother had come into the room and sat down in the corner chair of the room and was now engaged in a conversation with Frank. Liz tried to understand what her dad and mom were saying to each other but again it was hard for her to follow because they were both frightened and excited by that visit. Bobby peeked out from the bedroom and cried out to Liz, "Who were those guys? They were scary!" "Everything is all right now, little guy. It's kinda like a bad dream but it's all over and you can go back to bed."

Things did turn out okay. Frank continued to work at the same newspaper as the union voted to accept Frank's deafness as a conditional reason to work and yet continue as a member of the union. During that same year the owner of the Daily Herald decided to change their policy from unionized shop to open shop. Frank paid his union dues for the rest of his working life. Just a few years later when the Union went broke because of so many strikes across the nation; Frank lost the little bit of retirement money he had. So, perhaps keeping his membership in the union had not been a good thing after all; but rather, a waste of his money.

During the war and the later 1940s he felt blessed to have this job. He was even invited to play with the shop's softball league because so many of the younger fellows were gone to the service and he had shown himself to be able to handle the ball well. Liz and her brother enjoyed watching him play. Sometimes their mom would come too if she didn't have any hose to mend.

Saturdays changed from resting at home days to relaxation at the lake days. Evie and Liz would pack a picnic lunch of hotdogs, beans and potato salad. Of course an apple pie was included for dessert. It was just a five-mile drive from their new home on the East side of town. There was a swimming area where Bobby loved to go but Liz loved to sit on the shore with her dad and fish. She never caught anything big enough to keep but she enjoyed the feeling of closeness to her dad. They didn't have to talk, just sit and soak up the sun in the quiet cool atmosphere.

Sometimes Frank would choose these times to talk to Liz about something on his mind. For example, which did she think was the most difficult problem to endure, deafness or blindness. "Very difficult think about! What you think?" Liz asked as she realized she could not answer what she really thought! Of course Frank knew he wouldn't want to be blind! "If cannot see sun sparkling on water out there, see trees turning colors, see your sweet face." Frank hesitated as he puffed on his cigar and closed his eyes for a minute. Opening them wide he signed, "If cannot see Bobby hit home run, much sad!" Liz laughed and Frank joined her as he felt a pull on his line and soon the serious subject was forgotten.

While her hubby fished, Evie liked to stretch out on a lawn chair and look at a magazine or nap. Those times were very rare so Liz would take advantage of them to spend a little time with her mother. If there happened to be an area of grass with clover growing she would sit there and pick some to make a braid. Making a circle of the pretty white and violet flowers she would place it on Evie's head and sign, "Me crown you Queen of flowers." Evie would smile and pat Liz on the head, saying nothing in reply. Liz did this on three different occasions, once at home when Evie was gathering the clothes off the line. Each time she hoped her mother had thought of some reply but she never gave one. Perhaps she just didn't understand what it was like to "pretend."

At the lake, when it was time for Frank to go start the campfire and cook the hotdogs, Liz would walk on over to the swimming area to get Bobby. This could be a chore because he usually was not ready to quit swimming. Sometimes she would see some of her classmates and get into long conversations with them and it would be Bobby yelling at her to get back to the campfire for lunch. It was always a fun family day.

Soon, however, these family days were terminated and Liz was never sure why. Mom started making excuses that she was tired or dad would have to work overtime. Saturday nights the two of them would dress up and "go out on the town" they signed. One weekend they brought a deaf couple to visit while Liz was home. Liz was told that they were the Custers and had just moved to town.

They were showing pictures to Evie and Frank. Liz sneaked around behind her mother to look over her shoulder at them. She could see that it was a picture of a saloon and there were several people sitting there including her parents. Liz didn't like the way that her dad and the deaf visitor lady were sitting so close with Frank's arm around the lady's waist. Evie was in the picture too, laughing at the camera while the lady's husband was standing behind her. Evie watched her daughter's face closely to see her reaction to the pictures. She could see that Liz was disturbed but she didn't say anything, pretending that she didn't notice.

Liz did not feel comfortable with this couple but didn't have any reason to say so to anyone. She grabbed a book from the bookcase and said good night to them as she retreated into her bedroom. Unusual laughter came from the other room as Liz tried to get lost in her reading. She fell asleep before they left and wondered the next day how long they had stayed.

Another evening Evie and Frank took Liz and Bobby to the Custers' home for a visit. Liz sat in the dining room and watched as the four adults visited in the living room. She and Bobby began to play cards at the card table and Mr. Custer brought out wine for adults and soda for the kids. Liz saw him sign to her dad "My brother wine make many years ago. Very good." Liz knew nothing about wine and didn't really think her dad did either but again, she said nothing.

Mr. Custer used his voice when he talked to Liz. He wore funny looking wire hearing aids sometimes but there were times he did not have them on. Liz never spoke of them to anyone but she wondered why her parents didn't try to wear one. The Custers had no children. Liz never saw Mrs. Custer with hearing aids and deduced that she was too vain to wear such ugly wiring. She could speak too but her voice was rather raspy and not easy to understand. Liz was not sure why the Custers had chosen to make friends and use sign language with her parents. She knew they were able to understand people in public because she was with them one day when they went to the lumberyard and made a purchase.

She overheard one of the men in the store say to another, "You know, that's Art Custer. He's hard-of-hearing. He comes here a lot because they are remodeling their home. He reads your lips pretty good and if you listen close you can understand his speech." Hmmm, Liz thought, hard-of-hearing is a lot different than the terms people use for her folks. Most people think of mama and daddy as "deaf and dumb." Liz didn't like the "dumb" part! Her friends assured her it only means that someone cannot speak. "Then why not just say they are deaf?" That was all that Liz ever said when she talked of them.

The next time they came to Liz's home, Mr. Custer handed Liz a book and told her she might enjoy reading it when she retired that evening. He had brought wine over to their home this time and even offered Liz a glass. Luckily, Evie saw that and told him he should not do that because of Liz's age. He laughed and kept the glass for himself as he led Evie away from Liz. He turned his head and looked at Liz over his shoulder and winked at her. How creepy, Liz thought! When she went to her own room and opened the book she could not believe her eyes! There were pictures with stories under them of naked men, women, boys and girls, all doing strange things. Liz slammed the book shut and hid it under her bed. What nerve! She would burn it the next day! And that is exactly what she did. She took it down to the basement early in the morning and threw it into the coal furnace.

If anyone asked about it, she would tell them she didn't know what happened to the book. She didn't want to embarrass her mother and father or herself! But, later she realized the effect it might have on Mr. Custer. He might think she kept the book and looked at it when no one was home. He might actually try to touch Liz thinking that she liked it. Thank goodness the Custers did not come over to visit for a long time. As the weeks and months went by, Liz noticed more and more that her parents were not talking much together and when they did they always seemed to have an argument.

One evening in the fall, after one of these arguments, her mother went to their bedroom for a long while. Liz could hear her crying but she said nothing to her dad. She just didn't know how to handle these scenes so she pretended she had not seen them. Later, Evie came out of the bedroom and Frank came to Liz's room and asked Liz to join them in the front room. She followed him reluctantly to where he pointed for her to sit down with them at the table. Her dad looked at her sadly and softly signed, "Mom. Me. Separate decide." Liz jumped up and screamed at them, "You can't serious!" They couldn't hear her screams but they could certainly see that Liz was very upset. Liz continued in sign language, "You deaf. Not easy find other deaf. Only two other deaf here this town! Lonely. But you married. Father, mother, Bobby, me. No. Divorce sin. Call minister. No, he tell you, no!" Frank was shocked at Liz's words and emotions. "Custers blame. Bad people. Custers." Liz ran off into the bedroom crying. She could not believe what had just happened.

Thank goodness Bobby had gone over to his friend's house to spend the night. After a while she slipped down the hall to the bathroom and hearing nothing she decided to grab her jacket and walk over to Nita's house. There she shared all the evening's events and cried some more when her "Italian Mama" pulled Liz to her on the couch and hugged her hard. She had the warmest hug and always smelled like fresh bread. I sure wish my mom could be more loving like this, Liz thought. Mama Essie moved back and looked Liz in the eye. "Liz, these things happen sometimes and it's always hard for the children to understand. But, you know what? Nine times out of ten people don't go through with a divorce once they face the real facts. I bet your folks will be one of those nine. You pull yourself together and go back home now before you worry them. Tell them both that you love them and go on to your bedroom. Give them some space. Give them some time. Don't forget to say your prayers and ask God to show your folks a way that will keep them together. After a week you can come tell me how it is going. But if you need to talk to someone during the week that's okay too."

Mama Essie had been right. That Saturday morning Evie told the kids to dress warm and help her pack a picnic lunch because they were going out to the lake one more time before the weather got too cold. Fearful that these plans did not include her dad, Evie was not too happy. Then she remembered that her mother couldn't drive and sure enough when she looked out the kitchen window she saw her dad cleaning out the car. Bobby was excited even though he knew he couldn't go swimming. It would be an adventure to go to the lake with all the leaves on the ground. Maybe they could hike down that trail he always wanted to try.

Indeed, it turned out to be a great family day. The food tasted better than ever and they had fun throwing some crumbs to the squirrels who bravely came to the table. Daddy complimented mom on her apple pie and they were actually holding hands while Bobby and Liz packed up to go home. Liz looked at her mother in her freshly ironed plaid housedress and thought how neat she looked. But, she had never worn pants; not even on a picnic. Her aunts on the farms would wear blue jeans when out working with the animals or gardening; but if not working, they would be in housedresses too.

The only change that her dad ever had was wearing baggy old workpants on a Saturday like this. Liz wondered why she was even thinking about clothes except that she wanted this "picture" to be romantic between her mom and dad. She was so relieved that they seemed to really be together again. Of course, this traumatic event passed without any explanations to Liz. But she didn't care. She only wanted her folks to be happy and they seemed to be happier than ever. Liz did notice that the Custers never came by again and the Saturday nights "on the town" never happened again. To Liz that was good but she knew that it might mean lonely times for Evie and Frank. Liz prayed that God would send some new deaf people to town. Some good Christian folks.

Teenage years brought many changes in Liz. Most of the changes were physical, of course. What a nuisance monthly periods were. This was another trauma that her mother never explained to her except to buy her a box of pads and show her how to use the belt. Again she learned from her girlfriends and some from Mama Essie. Mama Essie and her husband brought more surprises into Liz's life as they hired her to work in their new business, an A&W Root beer stand.

What fun! The best part was that it was just two blocks from the Niklaus' residence so she could walk to and from work as long as she was home by ten p.m. What fun to walk (or, hop, as it was called) out to the car as it parked in the lot, give a big welcome word and write down their orders on her pad of paper. Root beer floats were the most popular item on the menu, with small size mugs for any little children in the car.

One responsibility of hers was to be sure those little glass mugs were counted right so that someone would not sneak off with one because they were so popular. Liz found the work challenging, hurrying as fast as she could to take a tray to a car window, smile and hope for a tip. She was a good worker and Mama Essie never failed to tell her so, at the end of her shift as she took off her apron and said goodnight.

Liz's side didn't hurt anymore either. Wow, that had been such a scare when she had the side aches all the time and couldn't figure out what was wrong. Then one day she had been walking to school with her friend, Mae, when all of a sudden the world started going around and around and the next thing she knew she was on the ground. A neighbor stopped her car as she viewed the scene and offered to take Liz home. Mae explained what had happened and offered to go with her to talk to Liz's parents. But the neighbor said Mae needed to go on to school as she noted Liz was awake and was able to get up now and into the car. "So, Liz can communicate the incident to her mother." Evie was frightened by Liz's story but she decided to wait out the day to see what Liz would feel like. When Frank came home he insisted that they take her to the doctor right away. Doc sent her right to the hospital and the next morning Liz had her very first surgery ever. In fact, it was the first time she'd ever been in the hospital except for Bobby's tonsils surgery. Appendix! She'd never heard the word before, but the next day she was glad she didn't have hers anymore.

It was a few days before she could get out of bed to go to the bathroom and she was told she would need to stay in the hospital a week! Her daddy came in on the third day and said that he and Evie wanted to drive to Milwaukee to the annual State Convention for the Deaf and assured her that she would be fine here. Bobby would go with them and they would be back on Sunday night to take her home on Monday morning. The nurses would take good care of her and she could teach them some sign language or at least the alphabet. Liz felt abandoned but there was nothing she could say. She knew these conventions were only once a year and her parents always looked forward to the event. For weeks afterwards their conversations would center around the gathering and the people who attended. Yet, Liz felt sorry for herself. This was the first time in her life that she felt so alone!

Mama Essie and Nita came to see her every evening and Sunday seemed to arrive fast. She still had to stay home another week from school and Mae brought her homework every day. She thought maybe this was a time her mother would become closer to her. However, mom had to work every day so Liz had to pass the time with schoolwork or reading a Nancy Drew mystery.

Then the war was over! What a day that was! Again Frank had to go to work to put out an "Extra" but this time it was with joy and pride that the paper was printed. After asking her mom's permission, Liz and Bobby joined their friends in walking downtown with their parents calling out to their friends with happiness, "The war is over! The war is over! Our boys will all be coming home soon."

There were so many people gathered downtown that day and soon an impromptu parade began marching through the city streets and over the bridge. The high school band and the local concert marching band members just brought their instruments and lined up as best they could and no one really cared. People began falling in behind the band in their cars and soon on foot. Confetti and paper ribbon streamers were floating out of windows above the stores where many store owners lived. What a festive mood everyone was in. The band stopped in the town square and began playing patriotic songs and after singing "My Country, Tis of Thee" most of the folks were tired and started their treks back home. Liz told Bobby that she would never forget this day, the end of World War II.

Bobby was happy because there would not be any rationing of candy anymore. The rest of the family were happy about more than rationing of sweet stuff but they all laughed along with Bobby that night as Liz did her best to describe to her parents what they had participated in earlier. Frank had seen some of it from the window of the Tribune; but Evie opted to stay home as crowds made her nervous. They both enjoyed reading the newspaper that next day that included pictures of the celebration downtown.

That fall, Liz entered high school as a freshman. Evie and Frank could not believe that their little girl was already a high school student. Liz loved her job at the A&W. All the high school boys and girls would come to the A&W after a movie or baseball game that summer. Liz was fifteen and only had an interest in one of the boys who seemed to have an equal interest in her.

Wade was an only child but not spoiled, because his folks appeared to be poor. It was later that Liz learned that Wade's mother was an alcoholic. Liz could not understand this because her husband, Wade's dad, had a good job at the Consolidated Paper Mill. Apparently he couldn't keep her satisfied or his monies were spent in the wrong places. Wade never talked about them so Liz tried to ignore the situation in his home.

Actually, that wasn't hard to do because they rarely stopped at his home. Liz knew it was because Wade did not want to embarrass her. Sometimes Liz thought that maybe the only reason he dated her was because her folks were deaf. That fact would mean that they would not know his folks or even want to meet them. Liz never was sure of Wade's feelings toward her. He had had other girlfriends before and never really asked her to go steady; but she had really fallen for him so she decided to take it one day at a time. Besides, she really had something to write about in her diary now! She had not gained any confidence in talking to her mother about such personal things; so, she continued to talk to her doll, to Trixie and her diary!

During their freshman year in high school, Wade showed his talents to be in baseball so Liz and her girlfriends would go out after school and watch the team practice. Sometimes they stayed until practice was over and Wade would sit down and talk to them and maybe even walk Liz home. Whenever Wade asked Liz for a "sorta" date she would agree to meet him at the soda fountain next to the theatre downtown. They would share a soda and walk up and down the main street window shopping or just talking. In the winter they would meet at the ice skating rink where they skated with friends and "waltzed" together to the music coming out of the warming house. Liz wasn't very strong on her ankles and tired sooner than Wade so she would sit and watch him do his fancy stuff.

Frank and Evie had given her these skates, beautiful white figure skates, for Christmas one year. It was the biggest gift she had ever received. She took good care of them, wiping off the ice and water and slipping the flannel cover over the blades as soon as she took them off. She realized she had become pretty responsible for herself now that she was working and able to buy herself some things such as a pair of pretty mittens and matching scarf to wear at the skating rink. It was silly to worry about how she would take care of herself. Each day seemed to bring a new experience that gave her opportunities to make decisions for herself and Bobby without asking her parents. Life seemed easier this way.

Liz was always worried that if she did bring home a boyfriend to meet her folks he may not react well to their deafness. She talked about it freely with her girlfriends but she did not want the boys to know. She wasn't sure why she felt this way and didn't want to question herself about these feelings at all, knowing that she would not like the answers.

But the first time Wade came to pick her up to go to a movie he was just fine with her folks being deaf. In fact he shook Frank's hand so long Liz thought he would never let go. Frank signed to Liz, "Ten thirty." Liz assured him they would be home before ten thirty and they slipped out the back door to start their walk to the theatre. After that it became a steady Saturday night date to the movies and home by curfew. But after a few months Wade began to make excuses for picking her up, asking her to meet him at the theatre instead.

He had a Saturday job delivering for a dry cleaners company that kept him busy until six p.m. and during the summer time Liz worked at the A&W from five to ten p.m. Liz wasn't sure but she thought maybe Wade was seeing another girl that summer. Again, she pushed aside these concerns and really enjoyed the carhop job. She would see many of her friends during the evening and even earned some tips that soon started adding up in her little bank at home. She knew she was a good worker even before her boss praised her as she informed Liz of her first raise.

That summer Frank surprised the family by announcing that they would all go on vacation for two weeks to one of Minnesota's thousand lakes, Lake Minehaha. "What a silly name!" said Bobby. "Did Daddy spell that right?" Liz laughed and asked her dad if that was what he spelled. He assured them that it was a correct name and that it was named after an Indian maiden of long ago.

Frank and his brother Karl had rented two cottages from a good deaf friend who owned a fishing lodge there. They would stop and see their brother and sister who lived in the area, Uncle Charles and his wife Lois, as well as Aunt Hazel and her husband, James. Liz and Bobby had never met them, because no one had ever come to Wisconsin to visit. Liz didn't know what to think about the plans but she was happy that their cousins, Dot and her brother, Bob would be included. They were a little older than Liz and always treated her so nice when they visited Illinois, which wasn't but once in two or three years. Liz got a big laugh when her brother was upset by the fact that his cousin had his same name! Bobby Niklaus. How could that be right? Liz and Dot tried to explain the whole concept of names to him and while he pretended to understand, they were not sure he did. When he became tired of talking about it, they all turned their attention to other things.

In fact, Dot was the only person in the world that Liz could feel comfortable with talking about their deaf parents and how deafness affected their lives. When they spoke of their dads they seemed to be talking about the same person. These two brothers were both in the printing business, loved sports, and spent a lot of time playing with their children. Even their language level was the same as they both were employed at newspapers as linotype operators. Liz said laughingly, "They are brothers! I don't think Dad ever uses any profanity. I probably don't know it when I see it but I have seen him make a sign for BS." Liz refused to say the words for this acronym. "I don't remember how I learned what that sign was and it's rarely I see him use it. Maybe he is a gentleman and tries to never swear in front of me. What about your dad?" "You know, that's a good question," Dot exclaimed. "I can't ever remember him using cuss words but, like you, I don't really know if I'd know one if I saw it." Their conversations were usually short and usually along with lunch sitting around a bonfire waiting for their dads to cook up those hamburgers.

When the subject turned to their mothers, there did seem to be some difference. Aunt Emily was a sweet woman who spent a lot of time talking with her daughter about "worldly" things. She liked to read, even the newspaper, so that she always had something to talk about when she and Dot were doing dishes or when they all sat out on the porch after supper. Dot never felt that she knew more than her mother. Emily dressed smartly and used makeup which enhanced her already pretty features. Superficially, it was Evie's black hair and fiery blue eyes that made her a natural beauty.

"Dot, my mom just doesn't have anything to talk about. Even when I ask her questions about her job at the clothing factory she can't seem to explain anything to me. It's like everything is a picture in her mind with no words with which to describe them. I get so frustrated trying to have a normal conversation with her. She seems to be in a world of her own. She will nod yes but I know she didn't understand me because she doesn't go on with the conversation. Do you have any idea what I mean?" Liz asked. Dorothy thought about this for a minute and quietly carried on this conversation. "Yes, I think I do, Liz. Mother's friend is that way too. So sweet but sort of ..hmm.. I guess you would have to say, limited, in her ability to communicate much. Let me tell you; she can give you the exact date of every relative's birthday, wedding date and death date! She really has a keen memory!

I have observed other deaf people at the deaf club hesitate sometimes in telling me a story. In fact, have you ever noticed that sometimes deaf people misunderstand each other?! I have seen someone get some information from another deaf person about a lady that was ill. That person then turned around and told another deaf person that the lady was not sick at all. It seems just a wrong expression on the face or the sleight of hand when making a sign can be read wrong by anybody, deaf or hearing. Ohhh, Liz, I wouldn't worry about your mom. She seems to be happy with your daddy and that's what really counts. Don't you agree?"

They had held a couple of other conversations like this over the years and without really realizing it, this was the very subject Liz wanted to talk about again at the Lake. She wanted Dot's opinion on how to talk to her mother about boyfriends and she was sure Dot would have the answer.

When they arrived at the Lake it was everything Liz had hoped for except that Dot had brought her boyfriend, Parky, along. So, Liz didn't get the attention or the time that she had hoped for. Bob was good to Bobby and took him fishing in the boat he rented for the day. Later that day Liz joined them and was surprised at how much fun could be had in a boat ride. After hours in the sun, they all went swimming while the adults fixed supper and later sat around the campfire singing. That was pretty much the way it was every day and the fried trout was delicious. Dot did spend some time with Liz late one afternoon as it was their turn to fix supper. Dot asked Liz if she had a boyfriend and after she answered shyly, "Yes, I guess I do." Dot said impatiently, "Well, if you only guess you do, then I would say you don't." "Why?!" Liz asked indignantly.

Dot laughed and told her not to worry, she was young yet. But when she turned seventeen she sure should know if she had a boyfriend or not. Liz wasn't satisfied. "Please tell me what you mean, Dot. You know my mom. She never talks to me about such stuff." Dot thought quietly for a minute and said, "Okay, I know what you mean. My mom used to be that way but she has come out of her shell a lot this past couple of years. I want to become a nurse, you know, so I'm talking to mom all the time now about the human body and all its functions. I think mom is learning right along with me and in fact, is excited about it. She and I are making up signs for certain parts of the body and everything. Isn't that great?" Liz was almost embarrassed but asserted herself anyway with more questions about the parts of the body and Dot was only too happy to answer them.

When she showed her signs for the boys and girls private parts they both giggled but Liz was learning a lot! She had never really heard the words vagina and penis, let alone ever thinking of signs for them. She would just sign "girl's bottom or boy's bottom," pointing to her front low part of her own body.

Supper was a little late that evening but no one seemed to mind. Later that night after everyone had gone to bed Liz still lay wide awake thinking of the marvels of the human body. She tossed and turned until she gave up, got up, threw on her robe, and stepped out onto the porch. After a couple of minutes of eerie silence she heard what she thought was a kitten crying or purring somewhere out in the trees. It was much too dark to try to find it and when she turned to go back into the cottage for a flashlight she heard the sound again but this time it was louder and most definitely not a kitten's cry. Crouching down near the ground, she stayed absolutely still not knowing whether to move or not. Maybe there are strange critters out here in the country, she thought.

The sounds became more distinct and then laughter took the place of the "mewing" cries. Oh, my God, Liz thought, that's Dot's laugh. Once again she looked into the darkness of the trees and then saw them. A small flashlight shone off into the deep part of the woods. It was Dot and Parky coming out onto the open field. Parky had his arm around Dot's waist, looking into her eyes so sweetly. Her frozen position became too difficult to hold so Liz carefully moved on her knees and opened the screen door and crawled back into her bed. She didn't want to attract attention from anyone.

Needless to say, Liz didn't get much sleep that night. This was entirely too much to learn in one day she decided and finally drifted off to sleep about two a.m. She had to get up early as this was the day they were all driving over to the farms of Uncle Charles and Aunt Lois. Although she had heard the term, Liz never really knew what poor dirt farming was. The barn looked like it was ready to collapse anytime. There were four pigs routing around in the dirt just a few feet from the barn with a little rail fence keeping them out of the driveway and sidewalk leading up to the house. The house didn't look too bad. It was obvious that they had just painted it and there were shutters propped up around the basement entrance which looked freshly painted too. The doors to the basement were wide open so Frank walked immediately over there and started down the steps. There he was met by an old man stooped over carrying two buckets full of fresh vegetables. When he saw Frank he set the buckets down and stretched out his arms to greet him.

A similar scene was happening at the kitchen door where an old lady came out to greet Evie and Liz. Bobby had already wandered off to a shed to talk to an old grey mare in the stall. Liz called to him and he came running in time to shake his Uncle's hand and hear the introductions all around. Liz thought the couple looked old enough to be Frank's parents, not his older brother. Liz found herself a go-between in the family conversation again. Most of the talk was about family members, where they lived now, and how their health was. Her aunt and uncle patiently spelled out all the proper names and used simple terms describing the various illnesses. It wasn't too difficult until Aunt Lois said, "Tell Evie I love her dress and I do hope she won't get it dirty around here. It's hard to keep things clean from dust because we've had a drought for the last six months." Liz paused half way through her signing and asked her, "Please.. just what is a drought? I don't even know how to spell it." "Oh, my goodness, child," Lois sighed, "I am sorry. Of course you don't know what a drought is. Tell your daddy that and spell it d r o u g h t. I'm sure he can explain it to your mom. Oh, Liz, drought means dry, no rain for a long time!" That proved to be the definition she needed, but it did slow down the flow of conversation. In fact Lois soon shooed the kids all outside saying that the women would get dinner on the table.

What a relief. Dot was already outside with Parky sitting on a tree swing and acting all romantic. Soon Parky started playing ball with the boys and Liz had a chance to talk to her more. Dot was really surprised at how much Liz would actually try to interpret conversations for her folks and told her so. "I never think about telling my mom and dad what everybody is saying. My folks don't ask me to do that. Why do you do it?" Dot asked. Liz couldn't answer that. "I guess it just seems natural to do it whenever I can."

"Dot, can I ask you something, do you call your mother 'mom' when talking directly to her? I don't think I ever do. When you think about it there is only one general sign that means mother, mom, or mommy; whichever one you might want to say. Don't you find that interesting? Come on, let's see the rest of this place." And with that Liz never talked to Dot again about deafness or about her mother. This just seemed like a private matter now and she would keep her thoughts to herself. She loved her mother and just knew down deep inside of her that Evie felt the same way about her.

That week at the Lake was the last time the two families got together and the last time she ever saw her father's family. For some reason they didn't even go to Dot and Parky's wedding two years later. Bob sent an announcement of his graduation from high school and that he would be going to college. Liz was too busy with school and friends to worry about why they didn't make a trip to Illinois to visit the two sets of dad's family there. She was always happy that they still would drive to Minnesota to visit Donna Mae's family as well as her cousins Gene and Glen. Life was good.

Liz and Wade were not a steady twosome in their sophomore year so she began to date other boys and found some to be fun. One night of fun ended up in a disaster. Oh, no one was really hurt but it had all been a frightening experience. She was with Billy and another girl was in the front seat with Billy's brother. He was older and could drive so they had borrowed their dad's car that was always thrilling at their age. He decided to take a romantic route taking them out in the country about five miles. The moon was so beautiful and they could smell fresh air. But as they were going around a sandy curve the car's wheels spun and slid so hard, it actually turned over on the side. She was on the passengers' side and felt pinned to the door! Liz yelled out as Billy's brother asked if they were all okay, "No! I can't move! Someone or something is on top of me!" Hearing everyone else respond in the affirmative, he told all to remain still. He somehow managed to push the driver's door open and crawled up and out. The car was near the edge of a small incline that did not appear to be dangerous. After looking over the scene he decided it was safe for them to crawl up and out just as he had. Thank God!

When Billy was pulled out, the weight lifted from Liz's body as she was the last one to crawl out. Billy helped her check her arms and legs and everything seemed fine. Yet, as Liz stepped away she could not believe her eyes. The car teetered with a big crack, tipping over the edge of the incline, down the hill until it hit the trees. Billy and his brother were devastated! What would their father say? Their car looked totally demolished. Liz said a prayer out loud, "Lord, thank you for saving us before the car rolled!" Everyone chimed, "Amen!"

They had to hike three miles to a telephone and when their dad did come, he politely drove the girls home before he started talking to the boys. Liz never did know how the boys were punished for that incident. But it was a long time before Billy asked her out again.

A neighbor boy took Liz to a drive-in movie one night. A lot of juniors and seniors went to drive-ins but this was Liz's first experience to go with a date. She was thrilled even though she didn't like to be alone on a first-date. This almost proved to be another disaster but in a different manner. Howie was eighteen and had ideas of necking in the back seat but she refused to budge. He tried to use the steering wheel as an excuse that he could not see the screen and they needed to sit in the back. Liz politely told him that she was not "that kind of girl" but he laughed and roughly pulled her to him. His hands were all over her so fast she could barely breathe. Since the windows were partly open she didn't want to embarrass him or herself so she quietly told him to stop as she had to go in to use the restroom. Thankfully he believed her and she slipped out quietly, headed toward the restrooms until she knew she was out of his sight. Then she slipped inside of the refreshments stand and asked to use the phone. She called Nita, intending to ask if her mom would come pick her up at the entrance to the drive-in but there was no answer.

Deathly afraid to return to her date, she found her way around the back of cars to the entrance. Once there she felt safe but this drive-in was on the edge of town and it would be a long walk home. She worried that Howie might get tired of waiting for her and come looking for her. However, she had no choice. Her brother was spending the night with some of his buddies and, of course, the phone was of no use with mom and dad. Liz didn't often pray but she did now. Staying in the shadows she half walked and half ran the two miles home. Her prayer was answered. She was finally home safe and sound.

Evie was still in the living room sewing and Frank was reading the newspaper. Liz walked slowly in front of them so as not to startle them and when they looked up she simply said good-night and went to her room. Her folks never asked her about her dates and she never offered to give them any details other than telling them where she was going and what time she expected to be home. She still had a curfew time and was good about adhering to that rule.

During her junior year in high school, the owner of the house told them he had sold the house and the new owner wanted to live in it so they had to move. There seemed to be no house available to them so Frank found a cottage at the lake to rent. Liz and Bobby thought this was a great idea! To live at the lake like rich people did. It was great during the summer. They had hoped to find a place by fall but had no luck. When winter arrived it was very cold in the bed-rooms as the house had only a potbellied stove in the living room. Evie found it difficult to sleep without shivering and she hated cook-ing on the old cook stove.

This didn't really bother Liz as this was her senior year and there were too many things to think about. She had fun telling everyone she lived at the lake. Every weekend some of her friends would come out and spend a day with her. She and Wade had drifted back together again with no drama involved. It was really a matter of convenience. Her popularity increased as she had a steady boyfriend now and they were members of a popular clique! Wade was really quite good looking, tall enough but not too tall, a nice smile and per-sonality with a cute wave in his blond hair falling over his forehead. Best of all, though, was that he was the catcher on their high school team and it was super to have a boyfriend in sports. The girls would meet with her at the games and cheer with her when Wade came up to bat or put someone out at home plate with a great catch.

Liz felt included more than ever. She worked on the school newspaper and was nominated for Homecoming Queen but didn't get enough votes to be included in the Queens' court. Liz was not disappointed at all; she was just thrilled that she had been a part of the whole thing.

Evie and Liz (1947)

7

Will Daughter Leave Us?

*A*round age eighteen, another potential beau was very good to Liz. In fact it was he that taught her how to polka and she became very good at stepping high and fast especially with him as her partner. George even had a home in the country out by the lake. He was twenty years old and had come into some inheritance so his first investment was this new house built out of oak and brick. It was a lovely place with a fireplace and big porch overlooking the water. Liz knew she was a fool for not trying to like this guy! Lake Wazeecha was *the* place to go after a movie or party; the place to park and watch the moon or stars while boys tried to grope you in the wrong places.

That's why it was so difficult to date someone you really didn't want to be intimate with. This house, this polite, generous fellow should have been a real attraction to Liz but try as she may, she could not become interested in him as anything other than a friend.

There were a couple of other fellows who tried to spark an interest in Liz but she felt nothing special for any one of them. In the meanwhile Mae moved back to the Rapids as her family came back from California. Immediately Mae started dating a neat guy, Bud, from the high school band and they became so serious that Liz didn't really chum with Mae anymore. But it was fun to see her at the local dance hall when she and George went there to polka. Liz felt like she was leading a double life. Wade never did know about George. He knew Liz loved to dance but he did not enjoy that activity so he trusted that she was just out with Mae to keep her company at the dances.

George was from another town and didn't know Wade. He was a freckle faced redhead who loved to dance. Liz loved to polka more than jitterbug or slow dance. The two of them "cut quite a rug" and sometimes people would stop and watch them circling around the floor. Liz didn't know whether to be embarrassed or thrilled. But George was enjoying every minute of it so she decided to go along with the fun and just have a good time. Now when she thought of Wade, she remembered that he only did a slow two-step and, frankly, was not a good dancer. So, it was almost easy to put him out of her mind when she came to the dance halls. She and George followed Bud's group around the area many a weekend. Bud played sax and clarinet in the polka band and was quite talented. Mae went to every dance and waited for him to go home late at night. Liz wasn't surprised when they announced their engagement during their senior year and planned to get married right after graduation. Liz made it very clear to George that she was not near ready for marriage. In fact, she was enjoying her senior year in high school too much to change her routine life at this time.

Somehow, just being someone's steady seemed more and more enticing now. It would be nice to know you had a date for every important event at school and every Saturday night for a movie. During her senior year that's exactly how it was for her and Wade. She was never sure if he was "true" to her but she remained his steady anyway. Nita told her that going steady was not good because one thing would lead to another. That was easy for her to say because now she was in love with a young man that had joined the navy and was gone to sea for six months. She wouldn't have any of the temptations that would face Liz from being with a boyfriend so much. Liz listened but she didn't really believe that anything would happen between her and Wade that she couldn't handle. Nothing that she couldn't control.

Control! Nita was right! How do you stay in control of your emotions when you are eighteen and think you are in love? Liz would have done anything for Wade. She was always there when he called and never questioned him about his whereabouts if he didn't call. One night all was almost lost as Liz did the unforgivable. She invited Wade into the house after her folks had gone to bed and things got out of hand. Soon they were in her bed and the worst thing happened. Her mother opened the door and saw them and screamed something that was very incomprehensible but it was enough to scare Wade ! He jumped out of bed, pulled on his pants, grabbed the rest of his clothes and was out the door before Liz could say a word!

Great, Liz thought! Great! Just leave me here to handle this all by myself. Liz pulled the covers over her and tried to ignore her mother's barrage of words. She couldn't believe her mom could even make her voice go on that long. Finally Evie closed the door and things were very quiet. As usual, nothing was said the next day. Nothing! It was as if nothing had happened. Another traumatic moment that Liz had to deal with by herself. This was probably a "blessing in disguise" Liz thought. She was sure she could forget it if Wade could. But she didn't hear from him for two weeks. Two weeks was a long time in their relationship, especially now. Graduation was just a month away and party plans were popping up every day at school. She couldn't decide which party to go to until some fellow invited her to accompany him. When friends began to ask about Wade, she was never sure how to answer them.

Finally he called. "Gollee, Liz, I didn't know what to do after that night! I know I was chicken. I'm still chicken. I don't want to see your folks again! There is no way I can communicate to them how I feel but I do want to be with you for graduation. Will your folks be there?" As always, just hearing Wade's voice melted her heart and Liz replied, "Ok, chicken! Yes, they will but it's sad to me that they won't know what's being said. I'm trying to convince Bobby to sit with them and fill them in once in a while on what's being said. They will just sit in the balcony until they see me go on stage and then they'll go home. They already gave me permission to go to a party. So, what party are we going to?"

What a party! Everyone who was anyone ended up out at the lake and Liz got deathly sick from drinking Mogen David wine and eating watermelon! That wasn't a smart combination, but once she regurgitated she felt fine. Liz wondered if Wade was even going to take her home but she didn't wonder about it long. He walked her down the lake road and said that he had asked Mae and Bud to take her home. He wanted to party on and knew that her parents would really be upset with him if he brought her home so late. With that he gave her a short goodnight kiss and she felt her heart tearing in two. Nothing was said of any future plans.

Liz really hated to think about school being out "forever." She had loved school. If she had tried harder she would have been on the honor roll. She didn't even know that she had been one point away from it until she saw her final report card that said her grade point average was eighty-nine. Liz knew it was her own fault for wasting so much time on her social life and working part time instead of doing more studying. Her parents did say they were proud of her and that should have been enough. Her English teacher had recommended that she apply to the University of Wisconsin and think about becoming a teacher to the deaf students in Delevan, where the School for the Deaf was located. Liz didn't even tell her folks about that because she knew they had no monies with which to send her to college.

Nevertheless, one day she had an opportunity to visit the teachers' college in Stevens Point, just a one hour drive from home. A friend was enrolling so she went along for the ride and walked into the school with her. There were brochures on stands in the hallway that covered the various courses the school offered. She stopped to look them over and found one that said "Deaf Education." This might be interesting Liz thought even though she knew she could not afford to attend classes now, she could work a year and save her money for school next year. While waiting for her friend, Liz sat down in a comfortable chair in the lobby and began reading about the course.

To her disbelief the descriptions of the classes did not include sign language. Rather, they included lip-reading, speech training, an entire program known as the "Oral Program for Deaf Education." What a disappointment. She asked her Dad about it that evening at supper and he was surprised too. Liz offered an idea, "Maybe good things, hearing-aids, lip-reading, oral program. Maybe kids don't need sign language anymore?" she signed. Frank then told Liz a story she would never forget. When he was fourteen a music teacher in their school insisted that deaf children could enjoy music and could learn to dance. He said that teacher did not use sign language and the kids were forced to watch his lips and his body movements learning to count their steps. There was only one child that could follow a lot of what he wanted them to learn. Others learned to follow that one student but Frank was one of a dozen that continually stumbled over his own feet. He laughed about it and tried to explain the one thing that he learned from that class. It was to enjoy every minute he could with the teachers who used sign language fluently.

Finally he signed, "Wait, Liz. Here stay." He disappeared for about five minutes and then came back with two objects that Liz thought were bowling pins. He grinned while waving Liz to follow him outside. She called Bobby to come too. Pulling himself away from his book, Bobby followed his sister asking what was so important. "Daddy has some trick he wants to show us. I have no idea what it is!" Liz felt happy because it was rare that Frank seemed excited about himself. In the backyard Frank had already set up two chairs and gestured for the kids to sit down.

Then he surprised them with quite an exercise using the two bowling pins. It was truly entertaining. In each hand he held a pin by the neck at the top and twisted his wrists so that they would swing forward and backward and then make a full circle. Liz could see that he was counting each movement on his lips without making a sound. Carefully raising the pins behind his back he pulled the pins forward in another wide circular motion. As he did this amazing feat he stepped forward, to each side, and back again like a neat dance step. By this time a couple of the neighbor kids had stopped playing and watched too. All the kids loved Frank and when he finished they came running up to him and gave him a hug around his knees. He tossed his graying head up with joy, smiling into each child's face. It was one of the rare times that Liz saw her father laughing with real pleasure in himself.

Evie was watching through the bedroom window and having memories of her own. When the family came back into the kitchen she wiped her hands on her apron as she met them with a smile. "Yes, daddy dance little. But, me, dance good," Evie signed to the kids. Liz sat down in a chair and laughingly signed, "Show us!" Her mother surprised her by walking away slowly and then gaining speed in her pace until she had circled the living room and the dining room table. Slipping off the apron on the way, she returned into the living room swaying gracefully to an imaginary music. The movements lasted a long while before she signed, "Imagine me with eleven girls. Standing this way making "V" shape. All coming back line straight." As she signed this she stepped slowly to an imaginary point and then back to the line gesturing a picture of all in a row.

Liz stared in awe. Her mother's black hair was damp with curls around her shiny face. It was not often that Liz saw Evie's face lit up with happiness. She looked beautiful! Frank smiled with pride but Bobby looked embarrassed. Bobby seemed bored so before he escaped the room Liz grabbed him and said, "Come on! Applaud!" They both waved their hands in the air as audiences do for people who cannot hear the clap of hands. Then Liz saw a scene she had never viewed before, Evie and Frank laughing together! Frank gave his wife a hug and asked her to take a bow. Liz joined them with a hug, enjoying a moment of happiness that seemed so rare in this house. It was not that Liz wasn't happy. She certainly had a comfortable home and good parents but sometimes she wished for a demonstration of love between her parents and for herself that was so rarely forthcoming.

Later that evening, Liz asked her dad again about the idea of deaf children learning through an "oral" method. Frank proceeded to give his feelings about the whole idea. It seemed that one music teacher was not the only one who could not sign with the children, pushing for the kids to read their lips for communication. Some teachers would write things on the blackboard expecting them to understand vocabulary that was almost entirely unfamiliar. "My humble opinion is this. A child must learn to communicate through a language he can understand. Sign language seemed to come naturally to me and my friends. It had started as a picture language, gesturing and pointing. As time evolved, we learned the alphabet and how to shape each letter into finger spelling. From spelling came words, unheard words. Words that are seen in the air and on the body, along with expressions of the face. That is my language!" Frank's wide grin and look of pride inspired Liz.

Those were not her daddy's exact words, of course; but that would be her English translation if Liz were asked to voice it or write it down. These words would stay with Liz for a long time to come. She felt the need to share her dad's words with her second mom, Mama Essie.

That was what she did the next time she was invited to a spaghetti dinner. She had tried to explain the way Nita's mother fixed spaghetti to her mother but was afraid to ask Mama Es for the recipe. Liz was happy with Evie's specialties such as sweet rolls, rhubarb pie, and her homemade buns for dad's great hamburgers. Liz told Mama Essie about her Aunt Alice's donuts, poppy seed cakes and sweet rolls that she sold commercially to a local store in Altura.

Another sister of Evie's sold bakeries to the local college in Winona. Aunt Erma baked apple, blueberry and peach pies as well as the holiday pumpkin and mincemeat. She worked in that college kitchen for a time, and then managed her own little diner downtown. Liz decided that her grandma had taught all the girls to be good cooks with sweets a traditional German specialty.

Liz still loved it when Mama Essie would invite her to stay for spaghetti supper, especially on a cold winter's evening. However if it was snowing hard or getting icy out she would send Liz home saying, "We can't call your folks and let them know that you are okay so it's best you go home so they won't worry about you." Liz knew that was very true. Even though there was a telephone in this house, there was none at home. She had been told that they would get one for Liz when they believed she was old enough to use it properly. So, with her coat and mittens in hand Liz was on her way.

Sometimes on a wintry evening, Frank would tell the kids of his experiences as a little boy with snow so deep they had to dig tunnels through to the barn! At times like this Liz would say to Bobby, "Daddy can be so funny sometimes. And yet sometimes I wonder if he's telling the truth. Do you understand, Bobby, this is one of those times I wish we could talk to someone from his family. A brother or sister who might relate the same stories but in a way we can really understand. I wonder why Daddy doesn't talk about his family much. We never go visit them like we do Mama's people. What do you think?" As usual Bobby had no opinion whatsoever. "How about a game of Monopoly? I'm bored." That was one thing Liz didn't mind playing with her little brother. It was fun to watch his little face grimace as if in pain when Liz bought Boardwalk. He was really growing "like a weed" as their Aunt Erma would say. Not a bad looking kid at all, but he didn't look like anyone in our family, except for his mother's blue eyes.

He was fair of skin and blond hair. Bobby loved to spend hours with Monopoly, sometimes days. They would leave the game on the card table set up in the living room and come back to the money dealings days later. Bobby never wanted to declare bankruptcy so when Liz became tired of the game she would be the one to give up.

Actually Liz preferred Chinese Checkers. Frank would play with her most any time she would ask him to but mama never wanted to play board games. She preferred cards. Liz could never understand why. Mama would only get mad when she was losing and blame it on her partner. Winning was so important to her. It was a rare occasion when all four of them played a game together. It would usually happen around the Christmas holidays. They all enjoyed a game of Canasta. If Liz and Bobby were partners, Liz learned to show her mother exactly what she was playing on her meld, counting the points "out-loud" on her fingers so that she could not accuse her later of laying down the wrong meld.

Liz and Bobby did not dare talk about anything or Evie would think they were telling each other what cards they held. When Liz thought about this later she realized that it was only when playing cards that she had to sign everything and anything she voiced. When

Mama was her partner, Liz would be careful to follow the "rules" that Evie added to the ones already in the book printed by the company.

Yet there was something special about an evening of cards with the family. To counter-balance mama's moments of frustration was the laughter at silly mistakes and at "lady luck" in general. Liz carried the love of card games to her friends and taught them some that they had never played. In fact she found that some of her friends knew nothing beyond "Old Maid" or "Go Fish"! How naïve! She was proud of the fact that her parents taught her how to count the cards and remember what had been played. She also knew that Evie and Frank were happy whenever Liz wanted to be included in an evening of fun with them.

There were two cliques among the girls. One seemed to have the "fast" girls who also happened to come from more well-to-do families. The second group was the one Liz and Nita belonged to. There were twelve members of a diversified background. They called themselves the Lamplighters. They met once a week in the School Library after school hours for just one hour. Most of the time they were just chatting about the events of the week at school, about who was dating who and about the upcoming events of the following week. Once a month they planned a party of some sort. Sometimes to be held at one of their homes and sometimes in conjunction with a school fun night of some kind. It was just innocent fun. But they also had a serious side to their girlish goals.

They were involved in community needs. For example, they gave time as candy stripers at the local hospital where they rolled bandages and put together first aid kits. They visited patients, taking them books, treats, and messages from family members. Liz always had a good warm feeling when she brought a smile to a patient's face as she read them their mail, or a few chapters of a good book. When she donned her striped uniform dress she swirled her skirt around to show her parents. Frank was so proud of Liz and told her so. "When I old man I hope pretty young lady same you help me. God gave you gift of smile with your eyes shows His love. Important you remember that." Liz promised she would.

Mae and Liz loved to go to the movies on Saturday afternoons from the days when they were little and would see all of Gene Autry movies. The songs of the Sons of the Pioneers would be sung over and over on the walk home after the movie. Frankenstein was a favorite movie subject of Liz's too. She could see scary movies with no after effects; but one friend of theirs, Susie, would have nightmares and would not go to any of them with the rest of the kids. As they got older their days for the movies changed from Saturday afternoon matinees to Sunday evenings' romances. Katherine Hepburn was Liz's favorite actress while a variety of mysteries were popular too. WWII brought G.I. Joe stories and the beautiful poster girl, Betty Grable. Most war stories were popular with everyone as well as the comedies featuring super stars such as Bob Hope, Bing Crosby, and Jerry Lewis.

Eventually, the all-time favorite movie came along, "Gone With the Wind"! Liz and her friends took their lunches to the theater as it was announced that the movie would be over three hours long. Movies were certainly a wonderful entertainment in the world of the 1940s. People were more sensitive to each other's needs. Love seemed to abound everywhere. Even though her parents did not see the movie, Liz told them all about it. Somehow it made an impression on Evie and she seemed to be more attentive to Frank and the children. Liz was glad to be a girl of her age experiencing such changes that the war seemed to bring to everyone. As a teenager Liz naturally learned to love to listen to the radio and to music. She told her daddy which movie stars she liked and who was a good singer as well. One day Frank asked Liz a question that was really difficult to answer. "Why are some stars better than others? Why are some singers better than others?"

Liz had to search her soul for a long while on how to handle this situation. Was her daddy really asking her what it was like to hear? How can anyone explain that to a deaf person! She carefully described that voices are of different pitches using just low to high as terminology and scrunching her face up while standing on her tippy-toes to show high soprano. Bending her knees and puffing her face she said this showed the bass voice of a man. Oh! Then she realized that a deaf person probably would not know that voices could be distinguished as male or female. He would not know that Liz could even perceive the age range of a person she talked to on the telephone! She would have an idea of a foreign voice and maybe even what country or race a voice belonged to. A hearing person recognizes family and friends by their voice.

Sometimes Nita's sister would answer her phone and Liz would think it was Nita! When Nita answered the phone Liz could tell she had been crying by the tone of her voice or she would know she was happy just the moment before she answered the phone. How fortunate hearing people are to be able to discern so many things through the sound of their voice. Was this too much information to give her dad? Would it make him sad to know what he was missing in life? Liz felt much older than her years as she tried to explain to her dad the many components of voices. Frank watched as his daughter went into such detail about the human voice. He remembered discussions with fellow deaf people about this subject.

Two members of the Wisconsin Valley Club for the Deaf had lost their hearing later in life and were interesting sources of information about how it was to be able to hear. However, they had never given Frank such a simplified meaningful description as his young daughter had just done. He felt the urge to pick her up and hug her tightly but she was too old to pick up and all he could bring himself to do was to take her hand and squeeze it. "Thank you," he signed quietly and turned to walk away. Liz didn't know if he was upset, angry or worried. His facial features were always the same for these moods. Pensive. She sat quietly watching her dad disappear into the garage.

Glancing at the old German clock on the wall she noted the time. He was probably going to drive over and pick up her mother after work so she should get busy and set the table. Liz continued to sit for a long while contemplating what she had told her dad about voices. This was really the first time she wanted to cry for her parents because they could not hear. So many things went through her mind.

Why wasn't there a better way to discuss such things with her parents? Maybe it was best not to try to discuss them at all. She would be careful from now on about what comments she made. She would try to be more empathetic and take time to analyze first if her words would require hearing or listening to be clearly understood.

This was not going to be easy. She did remember hearing the men at a meeting of their Wausau Deaf group talking about getting car insurance for their cars. No, she didn't "hear" them talking but she watched their signing as they seemed pretty excited about something and she was curious as to what it was all about. Now she thought about what it meant to them to get car insurance! Insurance companies probably did not have confidence in deaf people's driving abilities. That's why they were so excited to find a company that would accept them. If she remembered right it was through some National Association of the Deaf, a group called FRAT. Was that a short word for fraternity, Liz wondered. She didn't know what those initials stood for but she did know about the NAD.

Perhaps this was a fraternity of brotherhood inside of the NAD. Apparently it was a group of deaf people that had already proved they could drive with a good safety record. Right now Liz thought about how her dad drove that old Plymouth and took such good care of it. She had never seen so much as a dent in that car. Now she wondered how he did it! Of course they lived in a small town but still there were times when she had heard a fire truck when in the car with him. She had not even thought about how she should tell him she heard a siren; yet somehow he knew to pull over to the side of the road and let the truck go by. "He must have eyes in the back of his head," she mumbled to her little brother.

Liz could understand why her mother had chosen never to drive. Frank had taken her out a couple of times to try to teach her and she did see her mother drive into the driveway. But she had jumped out of the car after parking and declared in large gestured signs that she did not want to drive a car. Her dad had not encouraged Evie after that and it had been at least a year now since that incident. "Just think Nita, if I couldn't hear I don't think I would feel safe driving a car!" Liz exclaimed while confiding in Nita about her fears for the safety of deaf persons. "I never thought about this so deeply before!"

Occasionally, Liz's memories would seem to obsess her and she had to work hard to get them out of her mind. Like the night that she had gone to the Prom with that boy she really didn't think of as a prospect for an actual boyfriend. She didn't know him very well at all. However, since she was just a Freshman and Danny was a Junior, she was flattered to be invited to the Junior Prom even though she only had talked to him in school. She really knew nothing about him. Evie seemed more excited than Liz and together they went out to buy some material and a pattern for a formal dress. The bodice was black velvet while the skirt and puff sleeves were a beautiful light blue material with blue netting over the skirt. Evie didn't make the dress even though she had a sewing machine. There was a neighbor who did a lot of sewing and she offered to make it for her at no cost.

Even though the boy was no "dreamboat," Liz was thrilled to wear her first formal dress. Even more exciting was the beautiful white gardenia Danny brought her. She had to wear it on her left wrist like a bracelet because of the strong perfume that made Liz sneeze upon opening the plastic box. They all laughed while Evie took some thread and sewed it together like a bracelet. Liz had a surprisingly good time at the dance with a few boys signing their names on her dance program but there was not one boy among them all that could dance very well and none that she cared to talk to for more than a minute or two. When they arrived home that night Danny gave her a quick kiss on the cheek and said goodnight. As Liz watched him drive away in his father's Buick she thought she heard crying in the distance.

At first she thought it was a cat but soon realized there was someone standing across the street behind a tree crying. When her eyes adjusted to the darkness Liz realized it was her mother! Should she run to her? And if she did, what should she say? Should she approach her at all? It was obvious that she was trying to hide and of course she didn't realize that Liz could hear her crying. Liz decided it would be best to go on into the house but not until she looked into the garage where she saw that the car was not home. She still headed straight into her bedroom.

What was wrong with her mother? How did she get home? Where was Daddy? Bobby was spending the night at a friend's so she knew he wasn't home, thank goodness! Quickly Liz slipped out of the beautiful long dress and hung it up carefully on a padded hanger, hooking it over the door. Before ten minutes had gone by she heard her mother come in and go into the bathroom. Liz waited until she knew Evie had gone into her bedroom before she slipped into the bathroom to prepare herself for bed. She quickly crawled into bed, calling Trixie to join her. She told Trixie what she had seen, praying that Daddy was all right. She vowed not to go to sleep until he came in.

Liz looked at the clock showing one a.m. Physically and mentally worn out after all that dancing and worrying, she soon drifted off to sleep. Liz never did know what time her Dad got home that night and she never did know what had happened.

That was during the time that they were going out with that couple that she did not like; when all that talk about divorce had happened. But that was in the past. Yet now and then Liz would think about that night and wonder what trauma her mother had experienced.

Would I have asked them directly if they were hearing parents? Somehow she doubted that. Liz loved her Daddy so much but she never told him. He never actually signed that he loved her either but she just knew he did. Dad seemed to love life. He always took care of the yard, pushing that old lawnmower carefully around the two big elm trees in the side yard. He eventually taught Liz and later, Bobby, how to mow but Liz knew that he loved to do it and it would take just a little excuse for her to get out of the work. Evie didn't like the outdoors. She didn't want to plant any flowers or bushes. Of course when they were in the rented house on the west side of town they really had no desire to add anything to the landscape. But during the Second World War they did plant a little garden out back behind the garage and called it a "victory garden" as did all the neighbors. The mayor encouraged people to grow their own vegetables so that there would be more food for our soldiers fighting overseas. Liz relayed that message to her parents, but Frank was already showing them the story in the newspaper. Evie said she was growing vegetables to save money for themselves and because of the rationing of many items. Even here Frank did most of the work; all the spading and planting in even rows. Liz and Bobby helped keep the weeds out and Evie did not mind bringing in the harvest and cleaning and cooking the vegetables for all to enjoy.

Watching her mother work so diligently in the garden, Liz began to re-evaluate Evie's qualities. She remembered the day Bobby started kindergarten. On this first day, their mama went with them and when they stopped by the office, Liz approached the older lady at the front desk. She simply told her that Bobby Niklaus was to enter school at five years old. The gray haired woman handed Evie three sheets of paper and asked her to fill them out. She started to explain the details necessary to include; when Liz interrupted with self-confidence, saying "My mama is deaf. She cannot hear you but she can read and she can write, thank you." But in truth Liz did have to explain the vocabulary in some of the questions and help Evie to write out the answers in proper English form. She glanced at the papers that Evie had brought with her. One of the sheets was his baptism record. Then Liz noticed what her mother had written in for her brother's name!

It was not Bobby. It was Wallace! Wallace Frank Niklaus! Oh, my! She just stared at her mother and pointed to the name. She mouthed clearly along with her signs. "I name him Bobby," as she finger spelled B-o-b-b-y. Evie understood but simply smiled at her daughter and without a word, she picked up the papers, grabbed Bobby by the hand and marched up to the counter. The same office lady gave Liz a questioning look before carefully saying, "Tell your mother that I will take Wallace to his classroom. She is welcome to come along and watch the class for fifteen minutes if she so desires." When Liz relayed that to her mama it was the most fascinating thing

Frank, Evie & Liz

that the office personnel had witnessed in a long time. In fact, Liz overheard the two younger ladies whisper something about having never seen sign language before. All three women were somewhat taken aback when Mrs. Niklaus simply looked at them and shook her head no. In just another minute Bobby was walking down the hall crying softly, hand–in-hand with the older woman. Liz did not relay to her mother that Bobby was crying.

As they disappeared down the hallway, Evie walked out the front door without even waving goodbye. Liz walked silently to her own classroom that was in the next building. Something inside of her tummy churned as she realized another important moment was accepted in silence.

At home that evening, after Bobby gave his rendition of his day in class, Evie brought out the baptism record again. She showed it to Liz in silence. On this paper Liz read the name "Wallace Frank Niklaus born to Evie and Frank Niklaus on December 5th, 1936." Liz turned to her brother and said, "Sorry Bobby, guess I will need to learn to call you Wallace now. Looking at Evie and pointing to Bobby she asked as she signed, "Me name him all right? Wallace sounds like old man's name?" Evie looked at Frank with a question on her face, wanting his opinion. Noting the expression on his daughter's face, Frank smiled and with his usual expression of understanding, nodded his approval to Liz.

This change was never really comfortable to either Liz or Wallace so she often continued to call him "Bobby" and he always answered to that name. For the first time in his five and a half years, Bobby felt that his older sister really cared about him. He really didn't know what to make of this change in his name but it was good to be the center of attention. As it turned out, in the summer time Liz continued to call him Bobby because that was the name her friends and neighbors knew him by. At school she called him Wallace because his school friends did. He never complained. Having deaf parents did set them apart from everyone they knew in the small community of Merrill. Like any other siblings with an age and/or gender difference, the fact that their parents were deaf had no bearing.

Liz was usually just annoyed with her little brother for no real reason. It seemed to her that they just never would be close as brother and sister. Liz often noted that they didn't even look like brother and sister. Bobby was just as fair as Liz was dark. In Minnesota Evie's relatives said Bobby looked like grandpa when he was young so she accepted that. Liz and Bobby had a lot of arguments but she learned that a lot of her friends were the same way toward their younger brothers or sisters so she refused to feel guilty about it.

Mama did expect Liz to take Bobby places with her and keep an eye on him. This continued after they moved to Wisconsin Rapids even though they were both a little older now. Evie had taken a job so Liz was still expected to keep an eye on her brother. There were times when this was fun. They would walk together to the swimming pool and race each other crossing over the river on the railroad bridge. It only took ten minutes if they walked but knowing that their daddy had said they were not supposed to do this they ran as fast as they could to get to the other side. The town was spread out on both sides of the river with just two bridges adjoining them. The main bridge was in the center of the town, big with room for vehicles and a walk on either side for pedestrians. It was a beautiful view of the downtown area; overlooking the river to the east and west; with the paper mill on the north and lovely grassy banks to the south. To take that safe route it would require them to walk six blocks south from their home to the street leading them downtown. It was another mile to that bridge and then they would need to walk six blocks north to get to the swimming pool. The neighbor kids led them to the shortcut the first time. There they found the second bridge; a railroad bridge with a narrow board walk beside the rails. After leaving the railroad bridge it was just a half mile south to the pool. They were thrilled because it saved them more than a half hour walk.

Of course their Daddy never knew that they took this short cut but it was easy to hear any train that might be coming as well as to see it. He just didn't understand that. Other kids did the same thing. Besides, if a train did come, there was room to stand on the board walk and hang on to the bridge trestles while it rumbled by. They only experienced that one time and it almost convinced them not to take this route again. It was truly an adventure they enjoyed each time and Liz knew that Bobby secretly wished for the train to come again.

The public pool was really a part of the Wisconsin River that had been walled off with cement for the kids to swim in. Liz didn't know what she would do without this pool! The city provided a lifeguard, changing rooms and restrooms. The bank was covered in soft green grass on which the girls would spread out their towels to sunbathe. Shade trees prevented a sunburn so Liz and her girlfriends loved to tan most of the afternoon. Liz and Bobby had both participated in swimming lessons so Liz felt safe in allowing Bobby to go off and do his own thing. The day was filled with fun and water games with friends until their curfew of four p.m. The lifeguard knew them and would call down to Liz when it was a quarter of four. After responding with a "thank you" to him she would quickly change into her shorts and tee shirt, roll up her wet swimsuit in her towel, call to Bobby who never changed out of his suit and off they would head for the railroad track. They hurried over the bridge again, knowing that their mother would have arrived home from work by now.

On good weather days like this Evie walked the mile home, while during inclement weather she would wait for Frank to pick her up after he got off work. After a tough day of holding heavy army overcoats on the machine as she sewed along the inside seams; she was glad to punch the time clock and get out into the fresh air. Evie really looked forward to this time of day when she took the long walk home.

The large elm trees hung their branches over the sidewalks, giving her plenty of cool shade most of the way. She walked briskly so she could feel the breeze cooling her forehead. Evie slipped off her sweater, untied the ribbon holding her black hair and almost skipped her way home. She was convinced that this mile long walk helped her keep her figure trim through the years. Ignoring the fact that she wore an old housedress to work, Evie felt like a movie star waving a friendly hello to her fans along the way. It was fun to fantasize!

She recognized they were just kindly neighbors working out in their yards as they returned the wave. Feeling almost exuberant, she gave them a big smile as she continued her walk. Another reason she liked to walk home was to have time before Frank came home. She would brush her damp hair to look shiny, slip on a pretty clean apron and go into the kitchen. Evie would peel the potatoes for dinner, put them on to boil, slip the meat loaf into the oven and have water boiling, ready to pop in the corn on the cob that she had readied that morning. Finally, she rested on the porch swing watching for her children to arrive home.

She loved to see their beaming faces as they approached. To Evie this was a rare moment of brother and sister enjoying each other's company. Liz never forgot one particular day that her mother gathered them both to her breast with an encompassing gentle hug. She wondered what had caused this display of emotion from Evie, but asking no questions, she just savored the love.

Sometimes Liz and Bobby would be invited along by a neighbor who was going out to Lake Wazeecha, just southeast of the city. That was a real treat, one that required permission from their parents. Because they had no phone, the neighbor trusted Liz with a note to take to her parents. This note had to be written by the friend's parent and a note taken back signed by Evie or Frank. It was not easy for Liz to convince her mother that they would be safe because Evie had never liked the water. She would not even go out in a boat when given the opportunity. Frank loved the lake and often rented a small boat to go fishing. He persuaded his wife to allow him to sign the note and let Liz have some fun. The lake had a large sandy beach with a diving board attached to a floating dock out in the deep water. Liz could swim to the raft but she never learned to dive because she didn't want to. She disliked water in her nose and always held her nose when jumping in, bringing a laugh from her friends. The instructor of swimming lessons never did get that point across to Liz on how to hold your breath and then breathe out when hitting the water. Liz told herself that she really didn't care but this became an area that Bobby soon excelled in; so this bothered her for a long while. This was one subject that Liz could relate to her mother and get an expression of understanding in return.

Evie didn't take Bobby's side when he teased Liz about this because of her own fear of water. She would quickly change the subject. This was about the only thing involving Bobby that Liz felt she could share with her mother and expect her sympathy. Knowing her mother favored her little boy over her, Liz liked to think that her Daddy favored her over her little brother. Life seemed fair in this respect.

In the fall when asking her parents to let her take Bobby to the county fair, Liz felt she was fighting a losing battle. Merrill bragged about the nice fairgrounds the town had and rightly so. Bobby always wanted to walk through the animal barns before going on the rides. This was a good progression to take because he often got sick on the Tilt-a-Whirl. They would have to quit the rides then and maybe even go on home. If Liz met some friends she would politely tell Bobby that he needed to sit out while she rode the Tilt-a-Whirl with them. However, he would pout so badly that she considered that just as irritating as him getting sick!

One day their Daddy surprised them by going with them but only to go through the barns. Frank loved to sit and watch the horses as they were ridden around the arena. Liz assumed that this scene reminded her dad of his days on the farm when he was young. Liz found herself attracted to those beautiful animals too as they pranced around the ring. She especially enjoyed the young riders who amazed her with their skills at the reins. She turned to her daddy at one point and asked, "future me ride same that." Frank looked at her seriously for a second, starting to nod in assent, then shaking his head in disbelief, he said with his raspy voice, "No," and laughed out loud. Liz loved to hear him laugh so she didn't mind if he was agreeing with her or not.

She simply joined him in a laugh while Bobby looked at them in dismay and seemed to be embarrassed. This was one time Liz realized that Bobby did not use sign language in public any more than he had to. She wondered if this was because it embarrassed him. Or maybe he was just used to Liz doing all the signing for him. After all, being the first born, Liz had learned signs naturally directly from her mother and dad. When Bobby was born Liz was already six years old with a large vocabulary of signs. More than that, Liz could speak to him! Bobby could hear her voice over and above the signs his parents were using with him. So, it was natural that he might depend on her for clarification of what they were signing. Really, Liz thought, it might actually be her fault for not allowing her little brother to develop his signs directly from Evie or Frank, instead of from me!

The time soon came for Liz to have some driving lessons! She couldn't believe her father when he insisted he be her driving instructor. It was hilarious to Liz that her Daddy wanted to teach her to drive when he had absolutely no luck teaching her mother. But she changed her attitude the very first time Frank took her on the road. He went out to a country road and parked. Then he showed her how the shift and clutch worked. He drew a picture on some paper he pulled out of his pocket. Frank always had notepad and pencil in his shirt pocket so that he could write notes in communication with hearing people.

On this paper he drew a picture of the shift stick on the floor and the "H" pattern she would need to learn. The stick moved to what Frank voiced as "Lo and Hi," he wrote on the notepad, known as first and second shift. He then signed carefully pointing to the corners of the "H" that these two must be passed through before going to third gear where the car would then begin to move. The remaining point in the H was for driving in Reverse which would be the last thing he would teach her; how to back out of the driveway. Well, he changed that and signed, "No, last learn park between cars parallel curb." When Frank signed something for "parallel," Liz was not at all sure what he was talking about so she let it go, knowing that she could ask Mama Es about it later. Four lessons and Liz was driving!

One night after Liz had her license her daddy let her have the car to go to a basketball game at high school. She was so excited when she picked up her girlfriends and they all started cheers before they even got to the school. Liz finally told them to stop because she couldn't concentrate on her driving. The girls were miffed but they hushed as they approached the school and discovered a long line of cars waiting to go into the parking lot. Nita suggested that they jump out and go on in to save seats. "That was dangerous!" she called out to them as the back doors slammed. Liz had only slowed down without coming to a complete stop when they got out of the car but thank goodness all doors were shut tight as she advanced slowly in line. All of a sudden the car in front of her decided to back up and without thinking, Liz backed up too! Wrong reaction! The car in front of her did not hit her at all but she sure hit the car behind her. An angry man jumped out of that car and was at Liz's window in a flash spewing out some curse words. On further looking at the girl behind the wheel he calmed down and asked for her license. Tears welled up in Liz's eyes as she pulled her billfold out of her purse and handed her license to the man. He quietly looked at it and wrote down her name and address. As he handed it back to her he said simply, "I know your dad. In fact I work in the same place as he does so I will talk to him about this Monday." With that he turned away and strode back to his car. Liz didn't even know if either car had been damaged. She had only been driving about fifteen mph but she had no experience with this and only knew that she was at fault.

Liz finally got a look at the rear of the car after she got home that evening and told her daddy about the accident. Frank went outside immediately, and began rubbing his hand up and down the bumper, and shaking his head negatively. Evie was waiting for his decision when they walked back into the house and Liz watched him relay the facts to her ending with "damage none." Turning back to Liz he signed, "But Monday man tell me damage car his." Liz was relieved when he didn't punish her in any way; at least not now. Monday after school Liz hurried home and cleaned up the living room and dining room before starting dinner. Frank always got home before Evie unless he waited for her to give her a ride home on rainy days. But when Daddy came home he buried himself behind his newspaper and didn't communicate with Liz until dinner was over and the dishes done. Then he called Liz into the living room and pointed to the chair directing her to sit down. "Mr. Adams show me damage car his. Headlight broke.

Cost forty eight dollars fix. Me pay. Fridays you pay me from money job. You pay me five dollars ten times." Liz was astonished at how her daddy had solved this whole problem so fast. "OK will." She signed strongly in this response. "If finish not." Frank's signs were strong now too. "You drive car no. Drive car after fifty dollars paid." With that he left the room leaving Liz to brood over this new dilemma. She might forget how to drive a car in ten weeks! Oh, how she hated that sign he used for the word *if*. It looks like the scales of justice with each hand going up and down opposite direction of the other hand, like a scale. It was such a serious sign, especially when accompanied by the stern expression on his face. "If finish not," indeed!

Well, she would not let that happen. She knew what she would do and she did it. She was earning twenty to twenty-five dollars a week so she pinched her pennies and paid her father ten dollars a week so that it was completely paid off in just five weeks. Frank was both surprised and proud of his daughter but wondered if he had really won the fight. Perhaps she had not felt the punishment enough so he told her she had to wait one more week before she could drive the car again. Liz accepted that quietly and did not even ask to have the car again for four weeks.

Finally, one day Liz wanted to go to a friend's birthday party who lived on the other side of the city. She knew she didn't want to walk there in dress up clothes so she asked her dad politely if she could borrow the car. Frank was happy to give her the car because he was beginning to think that Liz would never want to drive again as a result of her little accident. During the party the hostess said she forgot to pick up the ice cream to go with the cake so Liz volunteered to go get it for her. A couple of the girls went with her just for the ride. They had just gone a couple of blocks when they met a car loaded with boys. Liz recognized one as someone she really didn't like so she turned on the next corner and drove the opposite direction.

The other car soon caught up with her and started following her slowly down the street. Liz drove fast for three blocks and once more turned the corner and drove down a strange street. Telling the girls to duck down, Liz turned her lights off and drove slowly hoping to elude the boys. But when she looked into the rearview mirror she saw the flashing lights of a police car and braked to a stop. The policeman swiftly walked up to Liz's window and asked, "What do you think you are doing driving without your lights on?" "These boys were following us and I was trying to lose them," Liz explained, smiling at the officer.

Not changing his serious demeanor, the policeman said curtly, "License please." Looking at the license a minute later, he continued "Liz Niklaus. I know your dad. What would he say if he knew about this? It is dangerous driving at night without your lights on, young lady!" "Yes, I know. My father would really be upset!" Liz replied as the tears began to roll down her cheeks. The policeman looked at the girls in the back seat and asked if they thought Liz was a good driver and they both quickly answered in the affirmative. "Okay, let this be a warning to you Liz. I won't tell your dad but if anything like this happens again you will be in trouble. Understand?" "Yes, officer. Thank you." With a huge sigh of relief Liz watched as he reentered his car and drove away. Thank goodness she would not be in trouble with her dad again. She must be more careful! He had taught her to be a good driver and yet she had two incidents within three months that would shame her. Liz had a moment of deep love for her father well up in her and told the girls how much she loved her dad. They were silent as she related some of her feelings about her parents being deaf and how lucky she was to have such special people in her life. They finished their errand and the birthday party was a huge success but Liz did not feel comfortable until she was back home with the car parked safely in the garage.

Neither Evie or Frank asked her about her evening as they sat in the dining room drinking their coffee. What Liz didn't realize was that Frank was telling Evie they would be going to a company Christmas party in December. The first thing Evie was concerned about was what she would wear. She shared that thought with her husband but admitted she was excited about going to a party. Not wanting to burst her bubble, Frank smiled his biggest smile as he signed, "You buy new dress for occasion, party if you agree it is my

Christmas present to you this year. Will that be alright?" Evie shook her head in the affirmative and gave him a big kiss on the cheek.

Over Frank's shoulder, she saw Liz come in so she gently turned Frank's head in that direction. Liz signed that she was tired and going to bed. Frank said "Okay. Car okay?" Liz tossed a big "Yes" on her hand and signed, "Good night." Evie said good night and was happy to get back to their intimate conversation about the Christmas party. "Would it be alright if I get red dress?" she asked planting another kiss on the opposite cheek. Frank knew he best pull his wife up from the table and make their way to the bedroom now. "You beautiful in red!" Frank signed as he gathered his wife into his arms for a loving kiss.

It was well known that Frank's boss was considered to be generous with his employees. They always had a large Christmas party out at the Country Club where a huge dinner was served to all. Evie had managed to find a simple red dress with a scooped neckline and three quarter length sleeves. She also found dangling red earrings to match perfectly. Then she had shopped for a red lipstick to match. With her black hair, Evie was beautiful. Even so, she felt a little out of place because of the finery in clothing and jewelry of the other women present. Then there was always the fact they could not communicate with anyone.

Frank had learned to communicate with his co-workers in a way they seemed to understand. He also wrote notes to clarify some thoughts. Evie was almost jealous of Frank's ability to do so. Evie was not as comfortable with communication and people always seemed to misunderstand her. At parties like this, attention was drawn by her beauty. Glancing at the ladies around the dinner table, Evie thought she may be the prettiest one there. Her thick black hair was neatly held back on one side with a large red barrette. Evie had read in a magazine that simple was beautiful and jewelry was not necessary for all occasions. Evie felt she was already lovely enough in this dress. A couple of the ladies stopped and gave her a compliment with gestures of one kind or another. One lady touched her barrette and gave her a big smile. The boss's wife took Evie's hand and clearly mouthed, "You look beautiful tonight, Evie!" She was not sure what the woman had said but she could tell by her facial expression that it was something complimentary.

However, Evie was very reserved and barely smiled at folks even when personally introduced to Frank's boss. He took her hand gesturing to her to stand up. He stepped back and looked her over from head to toe in a polite manner. With a big smile he slipped his arm around her shoulder, turning her to face the folks at the table. "Let's make Frank's wife, Evie, feel comfortable tonight!" Of course Evie did not have any idea what he said but knew it was something nice. Evie was flattered and didn't really know how to react. She couldn't believe that a rich man who owned a newspaper would be so sweet to her. Moreover, she could see that her husband was pleased too.

Another time, Frank's boss invited all the employees and their families to his home out in the country for a picnic in the yard. Liz and Bobby loved it. One of the men working there was requested to show all the children the racetrack and horses on the other side of the cranberry marshes. The man brought out a tractor pulling a trailer and directed the kids to jump aboard. They had a long ride around the marshes. Liz told Bobby that these were probably the very cranberries they ate for Thanksgiving and Christmas but Bobby could have cared less. He wasn't interested in the acres of plants flooded with water. What ugly fields this made. You couldn't even see the berries. He was impatient to see the racehorses. Liz enjoyed that part of the tour too and couldn't wait to get together with her girlfriends and to tell them where she had been that day.

That evening while relating the story to her parents about their ride around the cranberry fields, Liz stopped as she signed to her dad. "Dad, is there a special sign for Dad, not Father?" Frank thought about this a long while and slowly responded with a lot of words. "Well, there seems to be only one way to sign *daddy*. In fact there's only one sign for all the words: sir, dad, daddy, papa, pa, and pop. The same thing is true for mother, mom, mommy, mama, and ma."

"Oh, okay, I just wondered," Liz signed, trying to convey as little concern about it as possible. Later she couldn't help thinking that sign language could be so frustrating sometimes. There seemed to be no way to show special endearments except through your facial expressions and of course hugs and kisses which Liz didn't experience often. Liz also thought about how deaf people had signs for each other's names but she didn't have one that she knew of. So the next opportunity she had she asked her mother if she had a sign name for Bobby and herself. Evie looked surprised and perplexed as she signed her reply. "You hearing. Hearing not need sign names." So it was that simple? Somehow Liz did not think so. In her rationale she thought that deaf people got tired of spelling out names every time they talked about someone and a sign for a name was much quicker. If what her mother said was true then every time she was talking to another deaf person about her daughter she had to spell out her name? Or maybe she simply signed "daughter." All Liz knew for sure was that the reverse situation was also true. It was tiresome to have to spell out everyone's name when she talked to her parents about her friends or their relatives. Why couldn't she give hearing people name signs just as her parents gave their deaf friends. It wasn't fair.

Liz did a lot of singing around the house because there was no one to criticize her for doing so. When she was twelve she got her first radio. Well, it was the first radio for the family but she and Bobby were the only ones who could listen to it. When Bobby wasn't around Liz would turn on a station that played country western. She loved to hear Tennessee Ernie Ford singing gospel music or "Sixteen Tons." She would sing along with the radio while doing her chores around the house. One day she caught her mother staring at her and asked her what was wrong. "Talk, talk, talk you. Here no one?" Evie signed with an alarmed expression. "Oh, oh, me singing," Liz signed pointing to the radio, as she laughed. "Finish!" Evie signed as she walked out of the room. Liz stopped but she didn't understand why it upset her mother so much. Could it be that her mother was hurt because she could not sing? Could it be that it made her sad to realize she couldn't sing or even begin to understand why someone would sing to the radio? That night Liz wanted to apologize to her mother for singing and yet, she didn't think it was a bad thing to do. So, instead of talking to Evie about it, Liz simply had a new entry for her diary on traumatic moments.

The summer before entering high school, the church offered a week at their Youth Camp at Green Lake for just a nominal fee. Liz asked her friend, Mae if she would like to go and together they approached their parents, volunteering to work and earn the monies necessary to go. The Church paid a part of it so it was not expensive at all. What fun that was! Liz had no idea what a church camp might involve so she enjoyed everything as a new experience. The girls signed up for Crafts, Rowing, Swimming and Hiking. Each day was filled with this kind of fun and closed with a picnic supper with fifty other kids. One of the dozen leaders would always offer a prayer that was something neither of the girls were familiar with in their homes. It was nice. Then they would gather on the hillside and listen to other kids sharing their stories. These stories were always about a change in their lives because they had found Christ.

This was new to Liz. She really did not understand what they were talking about but the stories were sure fascinating so she listened intently. After sunset they roasted marshmallows over a campfire and sang songs. Liz thought this was the best time of the day and later, lying in bed she would think about the kids who had shared a story that evening. She did not discuss them with Mae or anyone. It all seemed a little too serious for her little mind right now. She would write about it in her diary and talk to Winki and Trixie when she got home.

At fourteen, Liz had another experience that was hard to relate to her parents. Nita's mother was doing some catering and asked the girls to help her serve a dinner on the island. Liz was thrilled be-cause not any one of her friends had ever been on the island that she knew of. It was on the Wisconsin River that divided the east side of the town from the west side. The Meaders owned that little piece of land and had a lovely home on it where it seemed only rich people were invited. Evie and Frank were happy for Liz too. This was one occasion they wanted to hear about upon her return. So it was with joy that she joined Nita in the big kitchen of this huge home. They had been instructed to enter through the back door so they had not seen anything but the kitchen yet.

Carefully the girls slipped on the white crisp aprons over their red dresses that were given to them to wear. Mama Essie had braided both of the girls hair with a tight French braid so that even though Liz did not really look Italian, they almost looked like twins that evening. Mama Essie was busy at the stove stirring a big pot of spaghetti sauce and readying water for the spaghetti. Nita was showing Liz how to set the tables set up in the large dining area. How lovely the table looked. The delicate china and sparkling silverware looked so elegant as they placed the deep green napkins at the left of each plate. Then they filled the green goblets with ice water and placed one at each place setting. Gold wine glasses were set on the sidebar but they were not allowed to fill them with the liquid drink because of their age.

Upon re-entering the kitchen, Liz froze in amazement as she saw a strange woman rolling out the bread dough to cut into biscuits for dinner. The woman was black! She was black like the people she had seen in the movie "Gone With the Wind." Nita held back a giggle as she nudged Liz's arm. Liz jumped and tried to look non-chalant as she asked Mama Essie what there was to do next. Mama Essie must have sensed Liz's discomfort; yet she took her by the arm over to the black lady and introduced her to Lucy, the Meaders' maid. "Oh, hello, nice to meet you," Liz stuttered and put out her hand to acknowledge the woman. Lucy declined her hand saying, "I have to keep my hands in this dough. Nice to meet you too, Liz." With that they all four continued their chores and served the dozen or so people who were seated at the tables.

Liz did not recognize any of the folks there. This actually made it easier to serve and she felt comfortable carrying out the work just as Mama Essie had instructed her to do. What an evening! Of course the clearing of tables was not as much fun as the setting had been. It was fun though listening to Lucy and Mama Essie gossiping about the folks who had been there. She tried to remember some of the names so that she could relate them to her parents when she got home. When Nita dropped her off at home she handed her a twenty-dollar bill that was equal to the amount she made in a weekend at the root beer stand. "Are you sure you are supposed to give me that much, Nita?" Nita laughed at that question from Liz and happily replied, "Oh, yeah! That family paid mama well for this job. Thank you and good night. I'm tired and I'm sure you are too." With that Nita drove away in her dad's old Chevrolet and Liz ran into the house to tell her mother and father about the party.

Her story would have to wait until the next day because her parents were already in bed. It was just then that Liz looked at the clock and realized it was after eleven! She had really worked six hours to earn that twenty dollars. This was another experience to write into her diary as an all-important occasion.

Liz's mother continued to work at the local clothing factory even after the war was over until something happened between her and a co-worker who was hard-of-hearing. Evie had talked about Adella just enough to lead Liz to believe she was happy to have someone who could sign with her during breaks and lunchtime. So it was a surprise to her when her mother came walking home from work one day and announced to the family, "Finish work. Tired work. Work no more." She had quit. She continued to tell Liz and Frank about an argument she had with this woman and rather than face the boss to defend herself, she simply signed a piece of paper stating, "Me quit! You know heavy Army overcoats!" Evie had tears in her eyes. Frank took Evie's hand and led her to the davenport where they both sat quietly side by side. Perceiving a serious moment for her parents, Liz took Bobby's hand and led him out to the backyard with the promise of playing a little "catch" with him.

When it was time for supper Liz went inside to help her mother in the kitchen and not another word was said about her job. The next morning Evie had lunches packed for Liz and Bobby and told them she would be home by the time they got home from school. They asked no questions and life continued with mother home every day which turned out to be rather pleasant for Liz. She didn't have to be responsible for Bobby any more. She could join the Girl's Club and stay for meetings after school.

Another part of being one of the girls was the fact that she had a reason now to buy one of those poodle skirts that swirled as she walked. She chose a black one that was flattering to her hips and on the front right side was a big pink poodle. Oh, how she loved that skirt and was very careful not to spill anything on it and to hang it up carefully after each time she wore it to let all the wrinkles out. A couple of the girls had pink angora sweaters to match. After pricing them, Liz picked out a soft knit sweater and a lovely rayon blouse, both in pink. She was so proud of herself as she wrote out her tickets for discount as a store employee. On her next payday she bought a pair of the penny loafers that were so popular too. Working at J.C. Penney's was of real benefit to Liz and her parents.

Sometimes she was bored with the stocking and dusting of shelves but she loved to help the customers find what they wanted. Every sale was a thrill. Her heart seemed to soar along with the cup containing the sales slip and cash as she attached it to the overhead wire, pulled the cord and watched it ride up to the cashier's office in the balcony above. She had no problem at all following the store's policy of "the customer is always right."

By this time Liz was going steady with Wade which should have made her happy. She was happy but it seemed life was becoming complicated because Wade wanted much more than just "necking." She thought it was fine to have a few kisses but she wanted to keep them less passionate. Her girlfriends talked about "going further" but she was never sure just how far a girl was supposed to go. She wanted to remain a part of the "in-crowd" and yet remain a virgin. Sometimes she wished the girls would share more of their own experiences. It might help. However, she also thought perhaps they couldn't because they had already "given in" and felt guilty about the whole thing.

Once or twice she had picked up a magazine full of romance stories. She didn't have to go to the store and buy one because her mother had some to read. When Liz asked permission to read one of her magazines, Evie was not sure if this was a good idea. She knew Liz had a boyfriend now and probably would enjoy some of the stories; so, she told her it was okay. Liz always wondered why her mom read such stories but after reading a few, she decided there was something to be learned from them. For example, it appeared when the girl gave in, the boyfriend dumped her soon afterwards. It seems men become bored with sex with one girl so they start looking for another conquest. Liz decided to stop reading romance magazines as they always seemed so sad.

She continued to go to the library and check out Nancy Drew mysteries or some historical novel. This was something she did not share with her friends because she was sure they would think she was very immature. She just told herself it didn't matter what they thought.

As a senior it was good to have a steady boyfriend so she could be sure of going to the parties and to the Prom. With a steady, she would know who would be walking her home from the football games and inviting her to the school dances. Yet, this year it was different. It seemed to be a game of which couple was doing it and if you were not in that group of names then it had to mean you were a prude. After their senior class party Liz almost lost all her inhibitions; however something held her back. Something Liz never thought of doing became an expected event for Wade.

It seemed that all they did was argue now over every little thing that they did together. Who would have thought that a little thing like sex could change the whole atmosphere of a high school romance? Liz thought she was crazy in love with Wade but she did manage to draw the line and end the evening without going all the way. She also could see that Wade was beginning to lose interest in her and flirting with other girls. Is this what they mean when they say boys want to make as many conquests as they can before they settle down seriously with one girl? Oh, how she wished she could talk to her mother about this.

None of the other girls spoke of talking to their mothers. If they couldn't discuss this subject with their mothers who communicated easily with them; how could she expect to discuss this with her mother? Things always became more complicated with breakdowns in their communication. Especially when discussing something serious. She did talk to Winki and Trixie more than once after a date turned out badly. Of course, her doll would have no reaction to her words but if there were tears, Trixie sure knew how to comfort her with her licks and cuddling. Those helped a little bit but not enough.

One day she came home from school and noticed immediately that Trixie did not greet her at the door. She walked through the kitchen and living room calling her name but the dog did not appear. Evie met her in the hallway and gestured for her to sit down. "Wrong. What?" Liz signed. "Trixie lost?" Evie could not look Liz in the eyes as she signed, "Trixie dead." She went on to explain that Trixie was lying quietly all morning. When Evie made her sound that she always used to call Trixie to her, Trixie did not move. Realizing something was wrong Evie had petted her only to discover that she was not breathing. "Suffer none. Thirteen years live." Evie signed. "Where Trixie now?" Liz asked. "Buried field one mile." "Ohhh, No. Wish see her me. Before buried." Liz escaped to her bedroom, flung herself on the bed and cried heavy tears.

"Trixie. Trixie. I'm so sorry I didn't get to say goodbye!" she said out loud. Bobby came into her room and told her he was so sorry. "She was always your dog, sis, and I know you will miss her. Let's you and I walk over to where Mom buried her. Want to?" "What a good idea, Bobby!" Liz said as she wiped the tears from her eyes. "Yes, let's go." Liz couldn't believe her brother was acting so kindly toward her. Bobby asked their mother where Trixie was buried and told her he was walking there with Liz. Evie simply nodded in the affirmative. The visit to Trixie's burial place was comforting. Liz repeated out loud her feelings to Trixie and thanked her for being such a good dog for so many years. She promised to visit her gravesite and leave flowers whenever she could.

She noted that Evie did put some lily of the valleys on the fresh dirt; so she promised to keep them watered if they took root. She thought better of her mother after realizing she had dug a hole, smoothed over the spot and left the flowers. After returning home she thanked her mother. "Guess you not want me see Trixie dead. Understand now. Thank you care her." That night Liz wrote in her diary, "Well, Diary, you will be the only one to hear of all my frustrations now that I can't talk to Trixie anymore." There was still her doll but Liz had reached the age where she was not comfortable talking to her anymore. She was just a pretty decoration for her bedroom now. One day she would give it to her daughter who could use her as a companion again.

After graduation, Wade continued with his job driving the delivery truck for a local cleaners. But this sure wasn't what he wanted to do for the rest of his life! He soon decided to join the Air Force along with many of his buddies. Things had sure changed around this town and around the whole United States because of this trouble in a little country called Korea. It was not easy saying goodbye with nothing but promises of letters to be written. Yet, Liz was relieved that she didn't have to argue about sex anymore. As the weeks turned into months she did miss him and the fun they had with their friends.

Liz's family had more time now for fun together during the early evenings. Liz especially loved to play card games. Maybe this was because Bobby never played adult games with Evie and Frank like Liz did. She learned quickly so that she was allowed to play Canasta and 500 Rummy with them and a neighbor widow who loved to be Frank's partner. Liz was wise in choosing her mother to be her partner because she knew that Evie's temper would flair up during card games. Liz tried to make light of it by doing such things as standing up, putting a hanky on her head, and walking around her chair for good luck. This made her dad laugh and her mother to cheer up a little when she was upset after losing a hand. However, Evie often remained sensitive to losing and would either go into the kitchen to fix a refreshment for everyone or send Liz to do it so that she could have a couple of minutes to calm down.

Sometimes during a card game they would actually begin a discussion about the events of the day. They would revolve around the neighborhood; school, city, or even Korea. Liz was surprised at how much her dad knew about surrounding events. Even Evie had started to read the newspaper enough to comment now and then on prices of groceries, what she saw the neighbor doing, and even the war. Liz began to feel humbled for the thoughts she had about deaf people not able to keep up with such things because of the vocabulary. Perhaps it wasn't that they didn't understand the words; it was really that there were no signs for them simple enough for their children to understand. When Frank used finger spelling, Liz did have a difficult time reading words that he put out there so quickly. She promised herself that she would concentrate more closely on that finger spelling and learn something from her parents. Actually, she was learning something about her parents. They were not dumb! They were smarter than she had given them credit for. She silently thanked God for that.

During one discussion about Korea, Frank turned to his daughter with a serious look and asked how Wade was doing in the service. Liz would always try to keep that reply as simple as possible because she really didn't get much information in his letters. Evie noted that Liz's comments were often the same, "He likes Air Force. They are good to him. He learns about Texas. Training is finished. He's going to New York!" Feeling brave, Evie asked her daughter if she thought she and Wade would marry one day. Unable to read Liz's expression, she became a little more forward and signed sharply, "If true, why he not give you engagement ring?" Feeling somewhat embarrassed, Liz simply retorted, "Maybe soon. I don't know! Let's get back to the card game!"

She continued to write to Wade, increasing her letters after he sent her an eight by ten picture of himself in his uniform. Proudly, she showed it to her parents, bought a frame for it, and set it on her dresser. He sure was handsome, her mother and dad both agreed. After basic training in Texas Wade was sent to Newark, New York. There he had an accident and broke his leg. Liz felt so badly for him she decided to surprise him with a visit. She had saved up some money from her summer job at Penney's, enough to buy a round trip train ticket to New York. She was over eighteen now so she didn't need anyone's permission.

However, she did take advantage of her parents again in that they had some deaf friends, the Browns, who had moved to Newark.

They arranged for her to stay with them for the weekend. They met Liz at the train and took her out for dinner that evening to a lovely little restaurant before going to their home. There she shared stories about her mother and dad as they had not seen her parents for several years. "Busy dad. Hobby make birdhouses from Readers' Digest magazines. Fun. Mother sews stuffed animals. Fun," Liz signed. She soon pled sleepiness and Mrs. Brown reluctantly agreed it was bedtime and showed her to her room. This couple never had children so they were enjoying Liz's visit. No doubt Liz had impressed them with her smooth signing and quick relay of messages with the waiter and taxi driver. It was a very pleasant evening for Liz too and she almost felt guilty taking advantage of their generosity like this. As she left the room they gave her instructions on where to go to the bus stop the next day and what name to look for on the bus that went out to the Naval Hospital. They were a little worried about her going on her own but she assured them that she knew what to look out for. Lying in bed she ended her prayer with a special plea to take care of her as she went out on a new venture.

The next morning she took a bus out to the naval base! How impressive! The red brick buildings were carefully outlined with perfect landscaping of green shrubberies with a scattering of bright flowers here and there. There were small signs in front of each building with information of what was to be found inside. The bus driver stopped at the military gate and indicated that his passengers were tourists from all across the United States. Nevertheless, they each had to show their identification to the military policeman who boarded the bus to see them. They soon parked in a spot that turned out to be close to the hospital where Liz was going.

The jovial driver explained what times he would be at this spot again to return to the city. Liz quickly jotted the information down on her notepaper pad that she always carried in her purse. Her father had been the one to encourage her to always have paper and pen with her just as he did. At first Liz had thought that was silly for a hearing person to do; but with time she realized there were moments when one needed to jot down information just like this, so they would not forget it or make a mistake in what they thought they remembered.

What a surprise Wade received when Liz walked into his hospital room that day! His roommates whistled when she walked in with a bouquet of flowers. Liz was embarrassed but she needn't be. She was an attractive girl with her dark brown hair curling around her face, emphasizing her big brown eyes and great smile. The yellow blouse and black dirndl skirt were flattering to her slim figure. Why shouldn't they whistle? Wade actually yelled out her name and a low whistle himself. "What are you doing here? How did you get here? I cannot believe it's you!" With that Liz reached over his bed to his cheek and gave him a kiss and small hug. "I thought you might be surprised," she said as she looked for a vase to put the flowers in. "Hey, guys, this is my girlfriend from Wisconsin, Liz," Wade said as he pulled her towards him in a possessive manner. He seemed genuinely pleased to see her. Liz was thrilled. She knew she would enjoy this visit because it couldn't possibly wind up with an argument about sex. He was stuck in that bed with his leg hanging on an overhead bar and would have to be happy with just a kiss and a hug. She was right. They had fun talking about old times and reviewing together where all their friends were. After two days of such innocent bliss Liz had to say goodbye. All the fellows said goodbye too.

Two of them had asked Liz to write notes to their girlfriends and tell them that she had seen them and could verify they were "out of commission" and to be trusted completely. She laughed at such requests but fully intended to carry out her promises. As Liz watched Wade's handsome face look so seriously at her, she felt somewhat proud that these young men would trust her to carry messages to their loved ones. It was the first time in their three year relationship that Liz felt Wade truly cared for her. It had been a mutual warm sensation for both of them.

They were both adult enough now to realize how short life could be and that they needed to make the most of every moment. Of course Liz knew that Wade was thinking more about having sex together than she was but she pushed that to the back of her mind and carried only pleasant thoughts with her on the return journey home. She also said a silent prayer for Wade and the other boys that God would keep them safe from any harm.

Her thoughts drifted to life and death and to the loved ones she had known who were gone now. Liz had lost both of her grandparents during her high school years. Aunt Mable explained that Granma Anna did not believe in doctors and would never visit a doctor's office or allow one to call on her. As a Christian Science member she believed that God would cure her of her ailments if He chose to do so. If not, then it was part of His plans that one would suffer or pass on to live with Him. She died on the operating table because she had suffered too long with gall bladder problems. She was too weak to argue with Uncle Ray when he had picked his mother up and carried her to the car and on to the hospital emergency room. But it was too late and later that same night she died. She was only sixty-seven years old. Liz believed that some people are old at fifty while others seem young at seventy.

Liz found the rest of the story about her grandmother to be fascinating. Anna had married, at age sixteen to a widower fifteen years older than her. She had raised his son along with the five that were born to Anna and Julius. All of her children respected her as their mother because she kept them clean and well fed as well as teaching them about the love of God. No doubt she worried that Evie would not learn about her Savior or how to worship Him. Liz thought how true that was as her grandma had often played hymns and sang the endearing words to Liz and her cousins.

However, she had not tried to influence Liz or anyone else that she knew of with her own particular religious belief. Apparently Grandpa Julius had always insisted that the children receive doctor's care when they needed it; and he had done the same for himself. But Anna had always used mid-wives for her children's births and never visited doctors for herself. True, Grandma had been the one to introduce Liz to religion but not to the Bible. She didn't preach the Word. Rather, her message was heard through the hymns. Liz remembered one in particular that she soon began to sing along with her:

I was sinking deep in sin,
far from the peaceful shore,
Very deeply stained within,
sinking to rise no more,

But the master of the sea,
heard my despairing cry,
From the waters lifted me,
now safe am I.

Love lifted me!
Love lifted me!
When nothing else could help,
Love lifted me!

Words: James Rowe (1865-1933) in 1912
Music: Howard E. Smith (1863-1915)

She remembered, of course, Grandma's homemade root beer and second to that, something she did not enjoy eating, tomato soup. Grandpa and Donna Mae both loved tomato soup so Liz would drown crackers in her bowl so that she could swallow it without getting sick. Grandpa lived to be 82. When he was ill, Evie took Bobby on the train to stay with him for a week. Unfortunately, she had only two days of visits with her father. Frank received word that Julius had died. He decided to take Liz and drive to Minnesota for the funeral, then bring his wife and son back home.

As they traveled Liz thought about her grandpa Julius. Liz didn't feel that she knew him at all because he spoke in German most of the time. All she could really remember about him was how he loved hard lemon drops of which grandma always kept supplied in a candy dish near his favorite chair. This memory included grandpa listening to a "soap opera" on the radio. Was it "Stella Dallas?" Or, was it "My Family?" She could remember the commercials about Ivory soap washing your clothes "whiter than snow." His life as a farmer had probably been much like Uncle Ray's was today but Liz did not remember him in that role at all.

Liz would not soon forget that trip to Minnesota with her daddy. After they were out on the highway an hour, an early snowstorm blew in causing problems for Frank's driving. Liz was frightened because she could see nothing through the window but snow swirling in the headlights. But she trusted her daddy's driving and noted that he had slowed down some. Suddenly she saw something in the headlights. Liz screamed as she saw the eyes and antlers of a deer! Frank slowed down but it was too late. His left front fender hit the deer hard enough to throw the animal to the side of the road. Liz was amazed that her dad did not stop. She didn't see how he could keep on driving. Then she saw the lights of a town and realized that he intended to pull off the main road into the town.

Soon he pulled up to the lights of a diner. Frank jumped out of the car and looked at the front bumper with a frown on his face. "Not bad," he signed as he pointed to the crack in the front left headlight. They both trudged through the thickening snow on the ground. Inside several people were eating or drinking a cup of coffee and chatting about the weather. Frank spied a tall man wearing a Sheriff's badge at one of the tables and told Liz to relay to him how they had struck a deer out on the highway about two miles east of town.

The Sheriff looked at this strange young girl, wondering where she had come from. Then he asked Liz why her father didn't come tell him the story himself. Liz hated it when people asked her such silly questions but she answered politely, "My daddy is deaf. He cannot speak." She walked back to her dad and instead of relaying what the man had said she simply nodded her head in the affirmative as to let him know she had given the man Frank's message

Listening to a couple of conversations in the room, Liz then relayed to her dad what people were saying about the road ahead being closed. He signed, "Ask road number. What?" Liz timidly asked the couple closest by, "My dad wants to know what the number of that road is that you say is closing." "Oh, just county road 34. If you are headed to La Crosse on the state highway you are okay. But I wouldn't head up the river road tonight if I were you." The gentleman who was kindly giving her father advice looked right into Frank's face as though he thought he could hear, or at the least, read his lips. Liz always appreciated it when people did that as long as they did not yell!

Unfortunately, only a few people had ever carried on a conversation in this fashion. They almost always looked at her, speaking in the third person such as "Tell him such and such." Frank smiled directly at the fellow and signed his appreciation so that Liz could easily see what he was signing. "Thanks for the information," Liz said confidently this time. Obviously watching this whole scene carefully, the Sheriff finally sauntered over to them and told Liz to let her Dad know that they would go out and take care of that deer. "Thank him for reporting this."

Finally Frank motioned for Liz to sit in the red leather booth, sliding into the opposite seat, asking what she would like to eat. This was a real treat to Liz because the only time they ever ate out was for a special occasion like someone's birthday. Better yet, this was to be shared with her daddy alone. She smiled at him and picked up the worn menu looking at the prices of hamburgers or chili. She chose chili and so did Frank. "Please me bottle Coca-Cola? New now," she asked. With a smile, Frank nodded, signing that he preferred coffee. After Liz relayed their order to the waiter she turned back to her dad, asking in signs, "What think you about snowstorm?"

Actually, Liz noted that her father's face had relaxed some since they came into this eating establishment. "Stay here one hour. Snow stop," looking at his watch he continued, "Arrive late Grandpa's." This seems logical, Liz thought, as they waited for their order. The soft spoken man who had talked to them earlier was putting on his fur-lined jacket and walking toward the door. He paused by the table, looked at Liz kindly and said, "Little lady, you sure are a help to your ol' man. It's such a shame that he's deaf and can't hear your sweet voice." With that he went out the door.

This was one time that Liz did not want to relay a comment to her dad but she could see that he was concerned about what the man had said. Thinking quickly, she simply signed, "He said he hoped the rest of our trip went well. He lives in town so he can walk home." Frank had his doubts, but did not respond because at that moment the waitress brought their chili with crackers and drinks. The waitress looked Frank squarely in the face and said, "This is quite a smart girl you have here." As if he got every word, he simply said out loud, roughly, but clear enough to be understood "Yes." Liz missed the whole thing as she was lost in thought. How she hated to fib to her dad but somehow she didn't think he needed to hear people say they were sorry that he was deaf. She hoped no one would ever write a note to him with such a statement.

Frank was right, in less than an hour the snow stopped, they bundled themselves up and were soon on their way. As they drove out of town Liz noticed a sign that said they were leaving the town of "Friendship." How fitting! The rest of their drive was slow but uneventful and they both sighed a big sigh of relief as they pulled into her grandparents' driveway two hours later.

Evie was shocked when her sister-in-law woke her up at midnight to tell her that Frank and Liz had arrived. Liz was proud of herself for carrying out her role as a responsible daughter to her loving daddy who deserved everyone's respect as well as hers. She tried to keep the strong spirit she had experienced during their trip while there for the next two days. She was able to relay the information read from Grandfather's will so that her mother knew a large part of what had transpired. It wasn't always easy to understand some of the language which caused her to frown a little while signing. She hoped her parents would accept that her frown was really just a moment's reflection on the meaning of the words so that she could sign it correctly. However, Evie seemed to have a different concept of the whole procedure.

Later, while the lawyer was reading a list of items and who they were to be given to, Liz could see her mother was following closely. She signed from her seat in front to Liz, "More me!" Looking Evie in the eye, Liz signed quietly, "wait later." After the reading of the will was complete; Evie, obviously upset, told Liz she was quite positive her father had left her much more than was quoted. Liz did not voice this to the gathering, deciding to sign only to her mother. "Please wait and we can talk to lawyer later. Do not want to upset your sisters."

Acting a little strangely, Evie turned her head away, staring off into space. Not sure what to do, Liz simply sat on the settee and waited for her mother to look at her and then quickly continued to relate the proceedings which were soon over. Alice came directly over to them and asked if Evie was alright. Instead of answering her or her daughter, Evie simply walked away and up the steps to the bedroom in which she and Frank were staying. Liz told Alice that her mother said grandpa had promised her mother more than he had left her. "Something about he would take care of her," Liz sighed.

Alice smiled and said, "Hmmm. I think that he probably told her this when she graduated from school. He just meant if she couldn't get a job or afford her own place to live that he would provide those for her. Do you think that might be it?" Liz sure didn't know what to make of her mother's attitude, so she simply said, "Maybe so." Alice continued with, "Liz, we are all proud of you for signing so well with your mother. It is not easy, I'm sure. While Evie was growing up with us in this house, there were several times when we knew she didn't understand fully what was going on. It's so wonderful that you can explain things to her."

Liz knew her aunt was being kind but there was no way that Liz ever felt her mother did or did not understand certain situations such as this one. Yet there was no point in carrying on with this subject at this time. Liz didn't know yet how to explain the rationale behind deafness and its relationship to communication. Sometimes it is too deep to analyze. So, she simply said, "Thank you, Aunt Alice. I'm sure mother will accept things eventually. She loves you so much and tells me that she's sorry I didn't have a younger sister to grow up with." Liz rose and headed for the stairs, saying over her shoulder, "I'd best go see that she's alright."

Liz soon realized that her mother had found her husband and was now deep in conversation with him in their designated guest room. She decided not to eavesdrop or to even interrupt their quiet time together. Liz did not pursue this any further that day or during their entire stay. She would always wonder why her mother felt that Grandpa owed her something more "because she was deaf!" Despite this incident and the gloomy atmosphere, Liz always enjoyed their visits to Minnesota where she could sit for hours and eavesdrop on the adults' conversations. It was only here or at Mama Essie' house that she could listen to the adults' perspective on events in the home, family or in the whole US of A. Oh, sure, she could learn a lot in the classroom from her teachers at school but it was not often she could anything to her own life or that of her family.

Nothing more was said about Liz going to college so she began looking for a job. She had been clerking part-time at J.C. Penney's for a few months, but they didn't need anyone full time right now. Besides she had really wanted to leave the store because of what had happened with her co-worker's husband. He was at least fifteen years older than Liz and she had just chatted with him during the times he came in to wait until closing to take his wife home. She considered both of them friends but only as casual friends because of working with Myda. The two ladies worked in the same department Monday through Saturday mornings but one of them would have every other Friday night off. On one of the free Friday nights that Liz was home she received a call from the husband asking her to meet him for a drink at a bar located some distance out of town.

Liz was horrified and told him so. He laughed and said perhaps she was just faking when she said that. "Maybe your parents are within ear-shot," he said. He continued, "You can slip out and meet me. You're a big girl now. I can show you a really good time." Immediately after she hung up the phone, Liz went to her dad and told him exactly what had transpired on the phone conversation. Frank was appalled but looked Liz straight in the face and asked, "Flirt you him?" "No! No! Never!" Liz signed angrily. Frank told her then that he believed her and if this would ever happen again to let him know. He reached for the phone book and handing it to Liz, he signed, "Name man, address?" Liz looked up her co-worker's name and underlined it for her dad. Frank copied it down and told her again that he believed what she had told him and that she should not worry. Liz never heard from the man again and his wife seemed to have no idea what had happened, thank goodness. Liz noted that Myda's husband did not come inside the store anymore but opted to wait for her outside. It made Liz uncomfortable though and she really wanted a full time job anyway, so she continued to read the want ads.

Before long she was answering an ad, sitting in a dentist's office filling out an application. She got the job and was elated to be working in an office instead of standing behind a store counter. Dr. Spate seemed like a real gentleman and kindly showed her the schedule of appointments and the bookkeeping of monies received. She was to answer the phone and greet the patients. She would then pull out their record from the files to notify him who was here and what work was to be done. After the work was done she was to record it in the book and if a payment was not received she would mail them a statement at the end of the month.

After a period of thirty days she felt quite comfortable with these duties and settled in very nicely. She had an hour for lunch and since the office was located right down town she could easily have lunch and time to do some shopping if she chose to do so. She even stopped in to see Myda a couple of times. Liz was always the last one to leave the office and would lock the door behind her. Doc expected her to be back at one o'clock sharp for the first patient of the afternoon who would be in at one fifteen. She was responsible for putting that patient's file on the counter in the inner office before Doc got back from his lunch.

One day she was just ready to lock the door when a man came from behind and grabbed her around the waist. "Let's just go right back in, sweetie, and have a talk." She tried to break away but his hands were tight and his body was pushing her and the door open at the same time. A scream broke out of her voice before she even realized it, even though he threw a hand over her mouth immediately.

Before he could close the door behind them someone came out from the office across the hall and yelled, "Hey, what's going on out there Liz, is that you?" The man swung around and fled down the stairs. But Liz had turned quickly to see his face. It was Myda's husband! Across the hall the attorney came on out of his office and asked if she was all right. Liz quickly replied, "Yes, thank goodness. Was that you that called out?" He nodded and told her he'd heard her scream. She was smart to do that! He also advised her to report the incident to the police.

When Dr. Spate returned after his lunch hour she had the opportunity to talk to him with the waiting room still empty because his one fifteen patient had called to postpone his appointment. She related exactly what had happened adding that she knew the man. "Did he have some personal reason to do this to you, Liz?" Doc asked. He was so kind that Liz had no problem telling him the whole story of the telephone conversation and of promising her dad that she would tell him if anything further happened. "Well, let me call the police and then after you make out the report you can go home and explain it to your father. But you can tell him that I know about this now and will be sure that you are not exposed to any such danger in the future. The police will talk to Myda's husband and I don't think he will ever bother you again!"

That evening Frank really was upset but he trusted that Dr. Spate would protect Liz as promised. Later Frank talked to Evie privately about the whole affair and asked her if she would speak to Liz about it. "You explain Liz. No flirt men. Married man no talk!" Evie was surprised at his strong expression but said nothing. She said nothing to Liz either as she actually felt intimidated by her daughter's understanding of having a boyfriend or talking to friends, both male and female. Evie knew no way of opening such a conversation so she preferred to forget about the whole thing.

Nothing further was said of the whole incident by anyone, not even Dr. Spate. This was somewhat of a relief and yet a disappointment to Liz. There seemed to be no real end to it. She didn't know what she expected, a phone call of apology? That was too much to expect especially if Myda found out about it because the police talked to her husband. Liz never wanted to hurt her but perhaps it was good that she learned the truth. It was a long time before Liz shopped at Penney's again. Then she found out that Myda had quit working there as she had moved to another city. Liz could not help but feel relieved. That night she included Myda in her prayers, asking God to be sure that Myda's husband did not bother any other girls. This was another traumatic moment to write about in her diary.

Working so many hours made Liz become tired of work, especially since the doctor wanted her to come in on Saturday mornings. Poor Dr. Spate worked too hard and his wife told Liz that he suffered with ulcers because of so many hours in his office. Liz was convinced then to look around for something with forty hours a week. Someone was always giving her some tips on positions available. The first one she applied for was in the Personnel office of the Nekoosa-Edwards paper company located in Port Edwards. The manager who interviewed her liked her positive attitude and hired her immediately. Frank knew a neighbor who worked in the same area so he arranged for Liz to ride to work with he and his wife.

Things worked out fine for some time. Then Frank told Liz that Dr. Spate's name was in the newspaper as admitted to the hospital! It seemed his ulcers were giving him a tough time. She heard that the new girl she had trained for him was not working out and he had to let her go. She felt so guilty. "Daddy, I must go to the hospital to visit him," she said as she grabbed her jacket from the coat rack. When she came home later, Frank asked her if the visit went well. "Yes. Doctor happy see me. Thanked me work hard for him. Feels good now. His doctor order cut hours office. New girl starts Monday and doctor Spate's wife will train." "Good. Good. All good," Frank signed with enthusiasm. He was proud of his daughter for handling this incident so well. She has become a wise young lady. Maybe we did alright as parents after all, he thought to himself.

Gerald King Powell
U.S. Air Force Bands (1952-1972)

8

Can We Keep Our Family Together?

Liz's friends became tired of the unwritten rule of "no dat-ing" just because their boyfriends were in the military. Nita preferred to stay true to her navy man and four other girls soon found excuses to go out without dates. They soon found that many other girls their age were also out just to have some fun. A favorite spot was Joe's BBQ. Joe was an Irish gentleman with a genuine interest in his customers. Most Friday or Saturday nights Liz would pick up her girlfriends to see a good movie. After the movie they drove out to Joe's for a BBQ and a beer. Listening to their favorite records on the jukebox they brought each other up to date on their specific boyfriends. Each girl had a letter to share, then they would all analyze the romantic phrases. Of course they would interpret them as positive statements from each fella because they did not want to hurt anyone's feelings. A couple of months passed in this innocent manner.

Just before Christmas, Ellie climbed into the car wiping her eyes of tears. "What's the matter?" Liz asked. "Sully broke off with me. They talk about the G.I.s getting a Dear John letter. Well, this is a Dear Ellie letter. Can you believe he has fallen for a Korean girl!" Liz turned off the motor and put her arms around her friend, quietly commenting; "It's going to be okay. It's going to be okay." Wiping her tears away, Ellie put on a half-smile and said, "Thank you, Liz. Let's not let this spoil our fun tonight. Wait 'til we get to Joe's to tell the others. Okay?" "Sure, whatever you want, Ellie. Here, use my compact and wipe away that mascara on your face, you'll be fine."

The consequences were not fine though. This break-up started a round of ideas as to what to do while their boyfriends were gone. Ellie wanted to go to some new places where she might meet someone who didn't know her. Dori said there was a state college just down the road so she might meet a guy over there because young men who were in school were exempt from the draft. So, they drove over to Stevens Point, only a forty minute drive down the highway. There they found a neat little place where a lot of college kids hung out. "Wow. There's some good looking kids here," exclaimed Ellie. They put some money in the jukebox careful not to choose the one song that Ellie considered hers and Sully's. After ordering beers all around Liz was surprised she was the first one to attract an invitation to dance. Ellie told her to go on. It was just a dance. Soon all of them were dancing and enjoying new company at their table. At midnight Liz said, "Hey, I'm driving so I'm not having another beer. It's time to head home." Everyone agreed and as they headed out the door their new friends told them to come back the following week. After three weeks of this Ellie and Liz were both asked on dates. "Let's double date and head to the ski slopes next Saturday," said Cody. "But I've never skied. Would you have patience with me and teach me how?" Liz asked; adding that she had always wanted to learn but was a little afraid of heights.

On Saturday, Liz picked up her friend and drove over to Stevens Point. She parked on the campus where they met Cody and his buddy. Liz checked out the back seat and saw nothing but Coca Cola and 7 Up with no signs of any beer. The four of them hopped into Cody's old Ford and headed north for Wausau and the little mountain ski resort. They sang silly songs along the way. The two fellows taught the girls college cheers and little was said about their personal lives. At the resort Cody checked out skis and ski boots for Liz and led her to the ski lift. Giving her instructions about sitting in the chair and helping her to hop off was okay. But when she stood at the top and looked down the hill she was struck with panic. Cody showed her how to move side to side slowly as in slalom skiing, something that would be a slow way to ski downhill. Somehow she skied down that huge mountain and found a place to sit down at the bottom. "Never again," Liz told Cody as he pulled her up and headed into the resort waiting room. Leading her to the fireplace he sat down beside her and told her it was all right. It was normal to have that reaction but he would like her to try again. "Not today. Please!" she laughed. "Okay, you're off the hook today. We'll try another time. I'm going back up and this time to the top. So, there are some magazines over there and a comfy couch. Would you like a cup of hot chocolate before I leave?" Liz was so grateful for his kindness and patience and wished him a good trip as he waved goodbye.

Liz really tried to like the guy but when he asked her to come back the next weekend she just had to decline. "I don't want to lead him on, just to hurt his feelings later," she told her friend. Ellie was not disappointed as she told Liz, "I'm not too sure I want to continue dating Ben either," she said quietly. "Oh, good. I'm glad. Let's just wait until we're really bored before driving over to the campus again," Liz laughed.

After two years in the Personnel Department at Nekoosa-Edwards Paper Company Liz had an offer to go to Florida with her classmates, Mae and Bud. How could she refuse? Bud was in the Air Force Band at Eglin A.F. Base near Ft. Walton Beach, FL. He and Mae had been high school sweethearts and married right after graduation. How romantic; but, yet, kind of foolish. However, these two people seemed comfortable with each other and ready to settle down. Liz was not one to question their wisdom. This was a chance to see what their married life was like in the military. Liz had never been south of Illinois where dad's two deaf siblings lived. She asked for her vacation of one week paid and then a second week without pay. Thank goodness her office complied because it was a two day trip to Florida and she wanted time to enjoy herself. The next day she packed her suitcase. Little did she know what adventure lay ahead!

The drive was long but fun. The first breakfast on the road Liz discovered a new food item, the first of many to come. Grits! After ordering scrambled eggs and bacon she assumed the grits was part of the eggs. However, after her second bite she looked at Mae and asked, "What is this? I see now that it is on your plate too." Bud laughed and said, "It's called grits. A lot of people in the south eat this stuff every day." "Well, all I can say is I don't think I'll ever eat it again. Thank you. Yuk." Liz replied.

Florida! This was like opening up a storybook and looking at pictures of palm trees and fruits like she had never seen before. Liz fell in love with the scenery before even entering the beach area. Ft. Walton Beach was picturesque with the white virgin sands running along the beach for miles and miles. This was a small town connected to two more villages with bridges spanning the backwaters of the Bay. Entering the town of Shalimar, Buddy turned into a small housing area of two bedroom homes. Liz was immediately curious about the houses all built on pillars with a space of two feet between the floor of the house and the ground. Bud explained is was because of sand.

Moments later, Liz forgot her curiosity as a big beautiful tri-colored collie came bounding from behind the house and jumped on Bud. "Hey, Lady. How's my girl? Yeah, we're happy to be home too." Lady ran around in circles barking before finally settling down by the front porch. As they unloaded their luggage Liz would talk to Lady telling her how pretty she was. Liz didn't realize how much she missed her Trixie. She had not given much thought to having another dog since she lived with her parents. That would be their decision, not hers. But now she felt drawn to this beautiful collie. She learned to brush Lady's long hair until it shone. She always laid still and almost purred like a kitten while Liz combed her. They became good friends in the two weeks that Liz stayed with Mae and Bud.

On the third day of her visit, Bud came home somewhat excited. The minute he walked in the door he told his wife they would have to evacuate for a couple of days. "Evacuate? Why? Who ordered that?" Bud continued, "Oh, I shouldn't say evacuate, and really, no one ordered it. But there is a hurricane sitting out there in the Bay that is heading right for us. They predict it will be here by the early hours of tomorrow morning. The guys and I have been talking and we've decided the best thing to do is get in our cars and drive north into Mississippi and stay in a motel for a couple of nights."

Listening intently, Liz hoped that Mae would agree to their plans. The next thing they knew they were on their way out of town. When they returned a couple of days later they found little damage to their house and others in the complex; but they were not a bit sorry they had "chickened out."

The next night a couple of the bandsmen came over to visit and they talked all evening about the effect the hurricane had on the base and how they had to go out and tie down things all across the base. They teased Bud that he hadn't had to take part in it. One of the guys talked more so than the other as he was giving the details of their chores. He looked at Liz as he embellished his story so she might think he was pretty brave to go out in the wind and rain to carry in all their band equipment into a sturdier building than their Quonset huts they used for band practice. He seemed a bit arrogant, but he did get Liz's attention. When leaving he asked Bud if he could come over the next evening to play some cards.

"Wow. Oh, Wow!" Liz exclaimed as she pulled Mae into the bedroom beyond the hearing of their visitor. "What's wrong?" Mae asked. "Mae, I just didn't realize; he's sooo cute! In fact, he looks just like Elvis Presley. Please tell me you can see that too," Liz whispered. "Well, then, let's get you two properly introduced," Mae answered as she took Liz's arm and steered her back into the living room.

"There you are, you two," Bud called out as he came around the corner from the kitchen. "Liz, you best meet your Canasta partner for the evening so you can get your heads together on how you cheat at the game!" Bud chided. "This is Jerry Powell, second to best sax player we have in the band. First best being me of course," laughed Bud. "Jerry, this is our classmate and good friend from Wisconsin Rapids."

"Hi, I've already heard quite a bit about you; but certainly nothing to indicate you are a cheater," Jerry said with a smile. Elvis Presley and a beautiful smile. How lucky can I get, Liz thought as she stretched out her hand. "Right back at you. These folks have said a few things about you but never told me about your cheating career either!" Liz responded. Laughing, Jerry took her hand and pulled out a chair stating that he was looking forward to beating Liz's old friends in a good game of cards. Already feeling comfy with this young man, Liz said she agreed; and by golly, they did win.

Jerry asked her if she would like to go to the drive-in movies with him the following night. That led to a first kiss surprising Liz with its intensity. She had only known him for four days; yet, she felt like she'd known him forever.

That was the beginning of a fast courtship by Jerry. He really had no trouble convincing Liz she should stay in Florida longer, giving them a chance to know each other better. After two weeks Liz decided she really would like to stay in Florida! She actually considered looking for a job and a place to live. Mae and Bud were more than a little surprised at her decision, but said nothing to discourage her. Bud felt sure that Jerry was a good guy and would treat their friend well. Mae wondered what Liz would do for transportation if she did find a job. Despite the questions that went through her mind, Mae put on a positive attitude for Liz's sake.

In fact, Mae had been working in the local "Piggly Wiggly" grocery store produce department. She introduced Liz to the owner and manager. After a short interview she was hired as a cashier. There were four registers in the store and the hours would be flexible according to the family schedule needs. At first Liz felt a little hesitant when she realized the whole family worked in the store and she might be at their mercy; but she shook off her fears and accepted the job. Now she could look for a place to live and start a new life.

The next day she found a place that looked absolutely adorable. After reading the ad in the paper Liz hurried to meet the owner who lived in this big old house in a secluded area of Ft. Lauderdale just off of the Bay. She was a widow, Elaine Smith, looking for someone to share the sprawling rooms. Liz fell in love with the lovely lady's charming manners and voice. She assumed this was part of that southern hospitality people often talked about. After chatting for fifteen minutes Elaine took Liz by the hand and gave her the grand tour. She explained that the rooms to rent would be a nice size bedroom and a small sitting room with a shared bathroom and kitchen privileges. There was a big overstuffed bed with a white wicker dresser and chest of drawers. Paintings of young couples dancing outdoors graced the wall opposite to the large picture window overlooking a lovely flowerbed. Everything worked together to give a feeling of sleeping outdoors. "Would I be expected to take care of those flowers?" Liz asked anxiously. "Oh, no! Please do not touch the flowerbed. That's my therapy. In fact, that's my life right now. I just retired and spend hours every morning out there. But, don't worry, you will have complete privacy. I'm out there in the wee hours of the morning and will be back in the house having my hot cup of tea before you even wake up. Now come on outside."

Just outside her sitting room door they stepped into a Floridian environment. Large cypress trees draped their branches over the large back yard. Lush flowers lined an old wooden walkway leading down an incline onto a small beach. This was all Liz needed. "I'll take it if you'll have me!" The rent was affordable on her meager wages so she lost no time moving in. Mae and Bud helped her move her personal things because her little Crossley didn't hold much. She really had fun driving this little vehicle around. It was a bargain that she purchased from one of Elaine's old crony friends. There was barely room for two people to get in and no space to move around when you settled in. Liz had never seen Jerry's old Cadillac because it had been in the garage for repair ever since she met him. Now she was glad to have the little Crossly as it fit perfectly into the single parking space about ten feet away from her private door. Life was beautiful. She only hoped her parents would not be upset when they learned of her decision.

Dear Mother and Dad...   *October, 1953*

I hope you will not be upset with me but I have decided to stay here in Florida! Fort Walton Beach is a beautiful little town right on the beaches. White sand covers the beaches and anyone can go down to the water to walk into the ocean as the waves come in. It is so clear it seems you can see for miles.

187

I only have to walk about twenty feet to get down to the water from where I live.! I live about four miles from Mae and Bud. They live in base housing so I could not rent anything close to them.

Yes, I have already found a place to live. An older lady owns this house and is renting out to me two rooms while sharing the bathroom and kitchen. I will take some pictures later and send them to you. I'm sure when you see them you will see that it is a nice clean house and a lovely Florida setting. I am so happy!

Mae helped me get a job in the grocery store she works in and the people there are so nice to me. I am working at the cash register and meet a lot of local people that way. I like meeting new people every day. I will write you more soon.

Hugs! Love, Liz

On Liz's twenty-third birthday, Jerry took her out to a fancy restaurant and ordered an expensive dinner. She was impressed because the only place they had gone before was the Open-Pit Bar BQ hut where they both loved their sandwiches and deep fried potatoes. The first thing they were to enjoy this evening was shrimp cocktail. Liz had never had shrimp in any form and ate it very slowly, savoring every bite. "That was delicious! Have you had it before?" she asked Jerry. "Yes, just a couple of times. Maybe they just don't have shrimp brought into that frozen tundra of Wisconsin!" he teased. At that point Liz stood up, covered her mouth with the napkin and excused herself as she hurriedly headed toward the ladies room. Jerry wondered if she had taken his remarks as an insult rather than a tease. However, when she did return she laughed. "I enjoyed the shrimp but it didn't like me! Sorry!" After that there were two more attempts at eating shrimp, both raw and fried. She learned that her body was allergic to this delectable food. The same held true for other shellfish she ate during her time in Florida!

Things moved along too quickly with Jerry. In just a few weeks he told her that he was in love with her. They were at the drive-in theatre cuddling closely as they watched the movie, "Creature of the Black Lagoon." Liz felt cozy and comfy with this young airman but she felt that they were both still on the rebound from their past relationships. Jerry had been engaged to a girl back in his hometown, Tulsa. She had broken his heart just as Wade had broken Liz's in Wisconsin. "Let's not rush into anything. We need to know if it is for real. Okay?" Liz said quietly. He agreed and they both relaxed for a few weeks just enjoying each other's company. It was fun going to Bingo or the bowling alley out at the base. They enjoyed the latest movies every weekend, or played Canasta with Mae and Bud. The four friends became very close. They celebrated with them when they announced Mae was pregnant, due in the fall.

In February, Bud's collie, Lady, gave birth to her first litter of puppies. Liz fell in love with them. They were so beautiful Liz decided to buy one for Jerry for his birthday which was in April. Liz asked Mae to keep the puppy until that date. She didn't know where he could keep the puppy! It would have to live with her but her landlady did not want any pets in their house. This was a dilemma but she was determined to have the puppy. Jerry and Liz filled out the registration papers for the new puppy and named her after the town that she was born in, "Princess Shalli of Shalimar."

Just a week later, Jerry surprised Liz with a ring and popped the question after just five months of dating. "I hope you will accept this ring. It was actually bought for my old girlfriend in Oklahoma but I have the set now and cannot see buying a new one." Liz could see the anxiety in Jerry's face and knowing that he could not afford to buy rings as Airman 2nd class she smiled and said, "That's fine as long as you will let me pick out a new one for our 25th wedding anniversary." He was thrilled with that response believing that she wanted to marry him.

However, Liz did not feel that she was ready for this. Not only did things move along too fast; but she had just found out a couple of days before this that Jerry was more than two years younger than her.

"I can't believe this," she said as she looked at his military identification card. "If I didn't see this with my own eyes I wouldn't believe it. I don't think this is a good idea. Let's call this off right now, Jerry. We are not ready for marriage yet." To her surprise, he didn't really argue with her decision. They hugged and parted quite amicably.

Liz was also not sure if she was completely over her feelings for her high school sweetheart. She wondered if any girl ever really got over her first love. Maybe Jerry still loved the girl in Tulsa who broke his heart. Who knows. She had dated Wade from the time she was sixteen until he joined the Air Force during the Korean conflict. They had written letters regularly but Liz felt their letters were not really love letters. Wade's words had been filled with mundane information of daily routines. Liz would write about what all their friends were doing and of any special events happening in their home town. Oh, to be sure, they would close their letters with the usual "I miss you," and "I love you," but Liz knew in her heart that Wade did not feel deeply about her as he never made any real statements of commitment to her. With Jerry, there were no doubts of his love for her.

Two weeks went by with no word from Jerry. Liz found herself missing him more and more every day. She felt lonely despite filling her days with work, shopping and visiting with Mae and Bud and their sweet Lady. She took Shalli out for a run around the school track that was right behind their house. Thank goodness Mae and Bud said they would keep Shalli for Liz until she found a place to live that accepted pets. During their third week apart, Liz broke down and called Jerry. After all, it had been her choice to break up with him; why should he call her?! Jerry was thrilled and told her he was thinking about taking a short leave to go and see his family. Liz thought he probably wanted to see his old girlfriend but before she could say so, he surprised her with an invitation to go along! "What?!" she exclaimed.

Jerry came right back with, "My car is still in the shop and I cannot afford to get the parts I need, but we can go on the bus. Come on, it would be fun! OK?" Not pausing long enough to let Liz say anything, he continued, "I can get ten days leave, it takes a day and night to get to Tulsa. You can meet my folks, and my sisters. They will all love you. My brothers will probably show their jealousy and we will be entertained all week long. Of course we'll go to the movies at the theaters where I used to work and those folks will like you too. Do you think you can talk your boss into giving you a week off?" Finally, Liz had a chance to say something. She was swept up in his excitement and answered as though she was out of breath. "I can certainly ask. I'll let you know tomorrow." Agreeing, Jerry replied "I'll pick you up around six. We'll go out for a burger and make our plans. Okay?"

It was an all night ride on a bus full of strangers. After some chit chat they soon fell asleep. The next thing they knew they were waking up in Tulsa. "My mom should be here to pick us up. Dad is at work of course." No sooner had he said the words than a tall lovely lady came up behind him and said, "That's right, son. Here I am. And this must be Liz. Jerry's told me so much about you, I feel like I know you already. Please call me Nan."

Liz hoped her future mother-in-law fell in love with her as fast as she had with her! She was so sweet and still had a Texas drawl even though she had lived in Tulsa for over thirty years. During their ride home, Nan pointed out the different buildings downtown and told her a little history of this interesting city. Liz told them one of her favorite movies had been "Tulsa" with Susan Hayward. "I loved that movie. When that oil well gushed, or whatever you call that, I was in awe! I never dreamed I would one day be here and see the oil wells in action!"

It wasn't a long ride at all to Jerry's home. It was an old white framed house with a large front porch with a porch swing that invited them in to sit down. Nan had canaries that were already singing in their cage when they heard our voices outside. Jerry carried their luggage to the spare bedroom which had been added on behind the kitchen just a few years earlier. "I know, Mom, I'll bunk in with Teddy while Liz gets this room. Am I right?"

Little did Liz know this would become the arrangement every time they came to Tulsa to visit. Hopefully, their next visit would welcome them as a married couple so they could share the guest room together. Later they shared it with their firstborn, and still later they had another guest room for the girls as Jerry's oldest brother had moved out into his own apartment.

Dear Mother & Dad...   *February, 1954*

I'm so sorry I haven't been writing regularly as I should be. But, maybe you will forgive me when you hear my news. The last time I wrote you I told you about this nice young airman I met when I first arrived here. He is in the Air Force Band just as Bud. Jerry even plays the same instruments as Bud. The saxophone and the clarinet.

Well, anyway, Jerry and I have been dating for a few months now. I was absolutely shocked when he asked me to marry him already! But I know we love each other.

He really is sweet! I'm sure you will like him. Mae and Bud are happy for us. They have known Jerry for over a year now. Bud says he thinks Jerry is a fine guy and will be good to me.

I could not believe it when Jerry planned a trip to Tulsa, Oklahoma so that I could meet his family. We had to take the Greyhound bus because his car was in the shop. But it was fun traveling and seeing a lot of interesting sights along the way. His older sister picked us up at the bus station. She is very nice.

He has two brothers and two sisters. Both sisters are married but not his brothers.

One sister lives right down the street from Jerry's parents and has four children. The other sister lives a few miles away with her hubby and one daughter.

One of his brothers has a physical deformity. It seems when Jerry's mother was pregnant with him, something went wrong. When he was born his feet and legs were overgrown! His mother was told that he might not live 12 years; but obviously they were wrong. Teddy is now twenty and living a pretty normal life. I will tell you more when I see you.

His other brother served in World War II and had a lot of trauma to work through when he got out of the Army. He now works for the Post Office and still lives at home with his parents.

We spent a week there and had so much fun. They are all good people. I really love his mother and dad. I hope you can meet them some day.

I will tell you all about them when I come home for a visit. I don't know when that will be, but I should be able to take another vacation from work in just a few months. Oh, and I should tell you. I really like Tulsa too.

Well, I must get some sleep as I go back to work tomorrow. We got back yesterday and I am still tired. Huh! I hope this finds you both doing well and that you will forgive me for accepting an engagement ring from a man you have not even met yet. I know that is not what you would like. But, I promise, he is a fine fellow and I know you will love him too.

Write when you can,
Love, Liz

Dear Mother and Daddy,   *April, 1954*

Well, we did it! Jerry and I were married on March 8th, as planned. Yes, it was a bit sad that no one from Wisconsin or Oklahoma came to the wedding. Of course I was happy to have my classmates, Mae & Bud as our Matron of Honor and Best Man. I just wore my light blue suit and a lovely corsage in the lapel. I also had some flowers made up as a headpiece. I will send pictures as soon as I can.

Some of Jerry's buddies from the band came too. About fifteen friends met us at the restaurant afterwards for a reception. That was something Mae and Bud arranged as a surprise for us. It all turned out to be good food and fun for all of us.

My landlady had even gone somewhere for the week-end so that Jerry and I could have privacy in the house. We do have a small house we will move into at the end of this month. It's only a one bedroom but it will do until we get into base housing.

Oh, I have other news. I quit my job at the grocery store. Well, I confess, I was actually fired. The boss had three daughters that worked part time at the store. On a busy Friday night one of them relieved me at the cash register without changing out the drawer or counting the money. The next morning the boss called me into his office and told me that when they closed the register Friday night and counted the money I was short over a hundred dollars!

He said he would take it out of my paychecks until it was paid. I told him that he wasn't being fair to me but he would not listen! I was so upset I immediately said I would not work for him anymore because he was biased toward his family. I decided to start looking for another job.

While interviewing with the manager of a Children's Shop, I told him all about what had transpired at the Piggly Wiggly store. He appreciated my honesty and gave me the position of Assistant Manager to this store. He also had a store in Panama City and will only be here two days a week. After one week of working here, I already know it is going to be better than the grocery store has been. At least for me, it is. It's fun helping parents choose clothes for the little children. Then it's fun to see the kids try on the clothes and hear the funny things they say about them. I enjoy this job so much.

Well, I must get dressed and get on over to the Shop. Ohhhh, I almost forgot to thank you. Thank you so very much for your check for our wedding present. We have not decided what to get with the money but you can be sure we will spend

*it wisely. We may get a new mattress and springs but then
we would have to leave them in this house. Hmmm. We will
shop soon.*

Love,
Liz

"Liz coming home! Next week!" Evie signed excitedly to her
hubby as he walked in the door. After reading the letter together,
Frank asked his impatient wife if she had the week's menu all planned
out and the bedroom ready. He laughed as he hugged her tightly with
mutual happiness. "Bedroom theirs wait. Bedroom you, me ready
now," Frank signed with a mischievous twinkle in his eyes. With his
arm around her waist he led her into the bedroom. Their lovemaking
was always enhanced when Evie was in a happy mood such as this.
Even their late dinner would be intimate as Frank brought in flowers
from outside and centered them on the table while his lovely wife
poured them two glasses of red wine. Lighting two candles, Frank
turned off the kitchen light before they sat down to enjoy their meal.

Upon their arrival, Jerry was tickled when he walked in the door
behind Liz and saw her handsome parents hugging her with joy. Evie
continued her greeting with a pleasant hug for Jerry. After a hearty
handshake Frank signed, "Beer after long drive!" Opening the refrigerator door he brought out two bottles of Budweiser handing them
to his daughter and her new husband. Liz laughed as she relayed her
dad's message to Jerry. Taking out two more bottles of beer, Frank
placed them on the table for his wife and himself to enjoy.

There was no room for awkwardness after this kind of intro-
duction. After some small talk about their two day trip; Frank and
Jerry unloaded their luggage from the station wagon. Without Liz to
interpret, the two men had no problem communicating with gestures
and facial expressions. At one point, Jerry pointed to his back with
a grimace on his face, and then pointed to his father-in-law's back,
changing his facial expression to look like he was asking a question.
Frank shook his head negatively and smiled back at Jerry.

When finished, Frank led Jerry into the garage to show off his new fishing pole. Then, he pointed to the car, then to Jerry, with a question on his face. Jerry replied with a frown, shaking his head, "No." He added a "Durn" by making that familiar gesture of twisting his fist downward. Both men were laughing as they returned to their spouses in the kitchen.

Their week was filled with fun and surprising ease of communication. Fishing and good meals were the highlights of their visit. Saying goodbye was beyond difficult but Evie and Frank were relieved to know that their daughter had married a good man. Even Liz was feeling better about her parents doing so well on their own. "You've heard said, 'After you visit home the first time, you will not be homesick again.' I'm inclined to believe that statement now," she exclaimed to her hubby. She only hoped that her parents would not be too lonely now that Bobby was gone too.

Evie checked her meat loaf in the oven and began to set the table for two. It had been only a few months since Bobby left for the Air Force and Liz had brought her new husband for a visit, but it seemed like years because the house was so quiet now. "Quiet" in the sense that there was no movement around the house. No one running through the hallway half naked in a hurry to go someplace. No one asking her to fix an early supper because he had to play ball at five o'clock. Evie sat down, turning on the news.

At least they had a television set now. Liz and her husband had brought theirs here as they were going overseas and could not take it with them. They had been married just one year when they were "shipped" out to Newfoundland. Evie and Frank had never even heard of that country; so they were relieved to find out it was just north of Canada and not that far at all. Liz and Jerry had acquired some furniture too but they had stored that in the Air Base storage unit. Liz said that the government did that for them free and whenever they returned to the states the Air Force would deliver all of their belongings to their new destination. Evie could not understand how they could actually look forward to moving around so often. Wait until they have children, she thought, they will not want to move so much then. I don't think they will even stay in the military like Liz says they will. Evie was disappointed that she and Frank had never gone down to Florida to visit them while Jerry was stationed there.

So much had happened in just this one year. Evie and Frank had been stunned when Liz decided to go to Florida with her good friends, Mae and Bud.

At the time, Liz had said it would just be for her two week vacation but after ten days she had written to say that she loved Fort Walton Beach and would look for a job there! Frank and Evie had both found that news tough to accept. Evie was trying to focus on the television. Her last thoughts were of Liz's wedding announcement. She couldn't seem to stay awake.

They had not even gone to their only daughter's wedding that took place in the Chapel of Eglin Air Force Base. Frank was working and could not take a vacation at that time. Oh, they could have taken a week off without pay but they could not afford that. Besides, it was still winter here in Wisconsin in March. Sometimes this month brought the worst blizzards of the year. They could not risk that. So, they had decided to stay home and sent them a wedding gift of one hundred dollars. They could purchase something they really needed with that money.

Slowly coming out of her nap, Evie's last thought was maybe this television we have now was bought with our wedding gift. How ironic! She jumped as she felt a tug on her shoulder. Frank was home and asking for dinner of course.

Jerry and Liz's Wedding (March 8, 1954)

9

Was It a Good Life After All?

Dearest Mother & Daddy,　　　　　　　　　　*September, 1954*

I love it here in Florida. I can understand now why Mae and Bud are enjoying their life here. It is really an easy one but I am not saying the fellas in the band are lazy. They have a lot of work in keeping their band organization in alignment with air force regulations. Each man has a job and Jerry loves his.

He is the liaison person between the band and the office that keeps their calendar schedule. He actually books (schedules) the band. Most of the time they are just going to another base and it is usually easy for him to arrange sleeping quarters on base. Or he may need to arrange transportation if the band is returning the same day.

Sometimes he is sent to another state to make arrangements for where the group will stay while they are entertaining because it is not a base. It is a city or town where they may be playing in a local parade or for the visit of an important person in the government.

But, now things will be changing for he and I. This is important news! Jerry received orders to go overseas! To Newfoundland. Have you ever heard of that? You can look on the map northeast of Canada. It will be a big change for Jerry because of the weather. For me it would just be cold like Wisconsin again.

Of course I'm not sure if I can even go with him. He says probably not right away. I will tell you more the next time

Frank, Evie & Liz

I write! Please don't worry about me. I knew Air Force life would be different before I even married Jerry.

Love, Liz

Evie laid the letter carefully on the table without reading it again. When Frank came home that evening, seeing the letter on the table waiting for him; he knew it must be important news from their daughter. The rest of that evening was spent comforting Evie and reassuring her that Newfoundland was not that far away and a safe place to live. Of course they found it on the map right away. Another letter came the very next day explaining that Liz would need to come home to live with them as there was no place for an Airman to bring his wife to live with him in that Newfoundland town. They did not have base housing for someone of Jerry's rank. So, Liz had come home to live and it was so good having her around again.

In fact, Liz thought she would stay here for the eighteen months that Jerry was to be based "overseas." She even found a job in a small bank in the bookkeeping department and life became a quiet routine of work and chats with her parents before bedtime. Liz's daddy comforted her some when he reminded her that many young men had gone to war when going "overseas" in years past.

Frank signed quietly as he tried to reassure her that Jerry would be alright. "Second world war, wife not know if husband come home alive!" He said she must be thankful that this was a time of peace and he was safe. Evie began to believe that it could become a permanent situation for Liz. Perhaps Jerry would like to live here in Wisconsin when his time was up. Surely Jerry would get out of the Air Force after this four year tour just as Bobby planned to do when his four years were done. However, this dream of Evie's soon ended as Jerry insisted that Liz come to Newfoundland!

After just two months, Jerry called one evening so excited he could barely speak. "Hon, I'm not the only airman who is pining for his wife! Four of us went out to visit this really sweet farmer in Stephenville, the small town just outside of this base. To make a long story short we found a place for several of us couples to live! Like I said, we talked to this farmer who owned an acreage that appeared to be rather poor. Somehow we convinced him to set up a park for trailer houses that we can bring in from the United States. It was a great opportunity to earn rent money on his land. So, we lost no time in ordering several trailer houses so that we can bring our wives here to join us!" Liz was floored! She couldn't believe her ears.

"Oh, no! I just started this job. I hate to let them down. But, don't worry, I will give them two weeks' notice. Is that alright?!" "Honey, this will take some money and time. Mr. Garner will need to put in plumbing and electricity first. We expect the trailers in a month. Then there's the setting up. I would say don't give your notice until two weeks from now. We will need every penny we can lay our hands on; for the down payment on the mobile home, you know. I doubt that either your folks or mine can help us out. Do you?

"In the meanwhile, we'll be figuring out just how we're going to get you here. Got all that?!" Jerry's excitement was still spilling over into his words so much that Liz wasn't sure if she understood it all but after their goodbyes she hung up the phone and plopped down on the couch. Her parents were looking at her anxiously, asking if she was alright.

Liz had related to Frank and Evie how Jerry had called one night a couple of weeks ago in tears and said he missed her so much that he got together with some of the other husbands there and devised a way in which they could bring their wives to be with them. Of course they were dismayed that Liz would be leaving after all; but they could see the excitement in her face and understood completely. However, they were not ready for her next remarks wherein she asked if it was at all possible that they could loan Jerry about $2,000.00 so he could buy a nice trailer house.

Frank and Evie looked at each other in utter dismay. Without hesitation, Frank signed to Evie that it would be impossible to do so. "You are old enough now, you understand the need to budget money and to have an emergency account in your savings. You know we love you, but we cannot help you out like that!" Seeing the tears in his daughter's eyes, he continued, "You must understand. I save for retirement some day." "Yes, yes, Dad, you are right. If we cannot do this on our own, then we will have to be patient and wait it out as long as necessary. It's okay. We will figure this out for ourselves."

With that, Liz gave both her parents a light kiss on the cheek and turned toward her bedroom. She would put this problem into God's hands.

Just a week later, Jerry called and said things were working out great. The Mobile Home Company had been thrilled to get an inquiry from these Air Force men. In gratitude for their service to their country, the company was willing to take whatever down payment each of them could afford. They worked out monthly payment plans that were satisfactory to all of them. "God must be happy with us right now, hon!" The plans were soon in place and the new adventure started.

Dearest Mother and Daddy,   *June, 1955*

Ohhh, my! We are taking pictures so that we can send them and you can see what a beautiful country this is! Newfoundland.. I will need to find the history of this country and see why they named it like it was found late ... ha.. Anyway, we have only seen a little of it so far and I will keep you apprised (informed) of what we find. Let me start at the beginning.

You remember I told you we were picking up another band wife, but I didn't tell you about the dog! Well, Helen lives in Michigan near Detroit. It was interesting seeing that part of our (Wisconsin) next door neighbor. Actually seems a lot like the Wisconsin countryside until you get near the city. Yet, we didn't have any problem following Helen's directions and found her home pretty easily.

We visited with her mother for just a few minutes while Jerry put the luggage into the station wagon. She offered us some lunch but Jerry was anxious to get on the road so we declined. Before I turned away, though, she whispered to me

that she was really glad to get rid of the dog. Without think-
ing, I said, "Oh, I bet!" Later I understood what she meant.

Helen is a pretty blonde, just twenty years young and fun.
She was good company on our trip. But, the dog was another
story! Of course I felt sorry for Rex (the dog) because he
did not belong to either Helen or us. Then we had our own
collie with us which didn't help the situation any. Rex is a
Doberman, really beautiful, but scary looking too! Ha!

His owners were both already in Newfoundland and he
brought the dog to Helen's two days before we got there. He
was nervous and would not settle down in the rear of the
wagon where Shalli had seemed comfortable before. After
four hours on the road we stopped at a small café close to a
motel where we spent the night.

After a walk with the dogs, I reminded Jerry that we
should talk about Rex's owners and he will feel more com-
fortable when he hears their names so that's what we did.
His ears would perk up when we said Jim and/or Jan and he
would look at us questioningly. We assured him that we were
taking him to see his "family" and he laid back down ready
for a good night's sleep. Daddy, you know dogs are smarter
than we give them credit for. Right?!

The next morning I offered Helen the passenger seat in
the front and brought Shalli into the back seat with me. That
way Rex had the whole rear of the wagon and settled down
right away. The rest of the trip went fine. Thank goodness!

Then we arrived at the port in Nova Scotia where we had
to get on a ferry to cross the waters to Newfoundland. Jerry
went to see about having the car go on board while Helen
and I watched the activity going on around the Ferry. The
dogs were to be crated and put down below. Rex was first to
go in his "kennel" and accepted surprisingly well.

But I was already shedding a couple of tears when a man
standing on deck called down to me, "Lady, is she a good
dog? Will she mind?" "Just like Lassie," she retorted with a

smile. *"I'm the Captain and would love to have her company in my cabin for the night! What do you say?"*

I couldn't believe it! He walked down the gangplank, took Shalli by her leash and walked her on board. I assured Shalli we would see her "after a while" (she always understood that). As it turned out we did see her in a short while. About an hour out, a little thunderstorm came up and I was afraid Shalli would be nervous, so I went for a walk until I found the Captain's cabin.

I knocked on the door and when he saw that it was me he placed his finger to his mouth to warn me not to say a word. Then he pointed to a far corner so that I could see that Shalli was sleeping on his bunk bed! Can you believe that? I quietly thanked him again and withdrew before she heard me. She was so lucky.

Jerry and I could neither one sleep in our small space and spent the whole night sitting at a table in their small dining room. I will remember that trip forever. Well, I will write you more after we are living here for a while. I miss you. I hope you don't miss me too much. Ha ha.

Love and Kisses,
Liz

Dearest Grandparents To-Be,   *August, 1956*

Yes, I am pregnant! Yes, you are going to be grandparents! Are you surprised? Are you happy? I sure hope so! Because God has blessed us and we are going to be a family!

Of course you wish that I lived closer so you could be with me when I have my first baby! I wish that could be true too.

The baby is due March 10th in the middle of cold Newfoundland winter weather! Not to worry! We only live two miles from the base hospital. It is a small place but they have new babies born there almost every day. Everyone says it is nice and clean with nurses and doctors who are in the

Air Force too. The good news is they are breaking ground for a new hospital. Maybe I will be one of the first to have a baby there. Maybe I will win a prize like people do when they have the first baby born in a new year. Ha.

We are not due to rotate back to the U.S. until the spring of '58 when the baby will be about a year old. However, Jerry said to tell you he may put me on a plane to come visit you when the baby is about three months old. That would be fun. We will talk about this as time moves forward.

For now, I want you to know I am happy and healthy. Please do not worry about me. I am not working now so I get plenty of rest. In fact, I am lazy!

I love you both so much,
Hugs and Kisses, Liz

After closing this letter a second time, Evie decided to answer positively. Now Liz was expecting her first baby! Again, Frank and Evie would not be participating in their only daughter's wonderful event. But they accepted these things as a part of their life pattern as deaf people. The world was a big place and it was hard for them to keep up with such movements as their children were making now. Evie wondered if hearing parents would feel the same way.

Dear Liz and Jerry,   *September, 1956*

Oh, My. We are so surprised that you expect our first grandchild born in other country! Wish you live close. We cannot drive to other country to be with you. But know not your fault. Not easy to plan when or where new baby born. It is disappointment we want to be there. True.

It is not disappointment that you are pregnant! That is wonderful news. You will be good mother.

You know I get this magazine named "Prevention" that has many interesting articles about our health. I found one today that reads about pregnancy. What to eat. How to exercise. You must talk to doctor about these things. I will also put some pages from this into this letter to you.

Please let me know if you have questions I can look in magazines for answers. I suppose you have friends who experience same as you so they can help you know things to do. I want to be your mother by mail. I want to be help if I can.

Your Daddy is so happy for you too. He says he wants to be a grandpa. Ha.

> *We will look for your mail all of the time.*
> *Love, Mother and Daddy*

Dear Mom and Dad,   *November, 1956*

Wow! We were so surprised that Bobby came to visit us! He sure looks neat in a uniform! That's what you said when he came home on leave after basic training. Of course he still looks like a boy to you and me. Ha. But he is twenty now and that's the age Jerry was when we were married.

I don't think Bobby even has a girlfriend though. Maybe you know something I don't know? Anyway, it was great to have him here for just one night. He had to go early this morning to catch his flight to Africa. It seems strange that his flight would come through Newfoundland to go to Africa, doesn't it? Bobby said it was strange to see me pregnant. I said what is stranger still is the fact that you, my parents, have never seen me pregnant.

But maybe next time (if there is a next time). Jerry says I should plan to fly home to see you after the baby is about three months old so you would see it before it is grown up! So maybe I will do that next summer. Would you like that?

Bobby was interested in how we live here. I introduced him to our landlord who is such a sweet man. He and his wife are good Catholics and have eight children. They live in a poor farmhouse and have only a potbelly stove in the kitchen for heat. But they all seem so happy and the kids are so well behaved.

Steve (landlord) has told Jerry and the other Airmen around here how happy he is that he can make money from this trailer court. He never thought of doing this until these men talked to him last summer. There are now fifteen trailer houses here so he charges rent money for the lots and is so good about keeping the grass cut and the snow plowed in the wintertime.

You remember that I told you how the men built rooms onto some of our trailers so that it would remain warmer in the wintertime. They decided to do that because of what happened with the water pipes one time. I wish I had taken a picture of Jerry. He had water frozen like icicles all over his face and shoulders. It wasn't funny to him but it was a funny sight to me.

We had been told that we must keep our water running a little bit all of the time. We even had a little note at both the sinks (kitchen and bathroom) telling us to keep water turned on. That was so it would not freeze under the trailer. Well, somebody, we don't really know who, turned it off. It could have been in another trailer near us because several of us are on the same water line and if one freezes they all freeze.

So Jerry went under the trailer to see if he could turn the pipe a little and get the water to flow again but he had no luck. What a mess Steve had to clean up then.

But he took care of it that next day. That's the kind of guy he is. We all like him very much. His wife is very quiet as are most of the women who live in this country. She is a good wife and mother.

You can imagine how she stays very busy taking care of all of those children. The children all seem so well behaved and help with all their chores. I never hear the woman yell at them. We American women don't know how lucky we are. We are all spoiled. Ha ha.

Well, that's the news for today. I'm feeling fine even though my tummy is getting bigger than a watermelon. The doctors tell me I am a very healthy pregnant woman. You know I see more than one doctor.

I mean I don't see the same doctor every month. We cannot ask to see a certain doctor. We simply write our names down on the list, sit down and wait. That upsets some of the girls but I say it is good. This way we can get the opinion of several doctors, not just one. I think that's an advantage. Anyway, my pregnancy is going fine. Bobby looks fine and we had a good visit so please do not worry about either one of us.

Love, Liz

The big day finally arrived. Evie could not wait to read this letter postmarked March 11th. Surely this would be an announcement of the arrival of Liz's first baby, our first grandchild, she thought. She tore the envelope open carefully, and then realizing she was actually afraid to read it until Frank came home, Evie closed the letter slowly and returned to her sewing. When Frank came home he always looked in the empty candy dish on the end table to see what was in the mail. Today he was tickled as always to see a letter from Liz. Evie brought him a cup of coffee as he settled into his blue wingback chair, opening the envelope and pulling out the single piece of paper. With Evie looking over his shoulder, they read:

Dear Mom and Dad, March 8, 1957 (Our 3rd Anniversary!)

Congratulations, Grandma and Grandpa!
Julie Lynn was born at 8:15 p.m. on March 5th. She weighs 7 lbs, 22 inches long and is beautiful. I can't wait for you to see her. We just got home from the hospital this morning. The baby is napping right now. Of course that is all she does is sleep and eat. Ha. We have her bassinet in the living room so that I can see her any time during the day.

Then tonight she will really be in her own room as we will not take her into our bedroom There is no room in there for the bassinet anyway. It will be good for her to have quiet. Do not worry though, she is close enough that I can hear her when she awakes during the night. I know she will need a diaper change and feeding. I can't wait until you see your first grandchild!

I know you won't feel like grandparents until we bring her to spend time with you.

And now for more good news! I will plan to come see you in June and stay for a couple of weeks. Jerry will come later. He wants to buy a car in Michigan and then come to Wisconsin.

And guess what? Then we want you to join us in a car trip to Tulsa to meet Jerry's family. That can be a fun trip!

Maybe we can even stop in Illinois and visit your brother, Karl and family. It's so great that Jerry gets a thirty day vacation each year. This will be a lot for you to think about now so I will close this letter. You let me know what you think of that plan. I am busy right now with diapers and formula but Jerry is a lot of help and the baby is good.

> *I love you both! Liz*

This was exciting to Evie. What fun it would be to take a trip with Liz and her husband and new baby! But she felt it would be impossible. Frank would not be able to get a vacation that long. Hmmm. How would they get home from Tulsa? If they stayed there a week and the trip took three days each way. It would be too long a vacation. But Evie couldn't stop feeling a little elated at the possibility and that Liz had invited them to do this. It was the first time that Evie could remember of anyone inviting them to join them for a trip. That just never happened. So she was still in a positive mood when Frank came home from work. She handed him Liz's letter with a smile on her face.

Frank couldn't stop looking at Evie's expression, one filled with happiness, an expression so rarely seen on her lovely face. Frank was happy himself. Life had treated him well; he had a good job with good people, he had a lovely wife who seemed to love him, he had good friends among the deaf people in Wausau and he loved his two children who were in good health. Now he was to become a grandfather! What else could a man ask for? Yet he continually sensed a deep sadness in Evie most of the time.

She was one who complained about her deafness and held it against the hearing people in her world. This was very obvious when her father died. Things had never been the same again with her sisters and brother, Ray. Frank didn't know if they just hadn't realized what deafness was like for their sister; or if they just chose to ignore it. Perhaps they believed that Evie was happy and naïve about the real world they lived in. Maybe it was something that Liz had said. Whatever the reason, they hadn't handled it very well after Evie's outburst at the reading of the will.

That day, so long ago, Evie had jumped into the car before anyone had even said goodbye. Since there could be no phone conversations she had to be satisfied with notes from her sisters apologizing for whatever they might have done to hurt her. Ray had written her a little stronger letter explaining how they had been taught since they were little to always treat Evie with special care as she was a "different" child. He stated that her sisters had always loved her and felt sorry for her because she was deaf. However, they had all watched her grow up into an independent woman. He admitted that they were very surprised that she found a good man to marry and she was now a woman who could bear children and take very good care of her family. Frank thought it was a good letter but he knew Evie could not be comforted.

But, that was then and this was today! A new day with new excitement on Evie's beautiful face. Whatever this letter brought today, Frank only hoped that the news was of something that would last for a long while. So, at this moment Frank felt warm all over just seeing the expression of happiness on his dear wife's face. "Read again!"

she signed excitedly. He laughed, reached over and kissed her on the cheek and remained in his chair to read the letter. When finished he realized what Evie must have been thinking.

Not that they were to be grandparents; but that she wanted to go on this trip with Liz and Jerry. Yet, how would Frank be able to take such an extended vacation? He only earned two weeks a year and they were asked not to take both weeks at one time unless it was an emergency. "Liz happy! Baby girl. We will see June here," he signed. "Yes, here," Evie continued to look at Frank with an anxious look. "Invited us with them Tulsa," she continued. "Nice. Wish," as she turned back to the kitchen where she was preparing their supper.

As she began to set the table Frank came over to sit down and gestured for Evie to sit down too. "Maybe. Maybe one week vacation." "Know," Evie replied. Later that evening as Evie joined Frank in the living room to watch the evening news, Frank smiled at Evie and said, "Idea me. Two days drive to Tulsa. Three days there. Train come home." "Ohhh! Idea! Good! "Evie signed as she contemplated his idea. The spark returned in her eyes and Frank said he would ask his boss about it the next day, then check on the train connections.

To Evie that was the longest day she could remember in a long time. She could hardly contain herself when Frank came home the next evening and grabbed her around the waist and signed, "Yes, we go with Liz and Jerry. Return train." She hugged her husband in a rare moment of emotion and kissed him on the side of his neck. Frank's heart warmed to his wife's show of happiness. She was so beautiful when she smiled and looked at him with love in her eyes. It was moments like this that made it all worthwhile. If he could only wipe away all bitterness from her personality they could be so happy.

Evie could not wait to sit down and write a letter to Liz accepting their invitation. Now that Liz was a mother, living so far away, and sharing her life in her letters, things seemed better with her daughter. She did not realize when it happened but thank goodness she had learned to love Liz over the years and felt close to her. Yet, her son was the one she had always loved with no reservation. She could hardly believe it. They were going on a real vacation. What fun that would be with the new baby too.

Frank was deep in thought because what Evie didn't know was that the National Association for the Deaf convention was to be held in St. Louis in June. Could that date be worked into their plans? Could they afford to include that in their trip? He would write to his friend in Wausau tomorrow and find out what week was scheduled for the convention. His friend was the President of the Wisconsin Association for the Deaf so he would receive this information. Frank often wondered why this kind of information would not be sent to him as Secretary of the group; but he never complained to Joe.

Evie still had her mind on her daughter. Oh, how she wished she could communicate her feelings better, both to Frank and to Liz. She wanted to share her own experience of her labor and hospital stay. Evie had been so frightened when she went into the hospital to have Bobby. The labor room seemed so big and cold with all those people in gowns and masks over their mouths and noses. She didn't have any idea what to expect from them but in the end they had been good people and helpful for the boy's delivery. There were some complications that Evie didn't understand. Months later her sister drew a picture of the fact that Bobby's bottom wanted to come out before his head. Then she knew why it took so much time for him to be born. Pointing her finger to the baby's head, Evie drew a curved line from there to the baby's little bottom and back in a circular motion over the top of the picture. This was to ask her sister if the baby had been turned around before he was born. Erma nodded her head profusely to say, "Yes, doctor turned baby around!"

Erma then displayed a relieved facial expression that indicated to Evie that the event had been a real ordeal. "Fortunate. Hurt not baby," Evie signed to Frank who was standing nearby. Frank nodded in agreement. Noting that these facts had not been communicated to them by the doctor or nurses; Frank continued signing, "Why tell us nothing hospital!" he exclaimed. He put his arm around Evie's shoulders and led her into the bedroom so they could discuss this further without interrupting the family who were enjoying the baby.

Evie stopped reflecting on her own problems and focused again on the visit from Liz and her baby. She had always been offended by the fact that Liz and Jerry had been married in Florida instead of here in her hometown. Did she think they could not afford to give her a nice wedding? Actually they could but it may have been a little problem convincing Frank. Evie's thoughts strayed to monies and how tight Frank was with their income. Even when she had gone to work those years at the Clothing Factory he had insisted that her money be placed into a savings account. She wanted to buy some pretty things for the house and maybe a new dress now and then but Frank had the money all budgeted and his budget could never be stretched to "buy fancy stuff not need."

Frank was a good man, a good husband and certainly a good worker. However, he just didn't know how to make Evie happy. Evie's mind wandered back to the time of Liz's birth. Evie had been frightened then too. Frightened about the pregnancy and then about the actual birth. She asked her sisters to tell her what to expect and they did so, but just in their limited way of communication. However, they lived in another state and were not available except through the handwritten language of a letter. Alice was the only one who could write words in a way that Evie would understand, but when she tried to explain what would happen at birth the words were just not there.

Evie could not understand. It was in her eighth month when Frank suggested she go to her mother's house to have the baby; Evie wasted no time in carrying out that plan. She was very much relieved to be in her mother's care again. In fact she acted completely like a child and allowed herself to become completely dependent upon her mother's every direction. She took morning walks around the neighborhood, afternoon naps in her old room, ate everything her mother put on the plate and retired when her mother said it was time for bed. Evie felt very relaxed until that wintry day when the labor pains began. Then and only then, did she begin to understand what her sister had been telling her to expect. There was no morning walk that day for two reasons; a blizzard had started during the night and her labor pains started early in the morning. Her mother told her to rest and that she had called the doctor who, in turn had contacted a midwife who lived in their town. She was on her way and would be here soon.

Evie wished Frank were there to hold her hand but he had already asked for his vacation time to be in two weeks and the weather would prevent him from driving now anyway. So it was that Alice, her mother and the midwife were in her room with a bucket of water and some towels. There was a bassinet in the corner awaiting the coming child. This bassinet had been in the family for years; in fact it held Evie as a baby when she was born down at the farm. Everyone was ready for this baby to come except Evie. The pains were close and sharp by sunset and she cried out with each contraction. Alice held her hand making signs that were to convey that Evie should relax between them.

Finally the big push came that she had been told about and the next thing she knew there was a wet sticky feeling on her legs and everyone around was smiling and crying at the same time. The midwife brought the baby around for Evie to see and showed her that it was a girl. Evie cried too and knew in her heart that Frank would be happy to have a girl.

But all she cared about right now was that the pain had stopped. Or so she thought. Her body had another contraction and pushed out something more! What was that? Another baby? No, she knew that was not possible. She tried to lift up her head to see what it was. What she did see was so ugly that she fainted.

She awoke again to find Alice standing next to her holding a wet cloth to Evie's head and smiling, signing a home sign that Evie knew to mean that everything was all right. She brought Evie a glass of water and propped her pillow up so that she could see the baby in the bassinet by her bedside. Evie pointed at the sleeping baby and signed "One?" Her mother and Alice looked at each other and could not understand why she asked that question but both looked back at Evie and nodded strongly, "Yes!" It wasn't until months later that she had a clear understanding of that second push. It was simply what they call "afterbirth."

Evie loved her baby daughter and took good care of her so there could be no question about a deaf woman raising her own baby. She had been told by some of the deaf club members in Wausau about another deaf couple who lost their baby because the father's parents had taken them to court. They claimed that a deaf mother could not take care of a baby or any child because they could not hear. The mother of the baby had no family so this set of grandparents sued to have full custody of the child. Evie couldn't believe what had happened in that family. It was so hard to fathom that anyone could be that cruel so as to take a baby away from his natural mother.

As the days became weeks and months Evie did have some second thoughts about her determination to be a good mother. It was not easy to keep an eye on the baby and still get her housework done to say nothing of her own physical needs. She found herself too busy to iron her cotton housedresses before wearing a clean one. Frank liked his shirts starched and the only way this would be done was to do one for him every day by leaving the ironing board standing in the dining room all of the time. The only time she had to take a hot bath was after putting the baby down to bed or under Frank's care. There never seemed to be time for a shampoo and her hair became straggly in need of a haircut. Oh, how she wished that her sisters or mother lived in this town instead of hundreds of miles away in another state! Indeed, it had not been easy learning to be a good mother, housekeeper and wife!

Frank offered for Evie to spend a month with her mother and have her teach Evie the necessary deeds to be done for a baby. But Evie declined. She was determined to raise her child without depending on a hearing person (hearie). By the time the baby was eight months old she had taught her signs for such things as milk, drink, mama, daddy, pain. It was amazing how quickly Liz caught on to her gestures. There were times Evie actually had fun trying to communicate something new to her baby. Time passed quickly as the baby learned to sit up, crawl, walk and then go to the door when she heard someone knocking or talking outside. It was a little difficult teaching Liz right from wrong but she rarely had to be scolded.

Frank was somewhat concerned about teaching Liz how to talk. He offered the same idea to Evie about visiting her mother for a few months when Liz was three years old. "Learn how teach Liz talk and behave." Again, Evie was determined to carry out her role as a mother without asking for help. Fortunately, Liz had been a good baby and a sweet little girl who seemed to recognize the needs her mother had. Liz had no problem facing Evie when she wanted to talk to her, always communicating what she wanted to say with signs and voice. It was Evie who had some difficulty communicating to her daughter what she had to say. It seemed impossible to convey her emotions whether they were of anger or love. Liz made herself known simply by running up to her mother and hugging her. She didn't have to say a word. However, Evie felt that it was not good for a grown-up to pass out hugs without a very good reason. Those good reasons rarely happened. Evie didn't know why she had such a hard time demonstrating her love for her daughter. Sometimes she was actually jealous of her own daughter. It was not only that Frank seemed to love her more than Evie; Liz could hear! She could talk! She could sing! Try as much as she could, she could not give in to simply loving and enjoying her daughter. She could not relax around her like Frank did. Yet Evie never talked to Frank or anyone about this.

Maybe that was why it was six years before Evie conceived again. However, this time, when Bobby was born, it seemed easier to love him. Little boys just need their mothers. He would come to her with a cut finger or a bloody nose and the very act of cleaning him up and wiping away his tears seemed to demand an immediate hug. He did not learn signs as quickly as Liz had but Evie tried not to dwell on such matters. She understood his gestures and knew how to take care of a small child now.

No one seemed to question her ability to be a good parent now so she relaxed in the role. The children always loved her cooking and baking. Both were good about keeping their rooms picked up and helping her with household chores. Both of them had found friends in the neighborhood to play with until their daddy came home from work. Then they would beg him to play with them before supper. Liz had always seemed happy.

10

Grandchildren Are Hearing Too?

*N*ow Liz was married and a mother herself! The day finally came when Evie and Frank drove down to the train station to meet their new granddaughter. It was a warm day but she certainly did not expect to see the baby half naked when Liz handed her to Evie to hold. "Baby cold?" she signed somewhat frantically. Upon closer look Evie realized that Liz had tears in her eyes and asked, "Wrong?"

"Tired! Long trip! Chicago hot!" Liz replied. She hugged her mother and dad and taking the child back into her arms again they all walked to the car. Frank was beaming from cheek to cheek and kissed the baby on her cheek as he held her while Liz entered the car. "Name again?" he asked as he handed her back to Liz. "I know! Julie. Beautiful," Frank smiled as he signed quickly before he turned and entered the driver's seat. Evie was already in the passenger seat still wondering why the baby was only half dressed and why Liz had been crying.

It seemed strange to Liz that Bobby was not here. He had joined the Air Force right after graduation. Yes, Liz missed Bobby being in the house. It was strange to have no one to really talk to. Again, she felt alone, unable to reveal fully the extent of her long day's travel. Liz mulled this over in her mind as she unpacked her suitcase and bathed the baby before dressing her in her nightclothes and preparing her supper. She was reminded of the times that she and Bobby would talk evenings about the events of the day until they noticed their mother watching them quietly. Now that she was older, Liz realized that when the two of them were chatting like that, Evie must have felt left out. Now that Bobby was not here perhaps she could relate more details to her mother and hope for some response.

Making this determination, she went on into the kitchen where Frank was already pouring some lemonade into three glasses, setting them on the table. It was impossible to carry on a conversation until she finished feeding the baby and held her over her shoulder for that final burp. During this time, Frank related some of the neighborhood news to Liz and all she could do was nod her head in acknowledgment. Evie started preparing supper for the three of them, stopping when she saw that the baby was asleep. Julie was so sweet when asleep.

Liz still could not believe she was a mother. Her mind drifted back to how frightened she was when she found out she was pregnant. She'd only been around Mae during her pregnancy without really paying attention to anything but her physical changes. Mae was a good mother, of course, but she had not really shared any of the details of taking care of a new baby. Now Liz was in a strange country miles from home; she had known there would be no one in her family there when the baby was born. More than that, she realized she knew nothing about babies. She'd not been around any of her friends or relatives when they had a baby to observe.

Liz never shared with her mother how worried she had been, nor did she ask her for any advice now. She wasn't sure why she felt this way but she knew down deep that miscommunication had something to do with it. By now, Liz realized she learned a lot by talking to other pregnant women as they waited to see the doctor. Well, so far things had gone well and here she was, learning day by day to be a good mother. So far, so good.

Suddenly Evie appeared beside her and motioned to Liz to follow her into the bedroom pointing to a crib in the corner of Liz's old bedroom. "Baby bed borrowed neighbor." Oh, thank goodness, Liz thought, as she carefully put the baby down on the soft sheet. Evie covered her with the baby quilt and since the house was nice and cool Liz did not say a word. She was so tired.

After a few sips of the lemonade, she proceeded to tell her family all the details of the trip and how she had been able to visit with Donna Mae in Chicago. Donna was an airline stewardess now for American Airlines, based out of Chicago. She just happened to be at home that weekend and had a neat apartment she shared with two other stewardesses. They were rarely all there at the same time so she had room for Liz to spend one night. It was a fun night but Liz admitted they had very little sleep. Then this morning it was so hot in Chicago that on the way to the airport in a taxicab, Liz had stripped the baby of everything but her diapers. She herself was *sweating bullets*.

This idiom brought a laugh from Frank but Evie didn't understand the explanation of that one at all. Most of the time when Bobby brought up idioms like that Evie just ignored them. But when Liz used one she always tried to get the meaning behind it. Liz was the same way when she saw her mother or dad or other deaf folks using a strange sign that was an idiom for them. Sometimes Liz would understand but she never thought it was funny. She decided the sense of humor of deaf folks was just not the same as that of hearing people. Finally Liz excused herself and retired to her room for the night. As she said her prayers she thanked God that she was able to enjoy an evening of silence completely absorbed in the language of signs.

Without anyone around to voice to, Liz felt closer to her mother than ever before. Of course she still spoke to the baby and sang to her as usual but tried to limit this to the times she was alone with her. This held true for the next seven days except for two visits that Liz made to show off her baby girl to some friends in town. These visits were fun and she relaxed as she chatted with them, catching up on the news of other friends she hadn't seen for some time. Her mother had chosen not to accompany her so no translation was necessary.

As she walked home from the second visit, Liz wondered why she even thought of the fact that she didn't have to translate. Did she actually resent doing that for her mother? Had she really loved the years in Newfoundland where she had met no deaf people to whom she needed to sign? No, she thought, she remembered how much she enjoyed signing with one salesman who happened by her door one day. It had been a real surprise to have someone come and try to sell her some sewing supplies by handing her a card with the American sign language alphabet printed on it. Of course he was equally amazed when Liz began to sign to him, "I know sign language. Do you understand me?" Liz had always asked that question of people when she met one peddling like this in the U.S. and they had immediately walked away. She had to assume that they did not understand her either because they were not a truly deaf person or because they were embarrassed. Once she had gone on and signed, "My dad deaf not like deaf peddlers. He knew deaf people can find work for pay." But this fellow, here in Canada, actually went on with a conversation in signs. He explained that his sign language was French and he knew very little English. He went to school in Canada and just decided he wanted to see what Newfoundland was like. It had been neat that day, meeting a deaf person, and using sign language for the first time in two years. So, in answering her own question, Liz decided she really loved signing.

Liz also reflected that she never had any problem signing with her mom when they were shopping or visiting her mother's doctor. But it was a real challenge to use her voice and her hands at the same time. Sometimes it was hard to understand her feelings about the language. It was just easier to do one or the other, speak with someone, or sign. Actually, when trying to do both simultaneously, it was not fair to one party or the other. With that she realized that sign language is really quite sophisticated because one can express a complete thought with just a couple of signs! Didn't that mean a savings in time? Wasn't that an important part of communication? Some day she might really study languages and the methods used in exchanging information, but not today.

Evie was hard to understand sometimes. She had been telling Liz a story about her father that Liz found hard to believe. Evie insisted that her father had written a special will to be read to just Evie whenever he died. She said he told her when she was young that he would always take care of her because she was deaf. "He knew I could never make a living earning a good income like my sisters and brothers would do. He probably didn't want a special bank account in my name because the people at the bank would think I could not handle money. You understand? People think deaf not know care money!"

Liz was appalled the first time Evie told her this story. It could not be true—could it?

If it was true did grandpa have a different lawyer handle a special will just for his deaf daughter? Did that lawyer just keep it quiet, realizing no one in the family would know about it? She tried to discuss this with her mother in a calm manner but Evie was so adamant! There were times when they had been shopping together and just out of habit, Liz would say, "I can't afford." Evie would sign, "When find my father's will, I rich, I help you."

Liz would try to explain that she didn't really need money! She and Jerry were comfortable. Their family's health was taken care of at their base clinic and hospital with no expense to them. They were able to buy groceries at their Commissary and everything else they needed at their Base Exchange. She did not need money. "I'm sorry, mother. I'm sorry no special will found. Grandpa loved you. Maybe lawyer cheat. But I want us to think about this carefully. Maybe grandpa only mean take care of you until you married. Long ago. Twenty years. Forget.. you must!"

Evie only stared at Liz in silence. If she could not convince her own daughter, how could she expect anyone else to believe her. Liz was truly the only hearing person who could communicate with her in her language. She was usually very clear in explaining and, or understanding what Evie was trying to say. Yet she didn't think her father only meant that he would be sure she was taken care of until she married someone who could support her. Who could she talk to that could look for a bank account for Violet Evelyn Hilke Niklaus. Who, indeed!

Liz's visit was coming to a close. The days had passed too quickly. As planned, Liz's husband drove into the driveway one day in a new station wagon. Evie had packed just one suitcase for Frank and herself with great anticipation. After packing everything into the back of the wagon they found a comfortable arrangement with Liz and Evie in the back seat with baby Julie and her belongings while Frank rode co-pilot in the front.

Their first stop was in Illinois where they spent one night and two days with Frank's brother Karl and his wife Emily. Their daughter was married to a friendly fellow who had learned quite a bit of sign language and was very comfortable with his in-laws already. Frank's widowed sister, Amanda, living nearby in Rockford, came over to visit for a few hours. They had not been together for over ten years when they had attended the Wisconsin Deaf Convention. Just like that had been a great time with old friends, this was a rare visit indeed; one that was enjoyed by all. Jerry did note that Liz seemed to tire easily but he knew the amount of energy she expended when she had to translate to him what all the deaf folks were saying and to share whatever he said with them in signs.

The same thing held true when they arrived in Tulsa and visited with Jerry's family. Liz did all she could to include everyone in the conversations. This was not often done simultaneously, but rather, consecutively. The result was sometimes confusing as Jerry and his folks would be onto another subject before Liz was caught up enough to be part of the continuing chit chat. She often asked him later in bed what was said by whom so that she could be sure she had not missed any important information.

Frank and Evie were truly grateful for their daughter's translations. They never felt left out. It was especially nice to get to know his parents. His dad was a bus driver in this large city and seemed to never run out of stories about some of his passengers. Brewer had a special knack for describing them, making them seem real to his listeners. Some were funny and some were sad. Evie loved Nannie and her cooking. They enjoyed Jerry's whole family.

His younger brother, Teddy, was a very special guy. He had been born with abnormally large legs and arms. Jerry told them that when Ted was born his mother was told that he would not live to be twelve but here he was getting along alright in his twenties. Evie could not imagine what a heartache that must have been for Nannie. Jerry's older brother, Don, lived in D.C. so they did not meet him. One sister lived out in California while the other sister lived here in Tulsa. She had the same name as Evie! They never called her Evie though, only Evelyn. When she and her hubby came to visit, they too, made Frank and Evie feel comfortable and relaxed. The highlight of the visit was when Jerry drove them all out to see the Will Rogers' Museum in Claremore. Frank learned a lot about the history of the West and vowed to read some books when he returned home.

After three days of pleasant visits, Frank and Evie were anxious to get on the train to go to the National Association of the Deaf convention in St. Louis. Liz helped them purchase their tickets and find comfortable seats aboard the train. She explained to the conductor that they were deaf so that if there was any special message to give them during their travel, they were to write them notes. After she was satisfied that the personnel understood about their special needs she kissed them both goodbye and got off the train. "Daughter good us," Frank signed to Evie as she wiped away the tears. She nodded in agreement and felt a real need to cuddle to her husband as the train moved away from the station. Frank pointed out the window and they both leaned close to see Liz, Jerry and baby Julie waving goodbye from the platform. Evie added, "Happy meet Jerry's family. Now know they good people."

The convention was held in a beautiful hotel and immediately after checking into their rooms they rode the elevator back to the lobby where they met many old friends and soon made new ones. The three days there went by in a whirl of fun chats, interesting meetings and finally, the Miss Deaf America pageant, Evie's favorite event of the whole week. There was a beautiful girl from Wisconsin who was one of the finalists. Evie had been told by the

Director of the pageant how difficult it was to entice young deaf ladies to enter their state pageants. They were often too shy but the state coordinators worked hard with them, teaching them how to walk, to present their talent and to answer questions with confidence. Evie couldn't help but wish that she had had that kind of opportunity when she was young.

This and many other happy thoughts stayed with Evie and Frank as they packed up to leave. They were too tired to sleep but the train ride home was smooth so they dozed off and on and saved their conversation until they arrived home. In what seemed a short while, the conductor came by with a note telling them that the next stop was their stop. Oh, my, it was good to arrive back home again.

Months later, Evie would still be telling her friends about that trip and showing pictures to her neighbors until they were obviously bored with them. The pictures were mostly of the new grandbaby which one neighbor never seemed to tire of looking through. Usually after everyone saw the landmarks and scenery of the trip that was enough. It was just so new to Evie to be the one showing the pictures and trying to communicate highlights of her vacation to her hearing neighbors. Until now it had always been them sharing pictures and vacations with her.

Every evening after supper dishes were finished, Frank and Evie would sit and look at the pictures, re-living the days of the visits in Illinois and Oklahoma. They both knew they would talk about this trip for a long while to come. It was almost necessary to go over the details of conversations together so that they felt completely sure of what had transpired. It was at times like this they realized how few friends they had. That is, friends that could communicate with them in their language of signs. But pictures conveyed a lot to them such as love, happiness and security.

Frank was so happy to have had the opportunity to see his brother and family near Chicago. It was an area of traffic on busy expressways in which he was hesitant to drive himself so it was great to have his son-in-law as the chauffeur. Liz didn't do badly either he mused, remembering how tough it had been to teach her to drive. Now she has driven all over the Northeastern States as well as Florida and Oklahoma. He was content that Liz had a good man and a healthy family and said so to his wife sitting across the room. "Yes," she nodded in agreement; "But live far! Two years what do, Liz husband? Blowing music horn life no good." Frank laughed as he wondered what Jerry would think if he knew his mother-in-law named his saxophone a music horn. He decided not to continue the conversation in a negative manner. He simply signed, "Wait – see." Looking at another picture of Jerry's parents in Oklahoma, he signed, "Good people. Hard workers same you, me. Jerry same. Not worry."

Dear Mother and Dad,　　　　　　　　　　　　　*October, 1957*

Well, I have some news for you! After our trip this summer and being busy with our new daughter, I really had not thought much about it but then I realized something was happening to me! I am pregnant again. Wow! It was three years after we were married before I became pregnant with Julie so I never thought I would get pregnant so fast again. Ha.

I went to the Doctor last Thursday and he confirmed what I suspected. I am in the fifth month now! I have felt so good all along with no morning sickness or anything. The Doctor says I am just fine and the baby is due the twentieth of February. It will be close to Julie's birthday! And it will be winter again. I hope this time we can get to the hospital easier than last time. Remember?

Our Henry J did not make it up the hill at the hospital so that I had to get out and walk with Jerry holding me so carefully. It was only about two blocks up that hill and around the curve to the door. Besides, it was good for me, as labor was increased! Ha ha.

The base now has a beautiful new hospital with a lovely decorated maternity ward. Also, our neighbor says when the time comes he will take us in his big Lincoln if there is a lot of snow, while his wife watches Julie. So, you see I will be safe.

Now I must tell you our other news. Jerry is due to be rotated back to the States in March. The doctor says we will need to wait until the baby is six weeks old before we can leave. This is for my sake. He says no new mother should travel before six weeks after the baby is born. Jerry does not know yet where we will go but he is trying to get Omaha, Nebraska.

That won't be far from Wisconsin or Oklahoma. You can drive there and see us anytime you want. So, you plan now about your vacation, Dad, for next summer. Of course we will have time to come to your house before we head to Omaha and spend a few days with you so you can get acquainted with Julie again and meet your new grandchild. A boy? I hope so!

Yes, you probably have wondered why we would like to go to Omaha. I told you before that we thought Jerry would get out of the Air Force when we leave Newfoundland. Change of plans. I hope you won't be upset with us but we have decided we really love Air Force life and will stay in it for a few years.

Maybe twenty or thirty years! It is a good life, really. There is free medical care. We will travel and see many places free. Most of the time we will get base housing with low cost rent. We can shop the BX for clothes and other household necessities, with food through the commissary at low prices. We have many friends and all are like family. Every year Jerry gets thirty days of vacation and we can visit you. Doesn't this sound good? I hope you will be happy for us!

Love, Liz

Frank folded the letter carefully, replacing it into the thin paper envelope. He looked at the Air Mail stamp and strange postal marks of another country, Canada. Evie was waiting patiently for Frank to sit down and discuss the newsy letter with her. She didn't realize that he had a hectic day at work with a lot of news to be typed before printing deadline. He tried to give her a kiss on the forehead as he stepped into the kitchen to pour a cup of coffee. Impatiently, Evie stepped ahead of him signing, "Liz pregnant again! Jerry Air Force stay!" Frank gestured for Evie to sit down at the table and brought her a glass of water. Sometimes he worried about his wife's blood pressure when she became overly excited or anxious. This was always his first concern.

"Minute, please. Coffee me." He stepped slowly to the counter where freshly perked coffee always awaited him. Only today the pot was cold. This news has really upset her, he thought as he rinsed out the pot, filled it up with cold water and reached for the canister and measuring spoon. He noticed the breakfast dishes still in the sink. She must have been unable to think of anything else since the mail came this morning. Plugging in the coffee pot he pulled down a cup and set it on the counter. Frank was trying to resolve the news in his own mind before beginning a discussion with Evie. There she was now standing beside him turning his head toward her and pulling his sleeve pointing to the other kitchen chair.

It was a long evening and already eight o'clock when they finished the dishes. Frank asked Evie to sit down in the living room with him and see if there was something fun to watch on television. Evie could not enjoy anything on the evening schedule. The drama shows were too difficult to follow and there were no cartoons to watch. But it was time for "I Love Lucy" and soon they were both laughing at the silly antics of Lucy and her friends. Sometimes Frank could actually lip read Lucy and her neighbors but never Desi! He would try to give the story line to Evie as best he could understand it to be. Yet they both agreed that the humor of hearing people was sometimes strange.

They probably would never have bought a television for themselves but when Jerry had his orders to go to Newfoundland, they had brought their television set to Wisconsin for Liz to enjoy while Jerry was gone. Then when they managed to have Liz go to Newfoundland too, they simply made the TV a gift to Frank and Evie. Of course the best of all the shows was that they could watch sports! Frank watched baseball every Saturday afternoon and Evie watched wrestling late at night. Frank couldn't get over the way that Evie loved wrestling! He thought of it as a "show," but she said it was real and the men were so mean! It was okay with Frank as he loved to see his wife really enjoying something even though it wasn't something he cared about. He would often go to bed while she stayed up all hours completely engrossed in the wrestling matches.

The next morning Evie only had one remark before Frank left for the Tribune. "Never see Liz pregnant! Two babies, never see pregnant!" Frank smiled and kissed her gently on the cheek. "Yes, true," he sighed. He could understand why this might be important to his wife, never having the opportunity to be with her daughter during the nine months she carried their grandchild. Somehow that was sad. Evie was so lovely. Even when she was in this strange mood her skin was flawless and her black hair soft and shiny as she leaned her head on his shoulder. She smelled like olive oil, her favorite way of treating her skin. Other men always told him what a beautiful wife he had. But they didn't know about her coldness and of course this was something he couldn't share with them or anyone. Sometimes he wondered what it would have been like to live with a woman like Molly who had shown such passion in the days of their youth. Frank never dwelled on such thoughts for long. His work and the energy expended to understand new vocabulary every day were enough to bring satisfaction to his middle-aged blood.

The following year went by faster than Evie thought it would. Just a few weeks ago the announcement came from Liz and Jerry. They had another healthy baby girl. Evie loved the name they gave her, Vicki Jo.

Dear Mother and Dad,   *March, 1958*

    Okay. We are packing our station wagon for our trip back to the good ol' US of A. We will drive to the train station and put the car on board. When we arrive to the port, we will board the same ferry that brought us to this country. I hope our dog will be treated the same way that she was when we came here. This time it will be a day time trip on the Ferry so we will look for a motel that night.

    We will start driving Monday morning so we hope to be at your place early Thursday. We will have at least a week with you. I bet we will want to sleep late that first day. Of course the baby will be hungry early in the mornings. She is so sweet and good. We will pack a bassinet and a crib into the station wagon. That should be fun. I will sit in the back seat with the girls. Okay, time to clean out the refrigerator and eat all the left overs for supper. Ha.

    I love you both. Cannot wait to be there for a nice visit.

Hugs, Liz

Liz came home with her family for a grand visit of ten days. It was so much fun having the little ones here. Frank enjoyed playing with little Julie, giving her rides on his knee, or on his back when he was down on all fours. How he wished he could hear her laughter even though he really had no idea what the sound would be like when anybody laughed. He would feel something vibrating in his own chest when he was happy or excited enough to open his mouth and laugh. Would he dare to ask Liz what laughter sounded like or would she think that to be a silly question. "Baby Julie laughs. Same sound me laugh?" he bravely signed to his daughter. At first Liz laughed but she quickly realized her father was asking a serious question. At the moment he had no laugh and barely had a smile on his face. He was actually turning his head away. Liz picked up Julie and tapped her father on his shoulder, gesturing for him to sit down.

"Oh, daddy! Please, wait. Put Julie down nap. Explain laugh." Jerry had driven her mother to the store and the baby was still sleeping when Liz put Julie in her bed.

Back in the den, Liz looked at her father in a different way. Her look almost frightened Frank. Had he said something so stupid that Liz had to have time to contain herself so she would not laugh at him in his face again?

"Daddy, I never think about you deaf. I mean I never think about what you not hear. It's ok. It's ok you ask me about sound of laughs. I stop think what sound of laugh. I know I am blessed able hear laughs. You happy me hear. Right?" Liz was not sure of her dad's facial expression this time, a mixture of love and fear. "Of course me happy you hear. I feel want you tell me what sounds laugh. Ok?" Frank signed slowly to his daughter. "Good. I love you daddy. Sounds like laughs are all different! Yes, each person different sound laugh! Miracle of God? Little voices mean small not loud not strong. Older child stronger voice and laugh. Adult stronger louder. Grandparents sometimes not strong or loud. But different from teenager. Baby Julie weaker, but soft and we call that *giggle*. Girls sometimes giggle, not laugh loud. Girls all ages.

Wow! Never me think about before! Laughs are different. Me hear man laugh in kitchen I know that Jerry's laugh, not Uncle Don's. Make sense to you, Daddy?" Liz was afraid she had been carried away in her own visions of sounds. Did she really explain this to her dad. Frank was quiet for a moment but his face was beaming. "I know! Like heavy log fall on ground make big vibrate! Chair fall on floor make small vibrate. Ball fall on floor make no vibrate. Right?" Liz thought about this for a minute and realizing it was probably the closest he could come to understanding her analogies, nodded a big yes. She walked over to his chair and gave him a big hug. With that, Frank took her hand and led her to the backyard where they sat in the lawn chairs to wait for Evie and Jerry to come home with the groceries.

It was obvious to Liz he did not want to hurt her feelings. No matter what she said about sounds, he would accept it. Liz was so happy that she could trust herself with him. It was not that easy with her mom. Evie made it pretty clear that she was disappointed to be deaf. In fact she seemed bitter about it at times. She had a tendency to say, "If me not deaf me could do that." Liz could not think of a comforting word to reply with because it seemed to her that Evie was right. There were things her mom could not do because she could not hear, such as using the telephone. The main problem, though, was she could not communicate. Yet, Frank could drive a car and seemed to communicate well through body language as well as the written word. Evie had told her that she was too nervous to drive. Liz knew her dad's job as a linotype operator gave him a lot more opportunity to master the English language.

One morning while lingering over a second cup of coffee with her mother in the kitchen, Liz asked Evie if it had been difficult for her when she had her first baby. "Was I a good baby? How did you know if I was crying? Was I okay with visitors? Julie sometimes seems frightened when she hears strange voices at the doorway. It's just for a minute and if the person comes in and talks to her she's fine. But if she has never seen that person before she cries until I take her. She's okay with friends though and now she goes right to you if you hold out your arms. I just wonder how it was for you when I was just a baby."

Evie looked at her daughter and smiled as she signed, "You good baby. But when company came you would not nap. Almost every Sunday afternoon someone visit. If hearing people, sit quiet with your big brown eyes wide open staring at them. Time nap you cry when I put you in crib until I brought you back out to living room with our visitors. I guess it was because you listen words from their mouths surprise but pleasant. Frank said let you enjoy our company because you quiet and good. That became habit through your first three years. I was truly jealous of attention you gave hearing friends. Now I realize it was natural and a good thing for you."

Liz sipped her coffee slowly as she absorbed that little communication. It was one of those rare times when she felt her mother truly loved her. Unsure of how to respond, Liz changed the subject.

"When Julie wakes up we will go and visit Mae and Bud for a couple of hours." Unfortunately, Evie was now jealous of Liz's time.

She couldn't seem to understand when Liz wanted to take the kids to go visit her old classmates. "Stay here talk with us. No time visit others," she would sign to Liz. "But good friends want see us. Just go two hours," Liz would reply as patiently as she could. Jerry was the lifesaver at those times. He would drag her out with the kids and off they would go, waving goodbye to grandma.

Jerry said Liz spoiled her mother. "How in the world can I spoil my mother? You must understand that she doesn't have friends like we do. She can't even talk to her next-door neighbor! She cannot pick up the phone and chat with her sister.

"It's so sad to me, Jerry!" Defending his statement, Jerry retorted, "I'm sorry, hon, but you do have your own family now and she shouldn't expect you to ignore your friends." This was one subject he hated to get into with his wife. He really did understand, but he also knew she could not let her mother dominate their time here. After all, didn't she realize how lucky they were to have this time at all? That was certainly something about Air Force life that was wonderful. Every time they had a move they got thirty days vacation in which to make the move. That gave them time to visit both their families before settling into their new home base. He knew it was hard on her though. "Sometimes I really feel guilty that I left home. Why did I go so far away? Do you think I was trying to get away from my mother?"

Liz's sadness was interrupted by Julie's crying. "Oh, mommy is alright, sweetie. We're almost there to see Auntie Mae. Her boys will make you laugh." They always enjoyed their visits, reminiscing about Air Force life, and finally playing a couple rounds of cards before calling it a night. Bud said he had never regretted getting out of the Air Force. He loved being a fireman. He acknowledged that he had always enjoyed the band. In fact, he continued playing his sax with a local polka band. If they were lucky enough to be in town on a Saturday night, Liz still loved to drag Jerry out to hear Bud play and dance a couple of polkas with someone. Jerry never had learned to polka but he enjoyed listening to the group. Mae and Bud had been good friends to Liz in her teen age days and to Jerry during their days with the Eglin A.F.B. Band in Florida. These visits were too rare now and they always found it hard to say their goodbyes.

Evenings were spent with the children until bedtime and then Frank would set up the card table and the adults would enjoy a game of Canasta or 500 Rummy until midnight. Evie loved to play cards but she was much too serious with the game. She wanted to be the winner and if she lost then woe to the person who happened to be her partner! Jerry got a kick out of it but Frank would tell Evie to calm down, it was just a card game. The week went by too fast for Frank and Evie but before their goodbyes plans were made for them to drive to Omaha, Jerry's new base assignment. At least this would be only a one day trip to visit them. Soon they made plans to drive to see Liz's new home in the fall.

When the leaves had fallen and been all raked up, Frank and Evie decided to keep those plans. They did make their visit to Omaha and found Liz and family to be happy in a little two bedroom house that they bought on the fringe of the city. It was called the "house of nines." It sold for just $9,000, a $99.00 down payment with monthly payments of only $199. In fact they had worked hard, painting the whole inside of the house themselves to save money on their down payment. But there had been one incident that wasn't good. Evie was somewhat shocked as Liz's story unfolded.

This event happened during the time of their painting project. One night they were completely worn out from the day's work. They put away their paint materials under the kitchen cabinet, latching them carefully, believing them to be safely out of the reach of the children. The next morning at dawn, Liz was awakened by screams coming from Vicki! When she opened her eyes she saw the youngest one covered with paint over her head and shoulders!

Liz picked up the screaming youngster and carried her to the bathtub where she turned the shower on her. To her great relief all the paint washed right off and Vicki had not even opened her eyes. She was fine. By this time Julie and her daddy had started scrubbing up the paint trail that led from the bedroom across the living room carpet into the kitchen where the can of paint lay on the floor.

They all laughed together but Julie was put into her crib for an hour to think about what she had done to her little sister. She was only three so it was difficult to be angry with her. Besides, Liz knew that it was her own fault for not taking the time to be sure the paint can was securely put in a safe place. As Liz related the story to Evie and Frank she signed over and over, "Fault mine. Fault Jerry!" Later they all learned to laugh about the incident since no one was hurt and nothing was permanently damaged.

Not long after that visit, a letter came unexpectedly from Liz that was quite short.

Dear Mom and Dad,   *June, 1958*

I have some sad news. Jerry's niece, Joyce, age 20, was killed in a car wreck Tuesday! It seems that she was on her way to pick up her brother, David, from his job at the grocery store. She was only a couple of blocks from home where there is a four way stop sign. It was clearly her turn to go on but as she did so another car came from the right without stopping and ran into her car hitting it so hard that she was thrown from the car. There was a woman witness to the whole accident and she called the ambulance. They tried to save her life at the hospital but it was too late. Isn't that sad?!

Joyce was Evelyn's only daughter and had just started nurse's training at the Hillcrest hospital there in Tulsa. Her brother, Dick was working at the time. He is an x-ray technician there and was the last person to speak to Joyce before she died. That was very difficult for him as you can imagine.

Jerry caught a military flight out from the base this morning and will be in Tulsa for the funeral Friday. His sister from California is flying in too so their whole family will help Evelyn through this sad time. We thought this was the best thing; just for Jerry to fly down by himself. He should be home sometime over the weekend depending upon when he can catch another flight out of Tinker A.F.B. over in Oklahoma City. He is so fortunate he can fly like that at no cost.

> *Keep the family in your prayers,*
> *Love, Liz*

Later that year, Liz surprised her parents by bringing her mother-in-law with her for a visit. Their road trip was so enjoyable as Nannie was easy to talk to and she entertained the girls, allowing Liz to keep focused on the road ahead. There were also times when Nannie drove and relieved Liz to hug her girls and rest as they napped.

Liz explained to her parents that a TDY means a temporary tour of duty. Sometimes the band was requested to play for some military function in another state and Jerry would be gone for a few days. This time he would be gone for a week so Liz thought it would be fun to bring Jerry's mother to her parents' home and let her learn about Liz's background just as her folks had been able to see what Jerry's home was like in Oklahoma.

Frank was sure glad that he and a co-worker had finished off the attic into two small bedrooms. Now they had grandchildren who could sleep upstairs allowing the adults to use the guestroom downstairs. They always enjoyed taking their company out to see the Rudolph Grotto and it's beautiful flower gardens just north of Wisconsin Rapids. Other sites to see were the cranberry marshes and Lake Wazeecha where the kids could swim while the adults fished. They could also tour the Nekoosa-Edwards or Consolidated paper mills of Wisconsin Rapids.

Of course we won't do that on a day when the wind is blowing the sulphur odors into the city! Oh, how Liz hated those days and was thankful they didn't occur often. In fact, it never did happen while they were here.

The week flew by and it was time to head back to Omaha. Their last evening together, Nannie asked Liz to be sure to tell her folks what good hosts they had been. Before she could say more, Liz interrupted her, saying, "Nannie. I want to try something. You look at my folks and tell them what you want to say. I will interpret your words. OK?" Nannie thought about it for a couple of minutes and said, "Sure. Let's try it."

Liz got her parents attention and noting that Nannie was, indeed, looking right at one and then the other; she began to sign what Nannie was saying. "I want to tell you both how much I have enjoyed my visit here. You have been wonderful hosts. Thank you for making such nice plans for us, for your good cooking Evie, and your efforts to communicate with me."

Everyone smiled at each other, then all eyes were on Liz. Deciding she would share her feelings with everyone, Liz simply asked, "What did you think of that? Instead of waiting for Nannie to tell me what she wanted to tell you and then me signing it to you; I signed the words immediately after she spoke them so you could be looking at each other and getting a true feeling of what was expressed by her… not me. Do I make any sense? What do you think about that?

"This way, you can get more of an idea what the person is feeling instead of accepting my interpretation of what they said." Of course, Liz was speaking out loud right now for Nannie and trying to sign in ASL simultaneously. She made a mental note of how difficult that had been too!

Immediately Frank said, "That is right. That is what happens at Club meetings. If we have a hearing speaker, we have a hearing interpreter who signs as the speaker speaks. That interpreter stands right next to, but a little behind, the speaker. We see the speaker's expression and yes, a truer sense of how the speaker feels." Evie just nodded in agreement with no added comment.

Nannie, however, was a bit confused. She arose from her chair, breaking eye contact from both Evie and Frank, and looking into Liz's bright brown eyes. Putting her hand on Liz's shoulder she said in low tones, "Wow, Liz, that's a lot of food for thought, especially for me! You'll just have to excuse me from this discussion. I'm tired and ready for bed. Hopefully, our plans are still to hit the road by 9:00 a.m. tomorrow?" And, with that, Liz turned to her parents and signed, "We really need now bed. Early leave morning! Girls now asleep so wake up 7:00 a.m. Good night." Stepping toward the bedroom, she looked back just long enough to see her parents both blow a kiss, signing "Nite!"

On their trip home a lot of conversation was centered around Liz as an interpreter, until Liz convinced Nannie that might be a career for her some day after the girls were older. She shifted the talk to Nannie and her family. Nan had met Brewer in Texas her home state, when he was in the Army. An Army nurse, no less. They married as soon as he got out of the Army and took a train to Tulsa, Oklahoma where they had heard there were jobs. Nannie was tall and thin then and was still tall and thin now, after giving birth to five children! Brewer was of average build and very good looking.

She learned a little about each of their children which were unique stories, each one. Of course Nannie had a lot of little stories to tell about Jerry's childhood which brought on a few laughs for both of them. Both of Jerry's sisters were married but neither brother had married yet. At this point, Liz really only cared about her mother and father-in law. They were both loving people and Liz felt blessed to have them in her life.

For some reason, Liz felt guilty at this point. Noting that the girls were asleep in the back seat, she said, "I need to tell you a story. It's really a confession of what a poor mother I am at times and I want to get it off of my chest. Okay?" Without waiting for an answer to her rhetorical question, Liz continued, "It's partly your fault too. You always make such darling little dresses for the girls that match. Right? Well, last April right after Easter I had an occasion to visit my neighbor's hometown with her. She has a girl a little older than Julie and she loves to play with her. Well, we were in this little town, just north of the city, enjoying a visit with Ruth's sister. The girls were playing out in the backyard with two of Ruth's nieces, all having a good time and all within view. All of a sudden, I realized I was seeing only one of those blue dresses you had sent them for Easter so I called out to Julie asking where Vicki was! She ran up to me and said, "Mommy, Vicki went for a walk all by herself down that way," pointing to the street.

Ruth's sister jumped up and yelled, "Oh, no! The highway is just two blocks up from our house. Come on, we all need to spread out and find that other blue dress just like the one Julie has on." At this point, Nan told Liz to pull over to the side of the road until her story was finished. She complied but keeping the motor running so the girls wouldn't wake up, Liz continued, "Well, let me tell you, I was scared to death. It was a good thing Ruth's sister stayed so cool and gave us all directions on where to look. I took Julie by the hand and headed toward the highway with my heart in my throat. After just one block I saw a patch of blue across the road moving along the highway toward oncoming traffic!

"Only there was no traffic. I didn't want to call out and cause Vicki to panic; so I asked Julie to stay with Ruth who was just one block to my right at the time. I crossed the road quickly and ran quietly up the highway. Just as I came within five feet of her, Vicki turned around and saw me. I quickly moved onto the grassy part of the shoulder, hoping she would be drawn into doing the same thing. It worked! She ran on the shoulder, back to my waiting arms. I picked her up and stepped further away from the road before collapsing onto the grass and burying my head in her sweet chest, bursting into tears! I thanked God right then and there.

"I waited until the next day before I explained to Vicki how dangerous that had been. I tried to sound a little angry, scolding her for leaving the backyard without telling me. I think she got the message, but at two years old it wasn't really her fault. Besides, the blame really falls on the pretty blue Easter dress!"

Nan took Liz into her arms and said soothingly, "Welcome to parenthood. I could tell you stories like that too. Like the time Jerry put his arm through the wringer of the wash machine. Unknown to me he was in the basement when I was outside hanging clothes on the clothesline. I should have noticed that he wasn't with me in the yard. I hope you feel better telling me your story. It's only by the grace of God that children grow into adulthood!"

Liz hated saying goodbye to her mother-in-law. They had shared other stories and the girls had grown to love their grandmother.

During their stay in Omaha, Liz decided to get an office job. They needed to start saving some monies if they wanted to get out of the military before twenty years. Everything seemed to work out for Liz to look for work. She had a good neighbor, Ruth, whose husband was in the Band with Jerry. She had mentioned more than once she would like to baby sit for some extra money. She was pregnant with her first baby so she told Liz she would come over to their home to watch the girls. This seemed like an ideal arrangement to Liz and Jerry so Liz began to scan the classified ads. Liz had office skills so she applied for a clerical position. She was hired in an insurance company office in the city.

It wasn't long until she was used to the routine of getting up early, kissing Jerry goodbye, feeding the girls their breakfast and dressing them before Ruth came over. After getting herself ready she would walk two blocks to a bus stop where she took the city bus to work.

She loved her job and was surprised that she didn't mind the routine of working and being a part-time mother. Of course there were times she would feel guilty when the girls would greet her with a cry of, "Oh, mommy, I'm glad you're home." And on some winter days she dreaded the trudge to and from the bus stop in deep snow. Then when Ruth had her baby, things changed just as Liz had feared it would. Her neighbor was not interested in babysitting anymore.

As it turned out, though, Liz didn't have to look for a way to quit working. After a year of this routine she was not disappointed when Jerry got orders to go overseas again. Secretly, Liz was thankful for a change. This routine was beginning to wear on her both physically and mentally. Jerry agreed with her reasoning adding that he was tired of the crazy weather conditions in Omaha.

This place had tornadoes in the summer and blizzards in the winter. Now they were to enjoy some beautiful weather in Guam!

Little did she know that Guam had its own kind of traumatic weather – typhoons.

11

Can a Quiet Life Be Good?

Dearest Mother and Daddy,   *September, 1961*

Please, try not to be upset because I have some news! Yes, we are moving again!

Jerry has received orders to go to Anderson AFB in Guam. This island is a possession of the U.S. and we have an Air force base as well as a large naval station there. We will miss Omaha because it is close to you, but we are tired of the weather here! Too many storms and tornadoes.

Guam will be like living in Florida again. I know we will enjoy the beautiful sunny weather and beaches of Guam. Mae and Bud were stationed there a few years ago. Mae said it will be easy living for me with the kids. They can wear the same clothes all year long as the weather is always warm. Interesting, though, there is a rain shower every day. She said we will get used to keeping our car windows shut even if the sun is shining. The showers are short and cause no problems.

We will have a better place to live in now than Mae and Bud did years ago. There is new base housing where we will live in a condo, three bedroom. It sounds so nice.

I should write you more but I'm really in a hurry as I must go on to work. I will give my notice to the boss to-day for one week. Then we will be busy packing things we want to go to storage. The Air Force will send people to do the packing and shipping and stuff to go to storage. I don't know the exact date we will leave yet but I think we

*will have time to come and see you for a few days before
we leave.*

Please don't be upset. We are happy.. really!

I love you both!

Liz

Evie could not believe her eyes. She was actually considering
tearing up the letter and pretend that they never received it. Frank
couldn't understand why Evie was so nervous when he got home
from work. Then she had to be honest and handed him the letter.
When Evie and Frank calmed down and actually talked about this
they were genuinely worried. A little island out in the middle of the
Pacific Ocean seemed like the end of the world to them. It must be
very dangerous out there in the middle of the ocean, in the middle
of nowhere!

Evie started to cry and her hands signed wildly to Frank, "If
my daddy would tell me where he put special will." "What?! What
mean?" Frank retorted. He could not imagine why she brought up that
subject again at this time. "If daddy gave me money I help Liz. She
come home. Leave husband. Not go strange island far away! If you
had money you could help her!" "Oh, my dear Evie," Frank signed
softly as he put his arm around her shoulders. "I wish you could believe what Liz told you. Your father just wanted to be sure you would
not go out into the world worried about how you would make money.
He didn't know if you could get a job. He didn't know if you would
marry. He just wanted you to feel the strength of your father's care for
you. I also wish you could believe in our Heavenly Father's care, His
love for you and me. We should not worry about our lives. We just do
the best we can and know that He will take care of us." Frank tried to
find the right words as he tried to reason with her.

Again, this was one of those times when Evie could think of
nothing but money. She honestly thought that Liz only stayed with
Jerry because she didn't have any money of her own. She could not
work with two little ones to take care of. So she took her family
with her to follow her soldier husband to other places. She honestly

thought Liz was unhappy. How could any woman be happy moving all over the world with children in tow?

As always, Evie waited anxiously for some word from her daughter to let them know they had made that long trip safely. Her first letter described the long hours in the airplane with a short stop on one of the Hawaiian Islands and Wake Island. She said it had taken twenty two hours but the weather had been good and it was not a bad flight. There were several other Air Force couples with families and some women without their husbands. Those husbands had gone on to Guam ahead of them but there were young Airmen aboard assigned to help these women who had children to watch.

Another letter came on the same day and continued with Liz's reaction to the island of Guam, itself:

Dearest Mom & Dad   *On Guam!*

Oh, my goodness, mother and daddy, I never realized what a change this would be for us. The first thing I noticed was a strange odor. It was a couple of days before I learned that this is an odor related to the humidity, because we are surrounded by the ocean waters and breezes that are sometimes cooling but most of the time just giving us a heavy warm humidity that almost feels like rain. They tell me we will get used to the smell and I think they are right as I can see a difference already.

The other thing that was strange is that the girls broke out in strange welts on the skin. We had to take them to the doctor and he said this happened with most of the children when they first came here. They were like boils and we had to break the yellow part, squeeze it out, and then cover them with tincture of violet. It was not as bad as it might sound to you when reading this.

After a few days they stopped appearing. The doctor said that their bodies have to get used to the different bacteria in the soil here. As they are playing outside they naturally get sweaty and dirty and the bacteria is in their skin before they come in and wash the dirt off. We adults don't have that happen to us at all. Isn't that interesting?

There is something else that has been new to all of us. There are little green lizards called geckos – cute little things about two inches long. They come into the house and crawl close to the ceiling eating little bugs or ants. They never bother people, so we are to consider that good.

Vicki is the only one who was frightened by them so much that she would wake up during the night and run to our bed crying that there was a gecko in her room. We learned to refer to them as our friends and protectors because they eat the little bugs that would bother us. She finally stopped crying when she saw one!

So, now we have a game to see who sees the most geckos in one day. Actually I can pick them up and throw them outside and they don't hurt me in any way. So, when they are bigger than two inches I do throw them out. All our neighbors do the same.

I'm enclosing some pictures I took of the girls playing with the little girl who lives in the other end of our condo. They love splashing in the little swimming pool we bought at the BX the first time we shopped there.

We have a great Commissary, Base Exchange, and Club. We have dinner once a week at the Club and play Bingo afterwards. We're also learning how to play Bridge with some friends of ours. That is a good card game but it's not easy to remember the rules. Ha. So, you see, we live a good life here. An easy life for me!

The girls love to go to the beach so we wives take turns taking our husband to work so we can have a car to drive down to the beach. This is really an easy life, I almost feel lazy; but it's so good to stay home with the girls.

I'm even trying to sew again. Jerry's mom sews dresses for the girls for their birthdays and Christmas and I can see how simple they are put together; so I am trying to learn how to read a pattern. Wish me luck! I'll also learn how to sew a loose dress for myself that is called a muu-muu. There is a lot of Hawaiian print material from which other wives here are making beautiful dresses like that. These dresses are so cool in this hot climate as they just hang loose from the body, like a bathrobe but cooler material.

I'm tired. Will write again soon, I promise! Love, Liz

A few weeks later another letter from Liz held a big surprise! She was pregnant again! "Oh, Frank!" Evie signed wearily that evening. "Again I won't see Liz pregnant! Another baby! Living on an island! Jerry's fault! He should know better!" Frank smiled to himself to see his wife so upset and blaming it on Liz's husband! Actually he was a little taken aback himself. It really was hard to imagine that Liz will have a third child to be born so very far from home. Liz is really a strong young lady and I will pray that her pregnancy goes as well as her others did, that a healthy baby will be born and that all will be well with her whole family! Frank knew that God listens to prayers, but he could never seem to convince Evie of that. Turning to her now, he signed softly, "I understand you feel worried. I'm surprised same. But she says sun shines every day, she is happy stay home children."

"I don't believe her. She not want you, me worry. I thought no more children. Liz thirty-one old!" Evie s blue eyes flashed a deeper blue as she forced herself to look at her husband. "Oh, I know! Jerry wants boy! Selfish! No brother with child. Want grandson, Powell name. Yes, Jerry's fault! You see? You men all same! Want boy, play ball. You disappointed Bobby not play ball pro! Now maybe grandson do!" Evie walked out of the room on that note not watching for Frank's reply.

"And, And, And," Evie had turned around and come back to face Frank up-close. "And did you see the pictures?!" she signed vehemently. "Little black girl in same pool water with our grandchildren!" Frank could not believe how angry Evie looked as she turned again heading for the bedroom. He picked up Liz's envelope and reached in for the snapshots. All he could think of, however, was Evie's outburst. He needed to calm her down.

Frank knew better than to follow Evie into the bedroom. She believed every word she said and there was no way to convince her otherwise. He may as well sit down and enjoy the pictures of his sweet granddaughters. Without really dwelling on the little black girl, he simply said a quick prayer for their health and happiness. After an internal debate on whether to discuss this with Evie right now, he opted to postpone that until after dinner. Instead, he grabbed the newspaper and tried to take an interest in the very words he had typed just that morning. But his mind stayed tuned in to his beautiful wife who literally was upset beyond consoling. This time his prayer was for her.

Evie was so thankful for another family event to distract her from Liz and that tiny island she lived on now. Bobby was getting married this spring! Frank was happy about it too. Bobby had brought his girlfriend home just a little over a year ago and Evie had liked her instantly. This was mostly because Jo had gone to the trouble to learn some sign language before coming, some signs and all of the alphabet. Furthermore she tried to use signs and gestures when talking to Evie and/or Frank if Bobby wasn't around. Evie was most pleased with her and told Bobby so. So, it was not a complete surprise to them when they announced their engagement and planned a spring wedding. Of course the wedding was to be in Jo's hometown, Oshkosh, Wisconsin.

Evie and Frank were pleasantly surprised that some of their nieces and nephews had come to the wedding. They were so proud to introduce their lovely new daughter-in-law when they arrived.

The reception was the highlight of the day for Evie. When invited to dance she was confident that her partners had been impressed with her charm and grace as she followed their steps around the ballroom. Frank knew that they would be talking about this day for a long time to come.

Dearest Mother and Dad,   *February, 1962*

Our new healthy baby girl was born on January 25th at the Agana Heights Naval Hospital. "We named her Marcia Lee. Have you noticed how we have given all the girls middle names that could be boys? We think it's clever and I told Jerry that if he wants to think they are boys he can call them by their middle names; Lynn, Jo, and Lee. Do you like their names? You never say what you think of the names we have chosen. Julie and Vicki like her name and they really do love their new baby sister.

Yes, of course we are disappointed not to have a boy but we are so thankful to have healthy girls and I have had no problems giving birth or even taking care of them. Jerry and I thank God every day for our girls and for our good life.

Oh, I must tell you what happened just the weekend before Marci was born. We decided to go on out to the NCO Club for dinner and Bingo. We were a little late getting there but we knew we could go in to Bingo anytime we wanted. The dining room is at one end of the building and the tables for Bingo are at the other end. While we were eating our dinner we heard a terrible loud crashing sound which I thought was a plane crash or something like that.

A military policeman came in and asked us to all line up and leave the building quickly but orderly. Jerry took my arm and when people saw that I was pregnant they let us out in front of everybody! Well, as it turned out the big glass ball had fallen from the ceiling bringing a lot of the roof down with it right over the tables where people were playing Bingo. The ball is huge, probably four foot in diameter and was all made of glass. It was a decoration as all the glass pieces would reflect all the colors in the room.

It just so happened that the airman who was sitting on the stage, calling Bingo, saw that the ball was swaying and he called out to everyone to get under their table as fast as they could and to not look up. He said it loud and clear and thank God, everyone did just as he said. Some people were still cut badly by the flying glass and debris.

Also, one woman had a heart attack and all were taken to the hospital by ambulance. How grateful to God I am that we had not gone into the Bingo hall yet. I would have found it impossible to jump under the table quickly in my condition!

Can you believe it?!

It has been an exciting couple of months. I must close now and get the baby ready for bed.

I hope you are both doing well. Please write and tell me all about Bobby's wedding. I hope there will be some pic-tures too.

Love and hugs, Liz

In the letters that followed, Evie realized that Liz was writing more often than before and assumed it was because she was not working and was staying at home with her girls. She always includ-ed some anecdote involving the girls.

Poor little Julie had gone down a slide on her tummy, landing just right to suffer a broken collar bone. Another time Liz described how Vicki loved olives and Liz had made the mistake of keeping an opened can of olives with a loose lid on it. It was on a low shelf in the refrigerator. Vicki managed to take the can out of the frig with-out spilling it but when she stuck her fingers in to get an olive she cut her thumb on the lid. "We both learned a lesson on that one. I won't put open cans in the refrigerator anymore! From now on Vicki will ask me when she wants something from the fridge!" Liz wrote.

Frank tried to keep his wife's mind off of their daughter's sit-uation. They became busy with plans for two events. One was his sister's fiftieth anniversary celebration in Minnesota. This was to be before Bobby's wedding. At first Evie didn't want to go to the anni-versary party but in the end Frank won that argument. It was just a two hour drive to his sister's home where they were invited to spend the night. The celebration was held in the church that his sister and hubby attended. Ida and Henry were proud to introduce Frank and Evie to their many friends. Frank was thrilled to visit with his brother William and his sisters Anna and Amanda. Of course it was good to be able to communicate in sign language with Amanda. Frank and Evie were so happy to catch up with all of her family news plus that of Karl and his family who lived near Amanda in Illinois. The time went by so fast that even Evie was not ready to go back home. Frank had only taken a few days' vacation time though so they had no choice.

Now the days were full of plans for Bobby's wedding. Evie was so excited for their son's wedding. The time had arrived for their rehearsal dinner. Since Evie and Frank really knew nothing about the restaurants in Jo's home town; they let Bobby and Jo choose one for themselves. It was a very attractive place and everyone seemed appropriately impressed. Frank was a bit shook up, however, when he received the bill. Bobby told him to be sure to add ten percent as a tip for the waiters. When Evie insisted on seeing the receipt, Frank pulled her aside and before showing it to her, he signed "Remember, we only do this one time in our lives! Please do not get upset!" Evie had to hold on to Frank's arm as she scanned the receipt. To Frank's amazement, she simply smiled and walked away.

The wedding day was just a little chilly but the sun was shining brightly as though God was giving his stamp of approval for this union. The church was quite beautiful. Jo's long white satin gown was gorgeous. Evie wished Liz were here to see the dress and her handsome brother in his tux. Frank and Evie both missed Liz more than they thought they would. Especially that evening when everyone helped clear the dining room after their lovely dinner; and the dance began. Frank was picturing Jerry as one of the sax players in the little band that Jo's parents had hired.

All in all, this early day in December would be a day long remembered by the Niklaus family. Evie wrote a long letter the very next day giving Liz every detail of Bobby's wedding day. Liz had never had a chance to get to know Jo well yet; hopefully, they could all get together for a long visit when Liz returned from Guam.

Some letters were full of exciting things happening on that tiny island of Guam. Well, they seemed to be exciting things to Liz but to Evie they seemed dangerous. Especially in the light of the fact that Frank brought home news of the events surrounding the area called the Bay of Pigs. Frank had tried to explain the politics of the day but it was a bit over Evie's mind and she preferred not to think about it because it brought immediate fear for Liz's safety.

Then it happened! No, there were no submarines in the area of Guam but there was a bad storm. In the Atlantic Ocean it was called a typhoon as opposed to the hurricanes that hit the East coast of the U.S. Guam was in the immediate path of this particular typhoon and it was a long time before they heard from Liz directly through the mail. Frank had related their concerns to his fellow workers and was surprised to see a story actually printed in the newspaper about Liz and her family being stationed on that little island.

The news was encouraging in that some information had come through that the Americans of the Air Force base and Naval station were safe. However, there was no electricity left on the island. Evie and Frank had no idea what kind of suffering their children may be going through until their letter came two weeks later. During those two weeks they prayed together as they had never done before.

Evie knew that Frank prayed and read the Bible almost daily but she had been reluctant to join him until now. When the red, white and blue envelope came in the mail that day she handled it gingerly and set it on the kitchen table without opening it. She wanted to wait until Frank came home so they could read it together. As she finished her chores around the house she would pass by the table and stare at the familiar handwriting with the words, Mr. And Mrs. Frank Niklaus and their address clearly printed beneath. This clearly showed that Liz had written this so Evie felt good that this would certainly mean Liz was well. At this point she picked up the letter and began to open it but returned it to the table quickly. It would be just one more hour before Frank came home from work.

Frank was beside himself with joy when he entered the kitchen and saw the letter. Evie wished she would see that look on his face more often. She knew he was a good man. He worked hard and always came home right after work. He had been faithful all their married life and always a good father to their two children. She knew she was lucky to have this man. She did love him and yet it was difficult for her to show him her true feelings. Today, though, she gave him a big hug and sat down beside him so that they could read the news together. Frank noted that the postmark was ten days ago, November 20th, 1962. Then, opening the letter he saw:

Hello! Dear Mom... Hello, Dear Daddy, November 14, 1962

> *We are still on Guam. It is now three days after that terrible typhoon hit this little island. I'm sure Daddy read about it in the news while he was at work. Typhoon Karen.*
>
> *I wish there had been some way we could have telephoned or sent you a telegram but that communication had very limited accessibility. Only priority calls could be made. So, they assured us that the mail would go out as soon as possible and to be sure to write our families right away.*
>
> *We are all fine! Really! Please do not worry about us.*

At this point, Evie saw tears in her dear husband's eyes and she hugged him again.

"Good. Family, all, okay," she signed softly to him. "Yes, seems true," Frank signed before returning to the letter.

> *It was very scary though! I'll be honest with you. I'm going to write some into this letter but will write again soon with more information.*
>
> *Some folks are leaving here because they were due to rotate (return to the states) before the end of this year anyway. We will stay until the end of our tour that is next spring. But, as I said, we are fine. Our home is still intact. No real damage. On one side of the duplex all the windows are blown out. Those were not what you think of as normal windows.*

They were made of thick glass and are about four feet above the floor. If you get out the pictures we sent you, you can see that the first four feet is made up of aluminum louvers. We just open and close those for sunshine during the day or keep them closed against the rain.

Amazingly, they are still working fine. So, the two bedrooms and bathroom lost their upper glass windows. The wind actually threw blades of grass and flowers into the walls opposite the windows! It was as though someone had a bow and shot long strips of grass, weeds and leaves straight as an arrow into the wood wall! That is hard for you to imagine, I know, but we will send pictures later.

When the base alerted us about the approaching storm we pushed all the furniture up against walls and pulled our own stuff like the TV into the hallway. Amazingly, all of that is just fine. The base furniture that we have is really quite beautiful. The rattan chairs and the couch all with the colorful cushions and the dining room table and chairs of the same materials are all good strong furniture.

Even the beds smell okay but we had to take all the mattresses and cushions outside for a day in the sunshine. They are fine now too.

The very first thing we were instructed to do was fill the bathtub with water. That was November 11th.

Anyway, that day all five of us were in our master bedroom because the radio told us that the southwest corner of our homes was the safest place to be. It was early evening.

When we lost radio contact we all lay on the bed and listened to the storm approaching. I put my arms over the baby and Jerry stayed close to the girls as we rode out the storm. We felt the vibration from the wind and it was much like riding on a train.

Actually, the girls were very good. They were concerned for each other and the baby. Marci was crying as though frightened so I made myself relax to help her feel more secure. We all said a prayer together and huddled even closer to the middle of the bed.

Despite the noise of the wind and debris hitting the bedroom windows behind us, Marci fell asleep and soon after that Vicki and Julie calmed down, shutting their eyes and quit talking altogether. I must have fallen asleep myself because the next thing I knew the sun was shining between the shutters, waking us all up.

I actually thought this might be the "eye" of the storm which means that the wind will come from the other direction soon. Jerry did not think so but told us all to stay on the bed as he tested out the water on the floor. I couldn't believe that this silence would be permanent. But it was; the storm was over! There were about two inches of water throughout the house but after we opened the two outside doors it all ran out slowly.

Jerry and I both took turns mopping the floor for about an hour and laid towels down to walk on. Thankfully all of our clothes were dry in drawers and closets and all that had to be done later was to change the sheets on the beds. We ventured outside to see if folks were okay and found them to be doing the same thing.

The first thing we focused on was the jungle behind our home. It was completely stripped of leaves with nothing but dark branches drooping, like ghosts staring, pleading with us to dry them off so they could smile at the sun again. Unfortunately there was nothing we could do for them.

But, we could smile and the girls were soon outside laughing and reporting to us their discoveries found in the yard. We had warned them not to pick anything up until we checked it out to be sure it was safe and not sharp or overly dirty to be handled. They were soon tired of this "game" as it turned out to be mostly debris from roofs or trees.

They wanted a challenge! Jerry turned the swing set upright again and they enjoyed that while we checked out our food situation and put together some breakfast.

Of course breakfast was cold cereal with milk that was still cool even though the electricity was out. Just as Jerry decided he would see if he could drive to the base, a truck came by with a loudspeaker announcing that no one should try to drive to work as the streets were filled with debris.

They were cleaning up the streets as fast as possible and would come back and let us know when people could begin traveling out of the housing addition. Then another big flatbed truck came by with some fellows from the band on it. Stopping by our house they called to Jerry to bring his sax and climb on board. Jerry asked me if I would be okay and of course I said it would be fine. So for the next two hours the band played some music up and down the streets to cheer everyone up.

After that the announcement was that the streets were cleared but we should tend to things at home. We should share our food with our neighbors as it would spoil in the refrigerator. They really thought our electricity might be out for a week.

Actually we had a good time sharing our stories. Some of us had grills and charcoal so we set them up outside on the patio and got together for our meals, sharing our meats and fixing our vegetables. We had long neighborly chats into the night until it got dark.

Then with flashlights, we all went to bed. The only problem we had was fixing Marci's formula. I had to boil water on the grill and mix it with the powder formula. I even began using some of the old cloth diapers I had; hung them out to dry after washing by hand. But we are fine. Jerry can drive to the Commissary tomorrow as he heard that they are well stocked again. So, please don't worry about us and we will write again soon. You know we can't get too many pages into this special Airmail thin envelope.

The girls send hugs,
Jerry and I send love, Liz

Evie and Frank looked at each other and hugged again. What a relief and yet what a dangerous time their daughter had been through. Why, oh why did they like Air Force life so well? How can she say that strangers are like a family? I hope when they leave there Jerry will decide to get out of the service forever! But Frank held in his heart real joy for his daughter. It was wonderful that she was able to travel and see the world with no real expense to herself or her family. Yet, it seemed to Evie that Mae and Bud were wise to get out of the Air Force when they did.

Frank had always liked Bud for his friendly smile and gestures toward him and Evie. He remembered that Bud was a fireman now with the Wisconsin Rapids Fire Department and also worked for his father laying cement driveways. They seemed to be doing fine with their three boys. Mae was working in the Produce Department of the new grocery store and Evie would stop, shop for a few things and write notes with her when she could.

Evie always carried notepads in her purse just like Frank carried them in his pocket. During this particular visit, she was surprised when Mae wrote her a note to say that she and Bud had been on Guam for three years when they were still in the Air Force. She said it sure had been fun, beautiful weather, lovely beaches and easy living. They lived in a small house off base and watched the new base housing developing just when it was time for them to rotate back home. "Liz was lucky to move into the nice cement block home safe through storm," Mae wrote to Evie. But Evie wasn't so sure that Liz was lucky at all. She wished that Mae knew sign language so she could tell her more about her experiences on that island. But of course this was not the time or place to do that. Customers were asking Mae for help, so Evie stepped aside. However, she nodded and smiled as she tucked the note back in her purse so that she could show it to Frank later.

True to her promise, Liz wrote letters regularly keeping her parents informed about their daily activities and general good health. She described the recovery of the whole island after the typhoon had left so much damage. Frank was surprised like Evie to learn that the island was only thirteen miles long and six miles wide with the

Agana Heights Naval Station at the very opposite end of the island as the Air Force Base. The two lane roads were good enough so that Liz and Jerry had joined a bowling league in the only bowling alley in town. Also, the kids could enjoy a ride out in the country once in a while and especially loved to go down to Tarague Beach. It would have been too far to walk there. Reading this in the letter, Evie could not imagine such a sight even when she looked at Liz's pictures of their two girls playing in the sand beside the ocean waters. Liz included a few interesting notes about that beautiful beach.

They couldn't help but remember the stories about these cliffs at the side of the beach. The story was that during WWII at least two Japanese soldiers had made their "home" in the cliff caves for years, not knowing that the war was over! It was eerie to think that they had looked down upon many American families spending time on this beach for years without realizing that the war was long over and they were living in peace now. Liz couldn't remember how that story ended but Jerry thought they had turned themselves in because they were starving.

Frank stopped reading the letter and mused how good it was of the government to allow the kids to take their car overseas even though they knew it would probably be left behind because of the rust. Liz had written that Jerry had the whole body painted with that orange stuff to keep it from rusting. However, as time approached for them to rotate back to the states he had already decided to sell it to one of his buddies who had another year on the island. Then he ordered a new station wagon to be waiting for them when they got to California where his sister lived. They were due to leave Guam on Memorial Day, meaning they would get to enjoy two Memorial Days because they crossed the dateline. Evie and Frank could hardly contain their excitement and anticipation as they began counting the days until their arrival back home. "Home not with us, natural, know!" Frank signed sadly to Evie. "But after they drive from California to Oklahoma they come here before go to Washington, D.C.!" "Never imagine our daughter travel much! Difficult believe," Evie replied, shaking her graying curly head in surprise.

Indeed, it was a weird experience for this young sergeant's family, celebrating two days of the same holiday. But the real experience was riding on a jet airliner instead of the military prop plane they had come to the island on. What a joy! Liz couldn't help but reflect back to their trip. Coming over here had taken them twenty-two hours and now they would be back in California in less than half that time. They landed in Hawaii and got off of the plane just long enough to look around the airport and enjoy a cup of coffee in the restaurant. The girls really could not remember being here before and Liz realized how everything would be so new to them when they started their drive across the United States.

Julie had just finished Kindergarten and Vicki would start school in D.C. Liz would probably be transporting everyone to work and school and she hadn't even driven in any real traffic for three years. Jerry would be driving on this trip on highways and in city traffic for the same length of time but always said, "When you learn how to ride a bicycle, and don't ride one for years, it will automatically come back to you." Liz had to shake it off and remember to be thankful they would be home soon! Their close friends from the band had already rotated to D.C. ahead of them and found an apartment for them to rent starting the first of July.

Jerry will go to school at the local base there for one year and then we will be moving again. This brought her out of her reverie as she turned to Jerry to say, "I didn't tell mom and dad about that because I just don't want to worry them with more information than they need right now." "About what, hon?" Jerry asked. "Oh, I was just thinking about how we're only going to be in D. C. for one year and then we don't know where we will be going." "Well, if it makes you feel any better, I'm pretty darn sure they won't be sending us overseas again," Jerry remarked, hoping against hope that this would prove to be true.

The wind gusts were strong and cold as they descended the plane at Travis A.F.B. in San Francisco that evening. Another Air Force couple was scheduled to meet their flight and drive them to their quarters for the night. But right now, Liz was having a tough time keeping Marci wrapped and warm in her arms as she trekked her way across the runway into the building. The girls were almost in tears as they ran with their Daddy into the warm building where their friends were waiting for them. It was such a big change coming from their warm island life into a late spring storm here on the mainland. However, after taking care of his paperwork, Jerry was soon herding his family into warm guest housing for the night. They were so grateful for the way the Air Force always had someone to meet them and arrange overnight stays at any new destination.

The next morning they were driven to the civilian airport where they had reservations to fly down to Los Angeles. There Jerry's sister, Dori, and her hubby, Lin, were to pick them up and take them to their lovely home in Northridge.

At the airport Dori was about to give up on their arrival as she walked right past Jerry and Liz. She had not even recognized them walking across the runway. "Oh, my gosh! I thought you were a black family, you all are so dark! I guess the sun hits that island more than it does our state," she laughed as she hugged her kid brother. Julie and Vicki were shy about meeting their aunt and uncle but they warmed up to them quickly when they discovered their home had a swimming pool. That was something they had never seen on Guam. Everyone there was satisfied to go to the beaches; but now they learned that the beach is not always that close to someone's home. Needless to say, the girls and Liz spent hours there the next afternoon while Jerry caught up with the family news with his sister.

Len had been shopping per Jerry's instructions and found a Chevy station wagon for the family to drive on the rest of this trip. All Jerry had to do was sign the papers, committing himself to the next few years of payments and drive it off the lot. Their visit passed quickly. They were packed into their new station wagon and off on a new adventure. What a trip this would be, driving all across the United States. Jerry had decided they should take the southern route this time since they had never been through this area before.

Dear Mom and Dad,   *June 3, 1963*

Well, we are on our way. But you do realize it will be ten days before we head out from Tulsa to Wisconsin. Our visit with Jerry's sister and husband was fun for the kids because they had a pool. Of course I enjoyed it too. We love our new station wagon. It offers plenty of room for our luggage and for the girls to play with their dolls or color in their coloring books in the back. They each have their own pillows if they want to take a nap. We expect to spend tonight at the home of some friends in El Paso, TX. They were on Guam with us last year. We've sure seen a lot of new sights as we traveled the southern route for the first time.

But, Wow! Yesterday we drove through a sand storm, a new experience for us. It was kind of scary with poor vision for the driver until we got behind a sand plow. Yes, it's just like a snowplow and it was actually plowing sand to the side of the road like drifting snow. What a strange sight! This slowed us down for about a half an hour and then we could see to drive a normal speed again.

We had to laugh at Vicki. She said she had to go potty and we didn't want to stop during this sand storm so Jerry just laughingly told her to go in her hands. Well, she did! Thank goodness there was a towel in the back and I threw it under her until we could get to a spot to stop and clean it all up back there. I really couldn't get upset with her because her daddy had told her to do it! I love it when unexpected things like this happen and we can all laugh about it.

That's about it for today and I will write you when we are at Jerry's folks to let you know exactly when to expect us there. We will stay with you for a few days if that is alright. We have to be in D.C. by July 1st. Our friends there have already found us a townhouse to move into on that day. A townhouse there means a two story duplex with three (apartments) side by side in one building. There will be two bedrooms upstairs for the girls and one down for us. It should be very comfortable. There is no base housing there so Uncle Sam gives us an allowance that covers us living "on the economy" in a suburb of D.C. known as Glass Manor, MD.

I must close now as we are stopping for lunch. Oh, we just discovered the McDonald's food places. They are so reasonable and fun for the girls. Have you seen them yet?

Love, Liz

Dear Mother & Daddy,   *June 8, 1963*

We've been enjoying our visit here in Tulsa this week. I must tell you about the first day when we were to pick up our collie, Shalli. You remember me telling you how Nannie and Brewer sold their house and moved to Broken Arrow, a little suburb of Tulsa. Well, first when we walked into the house everyone gave us hugs and I saw Shalli out of the corner of my eye to see that she was just looking at us and not recognizing us at all. She has patches of gray on her face now and looked tired. I was so disappointed in her reaction to us but after all she is eleven years old and hasn't seen us for three years. After we put our suitcases into the bedrooms that we would be staying in, Nannie insisted on giving us a tour of her garden. Shalli followed us outside and there we saw a beautiful boxer.

Well, we learned that when Dorlene and Lin had moved from Tulsa out to California they gave their boxer, Penny, to Nannie and Brewer. My oh my! What a surprise. That means Nannie had to take care of two big dogs. I'm sure that wasn't very easy for them at their age. But the two dogs seemed to be getting along just fine. Shalli kept following Nannie, looking quietly at us now and then. After seeing all the okra, green beans, carrots and the flower garden, we returned into the house for a glass of iced tea. As we all sat around in a circle enjoying our tea and all talking at the same time, Shalli began to perk up her head and ears to listen closely. Slowly she got up and started walking around the room, stopping at each of the girls, allowing them to pet her on the head. Then, she continued sniffing them closely, pausing at the baby's chair and finally coming over to where Jerry and I sat side by side. After smelling the two of us she suddenly went crazy with excitement while we hugged her and told her it really was us and we still loved her. Just like that she became our dog again!

So, now you know, we are bringing her with us to Wisconsin. There is no need for you to worry about it, really. She is quiet now and will be happy just laying out in your back yard. Daddy, you will probably enjoy her and maybe you can play a little "fetch" with her and the girls.

The girls have had fun at their Aunt Evelyn's house play-ing with their cousins and their toys.

Of course, Evelyn's kids are a little older than Julie and Vicki but they still have toys that the girls haven't seen before. It seems all girls are really into Barbie dolls like you sent them for Christmas. I can't believe you could sew such tiny outfits for them to wear. I would never attempt that. Ha. Jerry and I have gone to two movies; one as a night out for just us, and the other one with the kids at the Drive-In Theatre. That was their first experience with an outdoor theatre and of course they loved it. During our trip coming here we discovered McDonald's! The girls all loved their hamburgers and fries and I have to admit I love them too. For the price, Jerry and I decided it is a good place to get a meal for our whole family for just five dollars. Do you have one yet in Wisconsin Rapids?

I guess you are waiting for me to tell you when we are coming there! Well, we plan to leave here on Thursday and should arrive there Friday evening. Then we can stay until next Thursday before leaving for D.C. I hope this will be a good time for you. Please don't worry about what to have for food. We can go shopping on Saturday and buy the kinds of cereals that the kids like. It's so good to know that we can all sleep upstairs there. That should be a comfy arrangement for

*the kids in the front room and us in the back. The girls will
enjoy it up there with their dolls and games we brought for
them. Jerry and I are looking forward to playing some good
games of 500 Rummy with you both!*

Hugs... Liz

Little did Liz and Jerry know what lay ahead for them in the coming year. Evie and Frank would read and reread letters written about their experiences living in the East. The first letter was full of excitement about their lovely townhouse and great neighbors and getting the girls enrolled in school. Liz was correct when she had predicted that she would be a chauffeur but it wasn't full time work for her as she was in a car pool with other mothers. Jerry rode to school in the same kind of car pool so things worked out pretty smoothly. She wrote that she really enjoyed those days at home with just Marci to entertain.

The girls were all so pretty. Julie already showed her bright mind in class work and her pre-mature role as big sister to Vicki and Marci. She had soft, shiny brown hair that she loved to wear in different ways, refusing her mother's help. Sometimes Liz got upset with her stubbornness but she realized it just showed her strong nature and ability to be independent. She often worried about what Julie will be like when she is a teenager?

Vicki was different with her blond naturally curly hair and sharp brown eyes. She was as cute as a bug's ear. The opposite of Julie, she always did as told with no argument. Sometimes Liz feared she would not stand up for herself enough; especially when Julie caused her trouble. Is Julie jealous of her sister because of her cuteness or is it just that wish to be in control? Jerry really became upset when Julie bit Vicki's hand last year! He told Vicki to bite Julie back! Liz felt she had to step in when Vicki burst into tears and refused to do that! So, maybe this is what parenting is all about, Liz would wonder. Will Julie be bold, smart and witty like her dad and Vicki more accepting like me? These thoughts always ended with Liz determined to enjoy Vicki's sweetness. Besides, she would comfort herself with the fact that she'd always heard that the "middle" child will be prone to giving in to her siblings' wishes.

Marci already had thick brown hair which was best worn in "pigtails." Liz always looked forward to the time to braid her hair in the morning after the other two girls were gone to school.

With her daddy's blue eyes, Liz knew that Marci would be a beautiful girl. She was sweet natured but would know what she wanted and not give up until she got it. Liz decided it was normal for parents to spoil the youngest child so they didn't worry about this personality trait of their youngest. A big part of the morning for Marci would be playing fetch with Shalli who was quickly becoming acquainted with this new member of our family.

Another letter home expressed Liz's joy with a visit by Jerry's sister, Evelyn and her husband that included a lot of touring. Paul was a mechanic at the American Airlines in Tulsa and one of the perks of that job was the opportunity to fly to most any destination with his family at a minimal charge. This was the first opportunity Liz had to enjoy some real sight-seeing with just little Marci in tow. Then over the weekend the whole family was able to go to the Washington Monument and Lincoln Memorial as well as other sites.

At the Washington Monument, though, Liz would not go in the elevator to ride to the top! She had always experienced claustrophobia in a crowded elevator and a real fear of heights. When in the airliner coming home from Guam, she had locked herself into that tiny restroom and could not get the door open. She had to knock hard on the door to get anyone's attention and was almost faint with nervous perspiration by the time they were able to unlock the door. While visiting Evie and Frank that year, Liz had asked if they knew of any reason why she would have such a phobia. When Evie related a simple story to her, Liz thought that it probably was the reason.

The story was that when living on the first floor of a two story house there was another woman who rented the upstairs. A pot-belly stove in the corner of the dining room downstairs had a pipe that led up through the apartment upstairs. "You little, if cry, woman pound pipe, vibrate. Know, me, you cry." So, one day when Liz was about thirty months old and down for her nap, the pipe vibrated. Evie rose from her seat and went into the bedroom thinking that Liz must be crying. "But, you not there! Look all around, see bathroom door closed. Open, you crying." It seems that Liz had gone into the bathroom, closed the door, and could not get out. There was no way of knowing how long she had been in there but she had probably panicked knowing her mother could not hear her crying.

Liz had convinced herself now that she knew the underlying reason for her phobia, she could overcome it. Yet, she could not make herself ride on that elevator up the Washington Monument. The girls laughed at her as they disembarked with their daddy and their aunt and uncle. Apparently they all enjoyed the ride.

In November of that year, Frank thought about his daughter actually living in Washington, D.C. where she could go to the Rotunda to see President Kennedy lying in state. How disappointed he was when she wrote that they couldn't go. Jerry was supposed to march with the Air Force Band for the funeral but he was sick with the flu. It was such a rainy ugly day that Liz did not want to take the girls and certainly did not want to leave them at home with a sick daddy. So they watched the whole thing on television just like many other American families did on that day. It was still an event that they would never forget.

Dear Mom and Dad,   *November, 1963*

Wow, I have had the strangest experience and somewhat scary too. There was a policeman and his wife living in an apartment close by that had a new baby. When the baby was just a month old the mother wanted to go back to work so she was looking for a babysitter. Another neighbor I talked to a lot said she would do it but she had to be gone for a month before she could do it permanently. So, I told her I could take care of him for that month and the mother agreed to the arrangement. When they brought the baby to me he was six weeks old. He was such a good baby and Marci enjoyed helping me give him his bath, feed him, give him his bottle, and just keep him happy.

Well, the third day when they left I was ready to give him his bath when I noticed a weird looking bruise on his back. It was in the shape of a hand! So that evening when she came to pick him up I told her about it and she said oh, yes, that her husband had picked him up and almost dropped him so had to grab him hard. She said he really bruised easily. So, I accepted that as a reason. But, then the following Monday morning he was pretty fussy so I tried to rock him and calmed him somewhat. He had dirty diapers so when I was changing them I noted a huge mark on his leg. This really disturbed me and I faced her with that as soon as she came in that evening. I told her I didn't think her husband knew how to handle a baby and I certainly did not want to be held responsible for such bruises. I didn't want to babysit anymore. Again, she said the baby had this rare blood disease and bruised easily. But I told her not to come back again.

That next day another neighbor called me and said that Linda had left her baby with her and told her that I had hurt her baby and showed her not one, but two, bruised spots on the baby's buttocks and leg. I was livid! How could she accuse me? And, furthermore, how could I prove it was not me?! The nice neighbor said she knew I wasn't one to do that because she knew how I took care of my girls. I thanked her for calling me and told her my experience, warning her that the same thing could happen to her.

So, after talking to Jerry we decided we would call the number that we had seen announced on TV for reporting any suspicion of child abuse. That next day we had a visit from Jerry's C.O. (commanding officer) telling us we really should not get involved in civil cases such as this. I was shocked at his advice and said so. As it turned out, I had to ignore his advice because I had a call from that Child Protection Agency asking me to be a witness in a case against the policeman (the father)! It seems there had been more than one store clerk that had complained about him coming into a store while "walking his beat" as a policeman; then backing her into a corner to feel over her bosom or buttocks before striding quickly out to the street. One of these ladies had been accosted twice by him so she reported him to the police. So, now the other neighbor who had originally been babysitting for this couple came forward and said she had seen bruises on him before I had been babysitting.

With three witnesses against him, he was suspended from the police force and the baby was placed in a foster home! When I was in the courthouse that day I saw Linda out in the hall while I was waiting to be called in as a witness. I told her she really needed to think hard about staying married to a man that would bruise a little baby like that! She was very upset but with tears in her eyes she told me that her husband had very little patience with the baby's crying. However, she loved him and was sure that counseling would teach him how to care for a baby, so she had no intentions of witnessing against him or of leaving him.

Well, I really don't know how that story will end. I've heard that the baby would be allowed to come back to live with them after three months of counseling. We will be gone from here by then and I'm glad. I don't want to see that man again! However, one bad thing about being a military family is that sometimes we start things and never get to finish them; or we learn events in other people's lives and never get to hear the ending of their stories, such as this one.

I love my girls so much; I just cannot imagine how some people can do what they do to babies! If they don't have the patience for crying babies they should not have children of their own. But I know that's easier said than done.

That's enough for today.

Love & kisses, Liz

This was another letter that held their interest as Liz wrote about her babysitting job! Didn't she have enough to do without taking on a babysitting job, thought Evie.

Evie pondered over the sentence that said, "But I know that's easier said than done." What does that mean? She would ask Frank later because he learned a lot of things from his work as a linotype operator; although many times he would agree that he saw a lot of new words but did not have to learn what they mean, and often would just type them and continue his work. If his curiosity was peaked he would ask a fellow worker and they were always happy to write him notes of explanation. Evie wished that back when she was working during the war, her coworkers were that helpful to her.

Of course she didn't have to type sentences but sometimes there would be notes on the bulletin board or the supervisor would come around with instructions on some new piece of work they were sewing and she would be completely lost. Anytime she wrote a question to one of the people in her line they usually just came over, gestured for her to stand up, sit at her machine and complete the piece like it was to be done. They never had to show her twice; she always caught on after one demonstration. But they still seemed to have no time for her and there were only two or three that would smile and nod a good morning or a goodbye at quitting time. That was why she was happy when they moved to the East side of the city Frank had no problem with her quitting her job. Taking care of the house, finding new things to cook and fulfilling Frank's needs were really taking up most of her time anyway. Evie tried to convince herself she didn't need anything else.

Life was somewhat boring now though with the kids grown up and gone. She would often dwell on the fact that if it weren't for her deafness she could have an enjoyable job such as clerking at J.C. Penney's store. Frank never seemed to complain about being deaf but she was often bitter about this affliction. Why would a loving God allow such things to happen to babies? For that matter, why would God let bad diseases to happen to people? Why are some children unable to walk? Why are some people blind? She and Frank had discussed this many times and he was always able to turn to the

Bible and read some scriptures for comfort, but Evie was not in the least satisfied with that.

Someone once told Evie she was born deaf because of some sin that her parents or grandparents had committed. That person even quoted scriptures. In fact, they convinced Evie that God is not a loving God.

"If true God," she would sign to Frank, "then God is cruel!" Frank tried to explain about the God of the Old Testament trying to straighten out the people of that time; as opposed to the New Testament where one learns about our loving God through his son, Jesus Christ. With strong signs, Frank continued, "Yet, Jesus told his followers that becoming Christians did not guarantee them a perfect life. They would still experience disease as well as physical impairments. Jesus told us that he will always be with us. His grace will comfort us and give us the strength to become strong again. A Christian knows there will be a better life waiting for them when they get to Heaven. We must trust this to be true, Evie!"

Unfortunately, Evie chose not to focus on Frank's words. She preferred to sulk while her husband quietly and sadly prayed that his wife would understand some day.

A few weeks later a letter from Liz brought Evie out of her depression; a letter with some new excitement the Powell family intended to bring to Frank and Evie's quiet life.

Dearest Mother and Daddy,   *December, 1963*

You will be surprised to get this letter. Jerry gets a two week break from his classes and of course the girls get their Christmas break too, so we would like to come to visit you for Christmas! This will be the first time we've ever been able to come home to celebrate the holidays with you! I am so excited. However, we will not drive. It snows here a lot just as it does in Wisconsin and after talking it over we decided the best route would be the train. That will be so much easier for us and the girls will love it! I am enclosing our schedule for the train. It seems it would be best if you can pick us up in Adams-Friendship instead of us waiting there for hours to catch a train on up to Wisconsin Rapids. I hope this will be alright for you, Daddy. It looks like less than an hour's drive. If you do not feel comfortable with the idea perhaps Bobby would be willing to do so. If not, then we will wait there for the time it takes to get off the train, go inside and wait for the train to Wisconsin Rapids.

It will be grand to have a few days with you in your home with your Christmas tree. (Our neighbor says she will feed Shalli, so don't worry about her. Ha.) Please let me know what you think of this plan. I want to mail this letter today so I will close now.

With all our love, Liz

The first thing Evie said was, "See? If we not deaf could call Liz now. Make plans talk together." Frank ignored that remark and laughed instead. Of course this became fun for Frank and Evie. They replied immediately that they were as thrilled as could be to have their daughter and her family here for Christmas. The next two weeks went by rather quickly as they spent every evening getting ready for their visit. Shopping for groceries, a big turkey and all the trimmings, baking sugar cookies to be ready for the girls to decorate, a few gifts for the girls, getting the bedrooms ready and finally, they chose the most beautiful tree on the lot.

It was just snowing lightly the day they drove down to Adams-Friendship to meet the train. Frank silently thanked God for the clear roads to drive on and the promise of sunshine for a few days in the weather report. Frank thought he never saw a more beautiful display of happiness than on the faces of his granddaughters as they hopped off of the train and laughed at the snow hitting their faces. Julie and Vicki seemed to remember him as they ran up to him and hugged his knees. He stooped over to give them a welcoming hug, looking over their heads to see Liz smiling lovingly at them. She had Marci in her arms and handed her to Jerry so that she could hug her daddy too. Frank grinned at Jerry and pointed over to the car where Evie sat waiting for them. Just loading the car with the family and luggage was a tight squeeze but they all laughed and the girls started singing Jingle Bells as they headed toward the snow banked roads for their journey home. Liz wondered if her parents reflected back to the time they really did ride on a horse and buggy over the snow "to grandmother's house." Then it hit her! They couldn't hear the girls singing that song; they had never heard how sweet it was to hear children's voices singing Christmas carols.

Whenever thoughts like this came upon her, Liz could feel the tears swelling up but knew she could not explain that event so she would carefully swallow the lump in her throat and hope the tears would not show. If they did she would be able to say she was just so happy they were here; and if they didn't, then she would comfort herself by telling herself that deaf people didn't know what they were missing if they had never been able to hear in the first place.

Christmas was as wonderful as any one of them could have wished for. Evie and Frank were completely content. This contentment turned to ecstasy when Bobby and his family were able to come for a couple of days. Here they are with five little grandchildren in their home and it's really Christmas. Frank realized that he never had the experience in his own family growing up. There never been a time that every one of the family members were in his parents' home at the same time after his mother died. Of course he couldn't really remember much time with his mother because she died when he was just seven years old. She never knew how we three youngest children went to the school for the deaf. She never knew how we grew up just fine and got jobs and got married. She never enjoyed being a grandmother to sweet young children like these! Again, Frank prayed, this time a prayer of gratitude for his full life.

Liz enjoyed chatting with Bobby's wife and catching up on the news. They always shared bits about the children and then eventually would talk about Evie and Frank. Jo had accepted their deafness more easily than Jerry had. She remembered how Jerry was concerned that they might have deaf children; but Jo never mentioned that possibility. And here they were with six children between them and none of them showed any signs of deafness. The overall consensus was that neither Frank nor Evie had deafness in their genealogy so deafness was not to be expected to carry on in the family.

"There is one thing, I thought about today, though," Liz said quietly to Jo while watching her mother across the room showing her eldest granddaughter how she made a stuffed teddy bear. "I don't ever begin a conversation with either mom or daddy by saying their name. Did you ever think about that? I mean, sometimes I just say your name when beginning to tell you something. Like, 'Jo, I've been meaning to ask you about your mom.' I have never gone up to mom and said, 'Mother, how Aunt Lizzie?' I just simply say, 'How Aunt Lizzie?' Am I making any sense?" "Hmmm, I'll have to think about that one for a while," Jo answered.

"Maybe we say someone's name to get their attention and we don't really have to do that when getting a deaf person's attention. We wouldn't sign to them until they are looking at us and we know we have their attention," Liz continued. "Anyway, if they weren't looking at us, we couldn't just call their name, we have to go over to them and touch their shoulder to get their attention. I think it's interesting to think about. I will probably never change that either, after all these years." These kind of thoughts were seldom spoken of by Liz and she soon forgot all about this conversation with her sister-in-law.

The house was filled with joy and no real discomfort. Three comfy beds were upstairs while Bobby and family shared one bedroom downstairs. Of course there were toys everywhere. But Frank and Evie treasured every moment, knowing it would be a rare event in their memory book. They filled the days with games in the house including cards and a board game called Monopoly that Frank never tired of playing. Outdoors provided a great entertainment too, building a snowman, a snow fort, and making angels in the snow. Time went by faster than usual and soon it was time for them to leave. It was so difficult to say goodbye as Liz and her family boarded the train and waved until they couldn't be seen anymore.

The stillness of the house overshadowed them as they settled into their favorite chairs. Before Frank could take a nap, Evie engaged him in a long conversation, covering each and every detail of every day they had enjoyed their family. Evie was signing yet another story of one of the children when she slowly put down her hands because she noted that Frank was sound asleep. Thank goodness he had another day off before he had to go back to work.

Evie's thoughts soon turned to the future as she worried about where Liz and Jerry would be sent after he finished his schooling in D.C. She secretly wished he would quit the Air Force and attend the Teacher's College over in Stevens Point and allow Liz and the girls to come live with them. She suggested that possibility to Liz one evening but she seemed adamant that Jerry would be wise to finish out twenty years in the Air Force; moreover, she wouldn't mind if he continued for twenty five! Evie decided that it was not all Jerry's fault that they remained in the service after all.

In late spring a letter from Liz revealed their next assignment, Scott Air Force Base in Illinois, just East of St. Louis. Frank's reaction was, "Good. Close home." Evie had to admit that Frank was right; they could drive up here in one day. As it turned out it would be Frank and Evie that made that day's trip the first time. Liz wrote that they had no time to come to Wisconsin before reporting in to the Scott Air Force Base Band. Actually, they would have some time but they wanted to drive up to New York to the World's Fair since they lived so close now. The World's fair! As always, Frank agreed with that plan. He did not want to deny them that experience instead of driving up here to Wisconsin. "We drive Illinois after they settled," Frank said as he comforted his wife. "Cost money go to Fair!" Evie balked. "Just entry fee. Maybe Jerry get discount with school. Not our concern. Not need rides; just many sights many countries show," Frank signed as he sat down for dinner, anxious to end this argument if that is where it was headed.

After a good Friday night dinner of fish and fries, Frank changed the subject by asking, "Evie, I didn't know if Liz gave her girls name signs. Did they tell you any?" Evie's reply did not really surprise Frank.

"No, hmmm. I don't see why they need them." He knew she didn't understand the need for a hearing person to have a name sign. They hadn't even given one to their own children. Oh, sure they used an initial when they were talking together of one of them but they did not tag the sign onto Liz or Bobby. "OK, but when we are talking about them we need some name signs. We've done 'J' for Jerry but now we have 'J' for Julie. Then there is 'L' for Liz, and 'B' for Bobby's boy, Barry. We have easy with 'V' for Vicki, 'M' for Marci and 'C' for Corrine.

When Dianne becomes older 'D' will be fine; right now just a baby sign is for her until another baby comes along!" Evie smiled when she thought about the baby but she replied, "You right. Dianne always baby. Think no more grandbabies for us. Maybe put salute with 'J' for Jerry." Evie was proud for thinking this out while Frank had been talking and couldn't wait to see what he would say now. Frank simply nodded his head in affirmation and turned his attention to the TV evening news.

The trip to Illinois that Frank had promised waited for over a year. It was as if Liz and Jerry had heard Evie's comment on there being no more grandchildren to be born. She was pregnant again!

Dear Mom and Dad,   *February, 1967*

I've been so busy getting everything settled in our new home. We are so comfortable here now that we have the big house to live in. It wasn't easy living in that mobile home for six weeks while waiting for this house. It wasn't easy making two moves in two months but it was worth it. We have so much room here; two bedrooms upstairs, two down, a nice big living room, dining room and kitchen. It's the biggest home we have had in our married life.

We even have a garage to park our car in and a fenced in backyard. So, of course, we had to go out and find another dog! Ha. We still feel sad about losing Shalli. But she was thirteen and had a good life. It was tough on Jerry to have to take her to the Vet to put her to sleep. Well, now we just had to look for another dog to take her place. This one is a collie too and already a year old. The girls love him but I am a little annoyed with his barking all of the time. He barks at everything even airplanes flying over and birds! That's pretty silly, isn't it? His name is Max. Jerry got him through someone at the base that moved into base housing and had no room for a big dog. Well, we shall see if he settles down.

Now I have some news for you again! You will be surprised and believe me, I was surprised too! I am pregnant again! Maybe this will be a boy. Jerry's dad said that if we would have a baby born in the U.S. it would be a boy. So, maybe God has that in his plans, to give the Powells a grandson to carry on their family name! The baby is due the end of August. Maybe you can plan to come to see us then. We have an extra bedroom just for you! The girls love it that they have privacy upstairs and Marci has the most privacy with her own room because it is smaller of the two. She really thinks she is special now! Ha. I can't believe she will be starting school in the fall. But that does mean I will have a lot of time to take care of the new baby.

Please be happy for us to have another blessing from God. By the way, we are all attending church regularly now at the United Methodist Church just a few blocks from us on Main Street. It's so nice to live in a little town like this. Mascoutah is just 4 miles from the base and another 10 miles to a larger town, Belleville. Then we can always drive into St. Louis for a big event such as a baseball game, Dad! I know you would love that. We will see if they have a game scheduled after the baby is born.

Oh, it's getting cloudy so I must hush and go get the clothes off the line before it rains.

Love, Liz

Evie and Frank just looked at each other in surprise as they laid the letter down on the table and simultaneously picked up their coffee cups for a sip. This joint reaction made them both smile and relax into a conversation that they had experienced a few times before. Each and every time Liz or Bobby wrote a letter announcing the expectation of another child, Evie and Frank would read and re-read the news with mixed emotions. After all, they had been satisfied with two children; whoever would have thought that they would now be expecting their seventh grandchild! Frank would quietly say a prayer for his daughter and/or daughter-in-law for a healthy pregnancy. Evie would feel left out of her daughter's pregnancies. She just had to see Liz pregnant once! This prompted her to ask her husband about the possibility of driving down to Illinois before the baby was born so that she could see Liz pregnant! However, his reply was simply, "We'll see."

Unfortunately for Evie, that did not happen. Frank had decided not to retire at age sixty-two but to continue until age sixty-five; so, he had to wait his turn for vacation and the summer months were all spoken for before he had his bid in. His vacation could not happen until the third week of September which was satisfactory to him and of course, Evie had to accept that date too.

Another girl! "Oh, my," Evie signed, "Please not Liz try again try boy!" She did not want to see Liz go through life having babies. Evie thought about her nephew Buddy and his lovely red-headed wife, Flo. They were still farming Buddy's grandfather's land in Minnesota and wanted sons to help carry on the family tradition. Dairy farms demanded a lot of time and the more bodies to help, the less stress on the cows. They had the bodies alright but six girls were born before they had a baby boy. Of course Liz and Jerry didn't need a son to perform any special labor but Evie could still imagine Liz doing the same just to please the men in her life, Jerry, his father, and Frank.

But while they were visiting their daughter and family, this very subject came up in a conversation with Liz and Jerry. Without hesitation both said they were definitely not going to try again! Everyone laughed and continued to laud over the beauty of the new baby girl, Connie Jean. She was such a pretty baby and so good. She hardly ever cried, seeming quite happy with the routine that Liz laid out for her. However, everyone could see that five year old Marci was having a tough time accepting this new addition to the family.

Poor Marci had a scar on her chin now but it really did not change her sweet dimples on her pretty face. Vicki bravely started finger spelling and told her grandparents the story of Marci's fall off of the picnic table in the park. They had ridden their bicycles to the park to play on the swings and Marci had started climbing the wooden picnic table only to trip over the bench and fall on the corner of the fire pit, ripping through an inch of skin on her chin. "Me, Marci sit behind on bike fast home. Mom drive M to hospital, fourteen stitches!" Vicki signed what little she knew and finger spelled things like hospital. She was exhausted from this exercise in communication but proud of herself for pleasing her grandparents. It tickled Frank so much to see his grandchildren learning the alphabet in finger spelling, knowing that they would remember this all of their lives and always be able to spell words to talk to them.

Frank and Evie were pleasantly surprised to attend church services with the family, where Liz signed the sermon for them. She had asked someone in the church to place a folding chair in front of the front row so she could face them. Frank was so proud of his daughter doing her best to convey the message that the pastor spoke. Evie, however, had a little difficulty in following Liz and told her so after church. Before Liz could say anything, Frank interrupted by signing, "Evie, because you not read Bible. You not know people names in Bible. I explain later." Liz was busy gathering up the children from their Sunday School classes with Jerry, so she was not privy to any words that her parents may have exchanged after that.

That evening Evie simply told her daughter that it was quite nice to attend the service in a real church. She had been impressed with the pretty brick building and the comfortable seats. This was because all they had experienced for a worship service was a school room to sit in. There the visiting minister would come to hold a service with sign language.

The trip down here had been a tough one on Frank. Evie had no idea what was wrong with him until they arrived at Liz's home late that afternoon in September. He had told her that he was not feeling good a couple of hours before reaching their destination but since Evie did not drive, he tried not to let the pain get the best of him. Liz could see that her dad looked tired and a little pale so she suggested that he go lie down for a while before dinner. Evie walked into the bedroom with him while Jerry brought in their suitcases from the car after parking it into the garage. He told the girls to quiet down as their grandpa was not feeling good. Julie quietly laughed at her daddy as she said, "But, daddy, grandpa can't hear us anyway."

"You are right honey, but when I say quiet for grandpa, I mean no running around the house or peeking in on him. Understand?" Jerry stated in his parental voice. He looked at all three of the girls as they changed their moods quickly to satisfy their daddy. Marci asked if she could look in on the baby and make sure she was still asleep. With Jerry's approval, she walked slowly to her parents' bedroom where Connie's crib had been moved into while they had company. Connie was not asleep so Marci sat on the edge of her parents' bed and talked to her awhile before going out to tell mom that she was awake.

She loved her baby sister but she couldn't help feel a little jealous. "You are spoiled already because you're always getting compliments on how cute, or how pretty, or how good you are! And now you get to sleep in here with mommy and daddy! Lucky you! I have to sleep upstairs with your big sisters and listen to them talk about boyfriends, and stuff. Yuk! Maybe I'll ask mommy if I can share your bedroom when grandma and grandpa go back home. Would you like that?" Marci was hoping for an understanding smile on the baby's face but all she saw was a frown as Connie started crying. "Oh, no, we're supposed to be quiet, silly! I bet you need your diapers changed. Let me go get mommy."

She was out the door in a flash and ran right into her mother in the hall. "It's okay, sweetie, I'll take care of her little britches. Do you want to help me?" Liz realized that Marci was a little out of sorts since the baby arrived. Unfortunately, Marci had to start Kindergarten, her very first day of school, on the same day that Liz brought the baby home from the hospital. It was a little traumatic coming home full of the excitement of school only to find everyone focused on the new baby. Nana and Poppy Powell were here too, having just arrived from Tulsa. Marci could not help but wonder if they had come to see her when she was brought home from the hospital. But, of course that wasn't possible because she'd been born in a far off place in the middle of the ocean! Nobody was there except Julie and Vicki!

And now, Liz mused, just eight weeks later, here were her other grandma and grandpa just to see this new baby! "Marci, I'm so proud of the note that your teacher sent home with you today. She said that you are so anxious to learn whatever is new every day and that you are always attentive when she talks to you or the class. She's sure that you will be a good student with a real desire to do well. I am going to show that to grandma and grandpa right after dinner. That is so good to hear. I love you, sweetie."

Liz also realized how tough it was for Marci to have two older sisters so close in age to each other. They could have conversations that she could not participate in like talking about friends at school that Marci did not know. I'm sure they didn't mean to exclude Marci from everything but it would seem that way to her, a five year old girl.

Julie and Vicki still managed to see their special friends who lived just across the street from our old house, by hopping on their bicycles and riding the few blocks to their home. Julie had shared a little about her friend, Joy, with Liz. "She's somewhat jealous of her little sister because she was adopted when the family lived in some country in South America. I try to tell her I don't see them treating her any differently than you do our kid sister, mom! But she's convinced herself that Sherry gets everything she wants at a much younger age than she did. The worst thing is that she thinks she is so much prettier than she is."

Liz knew better than to argue that point with Julie and would simply say that it was very kind of Julie to listen to Joy's complaints. "The best thing you can do, hon, is to listen. Apparently she needs a friend who will just listen. Find every chance you can to pay her compliments. She really needs attention. Don't say too much, just agree quietly and she will get tired of talking about it before too long. Then just like you got used to sharing your life with your little sister, she will learn to do the same. In the meanwhile let's enjoy grandma and grandpa's visit. Hey, maybe you can get Joy to sit in on your next card game with grandpa!"

Frank and Evie were happy with this big comfortable house that Liz and Jerry had rented. They didn't feel that they were in the way at all. One evening as they sat on the front porch, Frank asked Liz what happened to the dog she wrote about last year.

"Oh, that collie!" Liz signed with a deep sigh. "Well, Max not happy here. Barked at everything, even birds," Liz laughed. "Neighbors complained. So decide try find better place for him. Put ad in paper. Funny thing happened. Jerry went Mascoutah's weekly newspaper write ad. One hour later employee there called wanted see our dog. Lives country now. Man name Bill, called two weeks later say Max so happy. Bill happy too. Max help with cows. You know collies good with cows. Bill teen-age son loves play with Max so all happy." Although surprised, Frank understood, while Evie remarked, "Maybe best wait baby grow three years old." "You right!" her daughter agreed.

Liz also told a little story about Marci's experience with a dog in the neighborhood. For some reason the dog was loose and approached Marci in the yard, sniffing her as dogs do. But this frightened Marci and she started running away. She even crossed our busy street and ran down the block crying and screaming loud enough that Liz heard her from the kitchen. When Liz saw the dog chasing her, she called him by name and he returned obediently home, letting her open the gate to his yard. By the time she reached Marci, she was shaking and saying she hated that dog. "I didn't know that Marci would be afraid of a dog. Maybe good wait another dog us."

Evie thought it was good they did not have a dog now. A collie loses so much hair that could be bad for the baby. "But dog good protection," Liz signed. "If we live here permanently, I would want dog now. But we have few years yet to retirement. We've been lucky live Mascoutah almost four years already." Liz tried to sign and voice simultaneously for her family which was not an easy task but they appreciated her efforts.

At dinner she noted that Frank only ate a few bites and excused himself to go back to bed. Then Evie told her what the problem was. Frank had not been able to urinate all day and had pain in his abdomen. When Liz relayed that to Jerry he suggested they take him to emergency at the base. After some discussion, Frank finally agreed to do just that. Jerry called the babysitter down the street and they were soon on their way.

Three hours later, Frank was lying comfortably in a hospital bed after the doctor ordered that he be admitted. He was feeling much better after having the pressure relieved while the bladder drained. A catheter was to stay in for the next few hours until they could run tests to see what was causing this problem. Liz really wanted to remain for the night so she could interpret for her dad but knew she needed to be home for the baby and the girls. After reassuring everyone that he would be fine with writing notes to the hospital staff, Evie, Liz and Jerry returned home.

Frank was so delighted to be able to go home after five days in the hospital. The doctor took care of the prostate gland as well as hemorrhoids with surgery and Frank felt like a new person. The only requirement was that he was not to travel for another ten days. Liz was sorry for her dad but at the same time happy that they could stay for a nice long visit. The plan was that Bobby would fly down and drive them home. He could not come for another two weeks so that worked out just fine. Frank would have more time to feel good enough for travel. The girls were so happy that grandma and grandpa could stay longer so that they could learn some more sign language with plenty of practice enjoyed immensely by all. The girls really got to know their grandpa as he loved to play cards and Monopoly with them. Liz was glad to have her mother in the kitchen making good meals for them as well as baking cookies for the girls. Luckily the September evenings were warm enough so that when Frank was feeling better they enjoyed walking slowly down to the local ice cream shop.

When Bobby arrived they enjoyed his company for just two days and before they knew it Evie and Frank were packed into the car and they were gone. Liz always felt a pang of loneliness after a visit from them, wishing deeply that they could have more times together like this. She realized it was her own fault that she didn't live near her parents. That's what unrequited love had done to her, she mused. Had she really run away from her broken romance or had she simply escaped from her life with deaf parents? No! She didn't want to add that theory to her already heavy load of guilt. Shaking her head, she turned toward the kitchen and found enough work to do to keep her busy until the kids got home from school. There was a lot of work to catch up on and her mind was soon filled with organizing her time to get it accomplished. Besides, life in the Air Force brought changes when one least expected it.

Back home in Wisconsin, Evie and Frank needed to relax for a few days before getting back into their old routine in life. Frank had not officially retired yet so he had to go back to work . He was proud to be there again and relate some of the events of his vacation. His co-workers seemed genuinely interested in how he and his wife traveled so easily. Some had notes ready saying they were sorry Frank had been ill while on vacation. Others wrote comments about how good he looked. More than one man wrote how glad they were that he was back and his boss wrote that he had been missed because he was such a good worker. With their questions and answers on notes, Frank was happy to share them with Evie when he got home. The only thing he couldn't share with her was the pats on the back that he had received from the fellas when he first walked into the Tribune that morning. Deep down he knew that they were really impressed that deaf people could travel like they did and to tell the truth, he was pretty impressed with himself! Little did he know that there was to be more travel in the not too distant future.

As it turned out, Liz's thoughts were like a premonition. When Connie turned six months old Jerry received orders to go to the state of Washington. The band out there was without a commander temporarily and he was needed to help re-organize their affairs. Washington State would be quite a trip again. The girls were now old enough to balk with disapproval at the thought of leaving their friends. Marci did not remember moving to Mascoutah but she remembered how difficult it was for her when we left the first house we rented here. She had three little friends she played with and thought she would not see again. After we came into this big house she started riding her bike just as her older sisters did and was able to visit them just three blocks away. Liz remembered that Marci was afraid she was leaving all her furniture and dolls at the old house and since we had to live one month in a mobile home before getting this house, our furniture was stored. She didn't know that we still had it until we moved into this house. Moving can be traumatic for a five year old.

The idea of moving again and moving far away was very scary to Marci. Julie and Vicki were also upset to leave their friends and especially to change schools in the middle of the year! With patience, Jerry talked to the girls. "Yes, girls, we will make this move during your Christmas vacation. I know it won't be easy but you will make new friends. We will have base housing and you will go to a school on base so all the kids there will be just like you, moving into a new school and needing to make friends quickly. That will be easier for you than it was coming to Mascoutah. Remember how it was attending a civilian school where a lot of kids already had their little cliques? It took time for them to get to know you."

"Yes, daddy, but will we be able to take baton twirling and piano lessons out there?" Julie asked, almost in tears. Vicki joined in with questions of her own and Liz had to walk away so that she wouldn't cry herself. This was really the first move in which the girls were old enough to feel some pain and when they were hurting, she was too. Besides, she and Jerry were leaving good friends too. They had lived here for four years and shared some very good times with people in the band. They had started bowling in a bowling league, attending church regularly, planning picnics, birthday parties, etc. Picking up Connie, she said, "Well, at least you won't be affected by this move." Liz was feeling some sadness herself for another reason. They knew they would just stay there one year or less. This would mean their furniture would not follow them to Washington after all; it would all be put in storage, including the piano.

DEPENDABLE WORKERS—Training they received in the school for the deaf in Minnesota prepared Mr. and Mrs. Frank Niklaus for productive lives, and helped them make the social adjustments necessary for those who can neither hear nor speak. Frank is a Linotype operator at The Tribune; his wife works at Paul Bunyan Outerwear clothing factory. (*Wisconsin Rapids Daily Tribune*, Oct 12, 1962)

Employ the Handicapped Week

Local Couple Has Normal Life in Soundless World

Mr. and Mrs. Frank Niklaus, 350 16th St. N., are a happy couple, devoted parents and beaming grandparents. Both are gainfully employed.

Nothing unusual about that, it seems, except … they raised their two children without ever hearing their infant cries; they dance to a tempo that they somehow instinctively sense; they must perform their daily tasks without being able to converse with their bosses.

Both Frank and Evelyn are deaf-mutes, although neither particularly cares for that term and the social stigma a few people mistakenly attach to it.

Not a Barrier

They offer dynamic proof that deafness is a minor handicap…and nothing more! It is definitely not a barrier to a rich and constructive life.

Frank is a Linotype operator at the Wisconsin Rapids Tribune. His wife operates a power sewing machine at Paul Bunyan Outerwear. Both win praise from their supervisors for the high level of their performance.

The manager at the clothing factory, Dave Morris,

says Mrs. Niklaus is "an excellent worker – dependable and reliable." She has developed, in her 12 years of employment there, an almost uncanny "feel" for the machines, says Morris. Occasional written instructions are all she ever needs.

In the Tribune's composing room, the unwritten rule is that if you want a story set into type in a hurry, "give it to Frank." He can "hang the machine," a trade term meaning that he can operate the keyboard faster than the machine can cast the lines of type. He's also the dean of the staff, having been here since 1942.

Almost an Asset

Mechanical Superintendent Al Wenzlaff attributes some of Frank's dependable skill to the fact that he is deaf. "Nothing ever seems to bother him," says Wenzlaff.

The noise from machinery eventually annoys most people, and they are distracted by conversations of fellow workers. Although deafness limits the types of work a person is qualified for, it can, in the right occupation, almost be considered an asset.

Although adept at talking with their hands to each other, the Niklauses do not lip-read as a general practice. With friends or co-workers who do not understand sign language, they communicate by writing notes.

"She loves to dance," Frank informed this interviewer when requested to tell something about the social life of a couple living in a silent wold. "We do not try to follow the rhythm; we dance step by step or do the Fox Trot." His wife, he added, was once an excellent fancy roller skater.

Enjoy Television

They have a television set in their home. Frank's preference naturally, is athletic contests. Evelyn's all-time favorite show was "The Price is Right."

Sound is caused by vibrations, and the deaf can "feel" certain sounds.

"We often put our hands on the radio when music is being played," Frank says.

Both of the Niklaus children hear and speak normally. Both are married. Betty (Mrs. Gerald Powell) is the oldest, and has three daughters. The family has lived on the island of Guam since 1960, but expects to return home in November of 1963. Wallace has two children and resides at Bensenville, Ill.

When they were infants, Mrs. Niklaus recalls, she kept a dim light burning in the room through the night so she could see them if they stirred in their cribs.

As they grew older they quickly picked up sign language, so there was no lack of parent-child communication.

Schools for Deaf

Frank is a native of Iowa and Evelyn was born in Minnesota. She was born deaf. Frank lost his hearing at 18 months from scarlet fever. Both attended the state school for the deaf at Faribault, Minn., which has courses from primary through high school. Many trades are taught, and Frank chose printing and type setting.

Unable to get a job in that field immediately after graduation, he worked on a farm for a year. Then he obtained a printing job at the Merrill Herald and worked there until his move to Wisconsin Rapids 20 years ago.

Both laud the special schools for the deaf that our enlightened society has provided. Wisconsin's school is located at Delavan, and has just been improved through the erection of a $369,500 rehabilitation center.

Their advice to parents of deaf-mutes is to see that these children attend such a special school where they can "acquire a number of skills and learn habits of industry that will stay with them through life."

284

12

She Is Moving Again?

(D)ear Mother and Dad,   *January 13, 1968*

Here we are all settled in our new home in Tacoma, Washington. It's lovely base housing, a duplex, two story stucco and wood townhouse. The living room had sliding doors opening onto a patio; a good size living room joining a dining area. There's a window size opening in the wall to the kitchen for passing dishes through. The girls think that is neat because they don't have to walk around the corner to talk to me in the kitchen and I can pass them the dishes and things to set the table with fairly easily. There are three comfy bedrooms upstairs, that means we have to watch Connie carefully so that nothing happens to her like Marci's fall down the stairs at your home in Wisconsin Rapids! Yes, all in all we like our new home.

Let me tell you about the trip out here. When we headed west out of Oklahoma it was already snowing and the further we drove the heavier the snow. We finally decided it would be best to stop for the night in Albuquerque. Our old station wagon was fine on the roads but that next day we were stopped by the local highway patrol and told that we must get chains put on the tires due to the heavy snowfall. We had a long wait at a local filling station to purchase the chains and have them put on the car. We only drove another hundred miles when the snow quit as we dropped down out of those mountains into California. There was no snow in sight, so we stopped at another station where they took the chains off.

Finally reaching our first destination, we were happy to get out of the car at Jerry's sister's home just north of Los Angeles. Dorlene was very relieved to see us because it had been raining for days with no relief in sight. She was also disappointed when we told her we could only stay two nights before continuing our trip. The girls enjoyed their swimming pool and Lin, Dorlene's hubby, loved cooking good food on the grill. They didn't even have to change out of their swim suits to enjoy their hamburgers outdoors. Dorlene has only one child, Nancy, who is ten years older than Julie but she had patience with the girls as she kept them entertained all day and evening. But time was marching on so we had to pack up again and be on our way. Just as Dorlene had predicted, it was raining that morning when we left.

Sure enough we ran into flood conditions but we continued to drive even though some water was seeping under the doors into our station wagon! We saw a little Volkswagen in front of us actually swept off the road that was a bit scary. By that point the police were stopping cars, announcing that this highway would be closed so we must detour over onto another road. We had to follow their directions and as soon as we got out of that deep water we stopped at a restaurant. Many cars stopped at this same place. All the people got out of their vehicles. We used some diapers to mop out the water from the floor and left the doors open for a while so the sun could dry them more. The girls and I went inside and had a light snack while Jerry looked at a map with some fellow travelers to figure out the best way to get back to our highway. Everyone agreed that this had been a strange trip, snow, ice and flood all in just a few days. Thank goodness the sun seemed to feel sorry for us at last. Shining brightly for the next few hours we drove on to our destination safely. In just an hour, Jerry had signed the necessary papers to get the keys to our temporary quarters. Needless to say, we all flopped on the beds for a nap! We really didn't care if they were comfy beds or not; just so they were clean, and they were!

We had to stay in an apartment for three weeks before our base housing was ready. Luckily the Air Force paid for that. It's been interesting to learn how much they will do for you when you are important to the band. It's nice being treated like VIPs. (Very Important People). It was a nice apartment on the second floor so I had some good exercise taking those steps with Marci and Connie down to the playground every morning.

Do you know, my dear mother and dad, I counted up the places we have lived since we were married and we are now in our sixteenth home! That's hard to believe, isn't it?! I am counting actual homes, not bases, i.e.; we were in three homes just in Mascoutah and now we have already lived in two in Tacoma so that's five. Florida (4), Newfoundland (2), Omaha (3), Guam (1), and just one in D.C. I have loved every one of them for different reasons. I wonder how many more homes we will have.

Well, I best hush. Besides, it's time to get something on the stove for supper.

Love, Liz

Dearest Mother and Daddy,   *March, 1968*

I have a cast on my foot because I broke my ankle at the bowling alley! All of us had gone bowling just for fun and I fell down when delivering my ball. I had a good score going too!

When I was at the base hospital the x-ray showed that it was just sprained so they wrapped it up and gave me crutches.

Well, the next day I fell down with the silly crutches and then the pain was so bad I had to go to the hospital again.

287

This time the x-ray showed that the ankle was broken so they set it and put a cast on. It feels so much better now. It's a cast I can walk on but I'm sleeping on the couch downstairs because it's too difficult to walk up those stairs. It's good for Jerry. He seems to enjoy helping the girls into their beds and listening to their prayers. Of course I still have to change the baby's diapers before he takes her on upstairs. Ha. Julie and Vicki are learning to make their beds in the mornings too.

Speaking of hospital visits, I have another story to tell you. Vicki had twelve stitches in her forehead a couple of weeks ago. She and Julie went bike riding with their friends on a beautiful, warm afternoon after school. They went into a wooded area which Jerry had told them was off limits to them. Off limits means they are not to go there. So, they learned a lesson the hard way. Julie came running home to tell us that Vicki had hit a rock causing her to fly off her bike into a tree. She was unconscious and bleeding from her head. Poor Julie was so upset and crying so Jerry took off running with her to go back to where Vicki was. I realized he had gone with no shoes on and had not taken even a towel with him; so I went next door and asked if the baby could stay at her place until one of us got back. Then Marci and I got into our car and drove the dirt road around the woods.

I was so relieved when we found Vicki sitting by the side of that road holding her shirt on her bleeding head. No longer unconscious, she was awake, waiting for someone to come to her aid! While Marci helped Vicki into the car I asked the neighborhood boy, Tommy, who was watching us, to wait there and tell Jerry that I had taken Vicki to the hospital. Jerry told us later that they had run to where Julie had left Vicki and then followed the bloody trail to where Tommy was sitting. Of course we felt sorry for Vicki and we were so thankful that she had not injured her eyes or any bones. The stitches just came out two days ago and it looks like she won't even have a scar. She is lucky and she knows it. The girls were grounded for a week because they were not supposed to go into that area in the first place. They didn't argue about that punishment. That's all for now.

Oh, have you thought any more about taking a vacation time to make a trip out here to see some of the Western coast of the United States. It really is beautiful here.

Hugs and kisses from the girls,
Liz

Frank read those words again about using his vacation time to visit Washington. Evie has already made up her mind as she would like to see some of our old friends who moved to Seattle a few years ago. He decided to keep these thoughts to himself for now.

"Surprise! Surprise!" Frank signed as he came through the door and spun Evie around from her stance at the stove. "You, me going California! I show boss Donna Mae's invitation and boss say, go! Use your vacation days before you lose. The two of us fly visit Donna two days then take a bus see Liz and family four days, then fly back home!" Frank was bursting with pride for having already made all of the arrangements at work, through Sally in the front office. Evie looked at Frank as though he had lost his mind. He had never surprised her with anything this big before. " Frank, tease me No!" she signed, with anxiety written all over her face. "Not tease! True!" Frank smiled. With that he took out two airline tickets from his pocket as well as tickets for the Greyhound out of San Francisco. "Finish cook, look later," Evie retorted, not wanting to believe her eyes.

After dinner that evening they read every word on all of the tickets, while Evie wrote down on a pad of paper just how much time they would be in the air, the wait time at the Denver airport and the flying time for the trip to San Francisco. Sally, at Frank's newspaper office, had even phoned their niece in Novato, her home just north of San Francisco! How kind Donna Mae and her husband were to invite them to visit! The next morning Evie wrote letters to Donna Mae, her sister-in-law Mable, and Liz.

What an exciting trip that was indeed. Donna had such a lovely home. Since her hubby was a Veterinarian with his own business place, Evie had surmised that they would have a home such as this. There was a big entryway leading to the stairway on the left, and into a huge dining room to the right. Beyond the stairwell was a large comfy den and kitchen. A fireplace at the end of the den held a huge clock that caught Evie's eye, while Frank took a seat at the kitchen bar as Donna gestured him to do so. She was already behind the counter fixing everyone a cool drink. Gesturing to the sliding doors, Evie could see a beautiful swimming pool. She turned to Donna with a questioning look which George picked up on; so he immediately took Evie's arm, opening the sliding door, and lead-ing her outside. The scene was breath taking to her until she saw the high bank! She signed to Frank through the glass door, "Lovely home with the exception of the back yard! Come see!" Puzzled, Frank stepped outside with Donna beside him.

On one side of the house was an in-ground swimming pool but all across the back was nothing but a hill that went straight up with no slope whatsoever. Of course Evie and Frank had noticed that a lot of California homes were built into mountain sides or above the cliffs. They looked dangerous but Donna assured them that her place was secure on solid ground and on an even plane with the majority of the town. George asked if they would like a little sightseeing trip and of course they both signed in the affirmative!

The ride into San Francisco was so interesting to Evie and Frank that there was no need for conversation. First they stopped by George's place right here in Novato. He was a Veterinarian and had three people on his staff. It was interesting to see what they were doing with a couple of dogs in the hospital wing recuperating after surgery. Evie especially enjoyed the area they had for animals to live and play while their owners were on vacations.

Then they returned to the road to see the city on the bay. They didn't want to miss any of the sights by writing notes; although, Donna did write down the names of special places that were familiar to them.

They enjoyed an evening with the children who were all fascinated with their signing of their names. The oldest son picked up on the alphabet quickly to please Evie. What a smart young boy, she mused. He was finger spelling his name and the school's name as well as the names of all the family members, including the dog. Donna's daughter, Peggy, was the delight of Frank's visit. What a cute little girl with blonde curly hair and a smile that never ended. But, like all good things, the visit came to an end the next morning as Donna drove them into town to catch their Greyhound bus.

The bus trip up the coast to Tacoma was perhaps the most beautiful one they had ever experienced, even though it made the heart beat a little fast when one looked down the side of the cliff into the ocean's bays located along the highway. On occasion when the bus turned a curve, Frank actually held Evie's hand in a caring manner. He had never done this in a romantic way or even on the airliner; so Evie felt contentment that he cared about her safety and chose to show it in this way. He certainly would never admit that it was just as frightening to him as it was to her. They even crossed some roads that were almost as high as the snowcapped mountains they could see off in the distance.

Soon the time came for the bus to drop down and drive into the bus station in Tacoma. Frank could see Jerry's station wagon in the parking lot but said nothing to Evie. As they descended from the bus Jerry was there to help Evie down the steps. Evie thought how handsome he looked in his blue Air Force uniform. She had seen pictures of Elvis Presley and told her daughter a long time ago that she thought Jerry looked just like him. Frank assumed from the uniform that Jerry must be taking some time off from work or on his lunch hour. But Jerry said nothing as he led them to the waiting room where Liz sat in a chair looking forlorn in her walking cast; but elated with her sparkling eyes and a big smile as they approached. The girls ran up to greet them with a hug as big as they could give. "Sit. Jerry get luggage and bring car front. We must hurry. Jerry must back work," signed Liz, as she gestured to some empty seats facing her.

By this time their movements had drawn attention from several people. This was not unusual and all of them had long ago learned to ignore the stares of strangers. For some reason, Vicki decided to just stare back at them until they looked away. Turning to her sister, she said, "I get so tired of people being so rude!" Frank saw the angry look on his granddaughter's face and asked Liz what was wrong with Vicki. Liz pretended to be busy with the baby and replied, "I don't know. We will ask her later. There's Jerry, need go." By the time they had packed the station wagon with their luggage and all eight members of the family, she knew Frank had forgotten about asking Vicki anything.

After they arrived home and showed grandma and grandpa that they would be sleeping in their room, Julie and Vicki picked up their backpacks and walked out the door. "They will stay nights with the neighbor girls while you are here so we are all comfy. They will be back here for breakfast." Liz finally convinced her parents they were no trouble at all. "The girls excited stay with friends. Anyway, closest hotel far. Jerry must work and we only have one car," she laughed.

Evie was impressed with the spacious condo that Liz explained was base housing. It was two stories with the three bedrooms upstairs and the comfortable living room-dining room combination taking up most of the first floor. There were big glass sliding doors leading out to an eight by ten patio. Immediately, inside the front door to the right, was the kitchen. She liked the way the kitchen was separated from the dining room by a short wall that included a pass-through window for food. Liz had done a good job of describing this in her letter.

The next morning was Saturday so Jerry took Frank to the Base Exchange where they bought some flowers to plant in the small space that served as their front yard. On the way back home, they stopped at another duplex and picked up Julie and Vicki to bring them home for the day. Frank explained to the girls that he wanted to plant the flowers by himself with a little help from the girls and they nodded in agreement. However, it turned out to be Frank giving a little help to the girls as they each grabbed a plant and put it into a hole that they had dug themselves. The three girls laughed at how dirty they were and lined up to wash up outside at the faucet hose before they entered the house. Julie picked up baby Connie who had been sitting in her stroller watching all the work in dirt, probably wishing she could be a part of it. Apparently she had enjoyed it anyway as she was laughing with them when they cleaned up afterwards.

The days were filled with laughter as they played games with grandpa and signed words with grandma. They had also made some serious plans. One day they drove over to Seattle to visit a deaf couple who had moved out here from Minnesota. Liz and Jerry had never taken the time for this trip before and thoroughly enjoyed the scenery. They had been lucky in securing a baby sitter for Connie for the whole day. The older girls were in school and would ride the school bus home.

Now Liz knew she could feel relaxed and communicate with her parents as much as she wanted to while Jerry enjoyed having a day off and relaxing with Liz. A warm greeting awaited them at their destination. It was such fun for Evie and Frank to catch up on their deaf news and for Evie to meet three sweet couples who were deaf. Two couples were the age of her parents but the other was just her age and when it was time to leave this couple promised to visit Liz and Jerry sometime. All the way home her parents chatted about their friends, their looks, their health, their home, and their friendship. Liz felt that they had enjoyed the day almost as much, if not more, than their whole trip to Tacoma.

The very next day, though, there was a change of plans. A phone call came from the daughter of the older deaf couple to say that they wanted Liz to interpret for a funeral that Friday in Seattle. When Liz spelled the name of the deceased to Frank he knew who the gentleman was and said they would like to attend the funeral. So, Liz accepted the challenge and carefully wrote down the directions to the church. Jerry managed to have another day off and made the same arrangements for the girls so that Liz could focus on her interpreting work.

Fortunately they arrived early and the piano player had the good sense to give Liz a copy of the notes that the minister had made about the order of the service. This included an obituary of the deceased which would be read with some additional remarks. Her parents were seated in a special section with their deaf friends and a folding chair was placed in front facing the deaf group. However, the group was large enough that Liz felt she would only be seen by all of them if she would stand. This was when she realized that for the first time in her life she was really going to interpret a service for a group, not just her parents! After the first few words that the minister spoke, her pulse slowed down as Liz relaxed realizing that the minister was quite articulate with his words and did not talk too fast.

The service was lovely and she was doing fine until the closing hymn. This was not presented by a live singer, but rather a recording which brought all eyes on Liz. A beautiful tenor voice began with "O Lord my God; When I in awesome wonder consider all the worlds thy hands have made," Liz froze! Music! A lovely tenor voice was giving such powerful sound to these words. I am supposed to interpret this to these sweet people in front of me, she panicked. I am supposed to bring all that profound emotion to these folks! I am supposed to make them feel inspired, through their sadness. I am supposed to give them comfort during this time of grief! How can I do that?! Then with a quick prayer to God to ask for the wisdom to do this, Liz began signing with her eyes closed. Thank goodness, the words were very familiar to her. Losing herself in this wonderful voice, focusing on each word, searching her mind for a conceptual sign and yet using graceful gestures; Liz gave all she could to the interpretation of this well-known hymn. She realized that God had just given her a little of his *amazing grace*.

It was over. Beginning in the back of the church the ushers directed people to the front to view the body and exit out the side door. When it was time for the deaf people to exit each one thanked Liz for interpreting. Her mother and father smiled at her and went on out the door. Liz sat down in the last row of pews and silently thanked God for being her guide today. She truly felt blessed as she headed for the exit to join her parents. Jerry was concentrating on the road so Liz relaxed and turned to the back seat where her folks were enjoying their chat instead of scenery just as she thought they would. It seemed Evie and Frank would never stop mulling through all the conversations that they had enjoyed with their Washington friends.

On the drive home she did not pay attention to her parents' conversation because she did not believe in signing while driving. It was not until they were relaxing after dinner in the evening that she had a chance to ask them if her signing had been understood well enough by all the deaf there. Had they learned anything about her interpretation skills from the other deaf folks there? Frank smiled and asked if Liz knew anything about the NRID (National Registry of Interpreters for the Deaf). Liz replied in the negative and Frank said he had not heard of them either but his deaf friend had given him a brochure to give to her. It contained information about a meeting of interpreters who were planning to set up a formal organization of professional interpreters.

"Much interest! I try maybe go," Liz signed enthusiastically. At this point Liz stopped to think how she really never addressed the person she was signing to. She didn't sign, "Daddy, that's interesting." She never said, "I love you, daddy." It was always just "I love you." She was just happy that she had finally learned to say I love you to both of her parents. She realized, too, one has to look directly at the person they are signing to when communicating with signs. That certainly implies that you are addressing the person you are looking at. Sometimes thoughts like this just went through her mind for no real reason. Just now it was probably because she was actually interested in the idea of becoming an interpreter for the deaf.

She was just beginning to realize how interpreting would not be easy just because she knew sign language; indeed American Sign Language was her first language. The difficulty arises when there is no sign for a word. You can just spell the word, that's true; however, it was much better if one could sign a word that has the same meaning. For example, while interpreting the funeral she heard the word *get* but knew that the sign normally used for *get* would imply *receiving*, while the meaning in the sentence she heard that day was *to become*. The sentence had been something like "He decided to get better educated." The word *get* could also mean *understand*, as in "Oh, I get it now!" These were simple examples and Liz knew there would be so many of them, all dependent on the subject area one is interpreting. Perhaps it was time to take some college classes and increase her vocabulary, she mused.

It was rather difficult to say goodbye to her parents after this busy visit. The girls hated to see them leave because they were just learning how much fun it was to play cards with their grandpa Frank. They all rode into Tacoma where Evie and Frank were taking the bus back to Novato again to spend a night with Donna. The plans were for Donna to take them to the airport the next day when they would head back to Minnesota.

After reading the brochure, Liz discussed it with her hubby and he arranged to have the day off from any duty at the base. It was just a month after her parents left, that Liz and Jerry drove to Seattle again. This time they took the girls with them and while Liz attended her meeting, Jerry took the girls sight-seeing and out for a late lunch. The meeting was such an ambitious idea set out by people just like her. Most of them were sons and daughters of deaf adults and some had a deaf relative. Liz could already tell this was definitely going to be a turning point in her life just as it was for others in the group.

The only difference was Liz still had four more years of military life to look forward to with Jerry which would postpone the time she could pursue this career. She also spoke out at the meeting that after just one solo as an interpreter she realized that just knowing sign language was not enough. "I know for myself that I need a broader education to gain vocabulary on which to draw for interpretation. I didn't go to college after graduating high school because of the likelihood of banning sign language from the schools; so I have only completed one semester of college which is not enough by a long shot. I will need to go back to school before I can feel comfortable as an interpreter in many

areas." Several people nodded in agreement and others commented on becoming lost in certain subjects they were interpreting in
school situations.

This would not be fair to the student. A whole new discussion
arose about qualifications of an interpreter. It was decided they
should include a college education for the interpreter himself!

Liz knew that having four children would leave her little time
to attend college classes; to say nothing of the workshops required
to enhance her skills in American Sign Language. However, she remained adamant that she needed to do so before one day applying
to the Registry of Interpreters for certification. This group discussed
such things as appointing committees to set up workshops, conduct
interviews and evaluate future interpreters. She signed her name to
the mailing list, wished them well and promised to keep in touch
with one of the attendees she had befriended. When Jerry picked
her up, the girls were so full of stories of their day in Seattle that
Liz found it hard to refrain from her news of the day; knowing only
Jerry would find it as exciting as she had.

Learning about the professional group of people who are interpreting for the deaf was such a great blessing for Liz. Not only
was she happy to know about the organization, but to understand
the role of an interpreter. Earlier Liz had only thought of the role
as that of a translator; for example, a person who changed a foreign language into English was usually known as a translator. To
Liz that was a scary thought when one considered a spoken word
changed into a signed word. Quite often there is not a sign for a
particular word, so now she understood that one would just be
expected to "interpret" the word. That would give more latitude
to the chore.

Liz tried to explain this to her hubby. "Jerry, it would give me
more leeway. If I don't know the meaning of a word I can fingerspell
it. I would give a definition or interpretation, if you will, of what I
think it is. Another good thing about signing is that it is a silent language with a silent audience so I could actually sign to them that I'm
not sure of the meaning and we would clarify the meaning as soon

as possible. A speaker often repeats important thoughts or words in layman's language, you know. I can look for that opportunity to correct any mistake I've made.

Speakers often read some text to support their subject and when they read, they always read faster than they do when speaking normally. I need to know if it is okay to interrupt the speaker and ask him to slow down when reading. Maybe an interpreter should request a short interview with the speaker before the event to discuss such matters.

Dearest Mother and Dad,   *February 2, 1969*

I wonder if you get tired of my letters always full of surprises?! Well, here is another one to add to the list. We are leaving here sooner than we thought! Jerry's duties here are coming to an end. And we are about to receive orders for Germany! Yes, the country of Germany. This will be our very best assignment yet because we will have the opportunity to visit so many historical places. Europe! How very exciting this is for our whole family. I cannot believe I will be visiting the country where your grandparents lived, mother. And I hope to visit Switzerland too, Daddy, where your grandparents lived. Maybe you two can come visit us while we are stationed there. Maybe Bobby can arrange a flight for you later this year, or next spring. Wouldn't that be great?! You will need to talk to Bobby about that possibility.

The one bad part about our move is that we must leave before school is out. In fact, they will have three weeks of school to complete before the end of the year. So, this means we will need to enroll the girls in school in Tulsa or Winona before we leave for Germany. They must finish their class year to receive report cards that will show them passing on into their next individual grades. Then we will take those to Germany for them to enroll in school there. The Air Force has schools on the base there. They won't be attending civilian schools because they would all be taught in German. Maybe the girls will all learn German while we're there. We expect to be there for three years or until the time that Jerry needs to decide if he wants to retire from the Air Force when he has twenty years completed. That would be in September of 1971. Anyway, for the three weeks of school now, I would prefer we come to Winona because there is really not room in Jerry's parents' home for all of us to stay for three weeks. Do you think that would be alright?

Of course we haven't even seen your new home yet but if you have a basement I think we can arrange something. What do you think? I know it sounds difficult but I am sure we will do just fine. I will let you know more details as we make our plans. I'm just praying that Jerry won't have to go to Germany before we do. It would be pretty rough on me to travel that far with four children and I do not want to stay in the states while he is gone for three years. I want to see Germany!

Love, Liz

Evie and Frank were dismayed and excited at the same time. Dismayed because they were worried about them taking such a long trip and to a foreign country! Excited because Liz and the girls would have a long visit with them before they leave. They would actually be living with them for a few weeks! There was so much to consider for their comfort. Also, excited because Liz was offering the idea that they could go visit them in Germany sometime! Evie sat down the very next day to write them a letter so that they would know how they could fix up the basement for the girls just fine. They had a fold away bed and a twin size bed down there and if Liz would buy a crib for Connie it would work out just fine.

Dear Liz,   *March, 1969*

Oh, my! Germany! Your father thinks wonderful you. Lucky you! But I think far away you live. How long you stay

Germany? Safe there? I want you come here, live with us but now own small house. Frank says it will all be okay. He wants to fix basement for girls' room. We already have three day beds down there with mattresses that can comfortable enough four children. But not you and Jerry. You sleep second bedroom. Do you think girls okay sleep downstairs themselves? Is nice warm down there; also, there's toilet and shower so not everyone lined up wait go potty. Ha. You think this good plan? Please tell us when expect you. We wait you arrive go groceries buy. Tell girls I bake apple pie know they love. We will so much enjoy you here for long visit!

Love, Mother & Dad

Liz read the letter from their grandmother to the girls when they got home from school. In doing so, she always read it with complete English sentences, thinking it was necessary for clarity. However, today she studied the sentence structure as written and thought how really quite simplified this was written. It was a lot like her own shorthand that she used many years ago before her boss had used a recorder for his letters. Shorthand was a great way to save time when the boss wanted to write a letter and get it into the mail the same day. Liz remembered how fairly easily she had picked up the subject while it was somewhat difficult for many of the students in her high school class. Now, years later, she realized that it was probably because she was, in fact, used to another way of quick communication, the American Sign Language.

Of course! Moreover, when watching her parents sign with their deaf friends, Liz would often think how sophisticated the language was. Not only was it a quick and easy way of communicating. With all the gestures and facial expressions ASL held more clarity of words. It would be extremely difficult to lie with signs because all of these areas need to melt together in the thought expressed. Yes, Liz thought, American Sign Language is the most sophisticated mode of communication that people can use.

Hopefully educators will encourage the use of sign language for all deaf children everywhere and classes will be held as well for hearing people of all ages.

The decision was made to go to Winona to live with Evie and Frank until the end of the school year. All of their household goods were once more packed up by the moving company that the Air Force hired with labels shipping to Wiesbaden A.F.B. in Germany. The only things they took with them for the next two months were their spring clothes which were packed in suitcases to travel with them in their station wagon. With the suitcases in the far back of the vehicle they still had three seats in which to put Connie's car seat with the older girls trading seats now and then to the back of the wagon. Liz even traded with one of them once a day for the front seat. They would sing songs, play "I see something green" games and take naps.

Two days and two nights on the road were required to reach Tulsa where they spent a few days before heading north to Minnesota. While in Tulsa, Julie sweetly thanked Dana for the dresses she had made and mailed to them for their birthdays and Christmas. "I love the material and pattern you picked out. I'll be glad when I am old enough to learn how to use the sewing machine. You know mother doesn't like to sew. She always runs out of patience!"

When they got to Grandma Evie's house, Julie remembered how to thank her for the dresses she had sent to them. She had to write a note. "But please don't send matching clothes anymore. I really liked the sailor dress. Yet, I think it was cuter on Vicki because she is little and looks like she's only eight when in fact, she is now eleven! We are older now, I am taller now and really are not anything alike. Ha! Thank you for all gifts you have sent us." Of course Evie read and re-read Julie's note and replied on the same note paper. "You are welcome. I understand. Maybe we go shopping one day and you can show me what you like. OK?" Julie shook her head in the affirmative and gave her grandma a big hug.

"It's really kind of fun down here, mother," Julie commented when asked how it was going down in the basement. "The beds are weird but comfy enough and it's great to have our own bathroom facilities. But we were wondering if we could, hmmm, could we have curtains of some kind over those windows? I know they are low when you are outside but you never know what kid might decide to kneel down and peek in on us!" "Oh, my goodness, honey, you are right! I'll see what grandma might have on hand and if there is nothing you can go with me to Woolworth's Saturday and buy some material. Maybe grandma will teach you how to use her sewing machine. Would you like that?"

Liz couldn't help but smile at her eldest daughter, noting how fast she was growing up. Just turning twelve this past month, it was more like Julie had turned sixteen. She always seemed to take on a mature role so she could feel older than her three sisters. Liz did not think she had required such a thing from her. She and Jerry did not go out much in the evening and promised each other that when they did, they would always get a babysitter so Julie would not have to feel responsible for the baby in the family. Liz was not really concerned about it, telling Jerry, "Julie is just like you, holds in her feelings while Vicki is just like me, spontaneous with laughs or tears. That's just their personalities and there is really nothing wrong with either one of them." Jerry tended to agree with her, grateful that Liz enjoyed her girls as much as he did.

She could spend hours with them indoors or out; sledding, skating and bowling throughout the winter with swimming, walking, and bike riding in the summer. Liz was always willing to play "Old Maid" or "Go Fish" when the girls asked. That was when they were little and as they grew older, board games and card games became a family fun time indoors anytime.

Liz knew Jerry appreciated her devotion to the girls while he was often gone with the band to various places. She always enjoyed it when he took her with him when the band played locally as often as he could. They enjoyed dinner and Bingo at the NCO Club following payday each month; and joined a local civilian bowling league wherever they were stationed. While on the island of Guam they learned Bridge, striving to find other couples who played; but if not Bridge then Canasta would suffice.

"Are you happy, Liz?" "All in all, yes, I am happy!" Liz signed in reply. She wondered what had brought on that question by her mother. Perhaps she was trying to persuade Liz to stay in Winona while Jerry served his time in Germany. "I not understand how you can move with four children far, far away again! Three years so long time not see you!" Evie did not waste any time getting into this adult conversation after the kids had gone downstairs to get ready for bed.

Jerry interrupted this discussion immediately with a side comment to Liz. "Tell her that she and Frank might think about coming to see us while we're there! Bobby could help them get their seats reserved along with information to the airlines that they are deaf and will need help transferring to another flight out East going to Germany!" With these words barely out of her husband's mouth, Liz acted excited and with wide eyes she interpreted Jerry's words to her parents. Pretending it was all Jerry's idea, she added, "Wow. Wouldn't that be great?"

Even though Liz had already mentioned that possibility in a letter, Evie seemed stunned with this information. She looked at Frank to read his response. However, Frank was just staring at Evie with a queried look on his face. Turning to Liz he said, "What that mean? What we do? How we fly overseas? Passports? Expensive? You pick us up airport Germany? Jerry time off? You drive ? Need German Driver's license? Far base from civilian airport? You live base?" Frank's signs flew so fast Liz just broke out in a long laugh! She forgot momentarily to voice to Jerry what her dad was signing so he remarked, "I'm glad you are laughing. I was afraid Frank was upset with me!"

The most difficult thing about this time in Winona was the school situation for the girls. All three of them were unhappy with their building, classes, and their peers. Jerry was most understanding of the cultural differences between their girls and the children from the rural area or this small town. It was also true that unlike moving from one Air Force base to another, there were not many occasions that children moved into this school district from out of state. This rarity caused the local students to have a negative attitude in welcoming "the new kids on the block." Even their accents and speech patterns were quite different from the Minnesotans.

Julie and Vicki were fortunate in being in the same building and would encourage each other to get through the day. However, Marci felt absolutely alone and often came home with a sad face. The only fun for her was sharing her day with her older sisters and getting their sympathy rather than their usual apathy. All Liz could seem to say was, "It's just for a couple of weeks. Hang in there and do the best you can on the finals so that you get that certificate to pass on to the next grade." Actually all three of them were finding classes to be easy and had very little homework.

They were happy when the weekends came and they could visit cousins in Altura and Rollingstone with all the interesting things going on at their farms. Actually, Liz was glad that the girls had an opportunity to see the different way of life on the farm. "Maybe they will appreciate the easy life they have when they see the amount of chores your children have out here," Liz remarked to her cousin while sitting in the kitchen sipping a cup of real brewed coffee. "I'll never forget the times I had with you on this farm and over at Les' place. Aunt Alice and Aunt Mable always found something for us to do. We were lucky to find one hour of the day to play with our paper dolls or get up a game of croquet or softball."

Liz laughed with the memory of it and then realized how most of her cousins had chosen to continue this very same lifestyle for their adult life. They seemed one hundred percent happy too! "Perhaps this is the kind of life God intended all of us to live," Liz mused as they drove home after an afternoon on the farm. "Love and be loved; what greater thing is there in life? Jerry, are you listening?"

Liz had learned long ago how to keep their "discussions" from becoming downright arguments. Jerry was always overly confident about a subject. Often Liz would simply drop the subject; especially if it held no real importance in their lives. She didn't like arguments, especially in front of their girls. She could still remember how hurt and lonely she would feel when she saw her parents having arguments, hating the looks on their faces. Her mother's soft beautiful face changed. Her blue eyes blazing fire and her voice sounding like a hawk squawking at a predator around her nest. Dad was not so vocal and instead of anger on his face, he looked sad, forlorn as though he wanted to give up; perhaps give up on their marriage.

Not allowing Liz to distract him from focusing on the dirt road full of ruts, Jerry answered reservedly, "Yes. Are we not doing that too? Just because we chose to serve our country in a different way, are we not pleasing God with the service? The farmers are supplying our country with food; we are supplying it with our support, or playing for the troops, helping their morale. Besides, don't belittle the fact that our girls are getting to see different lifestyles all over the world! They will have a wide range of experiences to draw from when they are deciding on what career path to follow." Jerry's voice was raised by now and somewhat defensive. "Oh, of course you are right, hon. I was just saying there is a lot to be said for the simple life. I wouldn't trade our lifestyle for theirs permanently; just maybe for a day," Liz said calmly keeping this conversation a discussion.

On other Saturdays, there was a movie theater not too far from their grandparents' home; and a little deer farm that Connie loved to visit. Again, after the homework was out of the way, evenings of card games with mom and grandpa were always fun.

As Liz promised, the time went by quickly and soon it was time to get on their way! Jerry managed to sign and spell to his father-in-law how they would be in New York in just two days. There the plan was to stay overnight in base housing after Jerry took care of the paperwork to ship the old station wagon to Germany. Frank had been so surprised when Jerry told him they could send their station wagon overseas on a ship. They would be given a "rent car" upon arrival until their own vehicle arrived about three weeks later. At absolutely no expense to them! Again, he marveled at the way the Air Force handled things for the families when they had to make a move. Goodbyes were very difficult for everyone and Jerry was the one to push his wife into the car, signing to his mother-in-law, "We must go!"

Frank just wished Evie could see the great life their daughter was having, instead of the fact that they didn't get to see them often enough. This had been a grand time having their grandkids here for a month; but he knew it was time for them to get back to their normal life. Besides he and Evie were pretty worn out after all the activities they had enjoyed with the girls.

The Powell family had a good road trip with absolute peace on board; not even one argument arising among the girls. Liz surmised that was because they were all happy to leave the Minnesota schools they attended and a little excited to be moving to a strange country. Their plans worked out exactly as they had hoped and soon they were on the big Jet airliner on their way to Germany. The smooth plane ride was uneventful until they landed in Ireland to refuel. Anyone sleeping was awakened with a jolt when the thick fog caused the pilot to make a rough landing. Yet they all laughed and sighed with relief as they came to a stop in front of a building with a lounge in sight. After a short break with sweet rolls, juice and coffee, they were all aboard again for the last leg of their trip. By the time they landed in Germany the sun was shining brightly in the East and a smooth landing here brought cheers from the passengers.

As scheduled, another Air Force couple met their plane in Frankfurt and after walking through customs they were on their way to their new home. During the drive they were enthralled with the beautiful countryside and the unique buildings. Liz was so grateful that the girls seemed just as excited as their daddy was when they all listened to their host driver describe the homes, villages, and gardens outside of their village. "Many of the residents do not have space for a garden at their homes so they rent a plot on the edge of town and keep their tools in a little shed there. You can see that along the road here. They are beautiful gardens because of the rich black soil and you will see markets in town where they sell their products.

"And, this is Koningstadten. In German that means *king's town*. This is where you will live until you get housing on the base. That may be three to six months. If school starts before you move on base you will catch a school bus to the base. No one attends the local school because they all speak only German. Your neighbors on both sides are German, with the exception of us. We live upstairs next door right now but we are moving on base next week. I understand there will be another American family moving in upstairs in your house so you won't be lonesome," he said as he pulled the car to a stop at the curb.

The whole family looked up at the house sitting just five yards back from the wrought iron fence outlining the property, crossing the front yard ending with a matching black wrought iron gate at the entrance. There was no driveway to indicate a garage. Everyone parked on the street. When they had unloaded the car and each adult had a suitcase in hand, their host pressed a button at the gate which opened slowly. After they all came through, he pressed the button again that not only closed the gate but also locked it. "If one of you were at home inside; this buzzer would tell you to open the gate to a visitor. That is the formality of the "natives"; however, we choose to leave it unlocked all of the time at our place unless the folks downstairs want to lock it."

When they came through the first door, they stood still in awe. There were two doors on either side of a hallway which would make one feel like this was an apartment complex. Liz's first thought was that their home would be very small if there were four apartments on this floor! "No," Duane commented, "It's not what you think, Liz. The first floor is all yours but each room has a door that the landlords keep closed to save on the heating bill. They even lock them but, again, we Americans find that mind-boggling to say nothing of time consuming! You will need to open the doors and allow the heat to flow through, that won't take long really. Oh, and I should tell you, your heat was turned off May 15th and won't be turned on again until September 15th. You'll find that there really are not many days in between when you will wish you had heat."

With this, he pulled a big ring of keys down from a nail high on the wall in the corner and proceeded to open each door with a different key. Then Julie and Vicki went into one room and yelled back that it was their bedroom; so Marci joined them. Jerry and Liz continued to walk from room to room, checking out the cabinets with some food already stocked for them. Noting the kitchen with a small table for four, a living room with comfortable furniture, and three bedrooms, one separated with a bathroom next to it in the hall, they were satisfied. On the beds were huge comforters and pillows, very inviting right now because everyone was exhausted!

Their sponsors, Duane and Terri, knew from experience that they would all want to take a nap, so they made their farewells and invited them to supper the next evening. After visiting each room again, the girls soon found their own comfy beds and with little more said, they were sound asleep. Even Connie was happy to lay her head down on that big feather pillow and said good night even though it was only four in the afternoon. Liz watched Jerry stretch out on the left side of the bed and realized she wanted to do the same on "her" side. Feeling a bit chilly, she first walked into the girls' bedrooms and covered them up before lying down and drawing covers over her hubby and herself. Jerry was already snoring! She supposed they all needed a good nap. It wasn't long after her thoughts settled down, about the trip they had just completed, and what she would find for dinner later, that Liz fell into a deep sleep too.

No one had seen any need to set an alarm clock so the night was completely gone when Liz opened her eyes again. Amazing! This seemed to be the morning sun shedding its bright rays into this strange bedroom. Looking at her watch, she thought it was eight o'clock in the evening but she knew the sun was shining from the direction of sunrise, not sunset! She was also surprised to see that Jerry was not in the bed! "Good morning, hon! Can you believe we all slept all night!" Jerry exclaimed as he set down a tray with two cups of coffee. "I found a coffee pot with coffee and water in it all ready to plug in. The girls are still sleeping. I guess we were really tired. How do you feel?"

"Oh, my gosh. This is unreal. We slept sixteen hours! I feel good. How about you?" Liz's voice was warm and inviting. "Great! I think we need to christen our new bed in our new home in a new land. I know the perfect way to do that and I'm not talking about hot coffee," he said as he closed the door behind him and gently pushed Liz back down on the bed with a long kiss.

What a beautiful morning it was. Liz was frying bacon and sausage when Julie and Vicki came out of their bedroom with sleepy faces and asked if this was our supper. Their unbelief at the hour was heard by Marci and Connie as they came running in to join the laughter and sit down for a big breakfast, their first meal in this country called Germany. Later they would find out that Germany was a name that Americans knew this country by, but European countries had different names for it; the Germans called it Deutschland while the French called it Albania.

This was just the beginning of all the things they would learn and see here in their new home. Yes, this would be their home for the next three years. After all, home is where the heart is. The days ahead would be filled with so many interesting sites to see. Liz couldn't wait to write a letter to her parents describing their new environment. Every letter that Liz wrote home after that contained some new place they had visited. She always had pictures to enclose so they could easily imagine what Liz was writing about in her letters.

Dearest Mom and Dad,   *Nov 9, 1969*

I do hope you can come visit us someday as there is so much to see here. We are very comfy in our house. It didn't take the girls long to discover that everyone in our neighborhood speaks German. Also, the children here are never out during the week because they are in school late and when they come home they stay inside and do their homework. On Saturdays we see a few boys playing ball in the street but the girls stay indoors and help their mothers do housecleaning, cooking and baking. The families are very strict and no one has swings or toys in their yards. The yards are full of vegetables or flowers. They do not waste any space with kids' things. Wow!

I'm glad our girls have two American girls upstairs to play with. Their dad and Jerry put up a swing set in our back yard. Although the girls have invited the neighbor kids to come over and swing, they just smile and walk away. Our landlord, Fritz, is a little man, about fifty years old; a good looking young German with thick dark eyebrows that seem to defy gravity. I think his wardrobe consists of nothing but overalls and a denim shirt, always clean. He used fluent English when he told us the Germans do not like we Americans having such play things in the yard. Thank goodness he said he has no problem with it at all.

Anyway, every morning after Jerry and the three girls have left for the base school and work, Connie and I quickly clean up the breakfast dishes. Then we love to take a walk around this small village. There is a nice little park just a few blocks away but they have no swings or picnic areas which is strange and disappointing to my little angel. She can't understand how there can be a place called a "park" with no swings or see-saws. "No wonder there are no kids here like me, Mom," she says every day. I've been told that is because they do not want anything destroying their green trees and grassland.

We do see some women riding their bicycles on the path though. They ride their bikes to do all of their shopping in town almost every day. Then I was told that their bread has no yeast in it which explains why the housewife goes shopping every day! We wait until payday and then go out to the base with Jerry to do our grocery shopping at the Commissary which stocks food mostly shipped here from the States. Not on a ship! On an airplane. Ha. There is plenty of good food to choose from and it's probably the biggest Commissary I've ever been in. Once in a while I will pick up some bread or coffeecake at the local bakery just a couple of blocks from our house. It is so good. I buy it on a Friday and it is all gone by Sunday. It reminds me of Aunt Alice's wonderful doughnuts or rolls.

The girls all love their school on base as everyone is just like them; far from homes in the United States, yet, still with family. They've all had the same experience as our girls, of

*visiting grandparents and making new friends in new neigh-
borhoods; often just getting to know them and then having to
say goodbye. I'm sure it has not been easy on the girls just as
it hasn't always been easy for Jerry and I; however, we still
feel it's a great experience for all of us. I do hope you both
can understand that.*

*We are making tentative plans to take a train to Berlin
next month! Yes, it may sound dangerous to you but just
know we will have armed soldiers on board to protect us at
all times. I'll tell you all about it when it happens.*

*I best close now as Jerry will be picking Connie and
I up soon so we can go out to the base and watch Marci
play softball at her school. Julie and Vicki will walk over
there from their school and meet us. Dad, the girls wanted
me to tell you that sometimes Julie gets to pitch and Vicki
makes a very good third baseman. Julie's not at all bad
as a pitcher but the team has one girl who is very good.
I love watching the game and chatting with other parents
while Connie finds friends her own age to play with behind the bleachers.*

*Have you talked with Bobby yet about a flight to Germany
to spend some time with us here? We don't want to wait too
long because I want you to see this village, Koningstadten,
where we live, before we move onto the base. Jerry says we
are moving up fast on that housing waiting list.*

*Hugs from the girls.
Love, Liz*

It was three months later, in one of her mother's letters, Evie said
that their plans were made, they really were coming to visit. She even
wrote ideas of their own they would like to visit while in Germany.
Liz was thrilled that Evie had enclosed their itinerary. Liz could
hardly believe it! She could feel that Evie had closed her letter with
excitement as she read on, noting improvement in Evie's English too.

"Yes, Liz, Bobby helps us all plans. He take us on plane in Twin Cities. Bobby give instructions to stewardess how communicate with us pencil paper notes. Someone guide us to right gate transfer in New York. We wait two hours next flight. So, time to use the restroom, eat and pick up newspaper to read. Of course I am nervous and excited both. Your father so proud to land on our grandparents' homeland. He wants to see everything while we there. I just want to enjoy the girls. Oh, but I would love go shopping! See you in two weeks!"

Love, Mother & Father

Needless to say, Liz and the girls worked hard cleaning up the whole apartment, especially the guest room which the younger two girls had to give up for them. They arranged some flowers on the dresser along with their cute china kittens that they knew Grandma would love. Marci and Connie remembered when they were living in Grandma's basement that grandma had several pictures of kittens that she had cut out of magazines and taped them on the cement block wall. That "daybed" of grandma's was so interesting to them.

Grandma said it was already thirty-five years old but the springs were still strong and the mattress was firm. It was really neat the way they could fold it up during the day and put a nice piece of cloth over it to hide it away in the corner. They reminded their mother of this bed and asked her to shop for one like that here in Koningstadten. It would be perfect for them to have while they had company just like this. But, alas, there was no bed to be found anywhere so sleeping bags were used on the floor. The girls always loved "camping out" on the living room floor and they didn't mind a bit giving up their twin beds to grandma and grandpa.

This would prove to be fun anyway even though Marci felt that she didn't get enough sleep to put in a good day at school. Thank goodness their visit coincided with spring break so she could sleep in when she needed. Liz wondered if Bobby had looked into the calendar for spring break in Germany!? So she called the school office where they confirmed that they tried to hold spring break here at the same time as public schools did in the United States. That was smart!

The day Frank and Evie arrived Liz and Jerry found the airport to be so crowded that they had the girls sit in the baggage area where they put Julie in charge. Liz could see that their flight was in and deplaning as they approached the arrival area. Keeping their eyes glued on all the people going through Customs, Liz and Jerry relayed back and forth that they did not see her parents anywhere! All of a sudden Liz felt someone tapping her on the shoulder and when she turned to look, it was her dad! "Oh, my, you must go through Customs," she signed to him. Just then a stewardess walked up with Evie in tow and explained that they were not required to go through Customs as they entered the area with her! "Much lucky, you!" Liz signed to her mother. Jerry thanked the stewardess and started to tip her but she refused the money stating that Bobby was an airlines employee and had taken care of all the arrangements, including tips.

On the ride home, Liz tried to point out the interesting sights as well as telling her folks a little of the plans they had made for their bedroom comfort and for their touring interests. Knowing how tired her parents were when they arrived at the house Liz immediately put a light supper on the table and suggested that they go to bed early. After they retired, Liz and Jerry discussed a schedule for the next two weeks. The girls listened in and soon joined in with their ideas on where to go. Of course their ideas were gained through the experiences that their peers at school had shared with them.

Jerry said he was not fortunate enough to get a spring break from his work. However, he managed to get four days away, so this was a perfect time for the whole family to take a trip to a nearby country; so plans were made to visit Holland. Packing up the station wagon so that there was enough room for six passengers proved to be a bit tricky but somehow they managed to do so. Actually, Connie and Marci enjoyed the rear seats as long as the luggage was strapped down and away from them. Driving north on the autobahn was a bit tiring for Jerry and Liz. Not because of the length of time; but for the intimidating speed of the local drivers that was hair-raising to say the least. Unfortunately there was no speed limit! Jerry would often say that the German people drove fast because if there was an accident no one ever lived to tell about it. They couldn't relate to others details about how or why it happened. No one survived with terrible injuries or pain, they were simply killed. The natives didn't seem to recognize that if they drove slower they might live through an accident if there should be one.

They arrived at their destination, Den Haag, before the sun had set so they could take in all the scenery before finding their hotel. Everyone but the driver enjoyed the sights, Jerry thought to himself, as he concentrated on finding street signs and numbers on the buildings.

Finally they pulled up in front of the hotel where they were to stay. Liz jumped out and entered the doors to walk to the front desk. The clerk found their reservation and checked them in. Evie watched through the windows, noting Liz pointing out to the car, while the clerk pointed upstairs. Jerry was already at the back of the wagon opening the door and reaching for the suitcases when Liz came out and said calmly to him, "Our rooms are upstairs and the steps look pretty steep. I do hope mom and dad can traverse them alright!" "Hmmm," Jerry murmured, "Perhaps we best take them in first and see what they think. Although I don't think there will be any other place to stay at this late notice!"

So, Liz explained the situation to her folks as carefully as she could. They both simply nodded and stepped out of the vehicle signing to each other to go see what Liz was talking about. The clerk looked at the couple coming in the door and knew right away they would have a problem. She started talking to them before Liz had re-entered the building. Frank pointed to his ears, shaking his head negatively and holding his other hand out to include his wife. The hotel clerk seemed not to understand the gestures but waited until the young lady returned. Addressing Liz, she said "Oh, I am afraid your parents are too old to go up those stairs. However, I can put them up in a separate room downstairs. Would you like to see that?" When Liz interpreted the remarks, her mother walked over to the steep stairs, looked back at her husband and shaking her head signed strongly, "We cannot climb these! Same ladder! Please see other room."

Jerry came in with the girls and their luggage just in time to see his mother-in-law's signs with an expression on her face that made it all very clear. The lady took Frank and Evie to see the room while he carefully climbed the stairs with a large suitcase in hand. Then he told the girls to come up without their suitcases and allow him to bring them up later. He knew they couldn't handle the climb with bags in hand.

Liz sighed with relief when her mother and dad came out of the room the owner showed them with big smiles, nodding a definite acceptance of the room on the first floor. The next morning everyone was in a good mood indicating that all had slept well. The hotel clerk led them into the big kitchen where they sat down at lovely wooden tables, decorated with vases full of yellow tulips. They could watch the cook as she worked around the old fashioned stove.

Breakfast was served with no menu having been presented; however, to the delight of all, it was a hearty breakfast that satisfied each one. A hot cereal was served first with boiled eggs sitting in their own individual egg dishes. There was crisp bacon, pork sausage, bagels and hot cinnamon rolls rounded out the breakfast. Frank ordered coffee and asked if it was okay to light up his cigar if he moved to the corner table where no one sat nearby. The waitress gave her permission and the family nodded an okay. They knew how important that cigar was to him.

"Grandpa looks so content," Julie commented to her sisters as they all relaxed around the table. They understood they were allowing mom, dad, and grandma to enjoy their coffee. They knew that in due time they would begin their tour of this strange but lovely city.

The first thing on Daddy's agenda was to visit a place called the Village at Madurodam. They were not sure of what to expect but when they alighted from the wagon they were immediately amazed at what they saw. This was a miniature village with buildings of all sizes and shapes but none taller than two feet. It was designed so that you were virtually walking the streets from downtown through a residential section to the airport at the edge of town which was full of real model airplanes moving in and out of the hangars. Near to downtown businesses was a castle. Around the property were little guards standing at the moat and entrance to the old castle. How fun this was to imagine oneself a giant visiting the folks on the streets of the city, thought Marci. Connie wanted to pick up the sheep out on the countryside but was reminded by their daddy of the sign telling them not to touch anything.

This tour ate up three hours of their precious day before they decided to go on to lunch outside a quaint café and continue with a tour of a doll museum. Actually the doll museum was at one side of the building with antique furniture on the other; offering something interesting to all members of the family. The girls noted how this museum was just one of the buildings right at the side of the street with very little signage to indicate what would be seen inside. Another such museum was really some famous person's home. Attending to both grandparents as they climbed the steps made of narrow stone, they entered the building slowly. There they continued the climb upward in a circular pattern. On the second landing they were allowed to look into individual rooms filled with antique furniture. However, there were ropes across each doorway barring their actual entrance into any room.

After descending this particular stairway, both grandma and grandpa were tired so they headed back to the hotel to rest. After another delicious meal at the hotel that evening, Evie and Frank declared their readiness to retire and said their goodnights to everyone early. Liz and Jerry discussed the possibilities for the evening, making a decision to go for a stroll in the nearby park. The girls were told to walk two by two, and keep an eye on each other. Julie and Connie; then Vicki and Marci with Liz and Jerry leading the way.

After a few blocks they were surprised to see a little band setting up on a small bandstand covered with vines of honeysuckle. "Can we stay and listen to the band, Daddy, please?" the girls asked in a chorus together. Liz always thought they must plan that sort of ploy before actually calling out in such perfect harmony but they denied having made such a plan together. "You know, Jerry, since my folks aren't with us we could stay for a little music. This would be a quiet enjoyable ending to an exciting day!" Liz's voice followed the girls' pleas as she whispered closely into her hubby's ear.

She knew this was probably not exciting to him because he traveled with the band so often to other countries where he would listen to foreign groups play prior to the Air Force Band giving their concert. Liz and the girls were fortunate in going into Wiesbaden a couple of times with him where they loved to hear the German bands blaring with the deep "oom pah pah" of their bassoons. Happy for an opportunity to relax with good music, Jerry laughed at the girls' demands as he headed toward the benches already filling up with local people.

This was one of those times that Liz could feel tears welling up in her eyes at the thought of her parents not able to enjoy music such as this. She would always tell herself to be rational; if they had never heard music they could not miss it! Comforting herself in this way she could enjoy music without feeling guilty that she could hear! Thank God all of her girls could appreciate music! For that matter, thank God they each have hearing. Sometimes Liz wondered if God had something planned for her because of having deaf parents; she always closed out these thoughts with the facts of her life in the here and now.

The next morning they packed the car early, starting out without breakfast so they could stop at a restaurant outside of town. The drive home was even more interesting than the Autobahn had been. Jerry said to really appreciate the architecture of Holland they should take the country roads home. This prediction was true as they drove through a couple of small towns where the notable thing was roofs of tile, unlike any they had ever seen before. They were large pieces of tile that looked more like sheets of tin. Many of the homes were made of rock with a variation of vines growing on them as though trying to give a warm welcoming look despite the cold appearance of the roof.

Evie had been constraining herself but when she saw the charming little gift shops on the side street she leaned over to her daughter and asked if they had enough time to stop and do a little shopping for souvenirs. Liz interpreted to her hubby and the girls immediately yelled with joy. Jerry found a place to park and they all disembarked for a couple hours of shopping. Coming out of one of the shops, Vicki and Marci called to their dad outside and asked if they could walk to the stone wall that seemed to surround the village. Jerry, Frank and the other girls walked just a block to the beautiful stone wall.

As they approached, they were amazed to realize this wall of stones was all that separated the village from the ocean waters. This was another sight they would report on in school next week. Other students would have similar experiences to tell about when the teacher asked, "What did you do during spring break?"

Now it was time to continue with their shopping. Time was running short. Each one of the girls picked out one thing to take home in the first shop while grandma and Liz looked over many counters of gifts and souvenirs in four different stores before making their decisions. Evie decided to buy three pairs of wooden shoes to take to her grandchildren back in Minnesota. Julie was a little jealous of this but held her tongue. Liz bought three little figurines of Dutch boys playing instruments, an accordion, a violin and saxophone.

Jerry and Frank were each enjoying an ice cream cone when the girls found them again so before leaving this village they all had some flavorful dishes of ice cream. Much to their surprise this little shop had some space behind where some music was playing. Liz and Jerry were not going to mention the music to her parents because they could not enjoy it anyway. However, the floors were wood and soon Evie could feel the vibrations so she asked if there was music somewhere. When Liz told her there was some coming from the back room, Evie got up and went through the door, returning in just a couple of minutes. "Come, Liz, dance with me!" she exclaimed. Liz laughed, joining her mother to see what was going on. There was a small band of musicians playing polkas with two couples on the floor dancing. Feeling somewhat embarrassed at first, Liz tried to turn her mother around to rejoin her dad and Jerry.

By this time, though, the girls had come through and asked if they could dance. Liz could not refuse them this fun time so she took her mother's arm and led them all onto the dance floor. Putting her hand around Evie's waist, Liz was pleasantly surprised at her mother's following her lead. Evie knew how to polka!

They didn't do a fast step as was necessary for the tune but somehow Liz cut the rate in half and still kept the pace right to swing her mom around the floor a couple of times before they both sat down laughing so hard they cried. "I can't believe you dance so well!" Liz signed to her mother. "I know, but now you do!" Evie signed with a smile. This was a moment to cherish Liz thought. Her mother rarely seemed happy with her life which led to very little laughter like today. Liz loved the fact that deaf people could enjoy music after all.

"I've never felt so close to her," she told Jerry on their ride home. "Good. Well, I have one more place to visit on our agenda in the next village. I'm not telling you what it is now but you will see it long before we are there," Jerry said. "That sounds like a puzzle, Daddy. What is it?" Vicki queried. "You heard me. I'm not telling you now but you will know before we get there," her dad replied.

"There it is! I know what it is, Daddy," a voice filled with pride was heard from the rear of the wagon. Vicki was the first to solve the puzzle; it was a windmill farm! They could see six or eight tall windmills in the distance and were a bit frightened as Jerry followed the road leading up and over the dikes. Julie, the budding artist, was already painting a picture in her mind as she looked down into fields of tulips that seemed to reach for miles and miles in all directions. They could see windmills scattered across the fields and by the time they pulled up to one of them, Evie and Frank were as excited as the rest of them. None of them had ever seen a real windmill before.

Here they got out and stretched their legs with a short walk up the road to the next windmill. There seemed to be no one around. The girls ran on the grass around the perimeter of one of the big objects, surprised to know just how large an area the base covered. A short fence surrounded the building with a front door and two windows making it look very much like someone's little home.

Not knowing what the propriety might be about these windmills, Jerry suggested they get back in the station wagon and continue their trip home. Disappointed, but understanding their daddy's military ethics in doing the proper thing as a tourist in another country; they ran back to the car screaming about who would get to sit in the back even though that decision had been made before they ever left home. Each one was to enjoy the rear of the wagon for 1 hour before trading with a sister who was sitting either in the front seat with grandpa and daddy or the second row with grandma and mom. Liz knew any one of them would become tired of the cramped space back there in anything over an hour so this was a fair way to kill two birds with one stone.

The next weekend was full of interesting history, especially for Frank. They visited the Gutenberg Museum in Mainz, just across the river. Here Frank studied the inventions of Gutenberg to do with printing. As a linotype operator, Frank could have spent hours looking at the machinery to do with the printing of newspapers. Evie was astounded as Frank said he wanted to visit the gift shop and take home a souvenir. However, it was not for Evie to choose, it was his choice alone. "This is it!" he exclaimed as he handed Evie the tiny object. "What this?" Evie could not even focus on the tiny print on the cover of this book. "It is the smallest Bible ever printed, printed right here by Gutenberg! I must have it no matter what the cost." Frank knew that Evie would not share his joy but he did not care. "You know cannot carry much home in suitcases but this need no space. I carry in my shirt pocket," he signed as he carefully withdrew his billfold from his deep pant pocket to pay the clerk. Evie had to agree to Frank's consideration of space. She honestly had not given that much thought when she bought her souvenirs. Now she began to sort out in her mind how she would pack her suitcase, promising herself she did not need any more souvenirs.

On that Sunday Frank opted to stay home. He seemed tired and did not want to go on this trip with the family. Liz was concerned but Evie reminded her that her father had problems with too much walking because of his one leg being shorter than the other. Liz felt bad when she realized why her dad wanted to stay home. Her mother had told her the story some years ago when Liz asked about him having a little limp. It was a very slight limp so that Liz had really forgotten about it.

The story Evie told was of Frank's childhood. He had contracted polio but they had done nothing for him because it had not seemed like a serious case to the nurse who had checked him out. Since he was away at school the family was not aware of any change in his gait. At school the change was so slow that it was not noted by any of the staff members; in fact, only his roommate became aware of it after watching him run the bases during a ball game. He asked Frank about it afterwards and was cut off sharply by his signs, "No, you are wrong. I was just tired. I'm fine!"

Evie joined the family on this little excursion even though she was not in favor of anything to do with water in a lake or a river. Reassured by Liz that it was a big boat and she would not feel any bumps in the waves, Evie kissed Frank goodbye. She knew that he would probably spend the afternoon trying to read that little print in that tiny Bible.

The cruise on the Rhine proved to be a smooth one thanks to the bright sunny day with just a little breeze. The sights were wonderful. There were grapevines growing on the high hillsides with people picking the grapes in such an awkward position one would think they might fall at any moment. The girls were enjoying some music which Evie could not hear of course; but watching the fellow with the accordion was fun. Soon they stopped and pulled ashore with no explanation given to Evie. Liz apologized for not having informed her of this part of the trip but she was really afraid that Evie may not have even come along if she knew that they were going to tour a castle! This did sound somewhat frightening to Evie but she could see the girls were bursting with excitement, so she told Liz to lead the way.

The tour did include some hiking uphill so Liz stopped with her mother for a break half way where there was a nice little nook with benches out of the sun. Evie insisted that Liz go on and enjoy the castle with her family and let her stay here to rest and enjoy the view. There was another couple sitting close by so Liz told them about her mom being deaf and asked if they would keep an eye on her.

Catching up with Jerry and the girls, she asked if each of them would take a turn in sitting for a little while with grandma who was only five minutes away. This worked out just fine and when they were satisfied with what they had seen, they all returned to the boat. They hadn't waited long before everyone was back on board and the cruise continued another mile before turning around and returning to Wiesbaden where they had started their ride. About half way on this leg of the journey Liz quietly asked Jerry, "Look! Watch the cook! See what he's doing?" The cook had come up from the galley with a big bowl of garbage, potato peelings, vegetable cores, lettuce leafs and some other unknown substances. He sat down on a seat in the front, almost hidden from their sight; and slowly poured it all into the river! "Don't say anything. We can't cause any trouble with civilians. Besides this must be their regular routine. Maybe the fish eat the stuff. Who knows?" Liz didn't agree but knew that he was right in not repeating what they had seen. Her mother had not seen any of it and the girls were sitting backwards watching the waves at the rear of the boat. Liz thought she might like to share that story with her dad that evening but that didn't happen.

The girls were full of stories about the boat and the castle they wanted to share with their grandpa. After attempting to do so with sign language, Julie and Connie decided to draw pictures. Ten years difference in their ages, yet these two girls were already alike in their love of art and both parents agreed that they had real talent. Frank was thrilled with their pictures and found this was something else he could put into his suitcase that would not take up any space!

Two weeks flew by and it was time for grandma and grandpa to leave. Truthfully, they were ready to leave as their old bones cried out for the comfort of their own bed. Marci and Connie were happy to have their beds back too; and Liz had run out of ideas for meals and entertainment. So it was with a contented and happy note that they all said their goodbyes at the airport.

Frank, Evie and 7 grandkids (1969)
Corrine, Julie, Barry, Connie, Dianne, Marci, Vicki

13

Are There Enough Precious Letters?

Dear Mother and Dad,   *Oct 2, 1970*

It was good to get your letter confirming your safe arrival back home. I'm so glad Bobby was there to help you again. I must write him a letter of thanks for all that he did to make your trip smooth. I know you must have been tired. We were all so happy to have you here because we love you and want you to have all the good trips that you can take during your retirement.

Well, we are planning another trip to Berlin! Please do not worry about it; we will be safe. We are planning this for summer before the local schools take their vacation. Here in Koningstadten they actually close the schools and the local car factory so that the parents' vacation is at the same time as their children. Their school summer vacation is only for six weeks. During that time the highways, trains and hotels will all be too busy. Yes, we will take a train all of the way and stay in American guest quarters in West Berlin. We will see the Berlin wall too! This should be educational and fun for all our kids. Our friends with their three children will go with us. I will write you all about it after we get back.

You remember our friend, Bob, who took you through the base print shop, Dad? It's his family that will go with us. Daddy, I remember when you were here I was so tickled when you met the deaf German linotype operator in that shop. You two seemed to communicate with sign language even though we know his was not American Sign Language. I know a lot of it was mime and gestures but that just goes to show that if two people share a common skill such as printing, you will find a way to communicate!

Oh, and also, Evelyn, Jerry's sister and her hubby, Paul are planning to come see us next spring. They want to take a road trip while here down through Bavaria and to the German Nazi concentration camp, Auschwitz-Birkenau. I don't know yet if we will be able to manage with all of our children or if we can find a baby sitter so we can enjoy the trip without them. Well, that is a long way off so we will tell you about that if and when it happens.

We are all fine and looking forward to our move into base housing soon. Please do not worry if you don't get a letter from me for a couple of weeks as that will just mean we are moving into our apartment on base and I will be busy getting everything settled in. I must hush now and get started on my laundry! Ugh!

Love, Liz and all

P.S. Marci says to tell Grandpa how much she misses him and their card games!

Dear Mother & Daddy,   *March 3, 1971*

Oh, my time goes by so fast here it seems. There is always something to do or someplace to go. We have so many friends and of course taking care of our four girls certainly means a lot of work. Oh, not hard work, really. It's just tiring some-times trying to think of what to have for dinner that doesn't take too much time or talent. I just never have learned to be the good cook that you are! But it is your fault! You wouldn't let me do any cooking at home. Ha.

Well, Evelyn and Paul were here for ten days and we did drive down to Auschwitz, where we saw the ruins of the concentration camp. You remember reading about Hitler and the Nazis killing so many Jewish German people during World War II. It is really sad to walk through there and see how they lived with bunk beds crowded into the long buildings.

We even saw the buildings where the prisoners took showers which were really gas chambers and the ovens where those poor people were cremated. That was quite a history lesson for the girls, something Julie, Vicki and Marci will remember.

We stopped a couple of other places along the way just to see a little more of this country of Germany. Evelyn wanted to go into the city of Wiesbaden and shop. They bought a couple of clocks that will be shipped to them in Oklahoma. You know, Evelyn and Paul have traveled many places because Paul works for American Airlines as a mechanic. He can get tickets at a very good price just like Bobby could from his position with North Central Airlines. They are very fortunate, aren't they?

I guess that's about all the news today. I want to be ready when Jerry picks us up to go to see Marci play softball on base. After that we will do our week's shopping at the commissary. You saw the commissary and the Base Exchange (BX) when you were here and know how big, clean and modern they are, thank goodness.

We'll no doubt have hamburgers at the little food place in the BX which is a real treat for the girls. It will be late when we get home, unload the groceries and put them away; so I won't have to worry about fixing supper when we get home.

I'm enclosing a few pictures that I hope you will enjoy. Take care of yourselves. We have just a little over a year here before we see you in good ol' Minnesota! Hope you are both feeling good as always.

Love,
Liz and all

In another letter a few weeks later, Liz had more news of travel.

Hi Mom and Dad,   *August, 1971*

Well, we are finally moved into Base housing. We were lucky and got a three bedroom apartment on the first floor. It was fairly easy to move all the furniture in and we even bought an old black piano that belonged to another couple who lived here before. The girls will all take piano lessons from a teacher who lives just two buildings over from us. There are three stories with two apartments on each floor so we already have six new families to get acquainted with.

Marci has already made friends with the girls who live right up over us. The mother's name is Hulda, and she is German. She married this military man ten years ago when he came here as a single American GI. They lived in the States for eight years and are now back here for his second tour. They have three girls and one boy. What a neat family they are because all speak German and English.

In fact one day a German friend of Hulda's was visiting so she brought her down to show me several lovely lace tablecloths that she was selling. I bought one. The dining room table is really "dressed up" now. We all like the way it brings a new beauty to the whole room.

We now have a telephone too! We really missed that while living in the village. The only thing is we have to pay for each phone call and the girls sure don't like that. But that's okay. Telephones should only be used for an absolute necessity. We live close enough to all of their friends now they don't need to waste time talking on the phone. They will get used to it I'm sure.

As I said before we are always finding new things to do. This last week we took a drive down to Switzerland! Yes, I wanted to see where your grandparents came from, Daddy. This time we got a baby sitter for the girls and went with our friends in our station wagon. It was a good trip.

First we stopped in Bavaria and spent the night in a love-ly old hotel there. It was romantic looking out the windows of the room to the mountains just beyond the town below. Jerry and I really needed that night away from the kids to just relax and have fun by ourselves. Jerry is a good man, a good father and husband but he is just not romantic! Ha. So I must be the one to remind him of what blessings we have in our lives.

I'm sure you must have felt the same way when you two would go to your deaf conventions out of town and leave Bobby and I at home. I think we are in a rut of just think-ing of what events the kids have on the calendar, helping them with their homework, cooking, shopping, and finding entertainment for them. So we forget about each other. Every couple needs to "stoke the fires" of love every now and then to remind themselves to fulfill their own needs.

Anyway, we drove into Berne, Switzerland and spent the night there in a big modern hotel. The next morning the four of us walked the downtown streets window shopping and dreaming of what we would buy if we had the money! Ha.

Something I noticed was that all the cities I've been in over here have a large clock centrally located tall enough to be seen by any vantage point in town. I do remember, though, that Wisconsin Rapids has a big clock like that on the corner by Johnson Hills.

I love clocks and hope we can take at least one clock back to the states with us. Jerry did buy a watch, but not in Switzerland because he could get the one he really wanted at a good price back at the BX. His watch shows the date and time in six time zones in the world, really fun and interesting to note.

We drove home on Monday, stopping only once for lunch. That was in a little village just over the border in France. It was so funny because after we ate at this little outdoor café we asked the waiter the best street to take to get us back to

Germany and he didn't understand us. He called over another waiter who seemed to use pretty good English but he didn't understand us either. So, we just paid our check and walked back to our car.

We started driving slowly in the general direction that we had arrived from but could not see any signs about Germany. Finally Jerry stopped at a gasoline station and asked the fellas there. They laughed and said in this part of the country they don't refer to Germany as Germany, they call it Alemania!

Then this guy just turned around and pointed to the road sign that read Alemania with a large arrow pointing due north, straight ahead of us. After we were on our way we laughed and poked fun of our friend, Bob because his heritage is French, to which he admitted he knew very little French.

Anyway, we got back home late that night but were thankful for a safe journey. And, I must close now and get ready for bed. I'm tired! Good night.

> *Hugs from the kids,*
> *Love, Liz & Jerry*

Just a week later, Evie was so surprised to receive another letter from Germany. Of course she and Frank were always glad to hear from their daughter. She had many interesting stories to tell us. Sometimes they were just sweet family stories and other times they were about other people in their lives who Evie or Frank would probably never meet.

This turned out to be one of those letters.

Dearest Mother and Daddy,   *September, 1971*

Ohhh, I forgot to tell you about meeting a deaf couple in Koningstadten before we moved to the base. I just happened to be shopping in the Bakery. I noticed them using sign language so I walked over to them and introduced my-self. The lady was not deaf and we tried to speak a little German to each other. (Did I ever tell you I took a class in German with a teacher who was German himself? It was fun but I didn't really retain all that we learned.)

Anyway, this lady finally used some English. This deaf man is her brother and when he was a young student, the war broke out and the school closed sending most of the kids to live with relatives or friends in other small towns. That's when she brought him here and they remained here ever since. Unfortunately there was no way he could go to school here.

The woman told me that her deaf brother really had no formal education, not even much sign language other than what she taught him at home. She was very nice and like most people here, very polite. Before I said goodbye she in-vited me and my family to come for afternoon tea and wrote down her address. I really didn't think we'd have time to squeeze in a visit to them before moving out to the base but Jerry said if we didn't pay them a visit it would be consid-ered very rude.

So, we all walked over there on a Sunday afternoon. She had cookies and milk for the girls and let them sit on her porch where they could watch some boys playing baseball in the street. Their home was a small two bedroom brick build-ing with a small sitting room, big kitchen, and one bathroom. Everything was spotless which was a trait all German women seemed to have.

We enjoyed a cup of coffee and some tiny delicious des-sert bars. They had a large globe and I pointed out where our homes were in the United States. The man, Ben, seemed to understand a lot of what I signed if I used a lot of gesturing and pointing. Ha. I explained to them how we would be mov-ing into base housing so that they would not expect a return invitation from us.

*They were fine with everything and we left after just a
little over an hour's visit. Too bad we didn't meet them before
you came here so you could have had that experience.*

Must hush now! Liz

Evie and Frank always read Liz's letters a second time to be sure
they understood every word and discussed the facts in the letters
during their long quiet evenings. Frank was wise enough to realize
they were allowing Liz's life experiences to become theirs. Now
that they could picture Liz's home, the village where they lived
and the base housing where they resided now; it was easy to picture every event she wrote about. Even though they had not been to
Switzerland, Frank enjoyed fantasizing himself visiting the land of
his forefathers. Liz's descriptions and pictures allowed him to imagine himself walking the streets that his grandfather had once trod.
He felt proud as he shared the pictures with his co-workers and read
their comments about how lucky he had been to visit Europe.

One quiet evening at home they were discussing Evie's latest letter. "You know, Evie, soon Jerry decide to re-enlist or get out of Air
Force after twenty years. I wonder what do. I think hard decision
because he will be thirty nine with no other experience, only theater
and band." Frank signed calmly to Evie. Immediately he was sorry
he brought up the subject because Evie was still so adamant about
Liz leading that kind of life. "No, no! He will not stay Air Force.
They must settle down sake of girls! Already Julie cries when leaving
friends, she told me!" Evie almost dared Frank to say otherwise. But
Frank was compelled to say "Funny thing! I'm thankful for you and
I able go to Washington state, Oklahoma, Nebraska, and Germany
because Air Force! I will miss travel see them." Frank was surprised
at what happened next. Evie was either too angry to continue this
conversation or just frustrated with the uncertainty of her daughter's
future; but she simply stood up, signed a good night and went to bed.

Another letter from Germany was especially interesting describing a train trip Liz and her family took to Berlin. Their friends

went with them and the girls had a lot of fun besides learning a little history.

Dearest Mother & Daddy,   *October, 1971*

The train was beautiful. There was just one incident that was a little scary. We stopped in the middle of the night and they collected our Passports to show the police inside the station house. We could actually see them through our window and watched as they went through all the Passports, said a few words to our Military Police, and placed all the Passports into a box for them to return to us on the train. Then we continued on, arriving in Berlin the next morning.

Oh, Berlin is so beautiful. I was surprised at how clean the city was with wide streets right downtown. Many lovely stores but we didn't really have time to go shopping. We had lunch in one of their nice little restaurants where the waiters treated us so politely. They were encouraging us to have another cup of coffee; not hurrying us to give our table to someone else like they do so often in the states. The food was delicious and dessert even better!

We all enjoyed walking some of the streets then before getting back on the train to start our journey home.

The girls will never forget this. We took a city bus to the Berlin Wall. In the tall buildings, we could see the Russian police standing in open spaces with machine guns, looking down on us! They did not look friendly at all!

Jerry and Bob were able to go on into East Berlin but we wives and kids were not allowed. So, we visited a small museum where we saw the history of the Wall going up after WWII. It was very interesting with pictures of people who had escaped through the Wall by hiding in the trunks of vehicles or digging a hole under the Wall. Wow!

We only waited another twenty minutes for our husbands to return. They had bought a few things from East Berlin stores. Jerry bought a musical instrument known as a zither. It has strings like a guitar but it doesn't look the shape of a guitar at all.

Well, I am so tired, I must get on to bed. It won't be long now and Jerry will be filling out his papers to retire from the Air Force. We need to decide what we will do, where we will live and how Jerry can finish his college degree to become a teacher like he wants to do. I'm sure I told you how he went to college classes everywhere he could. He finished two years while we were stationed at Scott, Omaha, Guam, and here in Germany. He will only need one more year in the states and one semester to do an "internship."

Love, Liz
Of course, the girls send big hugs to both of you!

14

❧

Are We Ready for Retirement?

etirement plans were going rather well for Frank. Yet, when the actual year arrived for Frank to retire, somehow he was not ready to do so. He convinced himself that just because he had turned sixty-two and the company had already wished him a good retirement with a gift of luggage; the decision was still his to make. When discussing this with his boss, he was actually encouraged to stay on until he could receive Medicare at age sixty-five. This also gave them time to get rid of excess furniture and ready the house to sell; as their plans included a move to their home state of Minnesota. Evie's siblings could search the market for a smaller house in Winona and let them know when to come look at them. Frank agreed with his wife that taking care of this two story house had become too much work for them. Still, they knew they would miss the comfort of space available here, especially when the grandkids came for visits.

Evie's mind drifted back to the year of living at the lake. That was a turning point in their lives. She was forever grateful to Frank's boss that led them to the decision of owning a home. That was when they decided to build this house. After years of renting here in the Rapids they realized how they were throwing their money away and knew it was not smart to do so. During the time they were looking around at homes to buy, Frank's boss had heard about their decision so he approached them about a plan to build one. He visited them one evening showing them different house plans and explaining the costs that would actually total out less than buying one already on the market. By the time Liz graduated from high school that spring their new home was ready.

Evie had hoped that whatever her father had left to her would be found now. They could use the money.

But, still, Liz told her the same story over and over. "Mother, your dad just wanted you to know that you didn't ever have to worry about being broke without a job or a place to live. Did you ever think about how he helped you become independent?" "Independent?" Evie remembered her conversation very well. "Independent? What do you mean?" she had asked her daughter. "He meant that you could earn a living for yourself. You could learn about the different jobs out there in the city that many deaf people have filled. Some jobs would not pay much but you could learn from them and move on into other positions that pay more. Independent means you do not have to lean on another person, not even a husband. Independent means you will learn much about social manners and how to behave around other decent people. So, don't you think he did that for you? Taught you how to get life's experiences for yourself? Sure he did!"

Liz stopped her lecture, suddenly realizing she was being too tough on her mom. "Oh, let's go back to Dad and his boss. I bet I need to translate some of that jargon to Dad." Happy to have Liz stop her long argument, Evie led the way back to the dining room where the gentlemen were having a cup of coffee. Frank looked relieved when he saw his daughter. "Come sit here and relate to me what Mr. C is talking about." The rest of the evening was pleasant enough, thank goodness.

Another kind thing Frank's boss did was to introduce them to a gentleman in the bank. He knew of a private way to set up a mortgage loan with a man who would not charge them as much interest as other companies would. Liz was brought into the bank with her parents to translate the important papers to be signed. Frank thought Liz did an excellent job of explaining the papers and translating the words coming from the mouth of the bank manager. She was just seventeen and had no idea what details there were to buying a house and setting up a mortgage. She was happy that her daddy was satisfied with the translations.

However, Liz was not so confident. "I do my best tell you what man say. What mean papers. Same time I realize I not understand deep myself. Difficult. Okay. I ask questions when I not understand. Please, if you not understand, please ask questions." She signed carefully focusing on her dad, knowing that her mother was not following the information after the first ten minutes. "Yes. Yes. Ask questions you not understand. Same me." Frank answered proudly. His brown eyes sparkled with pride. He was inspired by his daughter's attitude and watched carefully as the banker continued his instructions. The man was big framed with cheeks that bounced when he spoke. His smile was friendly and Frank felt he could trust him to be honest with Liz. Finally, Frank felt completely satisfied that he understood what was requested of him and it remained a good deal in his eyes, so he signed all the necessary papers. Evie smiled shyly at her husband and her daughter with only one thing on her mind; they were moving into a new home. This was exciting for all of the family.

The family was still a little crowded with just two bedrooms on the first floor. The second floor and walls were not finished yet. This was one way to save a little money. Frank was told that two of his co-workers were skilled in putting up drywall and finishing a floor. So it wasn't long before Bobby moved from his day bed in the living room to the finished room upstairs.

One night Evie brought up the story about her father leaving her a special will. Again she suggested that maybe there were actual cash or bonds lying in a bank safety vault somewhere. "Oh, you talk lawyers find one daddy used. He left me special will, special money. We could make house beautiful!" Frank ignored her plea. "We make comfortable. Don't worry. My job good pay. My job always there." Frank wondered what he could have done or said to convince his wife that there was no will hidden for her. Perhaps the first time she told the story he should have asked her sisters about the possibility of a real will or bank account for Evie. Sometimes he would imagine himself that some lawyer had cheated her out of the will. Maybe they should have taken the story to another lawyer and asked him to find the will. But most of the time Frank knew better. It wasn't that he didn't believe Evie's story. Her father probably did tell her that he would take care of her. By "taking care of her," he most likely meant until she got a job or was married. But the rest was something she had developed in her mind over the years and there was no changing her strong determination to find monies her father had hidden for her and for her alone.

Frank could see how much Bobby loved his privacy in his new room upstairs, hanging a sign "NO ENTRY" on his door. He convinced Evie there really could be nothing wrong with that. Hesitantly, she agreed as long as he brought his dirty clothes down to the laundry room and dusted his dresser and windowsills once a week; she would not intrude. Besides, Liz seemed to be getting along better with her brother now that he was not underfoot as she had so often complained about in the past. Life was good. Evenings were quiet. Evie could sew while Frank read the evening paper. Later the upstairs would prove to be a good place for the family when Liz or Bobby brought their little ones to stay for a nice long visit. Yes, this had been a comfortable house.

It was time to leave these memories behind and move on to their new life near their own brothers and sisters in Minnesota.

Of course, they did not need a big house anymore since both the children were grown and moved into homes of their own. Liz and Bobby were both sorry they could not be there to help them hunt for a home in Winona. Evie's sisters were familiar with the town and the prices of houses so they were able to help them more than anyone. They found a cute two-bedroom bungalow with a full basement. This would not be too much work for Evie to take care of now in their senior years. It was just the problem of communication again with the bank. However things went more smoothly this time than ever before. The bank even had a lady there who could sign well enough for Frank to follow. Bobby was able to come home for a few days and help them pack for the movers.

Bobby had married a sweet girl from another town in Wisconsin. They lived in the Twin Cities where he worked for North Central

Airlines. Their three children seemed well behaved, healthy and happy. It was just a two hour drive from their home to Evie and Frank's so they were able to check in now and then to see how they were doing. It was a comfortable relationship. Jo's parents lived in Green Bay on the eastern part of Wisconsin so of course Bobby was obligated to visit her family too.

Yet Evie harbored the thought that Bobby and his family should come here more often. Liz and her family could only come up from Tulsa a couple of times a year during Jerry's breaks from school. Why didn't they understand that? Then when Liz was here Evie wanted every minute with her that she could get. Liz knew that these thoughts were really her own guilt trips because of having moved so far away from her parents in the first place.

This coupled with the fact that time was very limited for a visit with both families here at the same time. Maybe it was because this was no longer home to them or because they had never been close as kids. Frank had the uneasy feeling that his daughter and son really didn't care if they had any time together. He couldn't understand this as the grandkids were fairly close in age and seemed to have fun together. Frank began to realize that Bobby and Liz never seemed to really enjoy each other's company when they were young either. Six years apart in age and of opposite genders would explain that, but Frank felt it was more than that. If it had just been a sibling thing, they should be past that now that they were both adults with their own families.

Maybe it had to do with the fact that years ago Bobby had told Evie he thought maybe Liz's husband was too lazy to get out of the Air Force and look for a regular job. Whatever he had said to Evie caused her to worry that it really must be easy work just play-ing his saxophone and clarinet and marching with the band. Evie seemed to believe that Jerry would not be able to hold a job out in the world. Frank disagreed with his wife and son on this subject. He tried explaining his opinion to them by emphasizing it was a secure position, working for the Air Force, and Liz seemed very happy with their life. The children were all healthy and happy and they were seeing the world! Frank sometimes envied his daughter's life, at least the travel part.

Then when Jerry had earned his retirement from the government he finished his Bachelor's degree and became a teacher. Wasn't that good enough for Evie? But no matter what Frank said it was always clear to him that Bobby was Evie's favorite while Frank all but admitted that Liz was his choice. Was there anything wrong with that? He didn't think so. So the years had gone by with precious time spent with the grandkids and keeping Evie happy during the times they were alone again. Frank knew something was missing, yet he wasn't sure. Sometimes when he would see one of the neighbor's children hugging his father for no apparent reason, he wondered if that was what was missing. Had he hugged his children when they were young? Had he ever told them how much he loved them? Had Evie done that? No! Why was that so difficult to do?

Retirement seemed to come easy for Frank as he found it fairly easy to let go of the stress of sitting at that linotype machine making sure the copy he typed from was correct English. He never wanted to appear lax in spelling either. Yes, retirement was okay. Frank loved working in the garden and flowerbeds. He also found a variety of crafts to work on without spending much money. His birdhouses were a favorite of the grandkids when they came to visit. Bobby was amazed at these as they were made from Readers Digest magazines. How clever, he thought. Evie required very little of her hubby except to keep his ashtray emptied after enjoying his evening cigar and keep his messes outside or in the basement.

He read his Bible faithfully and secretly wondered when and how he would die. Evie wasn't sure there was a God. Why would He let people suffer with deafness or blindness or a crippled body? She couldn't understand a God like that. She also remembered that her mother died in her sixties only because she believed in God! "My mother died because God mean." Frank looked at his wife's words hanging in the air and the look of doom on her face. "What you mean?" he signed. "Mother believed God care her. He not! She die!" Frank never knew that Evie had harbored such thoughts for so long. She actually blamed God for her mother's death. He knew it was really Anna's fault. Oh, she had been a good woman, a good wife to her husband, an excellent cook, a better than good mother and a keen Christian.

"You know," Frank signed carefully, "your mother Christian Science, not believe in doctors. We know better. God gave gift to doctors, help heal us."

With no reply, Evie changed the subject. Sometimes Evie wondered just what all was in her father's will. All she really received was some money that she immediately invested in a fur coat. Her money was all used for just this one item. Yet, now, her brother lived in the house that was her father's. It was a lovely big house with seven rooms downstairs and four comfortable size bedrooms and a bath upstairs. Her sisters had taken the furniture, linens and dishes that they desired. There were many other beautiful objects of her mother's which would stay in the house. Oh, Evie had been asked to look it all over and take anything she wanted; but she chose only a few as she had to decide just what they could carry with them in their car. It was too expensive to ship things to Wisconsin.

Evie was not the only one who lived out of the state of Minnesota. Lydi, the youngest daughter, lived in Tennessee where her husband had been an engineer with a good salary. At the time her only child was grown and gone. She had more furniture than she could find room for in her home already. Evie had always been a little jealous of Lydi because she was not only rich, she was beautiful. It had been Lydi that their daddy had asked for when he was taken ill and remained bedfast for a year before he died.

Before Julius had died, Evie had received a letter from Alice about that fact. "Daddy had really summoned Lydi to come to take care of him because her husband traveled so much on his job and she only had to care for one child. I know Lydi was lonesome. Evie, you will find it hard to believe, but she was keeping company with that bartender that she knew before she ever married. No one wanted to believe it but I know it's true. I don't think dad ever knew of this and that's just as well. It probably would have killed him long before he actually died."

Evie didn't know anyone who could tell her if this was true or not and since it was a long time ago there was no reason to dwell on this story of Alice's anyway. But it was so rare that any of her sisters took the time to write her a note, especially one with some gossip like this.

Evie knew she was the only one that could not carry any of the furniture or large sized decorations that she might have wanted from her parents' home. However, she kept this feeling to herself and accepted the situation because she was sure that one day some lawyer would visit her and give her a secret will directing her to some special riches that her daddy had hidden for her. After all, her father had promised to take care of her! No matter how much she tried to understand what her daughter had tried to tell her, she could not explain away the words her father had written down for her those many years ago. Evie felt strongly there was money somewhere just for her. Then her sisters and brothers would be surprised to see what nice things she had been able to buy with the monies. Someday!

15

Can Love Keep Us Together?

*D*earest Mother and Daddy,   *March, 1975*

I hope this finds you both feeling good these days. I am doing fine. It is so much fun in this new job working with the deaf. I know you, Daddy, told me you didn't think it would be a good job for me. I remember you saying that deaf people were different and that you were sure they would take advantage of me. In some ways you are right. There are a few people who want help from me when they can do it themselves. But, you see, that's the good thing about becoming a certified professional interpreter for the deaf. There is a CODE-OF-ETHICS that we are to follow.

Just like a lawyer or doctor we are not allowed to talk about the situation, no names, no story to anyone after we interpret for someone. Well, the fact that I must keep everything confidential helps me to avoid getting too close to a deaf person. When they ask me to do something special for them; or if they want my opinion about someone else, I can say: "No, my code-of-ethics does not allow me to do that."

Also if someone wants me to pick them up for an appointment or take them home I can say that I do not have business insurance on my car so I cannot do that. I will explain more to you when I see you next spring.

I know it is always a long time from our fall visit to spring visit. I wish we could be there for Christmas but we hate to take a chance on the weather. We are too spoiled to a milder climate ever since we moved here to Oklahoma. Oh, we had warmer weather before like on Guam and Florida but I like it better here.

Yes, because I like a change of weather during the year. I like a cool, warm, even hot and cold for the four seasons. We had a little snow here last winter. It was fun. The kids sure enjoyed it with the little hill we have out back. We love our new house.

Remember, now we have four bedrooms so we always have the twin beds for you. I hope that you will plan to fly down here soon to stay with us for a while. Anytime you would like to come is fine with us. Write when you can.

Love, Liz

Liz's prediction was true. They postponed a trip to Minnesota until spring break when the weather was somewhat better. The visit always meant that the girls used the basement for their bedrooms, so they wanted the weather to be on the warmer cycle of the year. Sometimes they would suggest they stay at a hotel but Frank and Evie said they would be insulted if they didn't stay at their home; so they always managed to do so.

Sitting in a comfy chair out in the sunroom of this rehab area, Frank began to dwell on his own health. Frank himself had been hospitalized, as a young man with an infection of the mastoid region behind his ear; as a middle aged man with prostrate problems; and now as an old man when he had broken his hip. Surgery had taken care of that quite nicely, but Frank never walked normally again. He always did have a slight limp from the polio he experienced during his childhood so this was not difficult for Frank to get used to, just escalated his gait a little. The only time Evie was hospitalized was to give birth to her second child. All during their married life they were so fortunate with their own health and the health of the kids. The grandkids seemed to have inherited this good trait too.

Thank goodness he was going to be released and heading back home tomorrow. Bobby would be there to pick him up at the hospital here in Winona in the morning. Hallelujah. He hoped his grandkids could come along and stay for a nice visit, even though he didn't know when their Easter break was scheduled.

Regretfully, Bobby was not able to take any time off himself and the kids were in school. There was only one day for Bobby to help get Frank settled in at home. Evie was so happy that Frank managed the wheelchair fine from his side of the bed into the bathroom and then out to the kitchen in the morning. Bobby had to move some furniture around in the living room so that his dad could get to his favorite chair in the living room. He knew this would be a real effort for his dad but was surprised to see how strong his arms were to lift him from one area to another. Everything seemed fine when Bobby hugged his parents goodbye the next morning and headed back to the Twin Cities. A promise was made that he and Jo would come back the weekend after Easter. They would stay for Frank's appointment with his doctor that Tuesday morning. Frank was feeling confident in himself and promised Evie he would not need help very often.

These positive thoughts were burst one week later when his dear wife had an accident in the garage. Evie had been sweeping out the floor when she pulled an old rug out from under the bicycle leaning against the wall causing her to fall hard on the cement floor. She lay there crying as the pain hit her in waves. There was no one to cry out to because their house was set back from the road with the unattached garage on the East side of their property. The home next door was on a small acreage with a big yard between the garage and their house.

After three hours, a little girl visiting next door heard strange sounds coming from the neighbor's garage. She ran in the house and told her grandmother that there was a kitten crying like it was hurt. Maybe it was stuck under the garage. What a shock it was when they realized it was a human cry and found Evie crying on the floor of their garage. After the ambulance came Evie asked for pencil and paper so that she could write a note, "Hubby in house. Take note. Hospital me go." Even though the neighbors took him to the hospital immediately, it was two hours later before Frank could see her as she was settled into her hospital room. What a strange state of affairs this was to be. The hospital allowed Frank to spend that night and two more in the same room with Evelyn until Liz arrived.

Evie eventually went into Rehabilitation for ten days while they taught her how to cope with the new hip bone! Life was not easy at home after that. Frank had never learned to walk without a walker but Evie did fairly well with pushing her wheelchair around. Liz had come up for a few weeks to help with meals and laundry. Liz was thankful she could take the time off from her interpreting. It was times like this that she was glad she was only doing freelance work. She didn't even have any appointments to cancel as she had kept her calendar open for a trip to Minnesota anyway.

Liz and Jerry had already planned to drive up here the very next week as Liz wanted to attend her high school class reunion in Wisconsin. Now she was not so sure she should leave her folks. Frank could sense his daughter's anxiety and was soon putting his mind to work. "Liz, I know what do! Contact cousin, Betty Lou. Ask about Stephanie, her daughter. Maybe stay three day with us. Help Evie."

Liz kissed her dad on the cheek, sending out a big thank you sign as she reached for the phone. But this call was to her mother's doctor. He assured her that Evie was doing fine and told her to go ahead and take some time off for herself as she deserved it. After arranging the time and duties with Steph, she could barely contain her excitement when she called Jerry to confirm the trip as planned. After looking around to be sure her mom was not in the room, Liz hugged her dad, explained all that had taken place on the phone and thanked him again. "I'm so glad you understand, Daddy. Now tell Mom, me. She not like."

Evie was more than disappointed when Liz told her she had hired a cousin's daughter to sit with them while she went to her class reunion. Evie thought Liz should stay home with them but when she learned that Liz had even spoken to her doctor she couldn't argue.

She had always respected their medical doctor. He was not only kind, he was handsome and pleasant every time she visited his office. Frank liked him too, especially the fact that the good doctor had never had any problem communicating with either one of them.

Most of it was written notes but he also used pictures and drawings to clarify the physical whereabouts with printed material to read. Then whenever possible he would ask Bobby or Liz to explain even more. Even though Frank typed words every day at work he did not always understand the meaning of them. The kind doctor actually longed for someone in their offices to learn sign language. Yet he knew it was often years before a person could become fluent enough to make clear interpretations for a deaf person. Sometimes he felt that only children of deaf parents could do this.

Still, Evie hated the idea of another woman in her kitchen as well as having to handle Frank and help him with his bath! Evie liked her privacy and could not understand the open ways that young people seemed to have about such things. So her mother would have no real objections to her leaving, Liz described Steph to her in glowing terms. "Steph good student in nurses' training here Winona. Excited. She wants work geriatrics. Means work with older people. She said this good experience for her. She happy come and have weekend with great aunt and uncle." With no arguments left, Evie grudgingly joined Frank in wishing their daughter a good time at her class reunion.

After driving the long trip from Tulsa by himself, Jerry immediately told Liz how proud he was of her for sticking to her guns and not giving in to her mother. He knew how difficult that was for her. Liz had not thought about this decision the way her hubby did and felt relieved by his remarks. She gave him a big hug and said, "Now I'm dropping the guilt, and feeling more excited about going, thanks to you!"

The drive over to Wisconsin Rapids was a beautiful drive and in just three hours they arrived at their hotel. The Mead met her reputation as the best place to stay in the city. It was great to get away from the kids and enjoy a beautiful room all to their own. In just two days they had great visits with several of Liz's old friends at the get together the night before the reunion. Later, Liz commented that this Friday night informal gathering was actually more fun than the formal one held the next day.

Liz had only missed one class reunion because they were in Germany that year. So, it was great to be here this year. The local Country club was a great place for the reunion dinner with a lovely background for the class pictures. Sunday morning they joined everyone for a brunch in their hotel before heading back to Minnesota. Jerry was fascinated by a car driven by a classmate and her hubby, a real antique, a genuine roadster. After more picture taking they headed back to the motel to check out and say one more goodbye to Mae and Bud.

Jerry had tried hard to convince the couple that they should attend the reunion but it seemed that ever since Bud's stroke a few years ago he could not handle crowds. That was sad, but he was fine with just Liz and Jerry visiting. They always managed a couple of visits with them while here in Wisconsin Rapids for the weekend.

One of their favorite spots was a little bar just across the street from the motel where they had the best burgers one could have with a cold glass of beer. Rapids had not grown that much but it had certainly increased in status with new, modern buildings, a shopping mall and large department stores such as J.C. Penney's.

It was a clean city with beautiful park areas along the green grassy banks on either side of the river. Liz knew that Jerry had fallen in love with this town the first time they came to visit mom and dad before her parents moved to Minnesota. But Liz loved Tulsa just as much; especially because there was more opportunity for the girls with colleges and businesses for whatever career they might choose in life. Liz herself was convinced that God sent her to Oklahoma because of the large deaf community where she could use the talents He had given her. Life was good despite the fact that they lived so far from her parents. Liz was almost able to shake off the guilt she carried because it had been her choice to do just that; live in Tulsa.

After returning to Winona, they stopped at a local restaurant to have a bite to eat before going to Evie and Frank's. They called Stephanie and told her they would be home in an hour and if she needed to leave that would be fine. As they were led to their table, Liz spotted her mother's doctor and stopped to say hello to him and his family. As introductions were made, Liz noted how charming his wife was. She immediately told him how she had followed his advice and taken the weekend off from her duties with her mother. He praised her for that as he shook Jerry's hand and said, "Liz has done more than she should be expected to; staying here and leaving you to fend for yourself." Jerry laughed and shrugging his shoulders retorted, "Well, it's just too bad we live so far away. But, I think she's planning to come back home in a week. Do you think Evie will be alright with that?" "Oh, no! She will not be alright with that or any length of time you can give her because she thinks Liz should live here," the doctor retorted with a big grin matching his warm personality.

Liz felt relaxed as they enjoyed their meal and waved to the doctor as he and his family left. Then feeling some tension returning, Liz told Jerry they needed to go on home and face the music. When they arrived they were surprised that Stephanie was still there but she explained that she only wanted Evie to be comfortable waiting for their return. "Well, how sweet of you," Liz said as she hugged her mother and father; "If u have a few more minutes let's chat. I feel like I have never really known you over the years." Fulfilling her role as hostess of the home, Stephanie surprised Liz by saying "Sure, how about a cup of coffee?" She stood up, tossed her short curly hair and walked into the kitchen with a confidence that said she knew where everything was. She proceeded to pour coffee for everyone while Jerry took on the waiter's role. She reported all the details of the weekend that seemed positive in every way. Liz interpreted their ensuing conversation centered around her experiences at college where she was majoring in social sciences. Jerry was comfortable with this kind of talk and hated to see her leave. After sharing some of his own experiences and passing on some minor advice that he was prone to do as a teacher; he walked her to the door. Handing her an envelope with a check for the agreed amount, he thanked her profusely for "parent sitting."

Frank was in a good mood and wanted to play some cards before retiring for the night but Evie said she wanted to hear from Liz about the weekend. "Who see you? What wear you? Where dance? Where dinner?" Liz laughed as Jerry carried in the luggage. "It's okay, hon, go ahead and tell her all."

They retired into the living room as Frank poured them another cup of coffee. The rest of the evening was really fun for Liz as she felt her mother's spirits were uplifted just imagining what a good time Liz had over the past three days. She seemed to remember most of Liz's old friends and was hungry for information about Wisconsin Rapids. Although engrossed in the news of the city, Frank soon lost interest in Liz's stories and nodding at his son-in-law, he turned on the TV and found a baseball game to watch.

However, Evie always enjoyed her daughter's description of the dresses that her classmates had worn and who was married to who. Evie could remember a few of Liz's friends and would imagine them in her mind as Liz gestured the style and sizes of each girlfriend she had known. Evie realized how talented Liz was with signs.

This was why she missed Liz. She has a way of making a picture for me that no one else can seem to do, not even the deaf friends we have in Wausau. Perhaps this was a skill that Liz developed growing up with me, watching my face and my hands, learning to give details to a story; she really knew how to make me happy, Evie thought.

While watching the game, Frank began writing notes to Jerry asking him how long he would stay. When Jerry said he must return to Tulsa on Friday, Frank gave him a puzzling look and pointed to Liz. Jerry knew he wanted to know if Liz would go with him then but he didn't want to answer that. He wanted Liz to give them her decision, so he simply shrugged his shoulders and smiled.

It was important they did take some time to discuss plans for her mother. The question became important as to how long Evie really did need her care here. Finally Jerry cornered Liz and asked when she was going to tell Evie she would be returning to Tulsa with him at the end of the week. Without signing what she was saying, Liz said under her breath, "We can wait a couple of days before telling her." Liz really tried never to say something to another hearing person in the room without signing; however, there were times it just seemed the best thing to do. There were other times when some folks might be signing to each other off in a corner of the room and she felt that she should keep her eyes averted or she would be eavesdropping on a private conversation.

Trying to solve this dilemma, Jerry and Liz wanted to convince her parents they should have a telephone installed so they could use the new Telephone Device for the Deaf (TDD). As Jerry demonstrated with a phone he had brought from their house, Liz explained how she had one at home to communicate with the deaf community. She had fun describing her first experience with the big old style teletypewriter like the one they used at Western Union years ago. Despite Liz's enthusiasm, Frank surprised them with his adamant refusal because of the monthly telephone bill, even though Jerry and Bobby both offered to pay the bill.

As a retired linotype operator, Frank was interested in the workings of this TDD, a new smaller device. As a member of the Wisconsin Association of the Deaf, he had read about the new TDD. The Deaf were happy about the machine itself but they had mixed feelings about the new name given to the device. Most of them wanted to keep the name *teletypewriter* or TTY. The controversy grew out of the fact that hearing people named the new TDD; whereas, the Deaf had labeled the first TTY after it's original role as a telegraph machine.

Liz had not heard her father's rendition on this subject before. Now she began to get an idea of what may have transpired. Maybe it was because the teletypewriter is a generic name with no reference to the Deaf. Telephone Device for the Deaf, however, suggests that this device is only to be used by the Deaf which isn't true at all. Both devices are used by both hearing and deaf people for communication.

(Little did Liz know that one day she would hold a device in her hand to type text messages to both deaf and hearing family and friends. This device would have no label to indicate use by any particular peoples.)

Some other terms had caused differences of opinion between the Deaf community and the hearing professionals involved in their lives. Hearing people referred to deaf people who had good voice with some loss of hearing as *hearing-impaired* while others still said *hard-of-hearing*. Thank goodness other terms had changed such as *deaf-and-dumb*, evolving into the deaf people. The National Association of the Deaf announced they prefer to refer to deaf people as the *Deaf*. A separate group of deaf people were known as the *oral deaf* because they preferred lip-reading with no use of sign language.

Of course Liz knew that all of these terms depend on the degree of hearing loss and ability to use one's voice.

Thank God, the powers-that-be finally recognized a child should be allowed to use any and all methods of communication they could be comfortable with during their years of education in the schools. Many times a graduate of public schools with the oral training would attend social functions of the local Deaf Club and become very intrigued with the American Sign Language, known as ASL. Some of them had been lucky in having friends while growing up and knew some signs; however, many others had a difficult time learning sign language as an adult. This resulted in the new Signed English which used the basics of American Sign Language but signs were added so that each word spoken was given a unique sign keeping an accurate display of English grammar.

Bringing themselves back to the moment at hand, Frank still insisted he did not want to pay a telephone bill every month whether he used the phone or not. He also rejected the idea that long distance costs would be there anytime he talked to his two children, even though Bobby and Liz insisted it would not cost them long distance to call him. "Sorry. We are not ready for this TDD. End of subject," Frank signed strongly. Liz told Jerry to back off for now, pack up the TDD and wait for a later date to approach this again.

Frank let his mind ruminate on what he had learned when he attended the Wisconsin Association Convention. Discussion centered around education focusing on the hearing grasp of sign language in various forms. With many hearing teachers in Deaf Education using what became known as Signed English; it was feared they still did not understand the one thing we need. Frank continued reading through the articles. Some teachers have forgotten that an English sign may not make sense. Concept is absolutely necessary.

One example was given to use when discussing the subject with other people, both hearing and deaf. This was the word, *sign*. Look at the four different meanings of this word: Sign language; outdoor signage; symbol; and signature. Each of these meanings held a different hand-sign to indicate concept in ASL; whereas, in Signed English, there is just one sign for the word *sign* no matter what it means.

Can you imagine if that one *sign* was *symbol*. Now use that sign in these sentences:

1. *Watch for the symbol at the corner.*
2. *Do you know symbol language?*
3. *Please symbol your name here.*
4. *The robin is the symbol of spring.*

The only sentence ASL would use the sign for *symbol* would be in number four. Again, in ASL the other three sentences would use a hand-sign clearly showing the meaning of the word, clarifying the complete thought of the sentence. For further clarification the article finished with the four sentences in ASL.

1. Careful signage corner!
2. Sign language, you know?
3. Write (point) your name please.
4. Robin symbol spring.

Frank knew from his experience with the words he would type every day at work the English language has multiple words that carry different meanings, so he was convinced that sign language for the deaf must be a conceptual signing of words. Thankfully, many educators did believe in this philosophy but there are also many deaf people who may become confused because of a lack of education in this area.

Realizing that Evie was not the avid reader that he was, Frank decided this TDD business might be a detriment to her way of life. She would only become more confused and frustrated, blaming Frank for her lack of understanding. Besides, he really did not want to spend the money for a phone line and would not bring himself to ask his children to pay for it with their hard earned monies either. If this had been a possibility years earlier, they could have accepted it much easier. However, at their age now, it was just a bit too much to ask of them.

Liz suggested that Bobby could share with them in the cost and it would be very minimal for each of the three of them. "But, charge long distance talk you, Bobby, you, Liz. No, no, no. No phone since you both gone. Need none now. You call neighbor if must. We fine," Frank signed adamantly. Liz turned to Jerry in desperation and agreed to let it go for now. She didn't want to aggravate her father even though she knew it was a mistake. She would give the TDD to Bobby and ask him to persuade them at a later date. Evie always said that the man of the family should handle any business decisions. She thought Liz didn't know as much as her brother about business costs and the cost of living. Aggravated by her mother's naïve, old-fashioned beliefs, she backed off from this subject. She was momentarily glad that her parents could not hear her big sigh of frustration as she set the TDD aside.

That was new food for thought; the fact that Liz could hear someone's sigh of emotion. It helps to analyze what someone is really thinking and feeling when you hear a sigh. A sigh could mean a huge frustration just as hers had been today; or, it could be a lighter sigh, meaning just a little frustration with a situation. Someone might sigh loudly with a little moan to accompany it when feeling sad; or it might indicate surprise, even shock at another scenario. Trying not to dwell on this new discovery, Liz catalogued the sound of sighs to the back of her mind for now.

As it turned out, Evie quietly accepted the news of their returning to Tulsa. Things settled down again after Liz and Jerry had gone back to their home because there were always little chores to be done before winter set in. Everything was calm and back to normal. Evie really had no problem getting around their small home and she felt good to be in control of her household again.

Little did they realize what that winter held in store for them. It was a long and cold one, with no less than three real blizzards inside of six weeks. During one of those blizzards they lost their heat. The gas furnace quit working on a Friday and by Saturday morning the house was feeling cold. Evie turned on the electric oven in the kitchen and Frank pulled their two comfy chairs in front of the stove for the night. This was easy to do since their small living room, dining and kitchen were all one open room. Wrapped in blankets, they managed to sleep for a few hours before dawn. After a light breakfast, Frank wrote a note to the newspaper boy and slipped it outside above the mailbox. It was in an envelope on which he had printed in big letters, "PAPERBOY HELP."

The paperboy came a little late that Sunday morning because of the drifting snow but he did see the envelope and when he opened it he went immediately next door where he asked the neighbor to read the note. "No heat us. Call fix furnace. Thank you, Frank Niklaus." Herb thanked the paper boy and said he would take care of it.

"Oh, no! Nellie, the Niklauses are without heat!" Herb remarked as he looked at his wife of forty years. "It's sad that they couldn't call anyone. We just don't realize how fortunate we are, sweetheart." Realizing that place of business would not be open on Sunday, he knew he had to come up with the owner's name. Thankfully his wife knew where they had it on file. She was always careful to keep all their bills and paid invoices in a file box and Herb was sure thankful for her habit of organization.

The call went through and when Joe heard about the Niklaus's dilemma he called one of his boys to pick him up in his repair truck. Soon they proceeded to traverse the plowed main streets without too much trouble. The residential streets were another story. But the truck driver slowly picked his way through the snowdrifts until it parked in the Niklaus's driveway.

As Joe pushed the doorbell, he noted a little card posted on it explaining there were special lights in the hallway that would flash to let folks inside know someone was at the door. Joe called out that they still were not answering the door. At the same time the other fellow caught sight of the two old folks sitting in the kitchen in front of their stove. "Well, they're sitting just where they could not see the hall light. I'll get their attention. This is a small house so I'll keep waving in the window until they see me." Sure enough, in just a minute, Evie stood up and hurried toward the front door. Another minute elapsed as she pulled out all the folded up newspapers she always slid into the drafty, open areas all along the side and top strips of the door.

She slowly pulled the door open to let the men in. Frank recognized one of them and gave him a big handshake, followed by an offer of coffee. Joe shook his head and pointed to the basement with a questioning expression that Frank understood clearly. He led Joe down into the basement and let him go to the furnace to do his work. This was one of those rare times when he was proud of Evie's housekeeping extending into the basement. Everything was neat and clean.

Evie had already started writing a letter to Bobby to relate the whole incident so when the repairmen were leaving she quickly finished the letter, quickly reached into her cabinet drawer for a stamp and handed it to them; gesturing to them to take it and mail it. Joe understood and nodded yes. Everything was fine now with the furnace and the house was soon comfy warm again. They even had a newspaper to read before retiring that night into their familiar beds.

But, this incident was not over as far as the neighbors were concerned. They began to discuss together how the Niklaus' deafness was certainly of danger to themselves and perhaps even to the neighbors, whether they realized it or not. What could they do to prevent such a thing from happening again? Herb's wife thought she had the right idea when she decided to call the local Department of Human Services. Perhaps a social worker would have some knowledge of ways for deaf people to "protect" themselves. And so it was that both Bobby and Liz received phone calls from the social worker accusing them of neglecting their parents!

It was difficult to explain to the well-meaning lady that Liz spoke to, how her parents really could help themselves but opted not to. Without sounding sarcastic, she patiently described her own status as a certified interpreter for the deaf in the city of Tulsa. "I've had years of experience as a professional helping people with hearing loss acquire independence in the community." She went on to give a quick summary of the equipment available to them such as the Telephone Device for the Deaf (TDD) that would provide them communication by phone in case of any emergency. If two people have a TDD this takes place quite simply but when calling to a hearing person or office, this would entail using a telephone relay service. "And why haven't you set up your parents with such a device and or service? Is Winona too small of a town to provide such service?" the worker's voice came across the line sharply. Understanding the woman's apparent anxiety, Liz continued, "Unfortunately, Ms. Ames, my mother is too paranoid about giving information to a third party. No matter how carefully I described the interpreters' Code of Ethics, Mother was convinced that everyone in the neighborhood would soon learn her business. My dad was a little more accepting but he always let mom have the final say. So, the TDD just sat on the counter. I believe they could have used a service out of Rochester as they do provide interpreters. However, I have been thinking about something we can do."

Frustrated, Liz had one more idea and with the help of the social worker, she made a recording stating a simple message they could send. This would be a voice saying, "This call is from a couple who are deaf. We live at 350 East McArthur. This is a recording used to call you because we have an emergency of some kind. Thank you.

For confirmation, call 459-6802." This was the phone number of the Department of Human Services in town.

This tape recorder sat next to the telephone on the kitchen counter and all Evie or Frank had to do was dial the number for whomever they wished to call; the plumber, police, fire department, or simply to one of their nieces or nephews in the area. Then he or she would need to place the receiver down on the counter next to the recorder and turn it on. As it turned out Frank used this recording one time when their bathroom commode backed up and there was water all over the floor. In just a few minutes, a pleasant looking plumber came to the door and Frank simply pointed out the water problem. All was taken care of in a matter of hours. Life was back to normal.

But what is *normal*?

16

Closer, My God, to Thee?

$\mathcal{A}$s a result of the call from DHS, Liz and Bobby were on the phone a few times, discussing the possibilities of security for their parents. They were not worried about them but apparently the neighbors were. Of course Liz and Bobby lived quite a distance from Evie and Frank with visits few and far apart. They owned homes, had jobs, and families; naturally keeping them busy.

Evie and Frank knew they could not expect either of their children to move closer to them at this stage in their lives. "But, perhaps we could move closer to either Bobby or Liz," Evie signed demurely one evening. Frank could not believe his eyes! However, he remained calm and readying himself for a possible argument. But he couldn't help the look of consternation etched in his face as he signed, "Hmmm. After visit Liz's place last summer, I thought you not comfortable. All traffic with grandkids cause you nervous. Remember?" Frank settled back in his favorite blue barrel back chair trying to look relaxed. He scratched his head as he would do when annoyed with something. However, just as Frank predicted, a lengthy discussion ensued. Evie did not settle back in her little green rocker at all and soon had Frank sitting at the edge of his seat. In the end Evie won her point, determined that they should approach their children with the idea. Needless to say, the subject became a discussion in their letters for the next couple of months with no solution made.

Finally, Frank was the one to make the suggestion. This certainly made it easier for his children; simply said, "Bobby, it is time. Check on the nursing homes. We want Sauer. Close. There our friends were. Mrs. lived to be one hundred there!" Bobby could never remember his dad writing to him. One time Liz mentioned that Frank had written into the middle of a letter Evie had written; a couple of lines about some sports event. So when Bobby read this short letter from his dad he knew Frank must be serious. He immediately called Liz and they agreed that he should check out the Sauer Home now. An hour later he called again, "There is no double room available now and they may only have one bed at a time in the months to come. After some frustration on my part, I checked into a nursing home in Lewiston. Liz, I put their name down for a double room available now! What do you think of that?" "Wow, Bobby! I'm really proud of you! Good luck with Mother!" Liz exclaimed.

It was not easy convincing Evie; in fact, her husband was the one who gave her no choice. "I will go and you know you cannot live here alone!" Evie knew he was right and as she cried quietly that night, she tried to think of positive things about this move. She could not believe she was actually ready to admit she was tired of cooking for two and worn out from trying to keep the house clean. Perhaps she would not need to nag Frank anymore and he could relax with his sports on TV as much as he wanted. "But live in nursing home? If Sauer, I feel better because know nurses," she lamented to Frank. "I know, I know," he replied with no further arguments in mind.

After another two days of tears, she perked up somewhat as Bobby came to help them sort out things in the house. He would not let them pack anything. "Jo and I will take care all later. Rent out house to good people for a while. Cousins will come visit you." The move was made. The room was nice. Within forty-eight hours they had set up the television and brought in two additional table lamps for plenty of light. One of the nurses wrote them a note that she knew one of their nieces and that led to a good conversation held with paper and pencil. Before leaving the room that evening, the same nurse said she was going to pick up some material with the manual alphabet and with their help she would learn them. That pleased Evie and Frank very much. Liz and Jerry came for a visit two months later and were quite pleased with the living conditions in Lewiston.

While there one day Liz went out for a walk and decided to venture out into the nearby neighborhood. She had a habit of saying hello to any of the local folks who were out mowing or working in their flowerbeds. This particular lady was very friendly and Liz explained the circumstances for her being here in Lewiston. Upon hearing the story, this woman introduced herself and said if Liz ever needed a room to stay in while visiting her parents, she would be happy to rent out her upstairs bedroom to her. "I just might take you up on that sometime. Thank you so much." With that the lady went into the house and wrote down her name and phone number, handing it to Liz as they parted. When she returned to their room, she related her visit to Evie and Frank. They wanted her name and said they would ask around to be sure they were decent folk. Liz loved the way they wanted to protect her, and told Jerry later that it was good to know that she had a place to stay because there was no motel in this little town.

It would save about a ten mile drive to Winona. Things seemed good. However, Frank and Evie were still insistent that they move to Sauer whenever possible. As it turned out, Liz did rent that upstairs room for herself for a week. She had the opportunity to bring a passenger out of Tulsa for about half of the trip up Highway 35. She spent the night with her friend at her family's home in Iowa, then drove on to Minnesota by herself. It all worked out rather well. The day Liz left, Frank and Evie were both a bit anxious about her driving alone even though she was stopping in Iowa again to pick up her friend. They watched for the mail every day and were thrilled that Liz had kept her promise to write soon.

Dearest Mother and Daddy,   *April 25, 1981*

Oh, my! What a week this has been! I want to tell you everything so this may be a long letter. First, I must tell you that I had a good trip home. I picked up my friend as planned but we did get tired so we did not try to drive all the way home on Saturday. We stopped in Joplin and rented a motel room. We were glad we made that decision as the clouds were getting dark and by the time we got our stuff unloaded and into the room, it was raining hard. You know how I don't like driving in heavy rain.

We left early Sunday morning and after dropping her off at her home in Owasso, I drove into our driveway a little after 3:00 p.m.

Jerry was so glad to see me, and I was surprised that he was the only one at our house. He explained that Marci and her friends had wanted to leave early as they were worried about the weather forecast. She had to make her classes tomorrow or she would be in trouble. Jerry reminded me again of what a good student Marci is and we need to tell her often how proud we are of her.

Connie had gone to the lake for the weekend with her girlfriend and her parents. Jerry was expecting her home late that afternoon. Julie had been here for a while but the baby was a bit fussy so she decided to take him home for his nap. Vicki and her hubby had gone home too.

You know mom, our new grandson is just a little over a month old now! He is such a beautiful boy. We will take some pictures next week to send you. I'm so thankful to have a grandson now! It will be so different watching him growing up compared to a girl. Ha.

I asked Jerry what the weather had been like on Saturday. He told me it was a bit stormy. He said some dark clouds looked scary but they went on by to Joplin. He was so glad that I had stopped there for the night.

So...Today they had us under a tornado watch until about four o'clock, when they lifted the watch altogether.

What happened next was really a shock to me. We heard the tornado siren blasting with the sounds that we recognized as a tornado warning; there has been a tornado sighted in the area.

The first thing Jerry thought of was the dogs. He brought all three of them into the utility room but they wouldn't let him get to the kitchen door so he could come back into the house.

Meanwhile, I had walked over to the TV to turn it off and unplug it. You taught me to do that whenever there was lightening around. Do you remember that?

By that time, it was getting so dark I couldn't see anything in the hallway so I got down on my hands and knees, crawling down to the bathroom. I crawled into the tub, pulled a towel over my head and prayed!

During the next few minutes, what felt like an eternity, I heard wood and glass crashing overhead with everything seeming to be going in one direction, East. Then I heard Jerry's voice calling out to me. "Liz! Liz! Where are you?" I yelled that I was in the bathroom and to be careful walking. When he found me I cried and hung on to him for dear life. I was so relieved that he was alive.

He told me how the dogs would not let him open the kitchen door. All three of them surrounded him in the utility room! It was a good thing the dogs would not let him come into the house as the wind was crashing through our glass sliding doors. They knew they should stay out in the garage where they would be safe. I think dogs have a sixth sense about things like weather. Don't you? Anyway, we were all alright but the house was a mess.! The house is still a mess!

The East side of the cathedral ceiling in the living room was blown off the house. The deck and back yard fencing all were torn up. Funny thing is that you can stand in the front yard and not see any damage. That is a good thing because there are always people out after a storm or any disaster, looking for damaged homes that they can loot, stealing anything they can carry.

Connie's friends drove up and after we explained what happened, her friend's mother invited Connie to come spend the night with them and meet up with Jerry at school the next day. That worked out just fine. We went on over to Julie's home to spend the night. Well, I did. Jerry was told by his security friends that he best stay in our house and keep his gun handy; so that was what he did!

I called Marci from Julie's to be sure they had arrived back at school safely. She said the weirdest thing happened. They had to stop driving for about fifteen minutes because their windows were bombarded by a rainstorm of grasshoppers! They could not see out the window. Can you imagine that?! They drove the rest of the trip just fine.

As I said, you don't need to worry about us. Our insurance agent came over the next morning and found us a place to live just a few blocks away. It's a two bedroom condo, very new and clean. We are very comfy. Some of Jerry's students came over and helped him move our furniture to the condo and boxes of stuff into a storage room. That sure saved us a lot of time and money. We may have to stay here for 3 months to give builders time to rebuild and re-roof our house.

We are so grateful to God that no one in our family was hurt. Not even a dog. One is with us in our Condo and the other two are staying in Julie's fenced in back yard.

Love and hugs, Liz

Evie and Frank read the letter at least three times until they could feel like they were there with Liz as she had waited out the storm. Later that evening when Frank was engrossed in a baseball game on TV, Evie started to reflect back over her life. She remembered the first time she had to visit a doctor after marrying Frank, was with her first pregnancy. She was absolutely terrified with the examination and would only go for one check-up after that. Frank tried to calm her during those visits but Evie told him he was a man and could never understand how she felt. Thank God that everything went smoothly with the pregnancy and at least her mother had allowed a mid-wife to be there when Liz was born. Years later when it was time for Bobby's birth, Evie had consented to be taken to the hospital. That had been a good experience with kind nurses who seemed to like her. In the years to come when the kids were sick with the measles or mumps, she would tell the landlady or the neighbor to call for the doctor. Doctors made house calls and put up the quarantine signs for all to see.

Liz was sorry she missed her mom's birthday celebration. Thank goodness her kind cousins helped to make it a joyous occasion for her. It had been very difficult for Liz to make the decision for her parents to enter a nursing home. But Frank was adamant about the plan. "Your mother worked hard care me. Now she not strong, not able walk. Now time we really retire. Our friends enjoyed their last years in Sauer Nursing Home Winona. We visited them often, played cards nice sunroom there. Please talk supervisor Sauer again about our admittance. You and Bobby need to make plans before you leave for your homes."

Evie started repeating again her story of having some monies that were lost or stolen. "My father never in nursing home. He ordered my sister, Lydia care him. I know he would not want me live that way!" she would sign. Frank reminded her that Medicare would pay some for their room and they could rent their house out to pay the balance.

"It seems Dad has all the answers," Liz said to Bobby. "You want to make the call or shall we go over there and talk to them in person?" In the end they all went, only to find out there was no room at this time but they could put their names on a waiting list. Liz actually felt relieved. This is just not the way I want their lives to end she thought as she turned to her dad, pulling him aside as they walked slowly back to their car. "Daddy, I love you and Mother so much. I am really sorry sometimes that I chose to live so far away. I don't know if I ever told you that Jerry would have been happy to live here in Winona if he found a teaching position close by. It was me that wanted to live in Tulsa and it is me that wants to stay in Tulsa. I think it offers more to our family. I hope you can understand that. Is there no way you would consider coming to Tulsa? We can find you a new kind of place. They call it Assisted Living."

Stopping his chair abruptly, he signed excitedly, "Oh, there is assisted living place here Winona. Was before big rich home, now changed, apartments with large dining room for all. Then moving his hands as fast as he could, he wheeled off to catch up with Evie and Bobby, he began talking to them about the place he described. "Can we go visit there now?" he asked Bobby. Liz stepped quickly into the office to sign her parents out for a couple of hours. By the time Liz caught up to them they were in the car and waiting for her to climb aboard.

Frank directed Bobby to the big building closer to downtown Winona. Looking around the area, Liz commented, "Actually, this is a good location. If mom wanted to walk to the grocery store she could. Dad could probably use his wheelchair just that one block to the park. Well, let's have a look."

Upon entering, Evie and Liz both commented on the pretty bright, yet soft colors used in the kitchen and living area. They were on an open floor plan with only one door, into the bedroom. The bedroom was large, spacious enough for two twin beds, a dresser as well as a chest of drawers. There were also two easy chairs, and a little table, with a desk and bookcase built into the wall. Everything was just as they had heard it to be but one important piece of information had been left out. The apartment was on the first floor with an easily accessed entry from the street; however, the dining room was on the second floor accessible only by a small elevator down the hall. After pushing the wheelchairs to the elevator, Bobby and Liz realized they would have to take turns as there was only enough room for one chair and one person standing. They followed this routine and when arriving at the dining room they were pleasantly impressed with the lovely open area and lots of space to wheel to a table. Service was provided by a waitress after choosing from a menu.

"Surely there must be another entrance into the dining room," Liz remarked to Bobby. "This is crazy!" Frank immediately stated that it would be too difficult to wheel oneself into that elevator and he could not imagine doing that three times a day every day! Evie was in tears just thinking about it. Liz immediately fell on her knees facing both of her parents to assure them both that this was not the only place they could live in; they would just have to look some more. Right now they were content with the room at Lewiston.

After just a few months in Lewiston, Bobby had a call from Sauer that there was room for one of his parents to come and room with another gentleman. Frank was not too keen on this idea and Evie said she would go crazy here alone with no one to communicate with. Bobby took that conversation back to the manager at Sauer; saying, "Can you imagine being a foreigner with no one else in the building that could understand your native language. Especially if you were not very good with English and had no interpreter available to you except maybe once a month. No, we can't expect my folks to live separately; so please consider them as having special needs and hopefully something here can be re-arranged so that they can have a room together. Thank you for your time and patience with us."

One month later Sauer called to say they had a room for both Frank and Evie, available as soon as they could make the move! Everyone was ecstatic over this news and with the help of cousins' near-by, the move was made. This was a good sized room with two twin beds and room for two easy chairs and a television. "Mom and dad seem quite comfortable, Liz," Bobby reported on the phone. "Oh, good news, Bobby. Good for you! Tell them Jerry and I will be coming up to see them at the end of next month." And with that, Liz felt like a load had been lifted from her shoulders.

After this move, brother and sister thought that it was probably just a matter of time before their parents would tire of this environment and their will to live. However, they proved them wrong. Frank loved the nurses and taught a few of them some sign language as well as the finger-spelling of the alphabet. Evie felt that he loved the girls a little too much but then she gained the friendship of a very nice gentleman who dropped in to see her every day.

This man's wife was in another wing of the home as she suffered with Alzheimer's. He committed himself to visiting her every day even though she did not seem to recognize him. This gentleman found out in November that he and Evie shared the same birth date and brought her a cake with candles. She was so thrilled. Some of her nieces and nephews came by that evening to share the cake and celebrate her 86th birthday with her.

The next day Evie had no trouble writing four pages to Liz letting her know that she had missed a beautiful day with her mother! Two pages were filled with the family news of each visitor which she knew Liz enjoyed reading. It wasn't really gossip, just newsy tidbits they had shared with her. All Evie had to do was copy the notes that had been passed to her by each of them. She also promised Liz pictures in her next letter.

That next summer brought visitors who really pleased them both.

Hi Mom and Daddy,   *July, 1987*

Just a quick note to let you know about when to expect us to arrive there. We have been having a great time up at this lake in this cute little cottage. Marci and Tom have only one complaint. The size of their bedroom is too small. We really had no choice as they had all the cottages rented out when we arrived with this one reserved for us. Otherwise all is comfy and they are having fun fishing.

We have caught some interesting fish that were very tasty. They have a service here that we took advantage of. They clean, cut and cook the fish for you when you are ready to eat them. We will tell you more about that when we see you. The weather was good to us too.

Anyway, we should arrive there Saturday around two o'clock and will stay until Monday morning. We have rooms reserved at the Days Inn close to you. Maybe we can take you out for lunch or dinner Saturday and then Sunday we are all invited out to our cousin's place for dinner. This should be a nice outing for you.

I hope you are feeling good and that we will see the sun shine all weekend. I think Bobby and his wife will drive down to see all of us too. I'm not sure when they are arriving but you probably have heard from them so you know. OK. That's all for now. I know you will love Tom. All of us do. We have to leave Monday as he must be back to work on Thursday. Of course Marci has the summer off just like Jerry as teachers. Lucky.

Love, Liz

Dear Liz and Jerry,   *November, 1988*

Oh, my time goes by fast! But we don't go out or really have much to do. I think it is because we move slowly to all three meals of the day and we both love TV game shows. Really love Price is Right. It is funny and fun to watch. Frank and I both guess about what will happen when people make choices. We don't agree so it is fun to see who is right...your Dad or me. Ha.

Right after you left last summer we looked at many pictures you sent us of your fun at that lake up north. Good pics. Yes, we agree. We like Tom so much. We wish he and Marci much happiness.

Soon there will be more grandkids for you. We are happy to show friends here at the nursing home pictures of grandkids and great grandkids. Of course they all do show us pictures too. Ha.

Some of these folks are good friends now. I think you know who they are. Next time you come I will tell you some news about their families. They sometimes tell me how they like your visits so they can chat with us more.

Soon is my birthday. I know some of your cousins will come with small gifts and birthday cake. They are always so good to me on my birthday. Then will be Thanksgiving, Frank's birthday and Christmas! Oh, my, we will be married 60 years December 22nd. I cannot believe! Maybe Bobby and wife will come and take us out to dinner if weather okay.

Well, no other news. We both feel good for our age! Even Dr. Parker says we are! We always look for your letters.

Love, Mother and Daddy

One mild Saturday in December of 1988, one of the nurses wheeled Evie to the elevator and handed her a note explaining that she had visitors downstairs. Another nurse was pushing Frank in the same direction. A bit annoyed on the ride down, thinking how she did not like surprises; Evie could not believe her eyes when the elevator door opened again and she saw the basement decorated so beautifully for some sort of celebration. In just a moment she saw the banner that read, "Happy 60th Anniversary Frank and Evie." She found it hard to feel any more perplexed when she saw the big grin on Frank's face as he looked around the room and saw so many familiar faces. She soon joined him in looking all around the room to see faces, especially those of Liz and Bobby and their families.

Frank recognized faces of loved ones from around the area; nieces and nephews and their families. And, more unbelievable, faces that he had not seen for a long time; those of his baby sister, Amanda with her two daughters and his lovely niece, Dorothy with her husband, all from Illinois! With little difficulty he soon found himself wheeled next to Amanda's wheelchair and outstretched arms found their way around each other as they hugged for a long while. "How u come here?" Frank signed to her. "Dear brother, I must come see you one more time. Norma and Jennie brought me. Much good see you," Amanda signed gracefully to her big brother.

People were all anxious to greet the anniversary couple but Liz quickly told them to wait until after cake and entertainment because there really was not enough room for folks to move around. Everyone agreed and the cake was cut, served and enjoyed with some group conversations around the tables as folks are likely to do. When Liz could see that her parents and her aunt had chatted awhile she started the "program" with a few highlights about Frank and Evie's lives.

After that, she introduced her family and Bobby's as well as her cousins from Illinois. When finished with that scenario, she laughed and said they were going to do a sing-a-long. One of her cousin's children had brought her portable piano to provide the necessary music. She had chosen some old songs with copies made for everyone and before long they all seemed to be enjoying the music. But the best entertainment of the day was still to come; little Tara, the first great-grandchild of Frank and Evie's. Tara was already a little actress. She had roles in plays since she was three years old in pre-school. What a natural she was with her blond hair and expressive eyes, she held her audience at attention. Everyone absolutely loved her rendition of signing the beautiful signs in the well-known song, "Jesus Loves Me." Tara basked in the applause and curtsied to her great grandparents, followed by big hugs all around. This led to rounds of goodbye hugs as many of the guests left the party. But a few cousins joined the family outside to enjoy a couple of hours left of this unusually warm December day.

Liz had signed everything she was saying to the guests which brought reactions from her cousins later. "How can you sign and talk at the same time?" they asked. These were her cousins who had deaf parents themselves; Aunt Amanda's two daughters and Uncle Karl's daughter. They were all fluent in sign language but had never become professional interpreters. Bobby had queried her before with the same question. "Well, of course it's not easy," Liz replied. "It became easier as I worked as an interpreter. I signed the words I was listening to at about the same rate of speed. However, if I was with an audience that needed or wanted ASL (American Sign Language) I would lag a little behind the speaker as I concentrated more on the real meaning of the words into the true interpretation with my signs. There are so many idioms in our crazy English language that must be interpreted to keep the message clear. Surely you can understand that. When just using ASL for my parents and Aunt Amanda today, I may have been a bit unfair to the words of the hearing person; but the ASL was understood by them, keeping them in the general discussion. Also today, I was trying to stay with English when signing the songs and was probably doing a little injustice to the deaf audience." Dot and the other girls were looking at Liz with amazement as she continued with a question, "Get it?" No one was sure they got it but they were definitely admiring Liz's talents on display today. Yes, Liz was sure this was a day for all to remember!

Before leaving for home, Liz found time to write an article about the celebration to send to the Minnesota Thompson Hall Newsletter.

Dear Editors: *December, 1988*

Please print this article in your next newsletter if possible:

Frank and Evelyn Niklaus (MSD graduates of 1924) were honored on their 60th Wedding Anniversary with an Open House Sunday, August 14th in Winona, MN. The celebration was held in the Community Center of the Sauer Memorial Home.

Their children, Bobby and his wife, Jo of Burnsville and Liz and her hubby, Jerry Powell of Tulsa, OK hosted the celebration. This joyous occasion was attended by over fifty friends and neighbors as well as family. Special guests were Frank's sister, Amanda Schmidt (MSD 1926) with her daughter, Norma Daugherty, both of Byron, IL. Frank's brother, Karl (MSD 1923), now deceased was represented by his daughter, Dorothy Parkinson and her husband, Parky; Evelyn's sister, Alice Schumacher and her five children all of Altura.

Frank and Evelyn have seven grandchildren and two great grandchildren. Granddaughters, Julie Watkins and

Connie Powell of Tulsa, OK. The great grandchildren, Chad, six and eight year old sister Tara Watkins were part of the entertainment as they signed songs for the guests of honor. Grandson Barry Niklaus and wife, Kathy of Burnsville as well as granddaughter, Corrine of St. Paul were all present.

Evelyn's many nieces and nephews living in the sur-rounding areas as well as residents of Sauer all joined in as the guests enjoyed a sing-along of old time love songs. Refreshments, including a beautiful cake, were provided by Sauer Home.

Friends may send cards to Frank and Evelyn at 1635 Service Rd Room#114 Winona, MN 55987.

Respectfully submitted with Thanks,
Mrs. Jerry Powell

Liz was so glad that Jerry was a teacher and had the summer months off so that they could drive up North around Memorial Day and then again before Labor Day. Any other time of the year would always include the worry of winter weather; now and then they caught a break and drove up during spring break. "But, you come one time Christmas," Evie would sign to Liz during a visit. Liz understood the tense of *come* as signed by her mother to mean past tense. This is one word that she interpreted to her family immediately as past tense because she understood the circumstances; changing that word (come) to include the word "have," voicing "But, you have only come one time for Christmas!"

Liz's mind became flooded with thoughts of interpretation and how difficult it could be. She realized that in the situation just experienced; if she had been interpreting for a deaf person she did not know very well, she would have had to ask that person what tense the word "come" was to be used. Of course she would not sign, "What tense are you using?" Seventy five percent of her clients would not understand the question. Knowing that, Liz would have signed, "Do you mean *now, or past, or future?*" Realizing this, Liz would often find herself arguing Pro for English signs in just such instances, that of tense! With English signs there are signs for the present, past and future by adding a little sign at the end of the word. For example, that sentence her mom had signed would have signed the same way, "But, you come (add sign for 'past' by throwing right hand over right shoulder behind you) only one time for Christmas." To complicate this subject more, there is more than one sign for the word "past!" One is to indicate "finished," another would show "before" and still another sign is to indicate "all this time"; the latter of which she could have used in this sentence of Evie's.

Yes, Liz knew her mother was right; this was true. They had come for Christmas to Wisconsin by train from Washington, D.C. in 1963; and they had driven up to Minnesota from Tulsa for Christmas in 1977. At that time, they also celebrated Evie and Frank's 50th wedding anniversary which was December 22nd. That had been a wonderful time with a celebration in the church by many of Liz's aunts, uncles, and cousins bringing their smiling faces as well as wonderful gifts. Evie and Frank were so proud which showed in their facial expressions caught by the camera for their Golden Anniversary portrait. Christmas had been neat too. By this time, Liz and Jerry's eldest daughter, Julie, had just been married earlier that month so it was like a family celebration for them too.

Unfortunately, the good times came to a sudden close on the very morning they were leaving to go back to Tulsa. Their suitcases had been stolen! Jerry had persuaded Liz to pack her suitcase and his along with some of Vicki's and Connie's clothes so that he could tie them down with a canvas cover on top of the station wagon. He wanted to do this the night before to save time. The girls said it was a bad idea because the car had to be left outside in the driveway, but their dad thought things would be okay. "This is a small town, nothing like that happens here!"

Jerry lived to regret those words as he went out to the station wagon the next morning with another suitcase to put in the back. Two of the girls always rode in the back end so they tried to keep luggage on the top, giving them more room. This time, though, they had not really needed the room because Julie and her hubby had driven their own car. They had reminded their father of that when he wanted to pack early but they still lost their argument. Thank goodness Julie had packed some of the Christmas presents in their car. Evie and Frank were also upset; even more than the girls. Liz was steaming but knew it would do no good to get angry because they couldn't do anything about it now and she didn't want to ruin the whole trip home. Jerry went to the local police and reported the incident while Vicki joined him in giving a detailed report of what was missing. Eventually they said their goodbyes to grandma and grandpa and started their long drive home. After twelve hours on the road they all fell into bed that night exhausted from all the events of the past few days.

Enough reflecting, Liz mused. That was ten years ago and circumstances are much different today. This visit to Sauer was quite different from that of visiting her parent's small but comfy home of that time. In fact, Liz reminded her hubby, today would be quite a serious visit since it included the State of Minnesota office similar to the Oklahoma Department of Human Services.

That afternoon, the manager of Sauer Home presented the facts to Liz and Bobby quietly in her office. She showed them that all of Evie and Frank's bank monies were gone from the sale of their home and what little savings they had was depleted. The only income Frank and Evie would have at the end of the month was that of Social Security. This was beginning to sound like some expenses Liz and Bobby would acquire very soon. But then the lady from the state office spoke up and assured them that there was financial aid available. Frank and Evie just needed to apply for next fiscal year, June 30, 1990 to July 1, 1991. Brother and sister inquired about the actual cost of the home with the answer a bit intimidating to both of them, over two thousand dollars a month! The house had been sold and all the proceedings paid out monthly to the home. Both sister and brother had families to support with college still looming for Liz's younger children. After a short discussion, Bobby and Liz decided to take advantage of the state's offer until they could make arrangements to cover the cost themselves. Of course, Medicare cost something each month and the administrator said they always gave Evelyn and Frank each forty-four dollars out of their Social Security check for "spending money." Liz and Bobby always gave their parents monies and went out to do any shopping for them each time they visited; so that wasn't any problem. It was that cost of the room, board and nursing care.

Remembering the scene with her father of a few years ago, Liz said, "Bobby, there is no reason to tell our folks about this money situation." She went on to tell him about the conversation with their dad. At that time Frank could not believe the cost of nursing homes when he was told the dollar figure by the Nursing Home director. He had told Liz that the director must have communicated that information wrongly. Surely she was mistaken about the cost. He insisted that the cost quoted must be a semi-annual charge, not a monthly one! Again, Liz said emphatically, "Bobby, there is no point in discussing this with mom and dad even now. It will only upset them." After some hesitation, Bobby had to agree. They also agreed that this perspective of their dad's about money was not because he was a profoundly deaf person. Rather, it was the attitude shared by many elderly people, especially patients in hospitals and nursing homes. The cost was prohibitive to many senior citizens.

"There would have to be cut backs somewhere if we are to help your folks," Jerry remarked later. "I've already signed my papers for retirement and you're just embarking on this new contract of yours in Oklahoma City. I don't see where we can come up with fifteen hundred a month unless your Relay business really takes off!" Liz had to agree as she quietly returned to her office that next week. Perhaps she should consider commuting the two hours from Tulsa instead of renting an apartment here in the City. Perhaps three times a week would be enough to keep an eye on things. Or, maybe she could take interpreting assignments from the Department of Rehabilitative Services as a free-lance interpreter a couple of days a week or even over the weekend and leave the office in Jerry's hands.

Jerry could also check into the Oklahoma City schools and apply as a substitute teacher.

They would need to work hard to earn an extra thousand dollars a month. There was even the possibility of teaching a class in the interpreter training classes held at the Oklahoma State University. Liz was soon immersed in the busy routine of this relay business that gave her very little time to worry about these opportunities available to her. She loved doing what she was doing and would spend ten to twelve hours a day taking care of this business so that it would serve the deaf community of area code 405 with the best service she could provide.

Jerry went ahead with his plans to move to Oklahoma City into the apartment Liz had rented in close proximity to her business. Julie and her two children were temporarily living in their home in Tulsa after her divorce which fit into the plan just fine. The house was no longer empty and they would not need to travel there every week-end for now. Jerry was proud to sit at the front desk at BP Services for the Deaf and take care of the outside phone calls coming into the business, giving Liz more time to help the other interpreter-operators on the relay calls. He didn't mind living in an apartment where he didn't have to mow the lawn or shovel the sidewalk. No, he didn't mind at all. In fact they were working so well together and giving the business all they could that he was sure they would make a larger profit within the year. Of course, the price of the computers had been costly, making high monthly payments along with the building rent and electric bills. There was a fine young Christian taking care of their accounting for them for a small monthly fee and it was a good feeling to be providing jobs for the young students in the local Oklahoma State University Interpreter Training Program. Fortunately, the school was located just a few miles from their office. Things were looking good.

Liz once heard a pastor say, "If you want to make God laugh, make plans." How true! Just as things were really rolling along smoothly with the business and with the routines of the day, a phone call came in from Minnesota.. Evie had been taken to the hospital to have a blood transfusion. It seems the doctor had just diagnosed leukemia and prescribed a blood transfusion immediately. Bobby was there with his mother the next morning, holding her hand as she cried while telling him how painful she thought the procedure had been.

Soon Liz and Jerry had a schedule worked out for the office. Jerry had to convince Liz that she could be gone for a week and things should run smoothly. Jerry was a bit anxious to let her go by herself but knew he could not leave this business in anyone else's hands. Actually, Liz was satisfied that the road trip had become routine. She was not nervous about driving alone.

Arriving in Minnesota late the next night, Liz did not stop at the hospital or the nursing home but went straight to her cousin's home in Winona. Kathleen and her husband had a lovely home not far from the nursing home. They had a roomy guest room that Liz found so comfortable she slept for ten solid hours. The next morning Liz awoke to find that Kat and her hubby were gone to work. So Liz enjoyed a leisurely shower before she headed over to the Home where she found her father at the breakfast table in the dining room. Frank was so happy to see her but she could see that he looked tired and somewhat sad. Liz soon realized how lonesome he was without his Evie. When they finished eating, Liz excused herself signing, "Will go see mother now and come back for lunch with you? OK?" "Yes, good," Frank replied. "Give her hug and kiss from me and tell her I miss her so much!" "Of course," Liz signed quickly, turning away before Frank would see the tears in her eyes.

Before leaving the building, a nurse caught her and told her that Frank was suffering with a toothache. The nurse had taken him to the dentist the day before but the dentist found the tooth to be infected. All he could do for him was give him some antibiotics, put some painkiller on the gums and tell him to go home until the infection cleared up. Liz thanked her for that info and explained that she would be back for lunchtime but wanted to be sure that her mother was comfy at the hospital.

Arriving at the hospital, she was relieved to find Evie dozing in a chair. All she had to do was touch her arm and her mother was wide awake holding her arms out for a hug. She signed, "Bobby drove home last night after called Kathleen's sure you here safely." "Oh, good. You look good this morning. You must be feeling better," Liz signed with a big smile. "Mother, now you and I are alone I want to tell you something that might help you understand about your father promising to take care of you. OK?"

Noting her mother's nod in the affirmative, she continued, "I heard Jerry telling his daughter that if ever there were problems in her job, or her marriage, she should always remember that he was always her father. That, as her father, he would always be available to her and that he would always take care of her. So, you see, that is what your father was telling you. Do you think you understand a little more now?" Liz's mother could see that Liz was really trying to make sense of this thing between Evie and her father. She was taking it so seriously. After a long pause, Evie signed quietly, "Thank you, Liz, for trying to explain. I think I understand a little more every time we talk about this. All these years have gone by and no one has found any money or bank account with my name, so I'm sure nothing will ever be discovered. I am okay with that." Not feeling at all secure in what her mother said, Liz felt the need to change the subject.

Liz explained about Frank's toothache which upset Evie. "No, will be alright! Dentist gave him medicine so he will not feel any pain. I will go back over there for lunch with Daddy and be sure he is ok, really!" Evie insisted she stay with Frank as long as she could and not to worry about coming back to the hospital until tomorrow. Unsure where her loyalty lay at this moment, Liz decided to play it by ear. She left at lunchtime as planned.

After hugging her father, she signed as sweetly as she knew how, "Mama sends you her hugs and kisses. She said to tell you that she misses you so much too and hopes she can be back here with you soon, maybe tomorrow. Liz enjoyed a lunch with her Daddy and walked back into his room with him but she could see he needed a nap. "I will go back to tell mother you are doing alright and then come back here later," she signed as Frank's head nodded sleepily. No doubt the pain meds were working.

Visiting again with her mother she was told again to stay with Frank and be sure to find out more about his tooth. That evening Liz sat with her dad to chat and watch some television together. He was unable to enjoy his dinner because of some pain in his tooth which Liz reported to the nurse immediately. For the first time in her life, she saw her dad actually feeling sorry for himself. He missed Evie, especially when he wanted her sympathy for his toothache. Liz tried to talk to him but he wasn't in the mood for conversation. Finally the nurse reported back that she had spoken to the dentist who said he could see Frank the next day at noon. So, the nurse gave him a pain pill and he crawled into bed. It was still early so Liz decided to stay and pulled her chair next to his bed to make some more small talk just to take his mind off of his tooth. For a while he held Liz's hand tightly indicating he was in pain; but after fifteen minutes he relaxed his hand. He finally fell asleep and Liz decided to go on to Kathleen's. Thank goodness Kat and her hubby were open to Liz sharing her frustrations about her parents situation and how it was not easy living so many miles away from them. Getting this out of her system helped so much. With tears in her eyes she asked to be excused so that she could get up early and check in with her dad.

The next morning, after Kat and George had both gone to work, Liz took the opportunity to shower. After a bowl of cereal, while dressing, Liz realized she had best go see Evie before taking Frank to the dentist. Getting into her car, she noted what a beautiful day it was with all the trees full of bright colors and a cool October breeze against her cheek. On her drive to the hospital she thanked God for his nature and for the blessings he bestowed upon her. She closed her conversation with her Lord by asking him to give a comfortable day to both her parents.

Before stepping into the hospital room, Liz watched from the doorway as Evie was enjoying a hearty breakfast, a good sign, she thought. "You feeling better!" Liz signed as she approached her mother's bed. After a short chat, the two women were pleasantly surprised when the doctor came in to give Evie a good check-up. Dr. Parker always seemed to lift Evie's spirits while Liz signed his words to her mom. "Everything is truly on the mend," (Liz could not sign the words *on-the-mend* because they would have no meaning to Evie, so she signed, *improving*).

Just then the telephone rang and the nurse came in to call Dr. Parker out of the room. Liz answered the phone to hear the voice of the nurse at the Sauer Home say, "Liz, your dad has passed away quite suddenly. You best come here and we will explain what happened." Feeling absolutely numb, Liz saw the doctor standing in the doorway and quietly said, "Wait, Dr. Parker is right here, why don't you talk to him," as she quickly handed the phone to him. She hugged her mother and said, "The phone call said I must go to Sauer now as daddy wants to go to the dentist." With that she grabbed her purse and coat and walked out the door. Dr. Parker quickly caught up with her and said he would take her to Sauer. "You do understand, Liz, your father has passed away." "I understand but I don't understand," Liz replied. Putting his arm around her shoulder, the good doctor said, "Liz, perhaps the toothache was just an indication of a heart attack last night. Often times the heart attack manifests itself in weak parts of the body. I am so sorry. Let me take you. You don't want to drive right now."

"No, please, I will drive. I just wasn't ready to tell mother yet. I'll come back later. I'm alright and it's such a short distance. I will meet you over there." With that she walked to the parking lot, got into her car and drove the mile or so to Sauer without realizing whether there had been a red light at the corner or any traffic on the road. Never a tear had formed yet. Finding a parking spot close to the entrance, she hurriedly walked through the day room, just two doors down the hall to her parents' room where she was met by two nurses at the door. "We're so sorry, Liz. Frank got up and wheeled himself to the dining room and even managed to eat a pretty good breakfast. After he came back to his room he was in his chair and slumped over. The reason we know this is because the lady directly across the hall noticed him slumped over and buzzed for the nurse. Liz, when we got to him he was already gone. We put him on the bed and performed CPR but he was gone, believe me. It was fast and easy if that helps any."

Liz could not believe her eyes as she looked at her sweet father lying on his bed but with his eyes still open. Dr. Parker came in at that moment and told Liz she could close Frank's eyes if she wanted to; so she did, giving him a kiss on each one as she did so. That's when the tears came! "Oh, my God, Daddy!"

She stepped over to the window and let them flow, gasping for air as she looked out at the scene that had filled her father's eyes for the past three years. Two birdhouses hung over their brick laid patio, covered lightly with an inch of snow that had fallen earlier that morning. The sun was shining brightly as she looked over this central area with the gazebo and benches arranged so that the residents could sit and visit with their neighbors or family members. In October it was a quiet scene and Liz finally spoke out loud, saying to anyone who wanted to listen, "This scene is just a preview of what Dad will be looking at in heaven. There will be flowers in bloom all year and angels all around. He will hear them singing. Oh, he will join in with their singing and he will shout praises to God with his own voice!"

With that the nurses said, "Amen" and without another word they left the room. The good doctor asked Liz if there was anything he could do for her. "I would like to be with you when you do tell your mother. Just to be sure that her reaction will not be too much for her heart. Okay? There is no hurry. I'm going to visit some folks here and I will let you know when I'm ready to go to the hospital." Liz nodded in agreement and sat down in the chair close to the bedside to say a short prayer for her dad's soul, that she was confident was in no jeopardy whatsoever. Then Liz began to realize some of the things she needed to do. First, she needed to call Bobby, of course; then, Jerry. But before she could do anything, the nurse returned to tell her they needed to call the funeral home to have the body moved, asking her which funeral home she wanted them to call. Since she knew of only one where her aunt had been; and having heard of more than satisfactory services there, that was an easy decision.

Going into the office, Liz asked permission to use a phone. She called her brother and her husband with just a brief message left on Bobby's answering machine. Liz was so glad to find Jerry at their office where he could go ahead and make the proper plans for their absence from the office. Jerry immediately said he was putting someone else in charge. He chose a lady who had proven to be reliable with integrity and the proper skills. Then he promised he would catch the first available flight. It was a relief just to know that Jerry would be here to support her through this time of grief. Of course Bobby would come as soon as he could make arrangements at his office too. He did have an important position in the control room, that much Liz knew. But she wasn't sure just what he did or whether he was in the Control Tower or another part of the airport. Jo would also have to get permission to leave her desk in the dental clinic where she worked.

Liz knew she needn't worry about all that; she just needed to take care of matters at hand. Upon returning to the room, she discovered that the men from the funeral home had just arrived. One gentleman asked if Liz would prefer to be out of the room as they had to put Frank's body into a zip up body bag. "No, I want to be right here," she replied. Later she realized why they had given her that option; it was not easy to watch as they did just that and put him on the gurney to take him to their vehicle. Liz made two more phone calls, one to her cousin who was a minister and the other to her cousin, Kathleen, before Dr. Parker came to announce he was ready to go to the hospital. Again, she opted to drive her own car there.

Dr. Parker met Liz at the front door of the hospital and they both walked to Evie's room together to find that Evie had just finished her lunch. As it turned out, that was not good timing because immediately upon seeing the words on Liz's hands, Evie screamed and tried to get out of bed before throwing up everything she had

Frank, Evie & Liz

just eaten. Liz buzzed for the nurse who came in a flash to help Evie into the bathroom where they stayed for a long time. After an orderly cleaned up the mess, Liz went into the bathroom to help her change into another gown. Evie asked Liz to please explain all that had happened to Frank. First they managed to get Evie back into a clean bed and make her as comfy as they could so that the doctor could check her heartbeat. He said a few kind words and then went back to his rounds at the hospital as Liz answered all the questions Evie had for her. The nurse soon came in to give Evie a sedative and after asking Liz to promise that she would stay right there, she closed her eyes to rest. The nurse further offered to order a lunch tray for Evie again and one for Liz too. Even though Evie said no, Liz said that might be nice. The trays came about a half hour later and they both ate a few bites as they tried to relax. Eventually Evie took a nap. Shortly after that, Bobby and Jo came in and the evening was filled with conversation about the day's events and some plans for a funeral.

Jerry rented a car in Rochester and drove in the next afternoon. Their next task was to go to the funeral home and make the necessary arrangements. Frank's body looked good, with just a hint of a smile on his face. To Liz that meant that he had seen an angel just as he died and knew he was seeing the rewards of his faithfulness. After another call to their minister cousin, all plans were set up without Evie. Soon all four went to the hospital and relayed all the information to their mother, carefully asking for her approval on each point that was covered. To Liz's surprise, Evie seemed satisfied with the plans and had no changes or requests to make.

Three of the girls had called with apologies for not coming to Minnesota. They all had full time jobs. Marci was a teacher, Vicki worked for Blue Cross/Blue Shield and had already taken all of her vacation. Connie was in Florida with no vacation time earned on her new job. Liz told them not to feel badly. It was so expensive to make the trip and to take unpaid vacations was just not sensible. Fortunately, Julie and her hubby were able to come. This was such a comfort to Liz throughout the next couple of days. Of course Jerry was comforting but it was nice to hear Julie talk about dad as her grandpa. Liz was able to keep her mind focused more on the pleasant memories of her dad as they chatted with their cousins off and on. The stories were also helping Evie feel better.

Just one question remained. Was Evie strong enough to go to the funeral and the cemetery? After receiving Dr. Parker's permission to do so, everything went surprisingly smooth in transporting Evie to the funeral home for the services and then to the cemetary for the burial. She did not get out of the car at the cemetery but could watch all that was going on. During the funeral services, Liz managed to interpret everything to her mother until the final hymnal was sung. Even though it was one of the most difficult assignments she ever had, Liz continued signing as the tears came for both of them.

The cemetery in Winona is on a hillside; well, actually a small mountain side, and quite beautiful. Frank and Evie had property within a family plot bought by Evie's parents many years ago. Their lot was high on the hill overlooking the tiers of stones and flowers with just a little view of the city beyond. There was a serenity here that caused Liz to feel close to God. There were large markers standing at the elder Hilke's site while the next generation all had flat stones with the usual information about each person lying there. A permanent vase on a stand would hold a green plant all year round. Large trees around the perimeter of the cemetery gave wonderful shade in the summer time. Late in the fall they loomed overhead with their branches hovering close as though protecting the stones from the inclement weather. Some colored leaves were still hanging on and covering the ground lending just enough brightness to this otherwise cloudy morning. Cousin Earl had just the right words to deliver at the graveside. His voice was sincere, carrying an image of the everlasting life that Jesus promised us. All her cousins hugged Liz before moving slowly to their cars. With true gratitude, Liz thanked Earl for his services as they walked to the car to give Evie some words of comfort. Liz had always had a warm spot in her heart for this caring man, the only minister in the family. She knew her mother loved him and had appreciated his visits to the

Nursing Home. Evie surprised Liz when she gave him a hug and signed, "Frank good man, believed in God. I want to believe too." Earl nodded and looked at Liz with a question in his eyes. "I will explain later," Liz mumbled without signing her words. She just didn't feel this was the appropriate time to tell him how Evie felt some bitterness over being born deaf. How do you tell a man of the cloth that your mother doesn't believe in God?

Cousin Glen and his wife, Helen, invited everyone to their home in Altura for lunch after the funeral. Evie's sister, Alice, was there along with several cousins and as is usually true of any family gathering, it was good to see everyone. Evie asked about the families of everyone attending which kept Liz busy, but this interpreting chore also kept the sadness from her mind.

Glen enjoyed telling Liz the story of her parents coming to their home to play cards. This had been when Evie and Frank first moved to Winona. Glen said he always had a good time with them even if he didn't know sign language. He sure knew how to mime! "Your mom was very serious about card games. The first time we played I learned something very fast. Helen was always my partner while Frank was Evie's. When Helen and I would say a few words to each other, Evie would lean over into my face and put her finger to her mouth, showing the well-known gesture for "Shhh. Shhh!" Liz laughed at her cousin's description of the scene. "I understood from the expression on her face that she thought we were cheating when we talked to one another. I waited until I noted Evie signing to Frank, and only Frank. Then I reached over and pulled her hand down! Boy was she shocked. But she had mixed emotions as she looked at Frank and Helen and turning back to me, she laughed a long laugh. She laughed so hard she cried. After that we always tried to keep our talking to an absolute minimum."

The world was still spinning a little too fast as Jerry had to say his goodbyes to get back to the business of BP Services for the Deaf in Oklahoma City to keep everything on course. Bobby and Jo had to go back to their home and jobs while Liz stayed on a few more days to be sure all was in order with her mother and the nursing home. Evie begged Liz to take her back to Tulsa with her but they both knew she was not in good enough health to take the trip. Liz took advantage of the time to clean out all her father's clothes and personal belongings, saving just a few items for her mother to keep.

Dr. Parker did discharge Evie from the hospital in a couple of days so Liz had an opportunity to get her settled in the nursing home again. The only problem was that Sauer was obliged to let another woman share the room with Evie. She would be moving in the next week. Liz's heart was heavy, knowing how lonely Evie would be. She tried to ignore that fact as she assured her mother she would come and visit at Thanksgiving.

Another two days found all paperwork in order and Liz had to face the fact that she must get back to her business in Oklahoma. She had only been in Oklahoma City for eight months and wanted to make a success of the 405 area Telephone Relay Service for the Deaf. She was determined to oversee the operation daily to be sure the deaf community was receiving the best of service. Unfortunately, she also was the only one who knew how to take care of all the paperwork necessary to turn in to the Department of Human Services at the end of the month. This led to an absolutely necessary paycheck which covered the payroll for all of the interpreter/operators. Yes, Liz knew she had to get back to her business. Yet, it was difficult to make the decision to go back to Oklahoma.

Liz knew Evie would receive better care here at Sauer Home and with her doctor; however, she also knew Evie would be lonesome. Lonesome because of the loss of her husband; but, more than that would be the bitter lonesomeness with the lack of communication. There would be no one using her sign language. The nursing home had promised to look for a roommate who was deaf or familiar with sign language but Liz knew this would be nigh onto impossible in this small community. There had only been one other deaf couple in Winona and they were now deceased. There was one lady and one man, both single, who were hard-of-hearing but knew very little sign language. Liz vowed to get in touch with them so they would at least visit Evie once in a while. She also knew that her cousins would keep in touch and see to it that Evie would have whatever she needed. Their gestures and notes were better than no communication at all.

Somehow Liz managed to get away from her mother's hold on her arm. She must be strong. She must go. She made the I Love You sign to Evie and kissed her on the forehead.

"Okay right, you, maybe," she signed slowly to her daughter. Evie had a sad look on her face that she tried but failed to change. "But, please stay awhile longer. Ask nurse you can go downstairs make toast and tea in kitchen." Liz tried so hard to keep her patience, but her thoughts were already organizing her time into packing her suitcase and crawling into bed. She needed a good night's sleep if she were to drive all the way home tomorrow. "I will ask the nurse to make you some toast and tea but I must go and get some sleep. Please understand!" she signed a little fast. Signing fast was usually an indication of impatience, Liz knew that but she just couldn't seem to regain her patience. Kissing her mother again on the forehead, she slipped out quickly without watching to see what, if anything, Evie might have to say in response.

She was relieved when the nurse agreed to fix Evie the snack she wanted. Climbing into her car, Liz was somewhat dismayed to see a little fog rolling into the area. Losing no time, she drove the country road up the hill toward Altura. Grateful to arrive at her cousin's before the fog settled, she accepted a cup of coffee and briefly explained her plans to leave in the early a.m. "Please do not get up or fix me anything to eat. I like to have a good reason to stop after a couple of hours on the road." They agreed amicably to her request as she said goodnight. With a hug for each of them, Liz felt almost as sad making these farewells as it had been with her mother. With dragging steps she climbed the stairs, anxiously falling into bed.

After a restless night in this lovely bedroom, she arose at five a.m. dressing quickly and quietly trying not to disturb anyone. However, having grown up on a farm, Glen and his wife were early risers so ignoring Liz's request, they had set their alarm to get up in time to set a breakfast out for one of their favorite guests. Liz never tired of visiting here, not just for the great hospitality, but for the closeness she felt to these two people. Helen always made her feel comfortable and the two of them were never at a loss of words.

They shared a lot about their respective family members and compared notes on the activities of their churches. Liz always teased Glen that he was so fortunate that a smart lady like Helen had actually accepted his proposal. Of course, Liz felt that they were really a well-matched pair. Glen had such a great sense of humor that carried the two of them through many tough times, such as the loss of their first baby girl at birth. Yes, Liz often thought, Glen and Helen are a hard-working, loving couple. They weren't bad looking either! Liz had always thought Glen looked just like a favorite movie star of hers, John Hodiak.

More than any other of the cousins in this area, Helen had even picked up on a lot of signs so that she could visit Evie and bring her news of the family. Liz was so grateful for this. Helen was a just a few months older than Liz, but had always seemed more mature in many ways. Her face was one of those rare ones to behold. Looking for the explanation of this, Liz noted that the tiny wrinkles around Helen's eyes and at each end of her small mouth gave her that ever present, expression of love. Helen had been a nurse in her early life career and carried all this experience and love over to raising her three grandchildren while their mother worked.

This was something Liz never had the patience for. She was fine keeping a child for one or two days but not every day for years! Liz loved to tell others about Helen, in her sixties, successfully donating a kidney to her younger brother. That makes her a heroine in my book! Liz felt that with every trip up here to her birth state it was always tough hugging Helen and cousin Glen farewell. This time Liz felt more than sadness, she actually felt lost. Perhaps it was the loss of Daddy.

She had packed her bag and placed it in the trunk of the car the night before so that by six in the morning she was on the highway heading home. Liz was not looking forward to this long drive by herself and decided she best stop in Kansas City early in the evening and spend the night before heading to Oklahoma City. With so much on her mind, though, the hours flew by as she readily gained mileage. She soon decided to drive on westward instead of driving into Kansas City and stay on the highway for at least two more hours. At that point she decided she may as well drive all the way home that night. This was the first time Liz was returning to Oklahoma City instead of Tulsa after a trip to Minnesota, so at least there was a little change of scenery to help her stay awake. At nine p.m. she drove into the driveway of the apartment complex. She couldn't believe she had driven all the way! Jerry greeted her with a big hug, "I'm so relieved you are here! Let's not ever do that again. We need to be together for road trips. Okay?"

After sleeping like a baby for twelve hours she wondered how in the world she ever made that trip so well. Before going to work that morning, she dropped to her knees to thank God over and over for His company on that trip home. She also asked Him to watch over Evie.

Things were a bit hectic at the office for the next few days but with Jerry's help and the super talented employees they had, things were soon back to normal. Of course *normal* was still very busy! Just two weeks after her return from Minnesota Liz had a phone call from the nurse stating that Evie had refused to have another blood transfusion. Dr. Parker had requested that Sauer Home notify me that things might go from bad to worse because Liz's mother would not co-operate. Liz told her that she would get away as soon as possible and be in Minnesota in a couple of days.

In reality, Liz had mixed feelings about the whole situation. First of all, her very good friend had passed away just two days ago and Liz wanted to attend her funeral in Tulsa on Monday. It was a shock to Liz because her friend had not shared the information about her health conditions. Liz wanted to see the family and give her personal condolences. Yet her own mother needed her. Or, at least, the doctor probably needed her to interpret to Evie how important this blood transfusion was. This was Friday, with a busy weekend ahead for the relay business. Please, God, let me make the right decision, Liz prayed.

She also realized that this was the perfect opportunity to let go of her control and trust her husband to handle the things at the office. When she called him, Jerry convinced Liz to go on home to Tulsa and check in with their girls on the whole scenario first. He certainly had to swallow those words he had spoken to her just a short while ago about taking that drive up North alone!

Liz was happy to comply, putting the office complex into his care. After packing a few clothes, she drove the two hours to their home in Tulsa. She always felt a little sadness when she walked into their house and realized how empty it was. Of course it's been an empty nest for years but we always had a collie to greet us at the door to let us know how much we've been missed. Now, there is just silence. But it's a good thing we don't have a dog right now. We would have to ignore him too much. I'm also glad we never opted to sell this house, Liz mused as she went directly to the telephone to relay the message about Evie to her three daughters here in Tulsa. Our house is in a nice neighborhood, quiet, yet so close to the real hubbub of the city; as well as to the hospital and clinics we both need.

Each of the girls was surprised to hear their mother's voice on the phone until she asked their advice on whether she should head up North right away or wait until after her friend's funeral on Monday. As usual, they all said the same thing, "It's your decision, mother." Liz expected this reply but typically they would give their own opinions first, knowing full well that Liz would do whatever she wanted to in the end. But, Liz argued with herself, sometimes I do listen to a particular piece of advice. My girls all have a lot of smarts. However, this time not a one of them gave her any thoughts on what she should do.

Things fell in place quickly as Liz made her plans to stay home for the weekend, go to her friend's funeral Monday morning and then take off for Minnesota. This was another time that

Liz thought of the old saying, "If you want to make God laugh, make plans." Early Monday morning the phone call came directly from Dr. Parker himself. "Your mother passed away peacefully this morning. Your cousins are here to take care of the things that need to be done now and then your brother will be arriving in a couple of hours; so rest assured that you do have time to drive here without hurrying." "Oh! No! I'm too late. Thank you for calling," Liz replied as she hung up the phone, stunned! She had to hold back the tears because her face was made up for the funeral. Or, perhaps she shouldn't go. How could she hold it all together through a friend's funeral?!

Still, Liz was relieved enough to attend her friend's funeral that day, glad for the opportunity to visit with the grieving family. As she was leaving, she had the opportunity to share her news of Evie's death to the grieving family's pastor. After comforting words from him Liz slipped out quietly to return home to her packing. The tears began slowly and then flowed freely as she chose a wardrobe for herself.

She didn't have to wait long for Jerry to come from the City. Since he was already packed, they left right away and drove to Kansas City this same day. Phone calls with her brother confirmed that all was taken care of and that the weather was looking good for November. So, they drove on the next day to Bobby's home in the Minneapolis area to spend Thanksgiving Day with them. It was a rare visit with Bobby's three children all there too. Like Liz, Bobby was fortunate to have two of his three children living in the Twin Cities area. The youngest girl was here from Phoenix with her hubby too so it was fun comparing notes about both families.

Ironically, Liz's promise two weeks ago to visit her mother was just one day late. Of course, it was to her funeral, not for pleasure! It was so hard to grasp, much less to understand! Just three weeks ago they were at Frank's funeral! This funeral did not require the services of an interpreter so Liz was relaxed, enjoying the words of the pastor. Again, Glen and Helen generously arranged a lovely reception for the families at their country home. A lot of stories were told lifting the somber mood to one of thanksgiving and praise.

Details came slowly from her brother about there being no life insurance on Evie and all the monies from their house had gone to their years at the nursing home. That was the end of a brief discussion as they covered the costs of the funeral together. They met the next day to quietly divide all the things left in Evie's room at Sauer. Her clothes were given to charity. However, Liz did take her father's chair! She could not remember a time when he didn't have that chair; he would sit in it every day after work and have his cup of coffee while Evie fixed dinner for the family. Considering it an antique, Liz would put it in their guest bedroom at home and pass it on to one of her daughters in her own will.

Her love for her mother and father wrapped up into a chair! Life is so fleeting. Life is altogether too short. However, just the thought that her parents would now be able to voice their love to each other, as well as all the other members of their families that were waiting for them, boosted Liz's morale. Surely they would enjoy loving days together in Heaven.

Their drive home included a long running conversation about Evie and Frank for two days. Theirs was a story that had to be related to their daughters and their children someday. There are really no words to describe the rarity of having deaf parents. Liz realized that in the time that she was growing up, people had a much quieter life than they do today. "We had no television, I had no radio until my twelfth birthday, and no telephone until I was sixteen. Therefore when I say it was a quiet home that I grew up in, it is not true for the CODAs of today," she mused with her hubby. "I'm glad that I lived in the era that I did. I've seen so many things change for the deaf; all for the better.

"Their education has improved over the last two decades. Mainstream has been good for a large percentage of the kids lending itself to the over-all social life of the deaf child. They may still miss out on some things but they get a lot better sense of

what is acceptable in today's society, even picking up a lot of the idioms that hearing kids use. Yet, there is still a need for parents and teachers to be patient in including their deaf child or student in every day conversations. Conversations with the child as well as those held between the hearing people around them. It is still difficult to include sign language in all communication; however, if everyone tries, the message will get across. I think it is still a mission to carry on for all advocates of deaf children and adults."
Jerry listened to all of Liz's comments, agreeing with her whole-heartedly. He withheld his own opinions because he could see that speaking all these thoughts out loud was a form of therapy for Liz. She didn't need any real conversation. The memories would linger for a long, long time. Thus ended the quiet era of two lovely deaf people, Frank and Evie.

Yet, Liz felt no real closure. She soon realized this was because she could not forgive herself for the way she acted toward Evie on their last visit. Liz could not shake the guilt she carried around in her own heart. She had actually been mean to her mother on the last night they were together. Selfishness and worry about the fog in the valley for her drive up to her cousin's place had caused her to "speak" a bit harshly to her mom. She knew her mother was trying to hold on to Liz for as long as possible, while Liz wanted nothing but to get away! Every time she thought about that evening, Liz would cry with heart-wrenching sobs.

Finally, Liz shared this heavy weight with her pastor. His suggestion was that she sit down and write a letter to her mom to ask for her forgiveness. "I know, Evelyn is gone; but she will read the letter and you will feel better. Trust me. The Lord works in mysterious ways, you know. Put her name on the envelope with no address and no return address. Try it, Liz."

Anyone who loves our Lord knows without my saying, that this worked! Liz could feel her mom's spirit looking over her shoulder as she sat at her desk in her little office at home and wrote her last letter to her mom.

Dearest Mom,

I know there were times when you found it hard to tell me you love me. That's probably because you couldn't say it quickly or quietly like I could. I think it helped a lot when deaf folks came up with the sign I L Y, putting all three letters on one hand and facing the palm out to the person or people you wanted to tell that you loved them. Of course, hugs are so much better!

Mom, I loved you so very much. Always. Sometimes I would wonder just what you wanted to say, or what you wanted me to do; but I always blamed that hesitation on the differences in our communication levels. I knew you loved me and I pray that you knew I loved you. Always!

However, I often feel guilty because I moved so far away from you and Dad when I should have realized I needed to live close to you all your lives. The only real excuse I have is that I never dreamed it would be permanent! The fact that I met a man I would marry and that his Air Force career kept us on the move for twenty years. Who could have predicted that you would never see me pregnant or be close by when I gave birth to each of my girls. Please forgive me for choosing a life that kept you and I so many miles apart.

I am writing you this letter because I also want to apologize to you for the way I treated you on our last night together! Please forgive me for not fulfilling your wishes when you asked me to go and make some toast for you before I left. I just thought the nurse could do it and I wanted to leave! Yes, I wanted to leave! I was concerned about the fog on that road up the hill to Glen and Helen's house. I was concerned about the lateness of the hour and I was anxious to get to bed so I could get up early to start my trip back to Oklahoma.

My thoughts were all of myself and not of you! I knew you didn't want the evening to end. It was always hard to say goodbye. Please forgive me. Again, Please know that I love you... Always!

I'm sure your father has explained to you why he said he would take care of you.

I know, too, that Jesus has explained to you things I didn't know how to explain. Like, why did he make you and some other people deaf? Why were there other handicaps such as blindness or diseases? Why were some people so poor? Jesus has the answers for you.

I feel good about you and Daddy being together again, and singing together your praises for our Precious Lord. I know your voices are beautiful!

I love you, most precious mother!

Your only daughter, Liz

EPILOGUE

*B*ack at work again in the City, Liz was able to renew her contract annually for four years with the State of Oklahoma Department of Rehabilitation Services before the large telephone companies saw the need to provide this service. It was with mixed feelings that she closed her offices and moved back to Tulsa in December of 1993. However, she was thrilled that the telephone service to the Deaf would be so much better now with many centers across the nation providing more manpower and state of the art equipment. In 2005, the service became one with video! How fantastic to be able to look at the video screen and use the deaf person's first language (American Sign Language), comfortably communicating to and from the hearing person's voice, still heard through a headset. Liz was proud to work for this Video Relay Service for another four years before completely retiring from her services for the deaf community. Again and again, Liz expressed to anyone who would listen, "I'm so blessed to have been born to deaf parents."

NOTES FROM THE AUTHOR

Among my fondest and proudest assignments were these:

- 1979 – Parental custody court case with Jewish parents desiring to have custody of their eighteen year old deaf daughter as she had learned about Jesus Christ and wished to become a Christian.   Story in *Tulsa World* newspapers

This case lasted two days. The girl's father was very upset because he believed his daughter was persuaded to become a Christian by a deaf man who claimed to be a Protestant preacher. The girl's father had raised his other children in the Jewish faith with no problems so he assumed it had something to do with her deafness, her lack of a good education, and because the preacher used her language, ASL. This story was picked up by the national Jews For Jesus group with stories appearing in the newspapers periodically over the next few years. This was a fascinating case!

- Late '70s and early '80s – I was included in a group of interpreters taking turns to do the News on Channel 6 KOTV. We also interpreted for Channel 8 KTUL for noon news. I was also fortunate to meet with a sweet little deaf girl who was doing an interview with Bob Hower on his special series, "The Waiting Child." Around this time, the service of closed captioning became the obvious solution for the deaf audiences.

I find it difficult to follow a show with closed captioning. It is nigh unto impossible to read captioning without missing a character's facial expression to "read" his mood. As an interpreter, when I "voice" and sign simultaneously, I am doing a disservice to one or the other. That is why after all these years I feel most comfortable with "consecutive" signing. This allows my deaf client a moment to look at the speaker's facial expression and body language. At this time, I discern the client's understanding of the subject at hand.

- 1979 – Interpreting for the first deaf juror in Oklahoma to serve on a civil case; the third one in the U.S.
  Story in *Tulsa World* newspapers.

- 1980 – Interpreting for a young Irish deaf man when he was sworn in as a United States citizen.
  Picture in *Tulsa World* newspapers.

- 1981 – With a team of interpreters we covered 24 hours in the ICU with a deaf patient after open heart surgery.

  Story in *Tulsa World* newspapers.

  "We" consisted of four qualified interpreters taking shifts, sitting by the patient ready to catch words he might sign or spell to us. I was on duty when he first woke up and spelled to me "what time." I was so thrilled to reply the time with more finger spelling; and interpret for the nurse that all went well. It was wonderful watching a big smile break out on his face.

- 1980-84 – Interpreting for the Miss Deaf Oklahoma Pageants – Tulsa & Sulphur, OK.

- 1982 – Chaperoning Miss Deaf Oklahoma to the Miss Deaf America pageant in St. Louis, MO.

- Interpreting for the Miss Deaf America Pageant in Cincinnati, Ohio.

- Interpreting at the 100th Anniversary of the National Association of the Deaf.

- 1994-95 – Interpreting for two neat deaf men as they took classes in a Technical School in hydraulics and electricity, two subjects I knew absolutely nothing about and had to learn the terminology along with them!

- 1996-97 – Interpreting in Tulsa Jr. College in Computer Science Class for a fine young deaf student. At the time, this subject was completely strange to me. As everyone knows today, computer language is a language unto itself. Thank goodness the teacher was very interested in how this language could be translated, so he called the National Technical Institute for the Deaf in New York to get their input on this important field. Today this is a great area of employment for the Deaf.

MORE NOTES FROM THE AUTHOR

While in Germany we did make the decision to retire from the Air Force upon completing our assignment there. So, I took the Civil Service test and did pretty well, despite the fact that I had never touched an electric typewriter! The officer in charge of my first position patiently allowed me a few days to practice on the electric typewriter before actually doing his work. I enjoyed the last eighteen months of our stay in Germany earning the best salary I had ever hoped to earn. With this experience under my belt I was bound to get into office work when we settled down in civilian life.

Tulsa was Jerry's home and even though he was willing to move close to my parents, I decided on Tulsa because it offered a variety of local schools for the girls, Jerry and me! While Jerry attended classes at the University of Tulsa, I found an office job working for a cemetery! For a short time I worked as a bookkeeper for a small photography business; and later left there to work at Nelson Electric, closer to our home in East Tulsa. I loved my job in Personnel.

There I met some deaf employees who occasionally asked me to interpret for them with Personnel Department questions as well as employee meetings. Seeing the need for interpreters, I thought about the Registry of Interpreters for the Deaf. I decided to search out other people in town who had any experience with interpreting as well. Finding a few, we formed the Green Country Interpreters for the Deaf. Eventually, I faced an RID evaluation board, receiving my Comprehensive Skills Certification.

One day I was contacted by Tulsa Jr. College looking for someone to interpret computer classes for a young deaf man from Ireland! Interpret in the educational environment? For a student from Ireland? Did he speak English? Or, rather, did he know American Sign Language? What an interesting challenge that would be. Without too much hesitation, I accepted, a decision I never regretted!

Later I became self-employed, gaining different contracts over the years, as "BP Services for the Deaf." My first contract was with the Department of Human Services to provide telephone relay service to the 918 area code. I rented offices close to home and hired four people who knew sign language. We each had a desk with a Telephone Device for the Deaf (TDD).

Another tidbit I would add here is how many things I have heard people say about deaf people and "their" sign language. Would you believe I heard a doctor say to an office personnel, "I understand *they* really need a close friend or relative to interpret for them. Another professional once said, "Yes, *they* are different from each other and must have someone in their own family to interpret because it won't be the same signs as another family would use." One more, "*They* really communicate with very few people."

You may be thinking that to work with the telephone relay service, all a person had to know was how to type? Noooo, we also have to understand the language of the deaf as it appears in print! Since most deaf consumers do not use Signed English, as a result they do not type in English order and very often do not include the timing, or tense, in their conversation. It is definitely a plus to let time lag as you read into the lines for just a few seconds before putting it into vocal words. Our duty is to vocalize good English sentences while reading a message written in American Sign Language.

I do not believe there is a formal written form for ASL although some folks do that in some kind of uniformity. I just told my employees to do their best to use good English and go ahead and make corrections when they realize they have stated something in error. We cannot make the judgment call of what is important; we do not necessarily know. So, it is best to repeat the sentence in better English if necessary. That does not mean we voice the fact that we are putting it into better English form, we simply do it. We do NOT want to belittle our deaf consumer by misreading the print we see from them.

Also, I find it best to "own" the error as the interpreter. Never blame the client or our use of ASL.

Does this mean we type back the hearing person's message in an ASL form? Absolutely not! This can be done when signing a message, of course; but, I do not believe we can type an English sentence into ASL.

In 1988 I lost out on my bid for the new contract for the 918 area code. Tulsa Speech and Hearing Association (TSHA) received the newly revised contract to extend the time from 11:00 pm to a 24 hour service. Theirs was an office that received United Way monies to match their fund raisers so they could actually cover this Relay service better and with less money. I was certainly disappointed that I lost out and a little bitter. Bitter? Yes, I never could accept the fact that any and all services for the Deaf should be under one roof. They already had the contract for Interpreter Services and Independent Living as well as working with the Hearing-Impaired community that did not use sign language.

My office was to focus only on telephone relay service. I had never intended to do anything else but the Relay service, focusing on this 24/7. Of course this would be covered only with the DHS monies. It was my understanding that everyone in Oklahoma who had a telephone would be paying an extra fee toward this service to cover both of the Area Codes in our state.

Regretfully, I had to close my public office and keep my small business contained in my home. For a few months I did free-lance work until I applied for a new position within TSHA. They had a new grant to work with deaf people on employment services, known as Project With Industry. This was a good service and I enjoyed the challenge of training and interpreting for a deaf person as he or she gained a new job.

Within a span of eight years, I went back to work for TSHA three times. Each time it was a new position under a different Director as well. First was as Receptionist, second was as Coordinator of Interpreter Services and this time as a Consultant for PWI.

However, I missed being my own boss. So, when the opportunity came in November of 1989 to bid for the 405 Area Code Relay service, I grabbed it, and won! This proved to be exciting in that I had to move to Oklahoma City. It was fun searching for the office spaces needed as well as an apartment to live in myself! I was fortunate to have a hubby who didn't balk at my cleaning out our little savings account to establish myself in Oklahoma City; to say nothing of the fact that we would be separated for a few months! We did not want to sell our house in Tulsa, so this would be a bit of a problem too.

At the end of the 1989-90 school year, Jerry took an early retirement from teaching and moved in with me. He found it challenging to sit at the Receptionist desk in my offices. It was especially tough for him to have to stop people from entering any further where they could see or hear the telephone operators on line. But it soon became known in the deaf community that our offices were small and only for relay services; so their visits became almost nil.

I felt good about our employees there because the position of relaying calls for the deaf was a good experience for those who were in interpreter training programs at the time. More than understanding their language they learned of their culture. Deafness does create a different culture from the norm because of the language; or, I should say, because of the lack of language! We hearing people forget how much we learn just from osmosis of vocabulary overheard, i.e. in the waiting rooms in medical settings. Conversations we hear between husbands and wives, between two or three friends across the room or on the bus tell us how other people live. We may hear and learn things we would never experience in our own homes or places of work, expanding our world. Therefore, many deaf folks have a limited knowledge of American culture.

All good things come to an end they say. Well, the good services didn't really come to an end. But the small businesses, the small mom & pop services, came to an end. Why? Because the service was so great that the large telephone companies finally woke up! Their bids were much better than ours and it was with a positive note our business closed again, knowing that the deaf community was to receive a much better over-all service than ever before!

No more would they be put on hold just waiting to find an operator free. (We always had someone on hold and yet we were not allowed to cut anyone's conversation off so that we could grab that next call. It was really difficult to sit with those long, one hour conversations between a couple of teen agers all the while looking at the board lit up with people waiting for our service!)

So, Jerry and I were happy to have our home still waiting for us in Tulsa after four years. Neither one of us wanted to stay in Oklahoma City even though he had some relatives there; and I was interpreting in the church there.

Actually, that was another employment I had. The Oklahoma Conference of the United Methodist Church Ministry with the Deaf had a full-time minister as the Director. He was not deaf but had a good mastery of sign language as his grandmother had been deaf. His ministry was not limited to one church but to several, as a traveling pastor. I was asked to go to some of the towns in outlying regions of Oklahoma, taking a Bible Study to share with them. Other trips were made to interpret for hearing ministers at funerals, weddings and other events for the Deaf. I did this for about three years until the Bishop closed out that phase of ministry and placed the minister into a permanent church in Oklahoma City. With the monies no longer funded for Deaf ministry, my position was also closed. I continued interpreting in the local church.

For many years, Jerry and I enjoyed traveling to Kiwanis Conventions in Texas, Oklahoma, Utah, Illinois and other places. I also was blessed to experience a variety of cities in the USA where I attended the United Methodist congress for the Deaf conferences.

In August of 2007, I had another thrilling employment. Sorenson Video Relay Service decided to expand their growing number of Centers to include Tulsa. The Manager of this new Center actually hired me at age 76! True, it was just part time but it was perfect for me. I already had to follow a schedule for my husband because of his needs.

Jerry was diabetic for years and now was diagnosed with heart problems. Apparently he had been missing an important valve for his heart, so he had open heart surgery to insert an artificial valve. Around this same time he was told he had congestive heart failure. In the next few years, he had problems with his kidneys which led to the necessity of dialysis treatments. These were four hour treatments done three times a week. I drove him to the Dialysis Center, then drove on to work for four hours at the Relay Center; then returned to pick him up. This worked out fairly easily for two years. Unfortunately, Jerry had to have a leg amputated due to lack of circulation. He had such a terrific positive attitude about all of this. There was no way I could let it get me down, so I did my best to make it as comfortable as possible.

I was thrilled to work a few hours a week at this new video relay service. What a great step up the video provided for real clarity of communication. We were no longer trying to make good English sentences from the typed words; we were actually reading sign language. If my parents had been able to use this method, we would have been so much closer. In fact, we would not have needed this service because we would each have the camera available on our computers and could call each other any time we wanted to, just to chit chat and relate events of the day. I'm so glad it is there for families to use today.

When you think of how many times the average person makes a call to a business office, then you realize how the deaf person needs this Relay service with a third party on the line for all those calls. Naturally this brings to mind the necessity of absolute confidentiality! That is why we interpreters have a Code of Ethics set up through our national Registry of Interpreters for the Deaf (RID). The many telephone video relay service centers throughout our nation employ only certified interpreters for confidentiality as well as skills in sign language.

I enjoyed this work for four years before I decided to officially retire. Celebrating my eightieth birthday helped me with this decision. Maybe I'll finish this book now.

GOD'S CALL

*W*ith these "employments," it seems I never really fulfilled my *call* from God. It was not until we became civilians again (1972) that I first felt God moving within me. My parents were here with us for their first visit to Tulsa since our residence here. They loved the fact that I had already met a few deaf folks and through visits with them they learned the location of the Deaf Club meetings.

At one of those meetings I met the director of the Deaf Education Department at the University of Tulsa. He also served as an interpreter for the deaf congregants at a neighborhood church on Sunday mornings; so I took my parents there for a service. I was impressed with the interpreting; however, I could see that my mother was not following very well. That was really my first experience with reading someone signing in English rather than American Sign Language (ASL).

Of course, I did not interrupt at the time but rather, I relaxed and watched carefully, changing phrases to ASL in my mind. I began to feel a warm rush of blood running throughout my body, feeling almost faint. Quickly this weak feeling became strong and spoke to me as in a dream, "Betty Jean, this is what you must do. Interpret God's words in ASL."

When the altar call came, I stood up and walked up to the minister and said I wanted to be baptized. It was as though I was outside of my body looking down on someone else going through the steps of disrobing, putting on another robe, walking into the water and hearing the words of baptism, making my own vows as though none had ever been said before.

Afterwards, my parents said nothing about what had happened. When we arrived home, Jerry had Sunday dinner waiting for us and nothing was said about my baptism. I don't know why I didn't share the "good news" with my family. To this day I'm not sure why I did not bring up this important subject with anyone! Perhaps it was because I was aware that in the Methodist church when one is baptized as an infant, has taken on those same vows as an adult through confirmation, and tried to become a better Christian; he/she is not supposed to be baptized again. I had gone through all those steps and perhaps my momentary decision to be baptized that Sunday in a strange church was not really a desire to be baptized but, rather, a desire to tell the Lord that I had "heard" him and intended to do my best to obey his request of me. Or, perhaps, simply to let my parents see the importance of following the Christian *call*. It was two years before I took the first steps in that direction. Even then I did not really go out and look for a way to begin, the opportunity came to me! A deaf man visited me at our home, introducing himself as the teacher of the Sunday school class of deaf people at Boston Avenue United Methodist Church. He invited me to visit the group which I did the very next week.

I fell in love with the deaf folks in that group and did my best to be there every Sunday. Eventually I interpreted the worship services and Wednesday night fellowship gatherings. We had great fun and the best thing was, I didn't have to help in the kitchen because my place was to interpret for anyone needing such services. I never was comfortable in a kitchen!

It was tough for him to get up on Sunday mornings because he played his saxophone with a dance band on Saturday nights. Our two younger daughters attended Boston Avenue with me, while our teen-age girls chose to attend a church on the East side of the city where they knew other students from Union High School.

During these years I was never sure if my role as an interpreter actually satisfied God's *calling* on me. In 1989 I lost my bid to renew my contract with the Department of Human Services to provide telephone relay services in the 918 area. In 1990 I applied for the Telephone Relay Service in Oklahoma City, won the contract for the 405 area and set up business as BP Services for the Deaf.

After settling into the offices in Oklahoma City, I soon realized that this was part of God's plan for me. I had received my first degree from Tulsa Junior College during my first few years of interpreting in the area. Subsequently, I earned a Bachelor's Degree from the Tulsa based classes of Langston University. Some of those credits were earned through Northeastern State University in Tahlequah. I earned several graduate hours for a Master's in Psychology Counseling, but moving to Oklahoma City forced me to take a break.

In just a few months I learned about the Diaconal Ministry offered by the United Methodist Church. I was told I could choose a field that I was interested in such as Music, Youth, etc. Of course, I chose Deaf Ministry and immediately visited the Oklahoma City University about the classes offered there. I was so excited about this possibility but did not see how I could afford to enroll. I learned that scholarships were offered by some churches and I could discuss this with the church I was attending. Dear God! He was with me all the way. I was blessed to have the support I needed from the local church and the Director of the Oklahoma Conference of the United Methodist Church, Ministry with the Deaf. My hubby, Jerry, said he could manage the office while I attended some classes and that's exactly the routine that worked for us.

After more than two years of classes at OCU which should have given me that Master's degree; other things changed dramatically for me. The first change was with the telephone relay service when I had to give up my small business. "This is great for the deaf community!" we continually repeated as we closed our offices with mixed emotions.

This also brought about our decision to move back to Tulsa. Four years of living in Oklahoma City did not change our belief that

Tulsa was the best place for us to live. So, as fate would have it, I never did complete a Master's degree; and even more importantly, things changed in the United Methodist Church. Diaconal Ministry was phased out.

Another challenge appeared when I had a call telling me that my paper written a year before about my *calling* was not satisfactory! I was shocked. Had I really not experienced God's *calling*? Was I mistaken? Is there something else in a *calling*?

After telling the office what my circumstances were now; I told that person I would need some time to pray about this. She accepted my simple reply without hesitation; and to be honest with you, I never called them again! I prayed I was not denying God my life. I wanted His blessing when making this decision.

I comforted myself, deciding that interpreting for the Deaf was my true *calling*. There were still times I thought I should have been a counselor, teacher or minister. I wanted to know I had actually helped someone along the way. Had I ever done that as an interpreter?

In January of 2012 the good Lord sent me a clear answer to that question. The Oklahoma Registry of Interpreters for the Deaf honored me with a Lifetime Achievement Award. An award from my peers that elicited congratulations from family and friends, hearing and deaf! Some folks even said I had been a real influence in their lives! There is nothing more important to me! I had actually positively helped someone along the way!

No one can possibly understand what this truly means to me. I pray this signifies that I have fulfilled my *calling*!

AMEN

Frank and Liz (1935)

Made in the USA
Middletown, DE
30 May 2023

31388041R00235